PERKEY'S
*N*ebraska
Place Names

NEBRASKA STATE HISTORICAL SOCIETY
Publications

Volume XXVIII

PERKEY'S
Nebraska Place Names

by Elton A. Perkey

Revised Edition 2003

Library of Congress #95-068748
ISBN 0-934904-19-7

Published by

J&L Lee Co.

P.O. Box 5575
Lincoln, NE 68505

FOREWORD

The first edition of *Perkey's Nebraska Place Names*, published by the Nebraska State Historical Society in 1982, followed its serial publication in Nebraska History magazine in 1977-78 under the title "Perkey's Names of Nebraska Locations." Society library and archival sources as well as postal records were combed by Mr. Perkey for names of territorial and state post offices and localities. Comments by readers and new works on Nebraska place names and post offices since then have enabled NSHS to add and revise selected entries. However, the work remains that of the author, and he assumes full responsibility. A bibliography is included to guide readers who wish to do further research.

A special note should be appended on railroad terminology. In the first edition, many localities were designated as "former" or "present" stations or sidings of a particular railroad. The editors of the revised edition have not attempted to update those designations to reflect the status of railroad stations or sidings in 2002.

The Union Pacific Railroad began construction across Nebraska in 1865, and it still operates under that name. The Burlington and Missouri River Railroad entered Nebraska in 1869, and consolidated with the Chicago, Burlington and Quincy in 1880. In 1970 a merger of several railroads including the CB&Q, the Northern Pacific, and the Great Northern created Burlington Northern, Inc. In this revised edition, the terms "Burlington" or "Burlington Railroad" have been used to designate the Burlington and Missouri River Railroad, the Chicago, Burlington & Quincy Railroad, and Burlington Northern, Inc. without reference to which name applied at the time a locality was established or named.

2002

Lawrence J. Sommer, Director
Nebraska State Historical Society
Lincoln, Nebraska

PREFACE

The study of place names has been my hobby for a number of years. After reading Lilian Fitzpatrick's Nebraska Place-Names, first printed in 1925, and Professor J. T. Link's Origin of Place-Names (1933), I felt the listings should be expanded. Perhaps they would have done so but for their untimely deaths.

I determined to extend the research, knowing the task would be an arduous one. It was an even larger undertaking than I anticipated, and I spent over ten years in assembling my list. Nebraska's great diversity of sources on places, people, and events, when canvassed thoroughly, I found to be a herculean task. Even so, there will doubtless be names which I have unaccountably failed to include. Perhaps other researchers will find occasion to extend my listings.

My entries cover: (1) the present population and the year of peak population; (2) dates of establishment and discontinuance of post offices; (3) circumstances of the foundation of counties; (4) notes on the origin of towns, hamlets, railroad stations, Pony Express and other stage line points.

The reader will notice that Nebraska place names fall into general classes. Miss Fitzpatrick points out in her book (see Introduction, page 5) that they fall into six categories: (1) Christian and surnames of settlers, railroad officials, postmasters, postmistresses, ranchers, prominent persons; (2) geographic features; (3) "transfer" names; (4) Indian names; (5) original or coined names; (6) miscellaneous names.

The majority of the post offices recorded were rural, many of them located in farm or ranch homes. Frequently they were transferred from farm to farm, sometimes across county lines. The discontinuance of small offices did not always occur at the given date and may have operated longer than recorded. Most were replaced in 1903 by Rural Free Delivery service from nearby towns.

So-called "ghost-town" entries dot the pages of this book. A term describing a village now faded from the map due to economic factors, they represent the shattered hopes of many entrepreneurs. They vanished for a variety of reasons: (1) failure to gain the county seat; (2) poor economic base; (3) lack of railroad; (4) inability to handle indebtedness; (5) fraudulent establishment designed to dupe the gullible; (6) Missouri River floods or abandonment of river trade due to railroad competition.

I hope this book will serve as a reference source well thumbed by school children and cherished by other readers of Nebraska history.

1982   Elton A. Perkey
                           Ojai, California

ACKNOWLEDGEMENTS

I desire to express my appreciation to the many Nebraskans who have shown a kindly interest in this volume, including Director Marvin F. Kivett of the Nebraska State Historical Society and members of his staff. I also wish to thank the staffs of the Los Angeles and Glendale, California, Public Libraries; and columnist Wilfrid Dellquest of La Jolla, California.

Special thanks is due those who furnished additional or corrected information on Nebraska place names after "Perkey's Names of Nebraska Locations" appeared serially in Nebraska History (Winter 1977 through Winter 1978): Thelma J. Hamilton, Geneva, Francis Gschwind, Callaway; Frederick Ware, Omaha; Ray Sall, Chappell; Mrs. Marion Shrader, South Sioux City; Mrs. Doris Jenkins, Lincoln; Mrs. Jess Meyer, Scotia; Mrs. Maxine Kessinger, Bancroft; E. E. McKee, Alma; Robert F. B. Diller, Steele City; Mrs. Rosalie Trail Fuller, Lincoln; Mrs. Golda V. Peckham Suttie, Omaha; Arthur J. Riedesel, Ashland; Keith Bryan, Columbus; Mrs. Gerald White, Doniphan; Etta Mae Giles, Elsmere; Jim McKee, Lincoln; John E. Sidner, Lincoln; Mabel Rice, Kearney; Mrs. Burt Kirkpatrick, York; Allona Pirnie, Weissert; Walter Feye, Creston; Dorothy Weyer Creigh, Hastings; Mrs. W. G. Reinke, Byron; Lillian Eley, Genoa; Mrs. Oswin Keifer, Guide Rock; Anna McElrany; Mrs. Margaret Darnell, Kimballton, Iowa; Pauline E. Bennett Saunders, Burlington, Iowa; Dennis A. Winkle, Pickrell; Leroy A. Walker, Gibbon; and Miss Mary Lou Peckham, Fort Collins, Colorado.

I wish also to express my gratitude to Mrs. Margaret Alagna of Los Angeles for her scholarly and professional help in editing and typing this work, and most of all to express appreciation to my wife, Marion, who spent these many years in helping and encouraging me in every way by hours of patient research, editing, typing, and proofreading.

I dedicate this work to the people of Nebraska and to the schools of Nebraska, where, I trust, it will be a help to future generations.

1982   Elton A. Perkey
                         Ojai, California

CONTENTS

Alphabetical List of Counties with their Place Names

NEBRASKA

On May 30, 1854, President Franklin Pierce signed a bill passed by the Congress of the United States which created the Territory of Nebraska. Nebraska became the thirty-seventh state of the Union by proclamation of President Andrew Johnson on March 1, 1867.

The word Nebraska is derived from the Oto Indian name of the Platte River: "Ni btha cka ke." One sometimes hears that the source of the word is Omaha Indian: "Ne'brath ke" or "Ne'prath ke."

ADAMS COUNTY

Created by legislative enactment on February 16, 1867, Adams County was named in honor of John Adams (1735-1826), U.S. president from 1797 to 1801. County officers chosen in December 1871.

Adams City. Probably a proposed town that never went beyond the platting and recording stage. Its location is unknown.

Assumption. Near Juniata, it was named by the Catholic Church for the Assumption of the Blessed Mary Church. A parochial school was constructed first and used for services while the church was being built. A general store operated by Matt Scholl opposite the church was built in 1899. Still an active community, Assumption was first settled by Germans.

Ayr. Peak population (1880), 275. Post office established December 20, 1878. Named in honor of Dr. Ayr of Iowa, a director of the Burlington Railroad at the time of the building of the railroad. The village was platted in September of 1878 by the South Platte Town Company and was incorporated in May 1883. Ayr Junction is north of town at the junction of two railroad branches. Crystal Lake, a state recreation area, is located one mile north of town.

Ayr Junction. A station and junction for two branches of the Burlington Railroad were located here.

Blaine. A former elevator siding probably named for James G. Blaine, statesman and presidential candidate at the time of its founding by Burlington Railroad officials. Located southeast of Hastings.

Brennans. A former elevator siding for the St. Joseph and Grand Island Railroad. Named in honor of Thomas Brennans, a farmer living near the elevator. Located southeast of Hastings.

Brickton. Six and one-half miles south of Hastings on the Burlington Railroad, Brickton was named for the C. H. Paul Brick Manufacturers, formed by a group of Hastings businessmen in 1886. Houses were built for thirty or forty employees and their families.

Bridgeton. Post office established December 20, 1878; discontinued April 23, 1879. The source of the name of this former post office has not yet been ascertained.

Deans. Located between Pauline and Ayr, this former elevator siding on the Burlington Railroad may have been named for one of these landowners: James M. Dean, James K. Dean, or Lucien Dean.

Farmers. Located north of Hastings, this former railroad station on the St. Joseph and Grand Island Railroad was so called because area farmers built an elevator here in 1879.

Ferrens. A siding on the Burlington Railroad, Ferrens is located near Hastings and was probably named for a local settler or railroad official.

Flickville. A former elevator siding named by Burlington Railroad officials for homesteader Joseph Flick, Flickville was located east of Hastings, near the Clay County boundary. Eventually moved from Adams to Clay County.

Galnes. Origin of the name of this siding of the Burlington Railroad located near Hastings, has not been learned.

Gilson. Post office established August 20, 1871, but moved to Ayr with the coming of the railroad on December 20, 1878. Gilson had a flour mill on the Little Blue River. Named by Postmaster Bigger R. Scott for his former home, Gilson, Illinois. Halloran. Station and former elevator siding named for its builder, Mike Halloran, in 1874 by Burlington Railroad officials. Located east of Hastings.

Hansen. Peak population (1880), 120. Post office established December 19, 1879; discontinued 1955. Mail served from Hastings. Village named for a Mr. Hansen of St. Joseph, Missouri, a civil engineer employed by the St. Joseph and Grand Island Railroad. Platted by A. B. Ideson and J. J. Wemple in 1879 on ground purchased from Charles and William Haines. S. J. Loucks built a hotel, the Hansen House.

Hastings. Peak population (1970), 23,233. Post office established September 19, 1872. Col. D. T. Hastings of the Grand Island and St. Joseph Railroad was instrumental in bringing the railroad to Hastings and inspired its name. The town was platted in 1872 on the homestead of Walter Micklen, whose land was located at the junction of two railroads. Incorporated April 2, 1874. A colony of Englishmen soon afterward settled the surrounding land. Hastings displaced Juniata as the county seat after a bitter election in 1878. Hastings College established September 1882.

Hayland. Peak population (1910), 33. Post office established January 31, 1914; discontinued 1943. Hay shipped from this former Union Pacific Railroad siding inspired its name.

Hazel Dell. Post office established April 7, 1879; discontinued February 21, 1889. The name of this former post office and community reminded residents of the hazel bushes which grew near the one-time home of Mrs. A. A. White. German settlers first located in the vicinity.

Holstein. Peak population (1910), 323. Post office established April 23, 1888. Town platted July 22, 1887, on coming of the Kansas City and Omaha Railroad, and incorporated June 6, 1889. Named in honor of Schleswig-Holstein, northern Germany, the original home of early settlers. The town also attracted Danish settlers.

Ingleside. Means fireside, but local tradition maintains that its meaning is "beauty" or "a thing of beauty." The Hastings State Hospital, sometimes called Ingleside, was established in 1888. Its fine brick buildings and beautifully landscaped grounds lie two miles west of Hastings. The town is now part of Hastings.

Inland. Post office established May 2, 1872; moved in 1878 to Clay County. Platted by South Platte Land Company, Inland was moved after the development of Hastings.

Jeffers. A railroad siding or junction on the Chicago, Burlington and Quincy, the Missouri Pacific, and the Union Pacific. Located near Hastings, it was probably named for William Martin Jeffers, former president of the Union Pacific Railroad.

Juniata. Peak population (1990), 811. Post office established December 26, 1876. S. L. Brass and A. H. Bowen located a colony from Michigan here in 1871 and 1872. Town platted by South Platte Land Company in November 1871 and incorporated June 15, 1880. Named for the Juniata River in Pennsylvania, Juniata vied with Kingston for county seat after a December 12, 1871 election; it was displaced by Hastings in 1877. Flour mill established in 1874.

Kenesaw. Peak population (1980), 854. Post office established December 5, 1872. Kennesaw Mountain, Georgia, battle site of the Civil War, inspired the name. Early settlers were from Virginia. Townsite platted by South Platte Land Company in June 1872; incorporated in 1884. Kenesaw at one time had two flour mills.

Kingston. Post office established March 12, 1872; moved to Pauline July 10, 1888. Named in honor of George King on whose land the post office was located. Kingston vied with Juniata in the county seat election of December 12, 1871. It was moved to Pauline with the coming of the railroad.

Leroy. Post office established February 4, 1889; discontinued January 22, 1902. Once known as a pleasure resort for Hastings residents. Named by A. H. Stone for his son Leroy. The station was later moved to Pauline.

Level. A Union Pacific station and former elevator siding, it was probably named for its level location.

Little Blue. Post office established March 7, 1873; discontinued March 4, 1879. Its location on the Little Blue River inspired the name.

Ludlow. Post office established January 2, 1880; moved to Clay County March 30, 1887. Named to honor Ludlow Huff, on whose premises the post office was located.

Martinville. Post office established August 29, 1870; discontinued May 5, 1873. Redefinition of county boundary placed it in Hall County in 1871. Named for George Martin, first postmaster.

Mayflower. Post office established July 9, 1877; discontinued May 5, 1896. Named for the historic ship that brought the Pilgrims to America, Mayflower was located on the farm of John Burlington, six miles northwest of Holstein.

Millington. Post office established August 17, 1877; discontinued February 1, 1881. Named for a mill built on the Little Blue River by John Dyer and two nephews, Eldridge and True Dyer.

Moritz. This former station and elevator siding on the Missouri Pacific Railroad was named for Charles Moritz, manager of elevators in the county.

Morseville. Post office established July 9, 1877; discontinued July 24, 1889. Probably named for Charles F. Morse, an early settler.

Muriel. Former elevator siding located on the Missouri Pacific Railroad south of Hastings. Origin of the name has not yet been learned.

Newmarch. Former elevator siding was located on the Union Pacific Railroad northwest of Hastings. Origin of the name has not been ascertained.

North Blue. Post office established June 3, 1872; discontinued November 29, 1876. Named for its location on the north branch of the Blue River.

Pauline. Peak population (1900), 175. Post office name changed from Kingston July 10, 1888. Post office discontinued 1967; mail to Glenvil. Named in honor of Pauline S. Ragan, wife of John M. Ragan, attorney for the Burlington Railroad, of Hastings. Town platted in 1887 on farm of James B. McCleery.

Prosser. Peak population (1900), 175. Post office established June 29, 1888. Named in honor of T. J. Prosser, construction superintendent of the Missouri Pacific Railroad building into Prosser, its terminus. Town incorporated August 13, 1907; declined after discontinuance of railroad in 1940s.

Rosedale. Post office established May 4, 1877; discontinued January 17, 1881. Named for the wild roses growing in the area, it was formerly called Sportville.

Roseland. Peak population (1980), 254. Post office established August 19, 1875. Platted April 20, 1887, and named by B. F. Evans, the first postmaster, for wild roses growing in the vicinity.

Sand Hill. Station No. 11 in Nebraska of the Pony Express, the name refers to the difficult sandy wagon road which called for double teaming. Possibly located one and one-half miles south of Kenesaw, it was sometimes called Summit Station or Water Hole. One authority termed it the most lonesome place in Nebraska.

Silver Lake. Post office established February 27, 1873; discontinued May 16, 1887. This former post office was named by Rufus Daily for a clear lake having a silver look.

Sodtown. May have been the former name of Mayflower or of another site nearby before Mayflower was established as a post office.

Spencer Park. Originally a siding on the Union Pacific Railroad. Early in 1944 the federal Public Housing Authority units in southeast Hastings became known as Spencer Park, named after the brothers who once owned the site.

Sportville. Post office established September 3, 1884; discontinued April 2, 1887. The first postmaster, Peter Volte, named Sportville for a popular baseball team.

Stroemer. Post office established August 4, 1900; discontinued January 22, 1902. A former post office and railroad siding, Stroemer was named to honor Dirk H. Stroemer, an early settler who purchased railroad land.

Thirty-two Mile Creek. Pony Express Station No. 10 in Nebraska, it was located six miles southwest of Hastings. A monument near the site refers to it as "Dinner Station I.O.O.F.E., Pony Express." A long, one-story building operated by George Comstock, it was abandoned after the 1864 Indian raids.

Wanda. Probably a proposed town that never got beyond the platting and recording stage in Wanda Township. Origin of the name has not yet been ascertained.

ANTELOPE COUNTY

Organized by legislative enactment June 15, 1871, after a bill approved March 1, 1871, for its establishment was introduced by Leander Gerrard of Platte County. Gerrard and others shot an antelope for food while on the trail of Indians. Recalling the incident, he suggested Antelope for the county name.

Antelope. Post office established April 25, 1872; name changed to Clearwater July 22, 1881. Named for the county; located near site of antelope-killing incident.

Barbor. Post office established May 14, 1887; discontinued April 27, 1890. Origin of the name has not been ascertained.

Beemer. Post office established April 16, 1884; name changed to Vickory August 4, 1884. Origin of the name has not been learned.

Brunswick. Peak population (1930), 362. Post office name changed from Clear Spring August 15, 1890. Named for Brunswick, Germany (world center for sugar beet seed) by Henry Nagle, settler who grew beets from imported seed.

Burnett. Post office established January 20, 1880; name changed to Tilden and office moved to Madison County, April 8, 1887. Named to honor a Mr. Burnett, first superintendent of the Sioux City and Pacific Railroad, later the Chicago North Western. Chicago. Post office established April 17, 1888; discontinued July 13, 1888. Named for Chicago, Illinois.

Clear Spring. Post office established December 16, 1877; name changed to Brunswick August 15, 1890. Named for the springs on Clearwater Creek. Office located at home of J. A. Douglas.

Clearwater. Peak population (1940), 568. Post office name changed from Antelope July 22, 1881. Town takes its name from the creek on which it is located.

Clyde. Post office established February 20, 1874; discontinued April 5, 1876. Origin of the name has not been ascertained.

Copenhagen. The Burlington Railroad named this railroad station and elevator siding for Copenhagen, Denmark. Many area settlers formerly lived in Denmark.

Cyrus. Post office established August 4, 1882; discontinued April 6, 1883. Named in honor of Cyrus Grant, first postmaster.

Elgin. Peak population (1970), 917. Post office established May 18, 1887. Named for Elgin, Illinois, and platted by Western Town Lot Company. Farmer William Eggleston desired a post office in his home and asked, as postmaster, that it be named in his honor but was refused. Postmaster E. Gailey of Oakdale picked Elgin from the Illinois post office guide, and it was accepted by the post office department.

Frenchtown. Peak population (1890), 100. Post office established April 25, 1872; discontinued May 31, 1890. Named for the French settlers who located here.

Gillespie. Post office established January 30, 1872; discontinued August 31, 1874. Named in honor of James M. Gillespie, first postmaster, who had the office in his grocery.

Glenalpine. Post office established May 25, 1882; discontinued February 16, 1905. Formerly located in a hilly, picturesque locality, near the headwaters of a branch of the Verdigris. First settlement made here in 1876.

Glenaro. Post office established February 7, 1877; discontinued April 4, 1878. Origin of the name has not been learned.

Glendale. Post office established May 28, 1887; discontinued November 30, 1888. Name signifies a narrow, secluded valley.

Griffith. Post office established May 27, 1887; discontinued 1888. Named in honor of Isaac Griffith, first postmaster.

Hering's Mill. Named for Julius Hering, native of Germany who located a mill on the headwaters of the Verdigris, four and one-half miles northeast of present-day Orchard. The mill continued until 1929; it served a large area and had a high reputation for the quality of flour and meal.

Hord Siding. This railroad siding was probably an elevator site on the Chicago and North Western Railroad. May have been named for T. B. Hord, who had a chain of elevators in Nebraska.

Jessup. Post office established June 16, 1877; discontinued March 15, 1905. Probably named in honor of Iowa State Senator Elias Jessup of Hardin County.

Mars. Located partly in Antelope County, while the post office was in Knox County. (See note on Knox County)

Mentorville. Post office established June 30, 1882; discontinued March 11, 1903. Name origin has not been ascertained.

Neligh. Peak population (1980), 1,893. Post office established June 3, 1873. Named in honor of early settler John D. Neligh of West Point, who bought the land on which the town is located. William B. Lambert suggested the name. Surveyed and platted by Niels Larsen, Cuming County surveyor. United States Land Office located here in the 1870s. Neligh Mills, erected on the Elkhorn River in 1874, is now a branch museum of the Nebraska State Historical Society. Neligh won county seat in election with Oakdale in 1883. Home of Gates College, 1882-99.

Oakdale. Peak population (1920), 707. Post office name changed from Twin Grove August 23, 1872. Located on the south bank of Cedar Creek and named for the presence of oak timber along the stream. Platted by J. G. Taylor, Oakdale was made the first county seat in 1872 and lost to Neligh in 1883. A cattle and grain shipping center in the 1880s and the headquarters for several freighting outfits.

Ogden. Post office established January 15, 1875; moved to Madison County April 8, 1878. Probably named for a local settler or for Ogden, Utah.

Orchard. Peak population (1910), 532. Post office established July 1, 1881. Named by D. L. Cramer, first postmaster, for an extensive apple orchard in the vicinity.

Royal. Peak population (1910), 250. Post office name changed from Savage July 15, 1881. Name changed from Savage to Royal to honor Royal Thayer, prominent Nebraskan.

Ryedale. Post office established August 27, 1886; discontinued May 13, 1887. Origin of the name has not been learned.

Savage. Post office established October 29, 1880; name changed to Royal July 15, 1881. Named for a Sioux City, Iowa, physician, who promised to build a school in any town named for him along the railroad. Mr. Bear, a local minister, objected to his Sunday School being called the Savage Sunday School, and because Dr. Savage didn't fulfill his agreement, the town changed the name to Royal.

St. Clair. Post office established August 20, 1877; discontinued January 23, 1904. Named in honor of George St. Clair, early settler.

Strickland. Post office established July 14, 1880; discontinued September 8, 1881. Probably named for a local settler.

Swan. Post office established January 11, 1886; discontinued August 20, 1886. Probably named in honor of Thomas Swan, first postmaster.

Twin Grove. Post office established May 9, 1871; named for two similar groups of trees, it became Oakdale August 23, 1872.

Vickory. Post office name changed from Beemer August 4, 1884; discontinued October 7, 1890. Named in honor of William Vickory, first postmaster.

Vilas. Locality probably named for Vilas, Michigan.

Vim. Post office established January 7, 1886; discontinued December 31, 1912. Named for the energy, spirit, and vigor of the settlers.

Willowdale. Post office established October 28, 1871; discontinued March 31, 1904. Named for its site on Willow Creek. Post office was located at the store of E. W. Waterman.

ARTHUR COUNTY

Named in honor of Chester A. Arthur (1830-86), U.S president from 1881 to 1885. Approved by an act of the Legislature March 31, 1887, but remained a part of McPherson County until 1913, when Arthur County was officially organized after the Legislature passed a second enabling act.

Arthur. Peak population (1970), 175. Post office established January 31, 1914. Named for the county and made county seat at time of county formation. Some people lived in tents during the building of the town in 1913. First courthouse in a shack; permanent courthouse, erected August 21, 1914, said to be the smallest in the United States—26-by-28-foot, frame building now used as museum. New courthouse erected December 30, 1961.

Braden. Post office established November 6, 1915; rescinded June 23, 1916. Honors Alfred Braden, an early settler, and his daughter, Mrs. Rhoda E. Twidwell, first postmistress.

Bucktail. Peak population (1940), 20. Post office name changed from Cullinan, June 29, 1916. Made rural station of Paxton, Keith County, in 1960. Named for deer and antelope in the vicinity. Buckingham, former name of Mrs. Bert Wakeman, was recommended to the U.S. Post Office Department, which considered it impractical, and Bucktail was selected. Town formerly called Cullinan, but after removal five miles east on Bucktail Lake, was given present name.

Calora. Post office established August 19, 1912; discontinued 1953. The postmaster and his wife, Carl and Aura Crouse, wanted this office called Carlaura, a combination of their first names. The post office department coined the name Calora.

Carman. Post office established March 11, 1916; discontinued 1947. Named in honor of the Rev. M. B. Carman, a Methodist minister.

Clenard. Post office established November 6, 1915; rescinded June 23, 1916. Name thought to be a local resident's first or last name. Postmaster was Otis B. McLaughlin.

Collins. Post office established June 30, 1909; discontinued March 30, 1929. Collins was one of three names suggested by citizens and selected by the post office department. One of the former postmasters was Charles J. Collins. Post office located in a sod house.

Cullinan. Post office established March 11, 1916. Name changed to Bucktail after removal five miles east, June 29, 1916. Office named in honor of George F. and Harry Cullinan, ranchers and mercantile store owners. George later became the first Arthur County clerk.

Edward. Post office established May 1, 1915, when moved from Garden County; discontinued June 30, 1919. Named in honor of Edward Fiesterman; Susan Fiesterman was first postmistress.

Fora. Post office established December 27, 1915; discontinued 1933. Named for the eldest daughter of Mr. and Mrs. William G. Brotherton. William Brotherton was first postmaster.

Glenrose. Post office established December 28, 1906; discontinued February 28, 1925. Named by C. E. Phillips, local resident, for the wild roses in a nearby valley.

Hillside. Post office established March 5, 1908; discontinued 1934. Named by its first postmistress, Lillie M. Grimshaw, for its location on the side of a hill.

Lena. Post office established April 25, 1891; discontinued 1961. Oldest post office in Arthur County. One source says the office named for Mrs. Lena Fellows, postmistress, but U.S. Post Office records do not list her. Another source says office was named for Miss Lena Keyes, first school teacher in the vicinity.

Melrose. Post office established June 10, 1916; discontinued 1939. Named for the abundance of roses in the vicinity by Mrs. Nettie Hart, first postmistress.

Read. Post office established April 13, 1908; discontinued September 1, 1916. Named to honor Henry B. Read, one of the early ranchmen. Probably once located in a store.

Rice. Post office moved February 7, 1910, from Keith County; discontinued 1933. Named in honor of Dr. Clinton S. Rice, an early settler in this part of the state.

Velma. Post office established May 4, 1917, when moved from Garden County; discontinued 1943. Named to honor the daughter of Mr. and Mrs. Henry Redlinger; Henry Redlinger was first postmaster while office was in Garden County.

Willett. Post office established October 28, 1914; discontinued May 31, 1930. Named for Willett, New York, former home of Charles F. Rose, first postmaster. Office located in his store.

Zella. Post office established here June 1, 1915, when moved from Keith County; discontinued July 31, 1920. Named for the first postmaster's wife, Mrs. Edmund Stone.

BANNER COUNTY

Created by legislative enactment November 6, 1888. Previously part of Cheyenne County, it was named by enthusiastic citizens who wished to make it the "banner county of the state." G. L. Shumway, deputy secretary of the Nebraska Department of Agriculture, helped promote the idea.

Ashford. Peak population (1890), 8. Post office established October 1887; discontinued July 24, 1902. Former town named for William Ashford, who located on Pumpkin Creek in 1885 on the stage road. Named first county seat of Banner County on January 25, 1889, it lost an election to Harrisburg for county seat on May 22, 1889.

Banner. Peak population (1890), 8. Post office established May 15, 1888; discontinued April 6, 1894. Former town named for the county by a Mrs. Robinson and Ebenezer Wells, first postmaster. Banner vied with Freeport, Ashford, and Harrisburg in the county seat election of May 22, 1889.

Bighorn. Post office established April 26, 1912; discontinued August 6, 1914. Mrs. Hope Brown, postmistress and proprietor of the Bighorn Ranch near Table Mountain and Bighorn Mountain, and the Grangers living in this area recorded the presence of bighorn sheep, which inspired the name.

Centropolis. Post office name changed from Randall February 1, 1889; changed to Harrisburg May 29, 1889. Called Centropolis because it was in the center of the county. Probably named by a Mr. Schooley, who owned the townsite, or by his nephew, C. H Randall.

Clyde. Post office established September 28, 1888; discontinued May 1, 1895. Office probably named for local resident. First postmaster was William Lowman.

Epworth. Post office established January 25, 1906; discontinued October 15, 1918.

7

Probably a Methodist community which used the name in youth meetings. Possibly named by Erastus and Elizabeth Cox, who had the post office.

Flowerfield. Post office established May 15, 1912; discontinued 1937. Former post office located on high table land which at the time of its settlement in the 1880s was covered with wild flowers. A homesteader chose the name, which was approved by the U.S. Post Office Department.

Freeport. Peak population (1890), 10. Post office established August 6, 1887; discontinued July 31, 1911. Elisha M. Cowen, first postmaster, named this former town for Freeport, Illinois, his former home.

Gary. Post office established June 22, 1897; discontinued October 31, 1921. Named to honor James A. Gary, postmaster general in President William McKinley's Cabinet. Post office established by William Reep, first postmaster.

Harrisburg. Peak population (1920), 140. Post office name changed from Centropolis May 29, 1889. Named for Harrisburg, Pennsylvania, by C. A. Schooley, early settler from Pennsylvania. Harrisburg won county seat in election over Ashford, Freeport, and Banner May 22, 1889. Centropolis was just south of Harrisburg. C. H. Randall had town platted on his land just north of his uncle's (C. A. Schooley) place. H. R. Stevens drew plans for the courthouse.

Heath. Post office established January 25, 1890; discontinued December 21, 1917. Derives its name from an early Scotch settler named McLatchky.

Hull. Peak population (1890), 15. Post office established February 26, 1887; discontinued 1930. Former hamlet named for Postmaster Albert B. Hull, an early settler who had a store with the post office.

Kirk. Post office established August 27, 1890; discontinued May 15, 1929. Former post office named for an early settler, A. O. Kirk. His wife was first postmistress.

Livingston. Post office established June 23, 1886; discontinued October 30, 1890. Named in honor of Lee D. Livingston, ranchman, whose wife Margaretta was the first postmistress. First post office in Banner County.

Loraine. Post office established May 16, 1888; discontinued May 18, 1895. Named for the daughter of Mr. and Mrs. Frank Edwards. He was the first postmaster and an early ranchman.

Myra. Post office established June 15, 1895; discontinued March 16, 1896. Origin of the name has not been learned. First postmaster was William Wisroth.

Randall. Post office established February 26, 1887. Name changed to Centropolis February 1, 1889. Former office named for C. H. Randall, who owned the site and later became congressman from Los Angeles County, California.

Rhoid. Post office established May 9, 1888; rescinded June 1, 1888. Origin of the name has not been ascertained.

Van. Post office established February 27, 1907; discontinued May 15, 1912. Named in honor of Thomas A. Van Pelt, the first postmaster, whose office was established at his ranch home. Mr. Van Pelt later served as treasurer of Banner County.

Vinlon. Post office established March 17, 1899; rescinded May 24, 1899. Origin of the name has not been ascertained.

BLAINE COUNTY

Boundaries were defined by an act of the Legislature approved March 5, 1885. The county was named in honor of James G. Blaine (1830-93), American statesman and 1884 presidential candidate.

Blaine. The locality never had a post office but was named for the county. Located three and one-half miles west of Brewster, it had a short existence.

Blaine Center. This town never had a post office but was located one and one-half miles west of Brewster. Vied for county eat with Ladora and Brewster in November 23, 1886, election.

Brewster. Peak population (1930), 287. Post office established September 18, 1884. Town possibly named for early pioneer and Civil War veteran George Washington Brewster, who came from Oakland, Nebraska, and erected several buildings, including a large hotel. A Republican, he was responsible for the county being named Blaine. A newspaper editor with interest in the town's progress, he boomed Brewster for the state capital because of its central location. Another source reports that the town was named for Elder Brewster of the Mayflower. Brewster and Blaine County lost a county seat election on November 6, 1886, with Ladora, which retained the county seat until another election in November 1887. In January 1888, Brewster became the permanent county seat. Most of the buildings in Ladora were dismantled and moved here. Town incorporated in 1947.

Cooper. Post office established January 26, 1906; discontinued February 15, 1914. Named in honor of Gilbert Cooper, first postmaster, on whose premises the post office was established.

Dunning. Peak population (1910), 450. Post office established June 10, 1887. Named in honor of R. A. and Sam Dunning, brothers. Platted by Lincoln Land Company after railroad built through here.

Edbell. The Burlington Railroad built and named this former railroad station for Ed W. Bell, master carpenter of the Alliance Division of the line.

Edith. Post office established January 26, 1885; discontinued 1919. Named for Edith Valley, which was named for Edith Randolph, daughter of a resident minister.

Frank. Post office established May 13, 1907; discontinued January 31, 1920. Named for Frank Thompson in whose residence post office was established. His wife was first postmistress.

Giles. Post office moved from Brown County, May 8, 1903. Post office moved back to Brown County, July 18, 1908 and from Brown County, July 21, 1923. Post office discontinued August 15, 1931. Mail served from Dunning. See note on Giles in Brown County.

Goldville. Post office established April 23, 1906; discontinued June 17, 1913. Named in honor of W. H. Gould, whose wife was first postmistress. The U.S. Post Office Department omitted the "u" in the name.

Hawley. Post office established June 14, 1880; discontinued December 29, 1884. Named for a Mrs. Northup, first postmistress, whose maiden name was Holley. An error by the U.S. Post Office Department caused the name to be Hawley.

Kaiser. Post office established May 3, 1906; rescinded August 6, 1906. Named in honor of Louis Kaiser, first postmaster. Ladora. Post office established June 10, 1884; discontinued and moved to Brewster September 18, 1884. Former county seat probably named for Ladora, Iowa, by E. W. Rankin. Made county seat November 23, 1886, Ladora lost it in election with Brewster in January 1888. After the election, townspeople either moved their buildings to Brewster or tore them down.

Lena. Located near Dunning, but was moved to Custer County after Dunning was founded and railroad established.

Linscott. Post office established November 30, 1887; discontinued November 14, 1921. Named in honor of two brothers, John H. and Charles Linscott, by Burlington Railroad officials.

Lucy. Post office established January 18, 1905; discontinued June 15, 1915. Named for the daughter of Mr. and Mrs. George A. Martin. Mrs. Martin was first postmistress.

Pritchard. Post office established April 26, 1905; discontinued January 15, 1914. Probably named for Laura E. Pritchard, first postmistress.

Purdum. Peak population (1940), 36. Post office established March 24, 1884, in Sioux County (including present Blaine County). Post office moved to Thomas County November 19, 1891; returned to Blaine County May 5, 1894. Post office and town named for Postmaster George F. Purdum, who homesteaded at Buffalo Flats in 1882. Purdum vied for county seat with Rankin and Brewster November 2, 1886.

Rankin. Post office established March 21, 1908; discontinued September 14, 1912. Named in honor of E. W. Rankin, early settler.

Scheding. Post office established August 31, 1907; discontinued November 30, 1919. Named in honor of a Mr. Scheding, German Lutheran minister. Also known as German Valley.

Valley Ridge. Community located near Dunning. Probably named for topographic characteristic.

BOONE COUNTY

Named in honor of Daniel Boone (1734-1820), noted hunter and Kentucky pioneer. Organized by legislative enactment March 28, 1871.

Akron. Peak population (1900), 27. Post office established February 2, 1881; discontinued November 21, 1905. Present railroad siding and former hamlet named by U.S. Post Office Department, probably for Akron, Ohio.

Albion. Peak population (1940), 2,268. Post office name changed from Hammond July 3, 1883. Named for Albion, Michigan. County seat located here February 25, 1873. Town platted by first postmaster, Loran Clark, on his land and surveyed by George W. Newberry.

Arden. Post office established June 15, 1881. Moved to Wheeler County May 15, 1918. Probably named for the English forest of Arden.

Beaver. Post office established March 28, 1870. Name changed to Waterville February 2, 1874. Named for its location on Beaver Creek, known for the presence of beaver.

Boone. Peak population (1930), 126. Post office established January 28, 1872. Town named for the county by M. E. Stevens.

Bradish. Peak population (1910 and 1930), 53. Post office established January 11, 1888; discontinued 1945. Site of this former town chosen by man from Chicago, Illinois. Town platted by Pioneer Town Site Company in 1888. Named in honor of George Bradish, engineer in charge of railroad construction.

Cedar Rapids. Peak population (1920), 740. Post office name changed from Dayton July 7, 1882. Named by Adam Smith, who platted town on the Cedar River with the construction of the Burlington Railroad.

Closter. Post office established February 21, 1880; discontinued January 31, 1917. Named in honor of Henry Closter, who owned the homestead on which the post office was established.

Coon Prairie. Post office established January 31, 1876; discontinued April 6, 1888. Named by Kettler Fumme for Coone Prairie, Wisconsin, where some of the original settlers had resided.

Dahlburg. Post office established February 20, 1895; discontinued August 27, 1898.

Dayton. Post office established August 17, 1873. Name changed to Cedar Rapids July 7, 1882. Probably named for Dayton, Ohio.

Denison. Post office established May 31, 1890; discontinued March 2, 1901. Origin of the name of this former post office has not been learned. Cities in Iowa and Texas and a college in Ohio are called Denison.

Dublin. Post office established February 11, 1874. Name changed to Primrose February 21, 1903. Irish immigrants who settled here named the town for the capital of Ireland.

Garner. Post office established February 15, 1881. Name changed to Ira June 25, 1890. Named to honor John S. Garner, first postmaster.

Hammond. Post office established December 1, 1871. Name changed to Albion July 3, 1873. Named in honor of John Hammond, early pioneer of Boone County.

Hardy. Probably named for a local settler. Formerly situated near Albion.

Ira. Post office name changed from Garner June 25, 1890; discontinued July 9, 1892. Origin of the name has not been learned.

Loran. Named for Loran Clark, early county settler; changed to Loretto to avoid confusion with another post office with similar name.

Loretto. Peak population (1930), 126. Post office established July 21, 1888. See note on Loran above.

Mauston. Post office established February 16, 1876; discontinued November 30, 1887. Probably named for Mauston, Wisconsin.

Mosside. Post office established June 10, 1880; discontinued November 30, 1887. Origin of the name is unknown.

Myra. Former locality probably named for a wife or daughter of a local settler.

Neoma. Post office established May 31, 1878; discontinued February 1, 1892. Origin of the name has not been learned. First postmaster was Hiram Snider.

Oadland. Former locality probably named for a local settler or for a place in Sweden.

Olnes. Post office established March 15, 1881; discontinued October 29, 1902. Probably named for the pioneer family of Lars Olnes.

Oxford. Post office established January 8, 1874; discontinued February 15, 1881. Probably named for Oxford University in England or for Oxford, Ohio.

Petersburg. Peak population (1940), 657. Post office established September 20, 1887. Platted by the Pioneer Town Site Company and named in honor of John Peters, who owned the land on which the town is located.

Primrose. Peak population (1930), 210. Post office name changed from Dublin February 21, 1903. Platted on land belonging to David Primrose and named in his honor.

Raeville. Peak population (1960), 100. Post office established January 8, 1874. Believed to have been named for two Rae brothers.

Roselma. Post office established April 6, 1875; discontinued April 6, 1896. Named for the daughter of Mrs. Marion Davis, first postmistress.

Sandalia. Post office established August 21, 1883; discontinued August 2, 1901. Name is probably Swedish in origin.

St. Edward. Peak population (1930), 1,029. Post office name changed from Waterville October 5, 1877. Named in honor of Edward Serrels, a Catholic priest who was prominent at Notre Dame University, Indiana. In 1871 A. T. Coquilliard of South Bend, Indiana, acquired the land on which the town now stands. He deeded it to the St. Edward Land and Emigration Company in 1876 and opened the tracts for sale.

Waterville. Post office name changed from Beaver February 2, 1874. Name changed to St. Edward October 5, 1877. Probably named for the stream on which it is located.

BOX BUTTE COUNTY

Formed from southern Dawes County by vote on November 2, 1886. The county was named for a large box-shaped or rectangular butte located about six miles north of Alliance.

Afton. Post office established September 10, 1906; discontinued May 31, 1907. Probably named for a local settler or inspired by Robert Burns's famous poem, "Flow Gently, Sweet Afton."

Alliance. Peak population (1980), 9,869. Post office established February 23, 1888.

Superintendent G. W. Holdrege of the Burlington Railroad named Alliance. He chose it because it was a single word, different from any other town in the state, and because it would be near the top of an alphabetical list of names. The citizens accepted the name and the town was platted by the Lincoln Land Company. Another source says the town was named for Alliance, Ohio. Alliance was made county seat after a March 1899 election contest with Hemingford. A U.S. Land Office was located here in the 1890s. Alliance is division headquarters for the Burlington Railroad.

Berea. Peak population (1960), 75. Post office established October 30, 1899; discontinued September 24, 1926; mail served from Alliance. Named by early settlers for their former home of Berea, Ohio.

Birdsell. Railroad station named after J. C. Birdsell, popular division superintendent of the Burlington Railroad.

Blackroot. Post office established September 15, 1916; discontinued February 28, 1919. Probably named for herbaceous plant found in the pine barren regions of the South.

Box Butte. Post office established April 10, 1885. Name changed to Marple April 25, 1905, after a man named Marple. Moved to Sheridan County April 23, 1908.

Buchanan. Renamed Nonpareil by newspaper editor Eugene Heath after a post office was established in 1886.

Burbank. Post office established August 12, 1889. Name changed to Burns July 23, 1900. Origin of the name has not been learned.

Burns. Census not available. Post office name changed from Burbank July 23, 1900; discontinued July 31, 1912. Former hamlet probably named in honor of Jack Burns, the postmaster.

Canton. Peak population (1910), 30. Post office moved from Sioux County December 28, 1891; moved to Sioux County March 10, 1920. Former hamlet probably named for Canton, Ohio.

Carlyle. Post office established January 20, 1886. Moved to Hemingford September 20, 1887. Probably named in honor of Thomas Carlyle, a Scottish essayist-historian. Post office was located at the homestead of postmaster Frederick W. Milck. Located four miles east of Hemingford.

Carpenter. Post office established November 13, 1889; discontinued November 30, 1900. Probably named in honor of Dennis Carpenter, first postmaster.

Corbin. Post office established December 13, 1880; discontinued September 12, 1889. Probably named in honor of Gen. Henry Corbin, whom Robert Gregg, the postmaster, admired.

Dorsey. Former station on the Burlington Railroad probably named in honor of Nebraska Congressman George W. E. Dorsey from the Third District.

Fleming. Post office established April 28, 1887; discontinued October 30, 1900. Origin of the name has not been learned.

Fowling. Post office established October 13, 1920; discontinued 1934. Named for a friend of Nels Peterson.

Ginn. Station on Burlington Railroad.

Girard. Station on the Burlington Railroad probably named for Girard, Ohio.

Grand Lake. Name proposed for Alliance, but postal authorities thought it might be confused with Grand Island, Nebraska.

Gregg. Post office established February 21, 1890; discontinued August 11, 1893. Named in honor of Robert Gregg, first postmaster.

Hashman. Post office established September 10, 1906; discontinued January 31, 1913. Named in honor of Alvin Hashman, first postmaster.

Hemingford. Peak population (1930), 1,025. Post office established September 20, 1887. Named for Hemmingford, Quebec, Canada, by former resident Joseph Hare. Post office department spelled the name with one "m." Hemingford won county seat election with Nonpareil in 1891 and then lost to Alliance in 1899.

Kelley. Post office established May 1, 1888; discontinued July 7, 1888. Origin of the name has not been learned.

Lawn. Peak population (1890), 10. Post office moved from Dawes County August 20, 1886; discontinued April 22, 1907. Origin of the name of this former hamlet, first called Sodville, has not been learned.

Letan. Station on the Burlington Railroad near the Morrill County line.

Libby. Post office established January 18, 1888; discontinued September 6, 1894. Probably named in honor of Samuel Libby, first postmaster.

Malinda. Post office established February 21, 1890. Moved to Sioux County June 16, 1910. First postmaster was Oren Shafter. One source says the place was named for Shafter's mother and another that it was named for his wife.

Marple. Post office changed from Box Butte April 25, 1905. Moved to Sheridan County August 23, 1908. One source says town named for a man who owned a skinning station. Another source says it was named for W. W. Marple of Beatrice, who opened a cream station here.

Nonpareil. Peak population (1890), 50. Post office established July 10, 1886; discontinued 1947. Former town and present station on the Burlington Railroad named by Eugene Heath for nonpareil or 6-point size of type (1/12th of an inch), used for his newspaper. Nonpareil was made county seat on formation of the county, then lost the county seat in election with Hemingford in 1891. Called Buchanan before a post office was established.

Nye. Station named by officials of the Burlington Railroad.

Quiz. Former station on the Burlington Railroad. Name probably chosen for brevity.

Reed. Post office established July 12, 1887; discontinued February 23, 1888. Probably named for Delbert S. Reed, one of the first county commissioners.

Sodville. Name mentioned for the Lawn post office.

Willey. Post office established March 27, 1895; discontinued July 14, 1900. Named in honor of George E. Willey, first postmaster.

Yale. Former station on the Burlington Railroad named by railway officials for its brevity.

BOYD COUNTY

Established in 1891, Boyd County was named in honor of James E. Boyd (1834-1906), governor of Nebraska from 1891 to 1893. Most of what is now Boyd County was part of the Sioux Reservation, Dakota Territory. An 1889 treaty prepared the way for white settlement in the area in 1890.

Alford. Post office established February 5, 1892. Name changed to Monowi July 3, 1902. Town named for William Alford, Sr., who settled here in 1890.

Anoka. Peak population (1910), 145. Post office established September 19, 1902; discontinued 1967. Anoka is a Dakota Indian word meaning "on both sides." Town named by Pioneer Town Site Company for Anoka, Minnesota.

Baker. Peak population (1910), 50. Post office established November 24, 1891; discontinued March 2, 1906. Former village named for Fred Baker, first postmaster.

Basin. Post office established November 24, 1891; discontinued March 14, 1904. Named for the low basins and lakes in the neighborhood.

Bristow. Peak population (1920), 255. Post office established November 24, 1891. Commemorates Secretary of the Treasury Benjamin H. Bristow, who served in President Grant's Cabinet. Town platted by Pioneer Town Site Company in 1902. Before Bristol became a village, post office was located west of present site.

Butte. Peak population (1940), 623. Post office established July 13, 1914. This county seat town named for the Twin Buttes located eight miles west of Butte and visible from South Dakota and five counties in Nebraska.

Doty. Census not available. Post office established January 20, 1881; discontinued February 11, 1902. Former town named for E. H. Doty, who settled here in 1879. He was responsible for many of the area post roads.

Gross. Peak population (1900), 325. Post office name changed from Morton February 28, 1895; discontinued 1960; mail served from Spencer. Town named by Postmaster Benjamin B. Gross, one of the first settlers. He homesteaded the land on which the town is located.

Keya Paha. Post office established August 21, 1877; discontinued February 11, 1888. Named for the Keya Paha River, on which it is located. Name is Indian in origin.

Kinkaid. Post office established October 4, 1901; discontinued September 25, 1902. Probably named in honor of Moses Kinkaid, author of the Kinkaid homesteading law.

Lynch. Peak population (1920), 589. Post office established August 22, 1890. Town named for John Lynch, first postmaster. Petitions designated the town Lynchburg, but U.S. Post Office Department shortened name to Lynch.

Mankato. Peak population (1910), 45. Post office established September 6, 1890; discontinued September 25, 1901. Former village probably named for Mankato, Minnesota, from Indian word "Mu-Ki-To" meaning "blue earth."

Monowi. Peak population (1930), 123. Post office name changed from Alford July 3, 1902; made a rural branch of Lynch in 1970. Town named by Pioneer Town Site company for Indian word meaning flower. Many wild flowers grow in the area.

Morton. Post office established September 1892. Name changed to Gross February 28, 1895. Probably named for J. Sterling Morton, Nebraska statesman and originator of Arbor Day.

Naper. Peak population (1910), 300. Post office established March 5, 1894. Named for Ralph Naper, who gave forty acres of his homestead for a townsite. First called Naperville.

Perry. Post office established May 29, 1899; discontinued March 9, 1900. Probably named for a local settler.

Postville. Former locality probably named for the post road to Fort Randall, South Dakota.

Ranch. Post office established September 24, 1891; discontinued December 22, 1894. Named by Ed Lewis, first postmaster.

Read. Post office established October 30, 1899; discontinued May 31, 1905. Origin of the name of this post office has not been ascertained.

Rochester. Post office established January 4, 1895; discontinued October 31, 1898. Probably named for Rochester, Minnesota.

Rosedale. Peak population (1910), 15. Post office established July 1, 1898; discontinued November 14, 1903. Former village named by John M. Anderson for a place in Minnesota.

Spencer. Peak population (1920), 728. Post office established May 12, 1891. Named for Spencer, Iowa, former home of many of the first settlers. A Mr. Sterns, first postmaster, suggested the name. Originally located near the dam south of town, the community was moved a year later to its present site on the slope.

Sylvia. Located two miles north of Rosedale but never a post office as some sources indicate. Named for Sylvia Rosburg.

Sunnyside. Post office established February 15, 1881; discontinued April 20, 1883. Descriptive word for sunswept area.

Tower. Post office name changed from Walther April 13, 1900; discontinued August 18, 1902. Origin of the name not learned.

Walther. Post office established February 5, 1892. Name changed to Tower April 13,

1900. Named by a Lutheran minister for the Walther League, a German Lutheran youth organization.

BROWN COUNTY

One source says county named for two state legislators named Brown. Another source indicates that there were five Browns. County created by legislative enactment and approved February 19, 1883.

Ainsworth. Peak population (1980), 2,256. Post office name changed from Bone Creek August 3, 1882. County seat town named for Capt. James E. Ainsworth of Missouri Valley, Iowa, chief construction engineer of the Fremont, Elkhorn and Missouri Valley Railroad. During World War II an army air field was located here. Alkali. Post office established January 28, 1909; discontinued September 30, 1910. Named for the alkaline lakes in the region.

Altai. Post office changed from White Cap April 16, 1909; discontinued January 5, 1918. Located on a divide, the name in Latin means high or elevated.

Anderson. Post office established June 23, 1884; discontinued April 19, 1886. Probably named for John Anderson, first postmaster.

Beardwell. Census not available. Post office established November 5, 1909; discontinued February 28, 1927. Former town named for William Beardwell, first postmaster.

Bone Creek. Post office established February 24, 1879; name changed to Ainsworth August 3, 1882. Named for the creek on which it was located. The creek, in turn, named for the numerous bones of buffalo and cattle strewn in the valley. Office located on the Cook and Tower ranches, which distributed mail on the Gordon Trail.

Burgan. Post office established November 25, 1908; discontinued April 15, 1929. Named for George Burgan, first postmaster.

Enders Lake. Post office established November 25, 1908; discontinued April 15, 1929. Former resort and seven-thousand-acre ranch named for J. E. Enders, who owned the ranch on which the resort was located. A hotel, dance hall, and cottages were built later on the lake front.

Evergreen. Post office established January 19, 1881; moved to Johnstown May 9, 1883. Named for the pine trees in the area. Located two and one-half miles from the present town of Johnstown.

Giles. Post office established January 8, 1896. Post office moved to Blaine County May 8, 1903; moved back from Blaine County, July 18, 1908. Post office moved to Blaine County, July 21, 1923. George Rodecker, the first postmaster, named office to honor his neighbor, George Giles, who homesteaded the area in 1886.

Halstead. Post office established June 14, 1888; discontinued October 1, 1892. Possibly named in honor of a local settler.

Huffman. Post office established May 9, 1906; discontinued July 15, 1914. Named in honor of Eck E. Huffman, first postmaster.

Johnstown. Peak population (1900), 480. Post office established May 9, 1883. One source says town named in honor of John Berry, a homesteader who later ran the mail stage to Fort Niobrara before the advent of the railroad. He participated in the construction of the railroad through Brown County. Another source reports town named for Harrison Junction, territorial legislator.

Koshopah. Post office established August 24, 1920; discontinued 1958. Name submitted to post office department was Koskopah for Koskopah Creek, an Indian word.

Lakeland. Post office established August 8, 1896; discontinued September 29, 1917. Named for its location in an area of lakes in southern Brown County.

Long Pine. Peak population (1930), 935. Post office established October 3, 1881. Town named for Long Pine Creek and canyon through which the stream winds. High symmetrical pines on its banks inspired the name.

Mabelo. Post office established January 16, 1836; discontinued January 14, 1895. Name origin not learned; probably a coined word.

Mary. Post office established April 10, 1908; discontinued 1939. Honored Mrs. Mary O'Neill, first postmistress.

Midvale. Post office established September 8, 1885; discontinued November 29, 1922. Name derived from location in the middle of the valley or vale of the Calamus River.

Pershing. Post office established September 15, 1916; discontinued November 29, 1922. Probably named for Gen. John Pershing, commander of the U.S. Army in World War I and prominent in military history of Nebraska.

Pike. Post office established April 23, 1906; discontinued 1933. Named in honor Frank Pike, first postmaster.

Pine Glen. Post office established June 23, 1884; discontinued July 1, 1895. Named for the pine trees growing in a glen or vale.

Raven. Post office established April 12, 1906; discontinued August 24, 1920. Named in honor of John Raven, first postmaster.

Sherman. Post office established April 16, 1898; discontinued April 1, 1899. Probably named for John Sherman, U.S. secretary of state at the time office was established.

Sunnyside. Post office established March 23, 1906; discontinued August 15, 1919. Named for its location, described as being on the sunny side.

White Cap. This was not a post office but a locality; Altai became the post office. Named for a landmark, a sand hill with a wind-scoured top resembling a white cap.

Winfield. Peak population (1910), 12. Post office established August 6, 1886; discontinued April 5, 1914. Probably named for son of H. J. Miller, first postmaster.

Wright. Post office established January 11, 1886; discontinued April 8, 1887. Probably named in honor of James E. Wright, first postmaster.

BUFFALO COUNTY

Named for the feeding grounds of buffalo herds which frequented this area in earlier times. County approved by an act of Territorial Legislature March 14, 1855, but not officially recognized until January 20, 1870.

Alfalfa Center. A former station on the Union Pacific Railroad named for the abundance of alfalfa fields; was probably a major shipping point for alfalfa hay.

Alliston. Post office established December 30, 1880; discontinued October 13, 1881. Origin of the name not learned.

Amherst. Peak population (2000), 277. Post office name changed from Greendale October 7, 1890, John H. Hamilton, first president of the Kearney and Black Hills Railroad, suggested Amherst for the college in Massachusetts.

Armada. Post office established October 25, 1875. Name changed to Miller July 25, 1890. Origin of the name not known. There is a town in Michigan by this name.

Baker. Post office established March 2, 1885; discontinued February 5, 1887. Possibly named in honor of Lee W. Baker, first postmaster.

Beaver Creek. Post office established December 11, 1878. Name changed to Ravenna July 23, 1886, upon completion of railroad. Named for a nearby creek on which beaver lived.

Berg. Post office established February 3, 1875; discontinued February 4, 1884. Origin of the name has not been ascertained.

Boyd's Ranch. Probably a caravan and supply station for westward-bound travelers, it later became a livestock shipping facility. Named for James E. Boyd, later governor of Nebraska.

Buda. Peak population (1910), 45. Post office name changed from Shelby October 23, 1878; discontinued February 29, 1924. One source says town named for a local settler; another, for Budapest, Hungary; and yet another, for Buda, Illinois. Another conjecture: Shelby was a railroad town with railway equipment, probably from the Buda Foundry and Manufacturing Company; the new name Buda could have been taken from the boxes or equipment.

Buller's Ranch. This large ranch located along the main line of the Union Pacific Railroad was a station for cattle shipping.

Butler. Post office established July 31, 1884; discontinued January 23, 1905. Honored Gen. Benjamin F. Butler, then a presidential candidate on the Greenback ticket.

Cartney. Post office established June 20, 1890; discontinued October 30, 1891. Probably named for the first postmaster, John D. McCartney.

Centennial. Post office established July 5, 1876; discontinued April 20, 1880. Named for our country's Declaration of Independence, promulgated one hundred years before the office was established.

Cherry Creek. Post office established February 7, 1879; discontinued September 20, 1880. Town named for creek near which wild chokecherry trees grew.

Crowellton. Post office established December 6, 1872; name changed to Odessa February 29, 1876. Town named in honor of Daniel A. and O. Allen Crowell, early home-steaders in the vicinity.

Denman. Census not available. Post office established June 27, 1914; discontinued 1957; mail served from Kenesaw. Town named in honor of Francis Marion Denman, a Civil War veteran and early pioneer.

Elm Creek. Peak population (2000), 894. Post office established June 9, 1872. Town named after a creek, tributary of the Platte River; many elm trees in the region.

Gage. Post office established July 1, 1899; discontinued November 18, 1899. Origin of the name not learned.

Gibbon. Peak population (2000), 1,759. Post office established June 21, 1871. Town commemorates Maj. Gen. John Gibbon, veteran of the Mexican and Civil Wars and Indian wars on the frontier. Town platted by John Thorpe and George Gilman who led to this site from Ohio the Soldiers Free Homestead Temperance Colony. County seat, first located here in 1871, lost to Kearney in election October 13, 1874.

Glenwood. Census not available. Post office name changed from Glenwood Park September 22, 1894; discontinued November 22, 1900. Railroad station renamed Glenwood Park.

Glenwood Park. Post office established November 18, 1892; name changed to Glenwood September 22, 1894. Named for a nearby park on the Wood River.

Greendale. Post office established April 11, 1879; changed to Amherst October 7, 1890. Probably named in honor of a local settler.

Kearney. Peak population (2000), 27,431. Post office name changed from Kearney Junction December 3, 1873. Named for Fort Kearny, which honored Gen. Stephen Watts Kearny. When the city was incorporated, the word "Junction" was omitted from the official name. Kearney won county seat in election with Gibbon on October 13, 1874. Kearney became transfer point for Texas cattle driven here for shipment by rail to the Chicago and Omaha markets. During World War II, an army air base was located here. Kearney State Teachers College founded, 1904. It is now the University of Nebraska at Kearney.

Kearney Junction. Post office established February 9, 1872; name changed to Kearney December 3, 1873. Junction between the Burlington Railroad and the Union Pacific Railroad.

Luce. Post office established September 28, 1885; discontinued November 21, 1901. Named in honor of John Luce, first postmaster, Civil War veteran, and storekeeper.

Mahilla. Post office established February 23, 1882; discontinued June 3, 1893. First postmaster was William Sparks. Named for William Sparks's wife, Mahila. Post Office Department added extra "l."

Majors. Post office established December 14, 1878; discontinued November 5, 1891. Named in honor of Col. T. J. Majors of Peru, Nebraska.

Miller. Peak population (1910), 330. Post office name changed from Armada July 5, 1890. Town named in honor of Dr. George L. Miller of Omaha, who had landed interests in the vicinity. Dr. Miller stipulated that if the town were built on his land, it should be named in his honor.

Nantasket. Peak population (1890), 25. Post office name changed from Trocknow November 9, 1887; discontinued October 11, 1895. This former town named for Nantasket, Massachusetts. It declined after the coming of the railroad to Ravenna.

Nebraska Center. Post office established 1854; discontinued October 26, 1868. Located on what was once Boyd's Ranch. Early settlers came here with the belief that proximity to Fort Kearny and the Platte River would give them some measure of protection against the Indians and offer opportunities for developing trade. The office, named for its location near the center of Nebraska, was a stopover for the Western and Holladay stage lines to Kearney.

Odessa. Peak population (1950), 150. Post office name changed from Crowellton February 29, 1876. Town possibly named for Odessa, Russia, where many settlers of the Mennonite faith had lived. Citizens met at the home of Mr. and Mrs. Theodore Knox when they chose the town's name.

Optic. Former station on the Union Pacific Railroad. Name origin has not been learned.

Peake. Post office established December 5, 1884; discontinued January 30, 1907. Named in honor of a settler who had secured the post office for his premises.

Platt's. No. 14 of the Pony Express stations in Nebraska, it was located five miles southeast of Odessa.

Pleasanton. Peak population (2000), 360. Post office name changed from Riverview April 18, 1890. This town located in the beautiful Loup River Valley, known locally in the early settlement of the county as Pleasant Valley. In 1890 a branch of the Union Pacific Railroad extended to this point, and the new town was named Pleasanton after the valley.

Poole. Peak population (1920), 337. Post office name changed from Poole Siding February 2, 1906. See note below on Poole Siding.

Poole Siding. Post office established June 23, 1892; name changed to Poole February 2, 1906. Town named in honor of W. W. Poole, who started a ranch in 1876. Town platted by Nebraska Land and Cattle Company, which had a siding on the railroad.

Prairie Center. Post office established July 2, 1874; discontinued April 7, 1902. A locally descriptive designation.

Ravenna. Peak population (1920), 1,703. Post office name changed from Beaver Creek July 23, 1886. This town platted by Lincoln Land Company. R. O. Phillips a member of the company, selected the name Ravenna after the Italian city. The streets also have Italian names.

Riverdale. Peak population (2000), 213. Post office established August 22, 1883. August Raymond, who built the first dwelling, named Riverdale because of the view of Wood River in the Platte Valley.

Riverview. Post office established August 21, 1883; name changed to Pleasanton April 18, 1890. Town named for the view of the Loup River.

Sartoria. Post office established January 14, 1886; discontinued February 2, 1924. This name coined by John Swenson, a homesteader. Swenson wrote that he made many combinations of letters before he finally decided upon the arrangement. His aim was to form a euphonious name. It came out as a French word, Sartoria.

Shafer. Post office established January 11, 1886; discontinued February 17, 1887. When this post office was established, Andrew Jackson Shafer, organizer of the Populist Party in this section, operated farms in Buffalo County.

Sharon. Post office established May 15, 1882; discontinued December 21, 1886. Origin of the name has not been learned.

Shelby. Post office established September 19, 1876; name changed to Buda October 23, 1878. Possibly named in honor of Paul Shelby, assistant general freight agent for the Union Pacific.

Shelton. Peak population (1980), 1,046. Post office name changed from Wood River Centre July 8, 1873. Town named in honor of N. Shelton, auditor in the land department of the Union Pacific Railroad, according to one source. Another source says town named in honor of Nathaniel Shelton, a local pioneer.

Sodtown. A locality east of Ravenna, possibly named for the sod houses that dotted the area in earlier times.

South Loup. Post office established August 24, 1874; discontinued January 9, 1877. Named for its location on the South Loup River.

South Ravenna. Two miles south of Ravenna on Union Pacific Railroad.

Stanley. Post office name changed from Huntsville March 15, 1877; discontinued January 1891. Origin of the name not learned.

Stevenson. Former station of the Union Pacific Railroad located west of Kearney.

St. Michael. Peak population (1940) 32. Post office established February 18, 1887; discontinued, 1956. Former town established by the Lincoln Land Company. An Irishman, Mike Kyne, who owned the land on which the town was built, told the company he would sell the land cheaply if they named the place in some way for him.

Sweetwater. Peak population (1930), 151. Post office established December 21, 1874. Made an independent station of Hazard, 1963. Village named for its location near Sweetwater Creek, noted for the excellent water found there in pioneer days. Trocknow. Post office established February 1, 1886; name changed to Nantasket November 9, 1887. Named in honor of the birthplace of the famous Hussite leader and Bohemian general, Johann Zizka.

Waltham. Post office established August 14, 1884; discontinued May 11, 1886. Possibly named for Waltham, Massachusetts.

Waters. Post office established December 5, 1883; discontinued June 29, 1885. Possibly named in honor of Henry Waters, first postmaster.

Watertown. Peak population (1910), 35. Post office established October 17, 1890; discontinued September 30, 1921. This former hamlet named for the water from a cistern on a hill via a trackside penstock or water crane.

Watsonawa. Post office established May 23, 1896; rescinded November 1, 1896. Possibly named in honor of H. D. Watson, who owned the Watson Ranch.

White Cloud. Post office established May 28, 1864; discontinued May 29, 1867. Possibly named in honor of White Cloud, an Iowa Indian leader. This was also a station for the Western and Holladay stage lines to Kearney.

Wood River Centre. Post office established August 20, 1860; moved to Shelton July 8, 1873. A small settlement that stood near the present town of Shelton, Wood River Centre was founded by English converts to the Mormon faith and led by Edward Oliver. A broken axle on a wagon forced Oliver to turn back. The Olivers spent the winter in a log hut on the banks of the Wood River, settled there and built a store. When Shelton was platted nearby, he and his group moved there, and Wood River Centre became another ghost town.

Wrightsville. Post office established January 11, 1886; discontinued January 15, 1887. Possibly named in honor of Samuel Wright, first postmaster.

BURT COUNTY

Named in honor of Francis Burt (1807-54), governor of Nebraska Territory in 1854. County founded in 1854. Boundaries were approved by the Legislature February 18, 1855, but redefined January 10, 1862.

Alder Grove. Post office established October 19, 1875; discontinued June 14, 1888. Named for a grove of alder trees in the vicinity.

Argo. Peak population (1900), 43. Post office established July 22, 1878; discontinued December 7, 1904. Former town probably named for Argo, Illinois, or Argo, Missouri. In Greek mythology the Argo was the ship on which Jason sailed to find the golden fleece.

Arizona. Peak population (1870), 89. Post office established July 15, 1867; discontinued December 12, 1899. Former river port formerly called Newton after a pioneer settler east of Tekamah.

Basford. Peak population (1900), 20. Post office established June 8, 1895; discontinued September 23, 1901. Former village named for a town in England.

Bertha. Post office established June 30, 1890; discontinued September 6, 1900. Named in honor of Bertha Hansen, whose husband owned and operated the blacksmith shop.

Bertrand. Post office established February 1879; discontinued June 22, 1881. Probably named for the steamboat which sank in the Missouri River below Burt County.

Blackbird. Post office established June 15, 1871; discontinued May 27, 1872. Named in honor of Blackbird, Omaha Indian leader.

Central Bluff. Post office established September 2, 1857; discontinued April 7, 1859. Named for a centrally located bluff.

Central City. Peak population (1870), 11. Post office established August 7, 1867; name changed to Riverside March 28, 1879. Former river town perhaps named for its central location as a Missouri River port.

Clark. Post office established June 23, 1874; discontinued November 29, 1880. Probably named in honor of William A. Clark, first postmaster.

Conkling. Former station on the Chicago, St. Paul, Minneapolis and Omaha Railroad named for Charles Conkling, who came to this locality in 1873 from Illinois.

Craig. Peak population (1930), 452. Post office established September 5, 1881. Named in honor of William Stewart Craig, owner of the land on which the town was platted when the railroad was built.

Crocy. Probably an early promotion town that never got beyond the platting stage.

Decatur. Peak population (1940), 905. Post office established February 28, 1857. Named in honor of Stephen Decatur, member of the Decatur Town and Ferry Company that founded the town on the Missouri River. Due to floods the town has moved frequently to follow the changing course of the river. At one time an important ferry linked this part of Nebraska with Iowa.

Essen. A railroad siding on the Burlington Railroad. Origin of the name has not been revealed.

Eureka. Former station on the Chicago, St. Paul, Minneapolis and Omaha Railroad.

Glen Dale. Former locality.

Golden. Post office name changed from Golden Spring May 4, 1894; discontinued August 1, 1901. See note on Golden Spring.

Golden Spring. Peak population (1880), 32. Post office established April 15, 1875. Name changed to Golden May 4, 1894. Former town so named for its proximity to a Golden Spring. Also noted as a stage depot.

Hollinsburg. Probably a proposed river town that never got beyond the platting stage.

Homestead. Post office established September 6, 1867; discontinued January 25, 1881. Probably named for post office located on a homestead.

Lake Quinnebaugh. Resort on the Missouri River.

Lyons. Peak population (1980), 1,214. Post office established June 19, 1875. Town named in honor of Waldo Lyons, who purchased land here in 1869.

Newton. Post office established April 7, 1871; discontinued October 12, 1871. Probably named for W. B. Newton, first postmaster.

Oakland. Peak population (1950), 1,456. Post office established May 11, 1868. Town named in honor of John Oak, who settled here in 1862 and owned the land when townsite was platted.

Ouren. Former station on the Chicago, St. Paul, Minneapolis and Omaha Railroad. Probably named for a company official.

Peak. Former station on the Chicago, St. Paul, Minneapolis and Omaha Railroad.

Riverside. Post office name changed from Central City March 28, 1870; discontinued June 28, 1875. This former town had a store and sawmill on the Missouri River. Named for its location on a river.

Silver Creek. Post office established May 5, 1863; discontinued June 18, 1875. Named for the creek and valley in which it was located.

Spur. Former station on the Chicago, St. Paul, Minneapolis and Omaha Railroad.

St. Paul. Probably named after a church in the vicinity.

Tekamah. Peak population (1940), 1,925. Post office established March 22, 1855. This county seat town founded by Col. Benjamin R. Folsom and eight companies from Utica, New York. One source says town named by an early settler, N. N. Byers, for a place in California. Town is located on old Indian camping ground.

Toxword. Former station on the Burlington Railroad named for N. A. Toxword, early settler.

Woodsville City. Former town on the Missouri River chartered February 10, 1857. Site of a sawmill and boat landing washed away by Missouri River floods.

Zion. Former station on the Chicago, St. Paul, Minneapolis and Omaha Railroad. Probably named for a church in the vicinity.

BUTLER COUNTY

Named in honor of William O. Butler (1791-1880) of Kentucky, appointed territorial governor of Nebraska. He declined the office, which was later accepted by Francis Burt of South Carolina. Boundaries were defined and county established by legislative enactment June 26, 1856.

Abie. Peak population (1910), 210. Post office established November 22, 1878. Named in honor of Abigail Stevens, first postmistress, whose husband applied for a post office and named it for his wife. Postal authorities changed the spelling to Abie.

Alexis. Post office name changed from Pepperville March 19, 1872; discontinued February 20, 1885. Origin of name is unknown. First postmaster was A. Gerrard. There is also an Alexis, Illinois.

Appleton. Post office established June 23, 1874; discontinued March 30, 1880. Origin of name not ascertained. There is also an Appleton, Wisconsin.

Bell. Post office name changed from Patron, July 12, 1880, to Bellwood December 30, 1881. See Bellwood.

Bellwood. Peak population (2000), 446. Post office name changed from Bell December 30, 1881. Named by Mrs. Mary Finch in honor of Jesse D. Bell, town founder.

Brainard. Peak population (1920), 468. Post office established October 16, 1877. Union Pacific Railroad named town for David Brainard, missionary to the Indians.

Bruno. Peak population (1910 and 1920), 468. Post office established April 7, 1888. Town named for Brno (now in Czech Republic), from which early settlers came. Railroad later changed Brno to Bruno, which was more easily pronounced.

Butler Center. Post office established January 15, 1871; moved to Garrison September 23, 1880. Founded by S. L. Russell and S. J. Oliver, the town was center of commerce until the selection of David City as the county seat. With the coming of the railroad to Garrison, it lost its identity.

Cairo. Post office established August 19, 1873; discontinued September 15, 1873. Probably named for Cairo, Illinois.

Carmel. Post office established November 3, 1873; discontinued January 10, 1877. Probably named for Carmel, a mountain mentioned in the Bible. There is also a Carmel, Illinois.

Connell. Site of this locality has not been learned, but it is listed in 1882 Rand-McNally Atlas.

Cottonwood. Post office established August 1, 1871; discontinued January 28, 1888. Post office probably located near cottonwood trees, which are native to Nebraska.

David City. Peak population (2000), 2,597. Post office name changed from Ollie August 4, 1873. County seat town named in honor of a Mrs. Miles (nee David), who deeded a tract of land for the townsite. Another source indicated the town was named for David Butler, first Nebraska governor. A third source says named for a Mr. Davids, relative of William Miles, who was patron and part owner of the site. The "s" was dropped for convenience. David City won county seat from Savannah in 1873.

Dwight. Peak population (1930), 323. Post office name changed from Lone Star August 22, 1884. Named with the coming of the railroad for Dwight, Illinois, where many residents formerly lived. Postmaster Henry Glover was instrumental in securing the name Dwight for the town.

Earl. This place was not a post office; the name was changed to Savannah on September 20, 1869. Previously named for William Earl, a settler who came here in 1858.

East Ellsworth. This former locality derived name from its situation east of Ellsworth.

Edholm. Post office established April 22, 1882; discontinued 1933. Origin of the name not learned.

Ellsworth. Post office established August 10, 1867; discontinued March 4, 1870. Origin of the name not learned; there are places in eleven different states with this name.

Foley. Post office established December 5, 1898; discontinued October 4, 1906. Probably named for a railroad official.

Gardner's Ranch. A stage stop which probably existed about 1859.

Garrison. Peak population (1900), 250. Post office established September 23, 1880; made a rural station of David City in 1966. Town named in honor of William Lloyd Garrison, leader of the anti-slavery movement prior to the Civil War, by a Mr. Sargent, an admirer of Garrison from Massachusetts.

Hennigan. Former locality two miles from Butler Center, named for Peter Hennigan, early settler. While never a post office, it once vied for Butler County seat.

Hiawatha. Post office established March 13, 1874; discontinued January 2, 1878. Named for the principal character in the poem by Henry Wadsworth Longfellow. Office located in the residence of Postmaster Perley M. Morse.

Kingston. A proposed town in early Butler County history.

Linwood. Peak population (1910), 329. Post office name changed from Skull Creek April 18, 1874. Named for the linden or basswood trees, rare in Nebraska, but growing in this area. Town platted by Waverly Town Site Company.

Loma. Peak population (1960), 60. Post office name changed from Spur, March 5, 1902. Loma, a Spanish word, means a "little hill or hillock rising from a plain." Town supposedly named by Union Pacific Railroad officials for unknown reason.

Lone Star. Post office established December 14, 1872; name changed to Dwight August 22, 1884. Post office located at the residence of J. C. Kerr, but after the coming of the railroad, name was changed to Dwight. Probably derived from nickname for Texas.

Mahala City. Never had a post office but was selected as county seat in 1858; Savannah was selected a short time later. Origin of name not known.

Millerton. Peak population (1910), 28. Post office established March 27, 1888; discontinued 1935. Former village named in honor of William Miller, early settler and landowner.

Nimberg. Peak population (1900), 25. Post office established October 9, 1888; discontinued November 7, 1895. Mail served from Linwood. Former town and present community named in honor of Nymburk, town in what is now Czech Republic. Name changed to accommodate English pronunciation.

Octavia. Peak population (1910), 200. Post office established January 27, 1888. Named in honor of Octavia Speltz, wife of Allen Speltz, a prominent farmer. Town platted by Pioneer Town Site Company.

Ollie. Post office established March 21, 1872; name changed to David City August 4, 1873. Origin of the name has not been learned.

Ora. Post office established December 1, 1875; discontinued July 23, 1878. Former post office located at a store owned by J. W. Latta when he was postmaster. Named for the daughter of a Mr. Latta, a homesteader.

Patron. Post office established November 6, 1874; name changed to Bell, July 12, 1880. Name possibly suggested for the Patrons of Husbandry or the Grange.

Pepperville. Post office established September 20, 1869; name changed to Alexis March 19, 1872. Probably named in honor of Hubbell Pepper, an early settler.

Prairie Center. Former locality named for surrounding prairie.

Reading. Former locality named for the precinct in which it was located, the precinct named for Reading, Michigan.

Ridgeland. Post office established April 23, 1879; discontinued December 29, 1879. Probably named for a geographic characteristic. There is also a Ridgeland, Wisconsin.

Rising City. Peak population (1880), 775. Post office name changed from Summit October 14, 1878. Named in honor of two brothers, A. W. and S. W. Rising, who owned the townsite.

Salona. Post office established December 27, 1875; discontinued August 13, 1877. Former post office located at the residence of Thomas Logan, first postmaster. Origin of the name is unknown.

Savannah. Peak population (1880), 25. Post office established January 17, 1870; discontinued March 21, 1882. Former county seat located on the old Gardner's Ranch. Town may have been named for cities in Georgia, Missouri, or Tennessee. Savannah lost county seat to David City in 1873.

Shinn's Ferry. A ferry to accommodate the stage coaches and freighters across the Platte River on their westward trek in early Nebraska history.

Skull Creek. Post office established April 20, 1868; name changed to Linwood April 18, 1874. This town played an important part in the westward immigration. Named for the numerous Pawnee and/or buffalo skulls found along its creek bed.

Spur. Post office established February 26, 1896; name changed to Loma March 5, 1902. Probably named for location on a railroad spur.

Summit. Post office established December 1, 1871; name changed to Rising City October 14, 1878. Named for Summit, Wisconsin, by C. C. Cobb, who established a mercantile business here. Post office located within the store.

Surprise. Peak population (1900), 348. Post office established February 28, 1883. So named because settlers were surprised by the good quality of the land.

Susquehanna. Post office established February 1, 1856; discontinued June 6, 1861. Probably named for the Susquehanna River Valley in Pennsylvania.

Ulysses. Peak population (1880), 700. Post office established October 5, 1869. Commemorates Ulysses S. Grant, president of the United States and Union Army commander during the Civil War.

Urban. Post office established February 8, 1870; discontinued November 26, 1877. Origin of the name has not been learned.

Wanatah. Former locality probably named for Wanatah, LaPorte County, Indiana. Name is Indian in origin.

Ware. Post office established May 18, 1895; discontinued November 19, 1903. Named for Ware family from Iowa.

Yanka. Former railroad station on the Union Pacific Railroad between David City and Brainard. Origin of the name has not been learned.

CASS COUNTY

Named in honor of Gen. Lewis Cass (1782-1866), American statesman and patriot. County approved by Territorial Legislature March 7, 1855, and redefined January 26, 1856.

Alvo. Peak population (1910), 250. Post office established February 12, 1891. The name of this town and post office chosen by the U.S. Post Office Department. Name probably selected because of its brevity.

Andrusville. Peak population (1880), 25. Post office established February 24, 1879; discontinued February 5, 1890. This former hamlet named in honor of Orasmus Andrus, first postmaster.

Avoca. This first Avoca was a proposed town, filed and recorded October 19, 1857. It never reached more than the promotion stage. Site was three miles east of present town of Avoca.

Avoca. Peak population (2000), 270. Post office established September 2, 1857. Town platted by George Fairfield, surveyor for Amos Tefft, owner of the land and first settler. The name is probably derived from Thomas Moore's poem "Sweet Vale of Avoca," extolling a river in Ireland. There is an Avoca, Iowa.

Belmont. Post office established May 6, 1872; discontinued April 3, 1888. Probably named for one of the eighteen U.S. post offices called Belmont.

Bluffdale. A proposed town that never got beyond the platting stage. Filed for platting March 9, 1857.

Bradford City. Proposed town recorded and filed February 13, 1857.

Brooklyn. A proposed town that never went beyond the recording and platting stage. Filed for platting February 3, 1857.

Bushberry. Post office established October 5, 1880; discontinued September 25, 1886. Origin of the name has not been learned.

Caladonia. A proposed town that never developed beyond the platting and recording stage. Filed for platting February 27, 1857.

Camp Harriet Harding. A youth camp located near Louisville.

Canotia. A proposed town which never progressed beyond the platting and recording stage. Filed for platting June 22, 1855.

Capitol City. Filed for platting August 3, 1857, but never went beyond the platting and recording stage.

Carlisle. A proposed town which never attained more than the recording stage. Filed for platting October 21, 1856.

Cassville. Former town filed for platting in 1855 by W. G. Gage, who ran a store and organized Western University, January 26, 1856. It did not acquire a post office. The university never went beyond the promotion stage.

Cedar Bluff. Proposed town filed for platting April 14, 1857, but never attained more than the promotion stage. Located south of the present town of Nehawka.

Cedar Creek. Peak population (2000), 396. Post office established March 20, 1872. Named for a nearby creek with cedar trees growing along its banks.

Cedar Island. Post office established May 5, 1857; discontinued August 5, 1858. Probably named for a single cedar tree on an island in the Platte River.

Centerville. A proposed town that never got beyond the platting stage.

Centre Valley. Post office established January 30, 1861; discontinued 1863. So named for its central location.

Clay City. A proposed town that never went beyond the platting and recording stages. Filed for platting November 14, 1856. Located west of Williamsport.

Cleveland. Post office established November 8, 1858; discontinued March 19, 1860. Probably named for Cleveland, Ohio; located on the Missouri River.

Concord. Census not available. Post office established December 14, 1870; discontinued January 15, 1880. A former town platted by Peter and Daniel Beaver on the Platte River. Probably named for towns in Massachusetts or New Hampshire.

Cullom. A station on the Burlington Railroad located near Plattsmouth.

Eagle. Peak population (2000), 1,105. Post office name changed from Sunlight October 7, 1887. Probably named for the American eagle.

Eight Mile Grove. Post office established August 22, 1868; discontinued August 31, 1893. Probably named for a grove of trees which extended eight miles in length.

El Dorado. A proposed townsite filed for recording in 1857 and never developed beyond the platting stage.

Elgin City. A proposed town filed for recording October 27, 1857, and never developed beyond the platting stage.

Elltown. A proposed town that never evolved beyond the platting and recording stage. Filed for platting February 1, 1857. Site later became North Rock Bluff.

Elmwood. Peak population (2000), 668. Post office established April 10, 1868. Town named by David McCaig, first postmaster, for a grove of elm trees. The first townsite was located on Stove Creek about two and one-half miles northeast of the present site.

Factorville. Proposed town that never advanced beyond the platting and recording stage in 1857. Site later became known as Factoryville.

Factoryville. Peak population (1870), 100. Post office established April 10, 1868. Name changed to Union Mills February 23, 1873. Name changed back to Factoryville June 14, 1880; discontinued prior to 1888. This promising town, which had most of the establishments that comprised any enterprising place, declined when the railroad was built on the other side of Weeping Water Creek.

Fairview. A proposed name for Murray, but there already was a Murray within the state.

Flora City. A proposed town that never got beyond the promotion stage in the 1850s.

Folden's Mill. A proposed town that failed to materialize in the boom period.

Franklin. A proposed town that never progressed beyond the platting and recording stage. Site was on the Platte River east of Concord.

Glendale. Post office established May 14, 1857; discontinued August 23, 1875. The post office was moved four times during its existence.

Granada. A proposed town that never went beyond the promotion stage. Filed for platting February 2, 1857.

Grand Rapids. A proposed town, filed for platting in 1858, located just west of Weeping Water.

Greenwood. Peak population (1980), 587. Post office established July 5, 1870. Town takes its name from a nearby creek named for an early settler, a Mr. Greenwood.

Independence City. A projected town of the boom period that never got beyond the promotion stage. Filed for recording July 11, 1857.

Inhelder Station. Projected town near Cedar Creek in 1850s; failed soon afterward. Probably named for John Inhelder, an early settler.

Iowa City. Filed for platting in 1857 on Wapahoo Creek but never went beyond the promotion stage.

Kanosha. Census not available. Post office established May 15, 1855; discontinued October 9, 1868. Early steamboat town on the Missouri River. A ferry boat provided a crossing to Iowa. Possibly named for Kenosha, Wisconsin, although a spelling error changed an "e" to an "a." The town's early promise faded with rerouting of the railroad, and Kanosha became a ghost town.

Kingville. Post office established May 27, 1879; discontinued October 10, 1879. Named in honor of Charles King, first postmaster.

Lewistown. Post office established July 11, 1855; discontinued October 5, 1858. Origin of the name not learned.

Liberty. Proposed town which never got beyond the promotion stage. Filed for recording April 10, 1857. Located on the Missouri River south of Rock Bluff.

Louisville. Peak population (1960), 1,194. Post office established January 26, 1857. Town thought to be named for Louisville, Kentucky, by one source. Another source says named for a Mr. Louis who operated a grist mill.

Luella. Post office established July 13, 1876; discontinued January 23, 1882. Origin of the name not learned. The first postmaster was George Haigward.

Manley. Peak population (1940), 249. Post office established June 4, 1883. There is a controversy over the naming of the town. There were three different ranchmen called Manley living in the vicinity, and each thought the town was named for him.

Mannland. Post office established June 7, 1876; discontinued February 29, 1888. Origin of the name not learned.

Marseilles. A proposed town that never moved beyond the promotion stage and was recorded for platting April 6, 1857.

Martins. A proposed town of the 1850s which never got beyond the promotion stage.

Moffitt. A proposed town of the boom period of the 1850s.

Montevalle. A proposed town which never attained more than the promotion stage in 1857. Located east of Wabash.

Mount Hope. Post office established February 27, 1871; discontinued September 26, 1872. Origin of the name not learned.

Mount Pleasant. Post office established September 20, 1858; discontinued January 12, 1888. This Methodist community may have been named for Mount Pleasant, Iowa.

Murdock. Peak population (2000), 269. Post office established April 3, 1891. Town named in honor of a Mr. Murdock, a member of the townsite company for the Chicago, Rock Island and Pacific Railroad.

Murray. Peak population (2000), 481. Post office established September 22, 1884. This town named in honor of the Rev. George L. Murray, pastor of the United Presbyterian Church.

Mynard. Peak population (1930), 304. Post office established March 1, 1894; discontinued 1939. Town named in honor of Mynard Lewis, former civil engineer for the Missouri Pacific Railroad.

Nehawka. Peak population (1930, 1940), 353. Post office established January 8, 1875. This town received its name from Isaac Pollard. On a trip to Washington D.C., he thumbed through a book of Indian names and chose Nehawka, which postal authorities accepted.

North Independence. A proposed town filed and recorded for July 13, 1857, but never advanced beyond the recording stage.

North Rock Bluff. An early community which later became part of Rock Bluff.

Oreapolis. Census not available. Post office established October 24, 1859; discontinued October 22, 1864. Name is probably Greek in origin.

Osage. This proposed town, filed for recording in the 1850s, never reached more than the promotion stage. Probably named for the Indian tribe.

Otopolis. A proposed town filed for recording December 24, 1856, which reached only the promotion stage.

Parabell City. A proposed town, filed for recording October 5, 1856, which never went beyond the promotion stage.

Parma. A proposed town, filed for recording October 5, 1856, which never went beyond the promotion stage.

Pickens. A former station on the Missouri Pacific Railroad located near Nehawka.

Platteau City. A proposed town filed for recording March 24, 1857. Located near South Bend.

Plattsmouth. Peak population (2000), 6,887. Post office established December 23, 1854. This county seat named for its position at the mouth of the Platte River, which empties into the Missouri. The town platted by Plattsmouth Town Company in 1854 and made the county seat at that time.

Ravenna. A proposed town filed for recording December 21, 1856, that never reached beyond the promotion stage.

Rock Bluff. Census not available. Post office established March 12, 1857; discontinued 1904. This former town, located on the Missouri River, took its name from the rocky bluffs in the area.

Rockland. A projected town of the boom period that never got beyond the recording stage. Filed for recording January 14, 1857. Located south of Rock Bluff on the Missouri River.

Salt Creek. Post office established June 19, 1864; discontinued October 9, 1868. Named for a nearby creek.

Smithland. A proposed town filed for recording July 13, 1857. Never attained more than the promotion stage.

South Bend. Peak population (1920), 142. Post office established October 29, 1856. Named for its geographical location on the south bend of the Platte River.

St. Charles. A proposed town, filed for platting January 7, 1857, which never attained more than the promotion stage. Located on the Missouri River near Concord.

Summit. A proposed name for the town of Manley.

Summit City. A proposed town recorded for filing November 28, 1856, which never got beyond the recording stage.

Sunlight. A proposed town filed for recording in 1857.

Sunlight. Post office established January 26, 1876; name changed to Eagle October 27, 1887.

Three Grove. Post office established July 31, 1861; discontinued May 1, 1884. Descriptive of a grove of trees in the vicinity.

Tobin. Station on the Missouri Pacific Railroad.

Todd's. Probably a former station on the Missouri Pacific Railroad.

Troy. A proposed town filed for recording June 6, 1857, but never developed further.

Tysonville. A proposed town of the boom period filed for recording March 30, 1857.

Union. Established in 1890 when the Missouri Pacific built north to Omaha. Shipping point for area farmers to Omaha hay and livestock markets.

Union Mills. Post office name changed from Factoryville February 23, 1873; switched back to Factoryville June 14, 1880. Named for Union sentiment held by residents during the Civil War.

Victoria. Post office established January 20, 1885; discontinued February 8, 1893. Former town commemorates Queen Victoria.

Wabash. Peak population (1930), 202. Post office established August 27, 1886. Town said to be named by settlers from Indiana for that state's Wabash River or for the Indiana town of Wabash.

Washington City. A projected town of the boom period that never attained more than the promotion stage. Filed and recorded July 23, 1857.

Waterville. A proposed town of the boom period filed for recording February 10, 1857, by Isaac Pollard and Lawson Sheldon.

Weeping Water. Peak population (1890), 1,350. Post office established September 1, 1857. Town situated on the creek called by the French L'Eau qui Pleure or the water that weeps.

Weston. A proposed town that never attained more than the promotion stage. Filed for recording November 15, 1856.

Wheatland. Proposed town filed for recording December 15, 1856, and never advanced beyond the promoting stage.

Williamsport. A proposed town filed for recording November 26, 1856. Located south of Plattsmouth on the Missouri River.

Woodland. Projected town of the boom period, which was filed and recorded November 3, 1856. It never evolved beyond the recording stage.

CEDAR COUNTY

Organized by an act of Legislature February 12, 1857. Boundaries were redefined January 13, 1860. County named for cedar trees in the region.

Andrew. Post office established March 17, 1882; discontinued January 18, 1902. Named in honor of Andrew McNeal, first postmaster.

Asbre. Former community, located near Crofton, named for an Asbre family.

Aten. Peak population (1890), 50. Post office name changed from Green Island January 11, 1882; discontinued July 3, 1906. Former town and present locality named in honor of John Aten, first postmaster.

Belden. Peak population (1920), 285. Post office established June 20, 1890. Town named in honor of Scott Belden, paymaster on the shortline railroad built from Sioux City, Iowa, to O'Neill, Nebraska, in 1890.

Bow Valley. Post office established December 11, 1871; discontinued April 4, 1903. Named for the creek on which it was located by postmaster Conrad Wisner.

Branch. Post office established August 27, 1884; discontinued October 12, 1895. Probably named for its location between two branches of the main creek.

Case. Former station on the Chicago, St. Paul, Minneapolis and Omaha Railroad. Probably named for A. B. Case, an early settler and Civil War veteran.

Center Bow. Post office established February 9, 1872; discontinued May 24, 1875. Probably named for its location near the center branch of Bow Creek.

Claramont. Post office established June 12, 1884; name changed to Laurel on May 28, 1892. Claramont is a misnomer, because the name presented by Louis Tolles to the Post Office Department was Claremont. Through a clerical error the letter "a" was inserted in lieu of the letter "e." Townspeople and the North Western Railroad used Claremont. Tolles, an early Cedar County settler from Ascutneyville, Vermont, who lived close to Claremont, New Hampshire, chose the name Claremont for the new town on land donated by Roger T. O'Gara. When the new site of Laurel was platted, some businesses in Claremont moved to the new site, and the North Western Railroad used Claremont as a flag station between Coleridge and Laurel.

Claremont. See Claramont.

Coleridge. Peak population (1920), 674. Post office name changed from Lawnridge September 10, 1883. Named in honor of Lord Coleridge from England, who visited the townsite. Mr. Whitten, general superintendent of the Chicago, St. Paul, Minneapolis and Omaha Railroad, named the town.

Constance. Post office established April 28, 1888; discontinued April 3, 1909. Origin of name not learned.

Curlew. Post office established December 11, 1871; discontinued October 7, 1872.

Supposedly promoted by easterners but never got beyond the platting stage. Origin of name not learned.

Elm Grove. Post office established May 1, 1858; discontinued October 1, 1868. Post office established by Philip Clark, first postmaster, and named for a grove of elm trees.

Fordyce. Peak population (1910), 250. Post office established March 26, 1907. Village named in honor of William Fordyce, train dispatcher for the Chicago, St. Paul, Minneapolis and Omaha Railroad.

Green Island. Post office established January 7, 1871; name changed to Aten June 11, 1882. This post office, located across the Missouri River from Yankton, South Dakota, was wiped out by an 1881 flood and moved to present Aten. Probably named for lush plants in the valley.

Hartington. Peak population (1980), 1,730. Post office name changed from Paragon October 17, 1883. County seat named by a Mr. Whitten of the Chicago, St. Paul, Minneapolis and Omaha Railroad for Lord Hartington of England. (Another town had been named for Lord Coleridge.) Lord Hartington visited the U.S. a year before the founding of the town. Platted by T. T. Linkhart, Hartington won county seat in election with St. Helena.

Havens. Post office established November 25, 1884; discontinued December 12, 1893. Probably named in honor of Alfred Havens, first postmaster.

Laurel. Peak population (1950), 944. Post office name changed from Claramont May 28, 1892. The Pacific Short Line Railroad, now the Burlington, built its east-west line with a junction of the North Western Railroad running southeast to northwest, about a mile east of Claremont. The townsite of Laurel was platted from farm land owned by William Martin and was to be named for his oldest daughter, Laura. There was already a post office called Laura in Holt County. As a compromise, the name Laurel was accepted.

The North Western Railroad failed to recognize the new town of Laurel and continued to drop mail and passengers at Claremont. Mail had to be transported by horsedrawn conveyance to Laurel. The State Railroad Commission ordered the railway to observe Laurel as a stop. The Claremont depot, water tank, elevator, and section house were then moved to Laurel.

Lawnridge. Post office established May 21, 1878; name changed to Coleridge September 10, 1883. First settlement made by R. T. O'Gara in 1870. Probably named for a grassy ridge having a lawn-like appearance.

Logan Valley. Post office established June 23, 1874; name changed to Norris October 3, 1881. Named for Logan Creek and Logan Valley.

Magnet. Peak population (1910), 178. Post office established April 21, 1894. Town named by B. E. Smith, townsite proprietor, for the "magnet stone" with the hope that it "would attract the people as the magnet attracts iron."

Menominee. Peak population (1890), 50. Post office established May 6, 1867; discontinued May 27, 1902; mail served from Fordyce. Village named for either Menominee, Michigan, or Menominee, Wisconsin; both named for Menominee Indian tribe.

Norris. Post office name changed from Logan Valley October 3, 1881; moved to Coleridge October 27, 1887. Named for A. Hart Norris of Batavia, New York, who wanted the place called Elm City for elm trees he planted. Most of the trees died, and Norris was adopted.

Obert. Peak population (1930), 117. Post office name changed from Oberton November 6, 1909. See note below on Oberton.

Oberton. Post office established July 3, 1909; name changed to Obert November 6, 1909. Town named in honor of a Mr. Oberton, Chicago, St. Paul, Minneapolis and Omaha Railroad official. Name changed to avoid confusion with Overton, Nebraska.

Paragon. Post office name changed from Smithland February 15, 1882; name changed to Hartington October 17, 1883. Town may have been named for the descriptive word "paragon," meaning to surpass or a model of perfection. There is also a Paragon, Indiana. Town first called Paragon City.

Plainfield. Post office established February 11, 1898; rescinded July 17, 1898. Probably named for one of twelve post offices or towns in the U.S. with the same name.

Randolph. Peak population (1930), 1,145. Post office established January 12, 1887. Town commemorates the famous English statesman, Lord Randolph Churchill (1849-95). Named by F. H. Peavey of Minneapolis, Minnesota.

Smithland. Post office established December 11, 1871; name changed to Paragon February 15, 1882. Probably named in honor of Michael Smith, first postmaster.

St. Helena. Peak population (1880), 300. Post office established June 29, 1857. Named by Carl C. P. Meyer, first settler in the vicinity (1857), probably for the patron St. Helena, widow of the fourth century Emperor Constantius Chlorus, mother of Constantine and first Christian emperor of Rome. St. Helena won county seat in election with St. James in 1869, but lost it to Hartington.

St. James. Peak population (1880), 81. Post office established July 13, 1858; discontinued May 31, 1909. Mail served from Wynot. Village platted by Col. C. C. Van and Moses H. Deming, formerly of Des Moines, Iowa, in 1856. St. James, first county seat, lost it in election with St. Helena in 1869. Probably named for one of seven St. Jameses in the U.S.

St. Peter. Census not available. Post office established May 21, 1875; discontinued January 18, 1902. Former village named in honor of Peter Abts, first settler who came here in 1870.

Strahmburg. Former locality named for Saby Strahm, early settler; probably intended for a townsite.

Taft. Former locality in early county settlement.

Van. Post office established March 12, 1883; discontinued April 7, 1884. Named in honor of C. C. Van, early settler.

Wareham. Post office established March 19, 1907; discontinued January 31, 1913. Former post office and railroad station probably named by railroad officials for Wareham, Massachusetts.

Washington. An 1880 map shows Washington as railroad terminus, where Hartington now stands.

Waucapena. Census not available. Post office established September 2, 1857; discontinued October 3, 1898. Former town probably named for a leader of the Potawatomi Indians.

Wynot. Peak population (1940), 416. Post office established December 16, 1907. Wynot, a shortened version of "why not," was suggested by a citizen who knew an elderly German settler whose answer to all questions was "Why not?" The boys and girls imitated him and later the older citizens caught their habit. The town was once the terminus of a now inactive Chicago, St. Paul, Minneapolis and Omaha Railroad line.

CHASE COUNTY

Created by legislative enactment in 1886, it was named in honor of Champion S. Chase (?-1848), then attorney general of Nebraska. County divided from Keith County.

Allendale. Named for a local settler, this short-lived town showed a population of thirty-two in 1890. Moved to Lamar upon completion of Burlington Railroad.

Best. Post office established June 12, 1902: discontinued 1939. Named in honor of Mrs. Ethel Best, first postmistress.

Blanche. Post office established June 18, 1887; discontinued February 28, 1920. Named for the daughter of G. C. Davis, first postmaster.

Catherine. Post office established April 2, 1890; moved to Hayes County August 7, 1891; moved back to Chase County September 3, 1896; discontinued November 14, 1914. Named in honor of the wife of Emmanuel Reisinger, homesteader of land on which the post office was established. Patrons suggested the name.

Champion. Peak population (1950), 140. Post office name changed from Hamilton May 26, 1887. Named in honor of Champion S. Chase, for whom the county is named. The Champion Mill is a state historical park operated by the Nebraska Game and Parks Commission.

Chase. Post office name changed from Eldridge November 28, 1887; discontinued 1939. Named for the county.

Colberg. Post office established June 6, 1891; discontinued April 3, 1893. Probably named for a locality in Sweden.

Eldridge. Post office established September 22, 1886; name changed to Chase November 28, 1887. Named for a local settler.

Enders. Peak population (1950), 100. Post office name changed from Martin February 8, 1890. Town platted by Lincoln Land Company and named for Peter Enders, a rancher.

Frease. Post office established September 6, 1880; discontinued February 16, 1882. Named in honor of Milton Frease from Texas, who established a ranch.

Hamilton. Post office established May 26, 1884; name changed to Champion May 26, 1887. Probably named for a local settler; vied for county seat at one time.

Imperial. Peak population (1990), 2,007. Post office established 1885. County seat named by homesteader Thomas Mercier, who donated townsite. Mercier, an emigrant from Canada, supposedly named the town after a place in Canada or for the British imperial government.

Lamar. Peak population (1930), 122. Post office name changed from Lennox October 31, 1887. Town commemorates Lucius Quintus Cincinnatus Lamar, secretary of interior in President Grover Cleveland's cabinet.

Lennox. Post office established November 23, 1886; name changed to Lamar October 31, 1887. Probably named for a city in New Jersey.

Manderson. Possibly a proposed town but was not identified as a post office.

Martin. Post office established October 19, 1888; name changed to Enders February 8, 1890. Named for a local settler.

Pearl. Post office established October 11, 1888; moved to Perkins County March 9, 1900. Origin of the name not learned. First postmaster was Henry Wagoneer.

Pezu. Origin of the name of this locality has not been learned.

Wauneta. Peak population (1950), 926. Post office established June 19, 1877; discontinued October 19, 1882; reestablished August 27, 1886. Named after popular song "Juanita." Because there already was a town similarly named within the state (Juniata), the spelling was modified to Wauneta.

Winchester. Post office established August 6, 1886; discontinued September 24, 1890. Origin of the name not learned; there are sixteen Winchesters in U.S.

Zell. Former railroad station on the Chicago, Burlington and Quincy line.

CHERRY COUNTY

Created by legislative enactment February 23, 1883. Named in honor of Lt. Samuel A. Cherry of the Fifth United States Cavalry of Fort Niobrara. He was murdered May 11, 1881, eight miles north of the fort near Rock Creek, South Dakota.

Albee. Post office established August 20, 1907; rescinded November 29, 1907. Named in honor of a rancher named Albee.

Arabia. Post office established October 9, 1883; discontinued July 19, 1920. Railroad station and former post office named by Henry V. Ferguson of Cedar Rapids, Iowa, auditor for the Chicago and North Western Railroad. He thought the sandy soil resembled the

Arabian Desert but soon discovered it to be fine grassland. Arabia at one time was a hay shipping point for army forts and private feeders.

Arlena. Post office established May 13, 1909; discontinued March 31, 1910. Named in honor of the wife of Fay James.

Audacious. Post office name changed from Dewitty April 15, 1916; discontinued April 18, 1918. A postmaster in this African American settlement told the people they were audacious for having settled there.

Ayers. Former locality established about 1940.

Bachelor. One source says this former railroad station named for Charles Bachelor, executive and rancher with land holdings of 30,000 acres. Another source believes the station named for J. H. Bachelor, a brother, who settled on a ranch in 1896.

Badger Lake. Post office established January 3, 1910; discontinued May 31, 1919. Named by rancher William Harman for the badgers found in the region.

Bailey. Post office established August 5, 1899; discontinued January 31, 1925. Named in honor of William Bailey at whose ranch the post office was established.

Balfe. Post office established August 23, 1915; discontinued 1945. Named by John M. Rose, first postmaster, for his wife, whose maiden name was Balfe.

Banner. Post office established June 20, 1903; discontinued December 31, 1915. Henry Murphy named this former post office because the word was brief and easy to read.

Bayonne. Post office established June 25, 1914; discontinued 1935. Martin Hansen, first postmaster, named the office for Bayonne, New Jersey.

Big Creek. Post office established April 1, 1908; discontinued March 31, 1925. Named for a valley and creek on which it was located.

Boiling Spring. Post office established May 19, 1881; discontinued September 18, 1883. Boiling Spring Ranch was owned by Carpenter and Moorhead in the open-range days. Foreman James H. Quigley named the office for the bubbling water at a spring.

Boulware. Post office established January 7, 1888; name changed to Kilgore April 8, 1890. Named in honor of Ira Boulware, first postmaster.

Britt. Post office established November 30, 1898; discontinued May 8, 1911. Named in honor of early settler John Britt.

Brock. Former station on the Chicago and North Western Railroad.

Brownlee. Peak population (1940), 86. Post office established January 21, 1888. Inland village established on the North Loup River. Named in honor of Jane Brownlee, grandmother of John R. Lee and William B. Lee, brothers who established the town.

Burge. Post office established May 25, 1904; discontinued 1937. Patrons suggested the name in honor of Tony Burge, livestock raiser.

Calf Creek. A locality and a precinct in the southern part of the county. Named after Calf Creek valley, an old river bed.

Capawell. Post office established August 7, 1915; discontinued August 30, 1919. Named in honor of Allen B. Capwell, early homesteader. How the extra "a" became included is unknown.

Cascade. Census not available. Post office established April 26, 1899; discontinued 1955. Name of hamlet located on the north bank of the Loup River submitted to postal authorities by J. F. Keller and citizens. Office established at the ranch home of W. E Cady but moved to various ranches during its existence.

Cashwan. Post office established July 17, 1918; discontinued June 30, 1930. "Cashswan" coined from name of first postmaster, Cassius Swan.

Cherry. Post office established August 20, 1907; discontinued 1941. Named for the county by Mrs. R. F. Osborne, wife of the postmaster.

Chesterfield. Post office established December 5, 1896; discontinued December 31, 1923. Established at the Boardman's Creek Ranch of a Mr. Waite, who evidently was an admirer of the English Lord Chesterfield.

Clement. Post office established November 1, 1886; discontinued January 18, 1887. Origin of the name not learned.

Cody. Peak population (1920), 428. Post office established June 4, 1886. Named in honor of Thomas Cody, foreman of the water-supply crew on the Chicago and North Western Railroad when the line was being built into the county. For a time this was the railroad terminus. Platted in 1885, Cody became a trading post for the Rosebud Indian Agency.

Compton. Post office established August 12, 1889; discontinued November 12, 1902. Named in honor of Weldon B. Compton.

Conquest. Post office established September 28, 1888; discontinued July 25, 1892. Reason for the name not learned.

Conterra. Post office established October 8, 1913; discontinued 1935. Named for the Latin word meaning "out in the country" by Max Wendler, first postmaster.

Cooper. Post office established September 6, 1893; changed to Irwin January 27, 1900. Probably named in honor of a local settler. Located two miles west of Irwin.

Corral. Station on the Chicago and North Western Railroad near Irwin.

Crookston. Peak population (1930), 373. Post office established December 2, 1886. Named in honor of W. T. Crook, yardmaster for the Chicago and North Western Railroad in Valentine and platted by Pioneer Town Site Company in 1885.

Curlew. Post office established April 8, 1902; discontinued 1930. Named by Hughes Carr, local settler, for species of bird found in vicinity.

Dandale. Post office established September 30, 1916; discontinued February 28, 1923. Named by Mrs. Mary Allen Schmidt for her father, Daniel Osgood. She combined "Dan" with "dale," a valley.

Dean. Post office established March 16, 1907; discontinued August 15, 1927. Named in honor of Marion Dean Fairchilds and submitted to postal authorities by Mrs. M. Simmonds.

Dent. May have been the former name of Kilgore or of a community close by.

Dewey Lake. Post office established December 1, 1911; discontinued March 3, 1916. Post office established at the ranch of Ulysses G. Welker and named in honor of Harvey E. Dewey, whose family built homes about the lake. Name suggested by patrons.

Dewitty. Post office established April 5, 1915; name changed to Audacious April 15, 1916. Origin of the name not learned.

Dough Boy. Post office established June 14, 1919; discontinued 1935. Name given by C. E. Barnes, a doughboy (infantryman) in the U.S. Army of World War I.

Douglas. Former locality of Cherry County.

Eden Springs. Former locality in Cherry County.

Eli. Post office established 1909; made a rural branch of Cody, 1918. Community and station on the Chicago and North Western Railroad named in honor of Eli Garner, pioneer settler. Another source says named for Daniel Webster Hitchcock, whose nickname was Get-There-Eli. He worked for J. E. Ainsworth, locating railroad engineer.

Elizabeth. Post office established May 19, 1906; discontinued January 14, 1928. Named by Postmaster John M. Uehling for his eldest daughter.

Elsmere. Post office established April 18, 1899. Parker Giles, store owner, suggested Elsmere after the novel *Robert Elsmere* by Mrs. Humphrey Ward. Giles homesteaded here in 1886.

Enlow. Post office established March 12, 1907; discontinued July 20, 1907. Named in honor of a local rancher, William Enlow.

Erik. Post office established April 14, 1908; discontinued July 31, 1923. Named by Mrs. Erik P. Erickson for her husband, the postmaster. Erickson was later elected a judge of Hooker County. Postal authorities used only the first name.

Ethel. Post office established February 17, 1913; discontinued January 15, 1921. Named in honor of the daughter of John Luenstra, first postmaster.

Fay. Post office established August 25, 1914; name changed to Tioga October 21, 1914. Origin of the name not learned.

Fee. Post office established December 16, 1916; discontinued May 31, 1918. Named by J. S. Ridgeway, in honor of J. R. Fee, state representative from Cherry County in 1891.

Fern. Post office established May 29, 1909; discontinued October 31, 1922. Named in honor of the second daughter of postmaster Kelsey F. Kime.

Fort Niobrara. Fort Niobrara was established by Maj. John J. Upham, Fifth Cavalry, on April 22, 1880, to guard Indian reservations in South Dakota. Discontinued October 22, 1906. Gen. John J. Pershing served as a second lieutenant with the Sixth Cavalry here.

Gallop. Post office established October 5, 1891; discontinued April 1, 1901. Named in honor of Peter Gallop, early settler.

Gard. Post office established February 20, 1919; discontinued 1943. Named in honor of Myrtle Gard by postmaster Dewitt C. Konkle.

Georgia. A present community and station on the Chicago and North Western Railroad. Named Georgetown but changed because another Nebraska station held that name. Located near Kilgore.

German Settlement. The locality south of Crookston and Kilgore settled by German craftsmen. A broom factory and sorghum mill were in the vicinity.

Gilaspie. A locality named in honor of Robert F. Gilaspie, a ranchman.

Giles. Probably a community named for P. R. Giles, who had a store in the area.

Goose Creek. A community named by cowboys for wild geese on this tributary to the Niobrara. Known as one of the best hay valleys in the county.

Gregory. Post office established July 8, 1897; discontinued December 14, 1903. Probably named in honor of Samuel Gregory, first postmaster.

Harlan. Post office established April 2, 1892; discontinued 1922. Named in honor of a local ranchman.

Harmony. Post office established January 21, 1908; discontinued March 31, 1925. Named after a district in Iowa.

Hire. Post office established April 29, 1911; discontinued 1945. Named in honor of John C. Hire, at whose home the post office was established.

Hood. Post office established June 18, 1914; discontinued January 15, 1918. Named in honor of Dr. L. T. Hood, former resident.

Idella. Post office established September 14, 1909; rescinded December 27, 1909. Origin of name not learned. First postmaster was Howard Wilson.

Irwin. Peak population (1940), 21. Post office name changed from Cooper January 27, 1900; discontinued January 9, 1917. Mail served from Gordon, Nebraska. Former town and present railroad station on the Chicago and North Western named in honor of Bennett Irwin, a cowboy during the open range days and later a successful rancher.

Junod. Post office established April 10, 1910; discontinued December 31, 1912. Named in honor of Melvie Junod, first postmaster.

Kennedy. Peak population (1960), 15. Post office established May 18, 1886; discontinued 1970. Mail served from Valentine. Town on Gordon Creek named in honor of B.E.B. Kennedy, first mayor of Omaha and a former homesteader.

Kewanee. Post office established March 15, 1888; discontinued 1934. Name was suggested by Joseph Bristol for Kewanee, Illinois.

Kilgore. Peak population (1920), 274. Post office name changed from Boulware April 8, 1890. Named in honor of the Scott and Columbus Kilgore families. Alice Kilgore was a pioneer teacher.

King. Post office established January 10, 1902; discontinued 1934. Named in honor of Charles E. King, first postmaster.

Kinneyville. Locality in the southern part of the county; named by men of the Standard Cattle Company, which had headquarters in this region.

Lackey. Locality named for a Mr. Lackey, an old settler.

Lake. Post office established June 25, 1904; discontinued May 31, 1922. Named for its location near one of the lakes in the region.

Lavacca. Post office established May 12, 1884; discontinued 1934. Named for Zeke Newman's ranch "Lavacca" (meaning "the cow" in Spanish), probably by Texas cowboys familiar with the Lavacca River in Texas.

Leat. Post office established November 17, 1915; discontinued August 14, 1921. Name suggested by Postmaster Oscar Smalley for his brother-in-law, whose last name was Leat.

Lewanna. Post office established December 21, 1907; discontinued 1934. Established on the Pete Lewellen Ranch. He chose the name Lewellen, but because there already was a Lewellen in the state, he coined Lewanna from his name and that of his daughter Anna.

Lombard. Post office established June 21, 1898; rescinded September 17, 1898. Origin of the name not learned.

Lund. Census not available. Post office established May 13, 1911; discontinued July 31, 1930. Former town named in honor of the first postmaster, Alfred Lund.

Marmora. Post office established April 25, 1891; discontinued October 30, 1895. Probably named for an island between Asia and Europe, off the coast of Turkey.

Martindale. Post office established June 8, 1910; discontinued October 14, 1916. Named in honor of James O. Martin, first postmaster.

Matteson. Post office established April 26, 1912; discontinued September 30, 1916. Named in honor of Clark E. Matteson, first postmaster and storekeeper.

McCann. Post office established December 6, 1880; discontinued July 23, 1898. Named in honor of D. J. McCann on whose ranch the post office was established.

Meldon. Post office established April 2, 1892; discontinued September 25, 1895. Origin of the name not known.

Melpha. Post office established February 27, 1925; discontinued 1939. Named in honor of Melpha E. Stoner. Name suggested by Ralph Otis.

Merriman. Peak population (1930), 361. Post office established March 8, 1886. Named in honor of John Merriman, trainmaster on construction trains of the Chicago and North Western Railroad.

Middle Prong. Former locality named after the middle fork of the Loup River.

Mygatt. Post office established November 24, 1916; rescinded May 9, 1917. Origin of the name not learned.

Nenzel. Peak population (1940), 125. Post office established January 27, 1885. Town named in honor of George Nenzel, early settler, postmaster, and owner of the land on which the townsite was platted in 1885.

Newton. Post office established June 22, 1897; discontinued October 15, 1928. Named in honor of Isaac Newton Russell, first postmaster.

Nodine. Post office established June 27, 1888; discontinued September 16, 1889. Named in honor of Charles Nodine, first postmaster.

Oasis. Post office established February 12, 1892; discontinued November 1, 1916. Post office established at the ranch of William H. Stratton. He named it Oasis because of the sandy location near a small lake.

Parmer. Former locality in Cherry County during the 1940s.

Pass. Post office established November 17, 1894; discontinued February 15, 1900. Named by cowboys and Bob Faddis, first postmaster, for the pass to the North Loup River.

Pearson. Post office established December 29, 1894; discontinued October 9, 1896. Probably named for B. W. Pearson, a ranchman.

Penbrook. Post office established May 8, 1884; moved to Keya Paha County October 3, 1892; moved to Cherry County February 23, 1898; discontinued June 15, 1912. Probably named in honor of a local settler.

Pleasant Hill. Post office established October 10, 1913; discontinued July 15, 1914. Location characterized by its pleasant features.

Poor's Ranch. Post office established June 20, 1879; discontinued August 28, 1882. Named in honor of Charles Poor, first postmaster and one of the earliest ranchmen in Cherry County.

Prentice. Post office established September 10, 1906; discontinued August 15, 1927. Named in honor of Benjamin F. Prentice, first postmaster.

Pullman. Post office established October 30, 1890; discontinued November 29, 1919. Named in honor of Philip and John Pullman, brothers who homesteaded the land on which the post office was located.

Putman. Post office established March 2, 1888; discontinued August 26, 1891. Named in honor of Scott Putman, early settler.

Red Deer. Post office established April 11, 1910; discontinued August 31, 1917. Named for the lake on which it was located by a Mr. Cumbow, on whose premises it was situated. The lake probably had been named for red-colored deer of the area.

Reeves. Former locality named for a local settler who came from Virginia.

Rex. Post office established February 14, 1914; discontinued August 31, 1915. Possibly named for Roy R. Russell, first postmaster.

Riege. Post office established June 27, 1888; discontinued May 31, 1912. Named in honor of Peter Riege, first postmaster, who settled near the Niobrara River in 1881.

Rita Park. Post office established November 3, 1908; discontinued March 15, 1916. Named in honor of Rita Stewart, daughter of A. L. Stewart, first postmaster.

Rolf. Post office established March 17, 1905; discontinued 1935. Named in honor of the youngest son of Charles N. Kime, first postmaster.

Roxby. Name of this former station on the Chicago and North Western Railroad near Cody is an adaptation of Roxbury, a Connecticut station.

Siding. Former siding on the Chicago and North Western Railroad located near Eli.

Simeon. Post office established June 11, 1885; discontinued 1954. Named in honor of Simeon Morgaridge, an early settler who built a sod house on Gordon Creek.

Soudan. Former station on the Chicago and North Western Railroad named after a region in Central Africa.

Sparks. Peak population (1890), 15. Post office established March 15, 1888. Said to be named in honor of five brothers: Eldon, James, Allen, Charles, and Levi Sparks. Situated on land owned by Eldon Sparks.

Survey. Post office established January 19, 1909; discontinued 1934. Located in the Survey Valley, so named because the Burlington Railroad surveyed the vicinity.

System. Post office established January 12, 1917; discontinued October 15, 1917. Named by William Ferndon because the ranch owners believed in operating systematically.

Thatcher. Post office established February 20, 1884; discontinued July 13, 1889. Named in honor of J. M. Thatcher, post trader at Fort Niobrara.

Tioga. Post office name changed from Fay October 21, 1914; discontinued February 28, 1921. Named by F. M. Tyerell for an Indian word meaning running water.

Trivey. Post office established June 15, 1908; rescinded September 24, 1908. Origin of the name not learned.

Trouble. Post office established December 16, 1916; discontinued May 14, 1921. Presumably named by Lerton Jay, first postmaster. Why he called the office "Trouble" has not been learned.

Tull. Post office established October 21, 1913; rescinded June 25, 1914. Origin of name not learned.

Valentine. Peak population (1960), 2,875. Post office established December 4, 1882. County seat town named in honor of E. K. Valentine, who represented the Third Nebraska

Congressional District, which included Cherry County. Until the Chicago and North Western Railroad was completed to Chadron in 1885, Valentine was a colorful frontier town in the open range cattle country where many ranchers pastured their stock. A United States Land Office was established here in 1883. The federal government built warehouses from which supplies were shipped.

Vian. Post office established March 4, 1910; discontinued 1936. Named in honor of Millard W. Vian, first postmaster.

Wells. Post office established July 22, 1909; discontinued, 1920. So named because a local settler had put down a considerable number of wells in the vicinity.

Wood Lake. Peak population (1920 and 1940), 323. Post office established November 26, 1883. Platted in 1888 and named after a nearby lake; originally called Cottonwood Lake but later shortened to Wood Lake. It was practically the only place timber grew in the area.

Wrage. Post office established September 30, 1916; discontinued 1935. Named in honor of Henry Wrage, ranchman.

CHEYENNE COUNTY

Cheyenne County separated from Lincoln County and was organized June 6, 1871. Named for the Cheyenne tribe.

Ancient Ruins. Probably an early settlement in the county.

Athena. Post office established January 11, 1890; discontinued January 7, 1892. Origin of the name not learned.

Boyer. Post office established August 12, 1889; discontinued December 23, 1890. Named in honor of John Boyer, first postmaster.

Brownson. Post office established March 2, 1887; discontinued June 6, 1895. Named for the precinct in which located. Perhaps named for a Union Pacific Railroad freight agent. Another source asserts the present railroad station and community named for Edgar Beecher Bronson, an early settler. The "w" may have been added in error.

Cheese Creek. Station on the Sidney-Black Hills stage route.

Clara. Post office established March 6, 1901; discontinued August 31, 1915. Named in honor of the daughter of Philip Higgins, first postmaster.

Cold Water. Former locality.

Colton. Post office established March 2, 1887; discontinued February 2, 1901. Former post office and present railroad station named in honor of Francis Colton of Galesburg, Illinois, former general ticket agent of the Union Pacific Railroad.

Dalton. Peak population (1960), 503. Post office established June 7, 1902. Named for Patrick Dalton, early settler, or for Patrick J. Dalton, official of the Burlington Railroad.

Dye. Post office established January 25, 1906; discontinued November 30, 1912; reestablished in Kimball County June 5, 1913. Named in honor of Lida F. Dye, first postmistress.

Eric. Former station on the Union Pacific Railroad.

Fort Sidney. Fort Sidney was established in 1867 to protect workers constructing the Union Pacific Railroad line westward. The fort, later important to the Black Hills trade, was discontinued in 1894.

Garman. Post office established June 18, 1887; discontinued May 28, 1895. Probably named in honor of Esaias Garman, first postmaster.

Greenwood Station. A former station on the Sidney-Black Hills stage route.

Gurley. Peak population (1960), 329. Post office established October 27, 1914. Town probably named in honor of Fred Gurley, superintendent of this division of the Burlington Railroad when the post office was established.

Hampton. Former station on the Burlington Railroad probably named for a county official.

Henry. Post office established June 30, 1892; discontinued September 2, 1902. Named in honor of Henry Weitenman, first postmaster.

Herndon. Former station on the Union Pacific Railroad probably named for a company official.

Higgins. Post office established November 26, 1889; discontinued July 15, 1912. Named in honor of Phillip Higgins, first postmaster.

Huntsman. Post office established December 26, 1919; discontinued 1935. Present station on the Burlington Railroad probably named for a local rancher or railroad official.

Ickes. Post office established April 8, 1890; discontinued January 18, 1894. Named in honor of Adam Ickes, county treasurer.

Lapeer. Post office established January 9, 1892; discontinued October 2, 1902. Probably named for a local rancher. There is a Lapeer, Michigan.

Laura. Post office established February 21, 1918; discontinued December 30, 1930. Named in honor of Laura Mathewson, first postmistress.

Leafdale. Post office established September 16, 1902; discontinued December 15, 1917. Named in honor of Martin Leafdale, first postmaster.

Lewis. Post office established June 10, 1895; discontinued November 16, 1904. Named in honor of Lewis Wilson, first postmaster.

Lodgepole. Peak population (1950), 555. Post office established January 20, 1876. Town received its name from Lodgepole Creek, so named because the Indians cut poles for their tepees from trees along its banks.

Lorenzo. Post office established May 23, 1916; discontinued 1934. Origin of the name not learned. First postmaster was William Frazier.

Margate. Former station on the Union Pacific Railroad.

Marlowe. Former station on the Burlington Railroad.

Nebraska Station No. 31. Pony Express Station No. 31 was located within Sioux Ordnance area near Gurley.

Ordville. Home of Sioux Ordnance Depot, located twelve miles northwest of Sidney. The depot, established in 1942, was a military installation with warehouses. A government-owned housing facility was situated adjacent to the depot.

Panhandle. Station and junction for the Union Pacific and Burlington Railroads. Named for its location in the Panhandle of Nebraska.

Pole Creek No. 2. Pony Express Station No. 29 in Nebraska. Location in Lodgepole vicinity. Site could have been the E. Farrell Ranch in 1865.

Pole Creek No. 3. Pony Express Station No. 30 in Nebraska. Its location would have been at the old St. George Cattle Ranch three and one-half miles east of the present site of Sidney. This important station was at the junction of the Old California Road stage route.

Potter. Peak population (1960), 554. Post office established August 14, 1885. A 1924 issue of the *Potter Review* (newspaper) says named for early Union Pacific roadmaster, not for General Potter, one time troop commander in western Nebraska and Union Pacific shareholder.

Sextorp. Post office established July 1, 1898; discontinued November 30, 1920. Probably a Swedish word for Swedish settlers who established themselves here.

Sidney. Peak population (1960), 8,004. Post office established August 9, 1869. Named in honor of Sidney Dillon of New York City, general solicitor for the Union Pacific Railroad. It became the county seat. Sidney, at first a small cattle town, grew up around Fort Sidney. When gold was discovered in the Black Hills, the town became the closest railhead to the gold fields and was headquarters for freight and stage lines. Sidney's frontier lawlessness was well known but eventually subsided.

Sunol. Peak population (1940), 299. Post office established September 23, 1910; discontinued 1974; mail served from Lodgepole. Origin of name not learned.

Tabor. Former station on the Union Pacific Railroad.

Thirty-one Station. See Nebraska Station No. 31.

Water Hole Ranch. Station on Sidney-Deadwood Trail.

Weyerts. Post office established January 19, 1888; discontinued March 15, 1924. Probably named in honor of Cornelius Weyerts, first postmaster.

CLAY COUNTY

Originally a county situated between Lancaster and Gage counties. Established March 7, 1855; partitioned Feb. 15, 1864. Named in honor of Henry Clay (1777-1852), Kentucky statesman.

Alma Junction. Station point for St. Joseph and Grand Island and Burlington Railroads.

Annandale. Post office established November 6, 1879; discontinued October 5, 1881. Probably named for town in Minnesota, New Jersey, New York, or Virginia.

Clay Center. Peak population (1910 and 1920), 1,065. Post office name changed from Marshall July 21, 1879. Named by R. L. Brown for its central location in Clay County. Town Site Company purchased land from the Burlington Railroad. County seat moved here in disputed election with Sutton in 1879.

Davis. Post office name changed from Dilworth January 10, 1877; discontinued November 9, 1887. Named in honor of a local settler.

Deweese. Peak population (1930), 156. Post office established January 26, 1887. Named in honor of Joel W. Deweese, attorney for the Burlington Railroad and member of the law firm of Marquette, Deweese, and Hall.

Dilworth. Post office established April 14, 1875; name changed to Davis January 10, 1877. Named in honor of C. J. Dilworth, Nebraska attorney general.

Eden. Name changed to Edgar after a post office was established.

Edgar. Peak population (1890), 1,105. Post office established November 25, 1872. Town, previously called Eden, named for the son of Ed Graham, pioneer settler. Preempted by Henry Gipe for the Nebraska Land and Town Site Company and surveyed by A. R. Buttolph in May 1873.

Eldon. This community never had a post office, but William Stockham opened a general store here in 1889. It was also a station east of Harvard on the Fremont, Elkhorn and Missouri Valley Railroad.

Eldora. Probably the railroad name for Eldorado.

Eldorado. Peak population (1910), 100. Post office established October 22, 1888; discontinued 1943. Mail served from Aurora, Nebraska. Name of Spanish origin means gilded or golden. Reason for the name not learned.

Fairfield. Peak population (1900), 1,203. Post office name changed from White Elm June 25, 1873. Change from White Elm to Frankfort was rejected because of prior Frankfort in Nebraska. Town named in honor of George Washington Fairfield, civil engineer and surveyor of the Burlington Railroad. Fairfield also conformed to the railroad's alphabetical naming system ("A" through "N") in four counties along what is now the Burlington Northern line.

Flickville. Former station on the Burlington Railroad moved from Adams County to Clay County. Named in honor of Joseph Flick.

Frankfort. See Fairfield.

Georgetown. Original name of Glenvil. Because there was already a Georgetown post office within the state, the name was rejected.

Glenvil. Peak population (1920), 400. Post office established May 13, 1873. Named by the Burlington Railroad to conform with its alphabetical name system along the line. Original name was Glenville, but changed to prevent conflict with identical names in other states. Spelling upheld by court action, June 1984.

Greenberry. Post office name changed from Joong August 24, 1888; name changed to Ong November 12, 1888. Probably named in honor of Greenberry L. Fort, landowner in the vicinity.

Harvard. Peak population (1960), 1,261. Post office established December 6, 1871. Named to conform with the alphabetical naming system of the Burlington and Missouri River Railroad for Harvard University in Cambridge, Massachusetts. Platted by South Platte Land Company in 1871. An army air field was located in Harvard during World War II.

Inland. Peak population (1920), 105. Post office moved from Adams County January 13, 1879. Named by the Burlington Railroad in conformity with its alphabetical system. Name thought to refer to the town's inland site.

Joong. Post office established August 20, 1886; name changed to Greenberry August 24, 1888. Probably named in honor of a local settler.

Liberty Farm. No. 8 of the Pony Express stations in Nebraska. Located one-half mile northeast of present site of Deweese.

Liberty Farms. Post office established January 9, 1871; discontinued September 14, 1874. See Liberty Farm. Probably located on site of former Liberty Farm Pony Express station.

Ludlow. Post office moved from Adams County March 30, 1880; name changed to Trumbull March 30, 1887. Named in honor of Ludlow Huff, early settler.

Marshall. Post office established March 17, 1873; moved to Clay Center July 21, 1879. Name origin not learned.

Ong. Peak population (1910), 285. Post office name changed from Greenberry November 12, 1888; discontinued 1966. Mail served from Shickley. Named in honor of Judge J. E. Ong, who owned the land on which townsite was located.

Saronville. Peak population (1900), 176. Post office established October 3, 1882. A Swedish Lutheran minister named Haterius called the local church Saron after a village in Sweden. When the post office was established, it was called Saronville.

School Creek. Previous name of Sutton.

Spring Ranch. Peak population (1910), 57. Post office established December 14, 1870; discontinued 1940. Former town probably named for the numerous springs in the vicinity.

Spring Ranch. No. 9 of the Pony Express stations in Nebraska.

Sutton. Peak population (1910), 1,702. Post office established August 8, 1871. Named after Sutton, Massachusetts. The first county seat after an election with Harvard, Sutton lost to Clay Center in 1879. Many settlers came here from Odessa, Russia, in the fall of 1873.

Sweden. Named Verona before a post office was established by Swedish settlers.

Trumbull. Peak population (1920), 236. Post office name changed from Ludlow March 30, 1887. Named in honor of a Mr. Trumbull, Burlington Railroad official.

Verona. Peak population (1910), 150. Post office established August 19, 1887; discontinued 1954. Former town and present railroad station originally called Sweden. Named in honor of the Veronica family, which played a major part in its early development.

White Elm. Post office established March 5, 1872; moved one mile to Fairfield June 25, 1873. Probably named for a species of elm tree in the vicinity. Post office moved when railroad built to Fairfield.

COLFAX COUNTY

Colfax County was originally part of Platte County. By an act of the Legislature approved February 15, 1869, this county was divided, and Colfax County was named for

Schuyler Colfax (1823-85), U.S. vice-president from 1869 to 1873. The boundaries were redefined March 3, 1873.

Abington. Post office established May 2, 1872; discontinued November 19, 1887. Probably named for a town in Connecticut or Pennsylvania.

Benton. Name of the Union Pacific Railroad station for the town of Richland. Probably named in honor of Missouri Senator Thomas Hart Benton.

Bissell. Post office established September 7, 1899; discontinued June 25, 1904. Probably named in honor of Thomas Bissell, early settler.

Bohemia. Community named by Czech settlers from the province of Bohemia in what is now the Czech Republic.

Buchanan. First county seat of Colfax County. Probably named in honor of James Buchanan, candidate for president at the time the town was platted by Isaac Albertson and E. W. Toncray in April 1856. A short-lived town at the junction of Shell Creek and the Platte River near present town of Rogers and a stage coach station on the Western Stage Lines.

Clarkson. Peak population (1930), 913. Post office established January 24, 1882. Named in honor of Schuyler Postmaster T. S. Clarkson, who helped establish the town. Later he became postmaster of Omaha. Town platted by the Western Town Lot Company in October of 1886.

Curry. Post office established May 18, 1882; discontinued October 23, 1890. Named in honor of a local settler.

Donovan. Post office established February 16, 1898; discontinued September 7, 1899. Possibly named in honor of a local settler.

Eldorado. Post office established August 12, 1870; name changed to Richmond February 14, 1879. Spanish name means the gilded or golden. Why this office was thus named has not been learned. Station on the Western Stage Lines from Omaha to Fort Kearny.

Franklin. Probably a proposed town that never got beyond the platting stage.

Fulton. Post office established May 13, 1875; discontinued May 18, 1900. Origin of the name has not been learned.

Heun. Post office established December 3, 1885; discontinued February 24, 1903. Probably named in honor of William Heun, early settler.

Howells. Peak population (1930), 952. Post office established November 20, 1886. Named in honor of J. S. Howell, early pioneer. The "s" added by the railroad company and adopted by postal authorities. Town platted by Western Town Site Company.

Lambert. Former station on the Union Pacific Railroad. Located near Schuyler.

Leigh. Peak population (1930), 688. Post office established March 18, 1875. Named in honor of Mrs. A. M. Walling, whose maiden name was Leigh. The Wallings owned the townsite.

Marion. Post office established January 8, 1873; discontinued March 12, 1877. Origin of the name not learned.

Midland. Post office established May 6, 1872; discontinued September 26, 1884. Located west of Glencoe midway to a point farther west.

Neenah. A former locality probably named by Wisconsin settlers for Neenah, Wisconsin.

Olean. Post office established June 3, 1873; discontinued August 20, 1877. Probably named for Olean, New York.

Oleyen. Post office established June 26, 1895; discontinued May 31, 1904. Origin of the name not learned.

Praha. Post office name changed from Reno December 6, 1880; discontinued October 29, 1902. Established by John F. Sobotka, an early settler, it was named by Czech settlers for Praha, capital of the Czech Republic.

Reno. Post office established April 3, 1879; name changed to Praha December 6, 1880.

Probably named for Gen. Marcus A. Reno of Civil War and Indian War fame. Name changed to avoid confusion of mail with Reno, Nevada.

Richland. Peak population (1930), 174. Post office name changed from Eldorado February 14, 1879. Probably named for the rich soil in the vicinity. The name Spitley previously rejected.

Rogers. Peak population (1960), 162. Post office established July 31, 1883. Named in honor of a Mr. Rogers, Union Pacific Railroad official.

Sangco. Post office established January 12, 1885; discontinued April 23, 1890. Origin of the name not learned.

Schuyler. Peak population (2000), 5,371. Post office name changed from Shell Creek July 1, 1869. Named in honor of Schuyler Colfax, vice president during President Ulysses Grant's administration, it became the county seat. In 1870s a rail shipping point to the East for cattle trailed in from Texas.

Shell Creek. Post office established March 6, 1869; name changed to Schuyler July 1, 1869. Named for the creek on which it is located.

Skinner's. Stop on the Western Stage Lines from Omaha to Fort Kearny located eleven miles east of Columbus. Probably named for early settler Joseph Skinner.

Spitley. Name proposed for the town of Richland.

St. John. Probably a community located near a church of this name.

Tabor. Former locality probably named for a city in Bohemia now in the Czech Republic.

Wells. Post office established November 25, 1895; discontinued June 25, 1904. Named in honor of a local settler.

Wilson. Post office established April 28, 1875; discontinued February 16, 1892. Probably named in honor of a local settler.

CUMING COUNTY

Boundaries of Cuming County, defined by an act of the Territorial Legislature, were approved March 16, 1855. Boundaries were redefined by an act approved February 12, 1857, and January 10, 1862. County was named in honor of Thomas B. Cuming (1827-58), acting governor of Nebraska Territory from 1854 to 1855 and from 1857 to 1858.

Aloys. Peak population (1910), 15. Post office established March 19, 1885; discontinued December 28, 1904. Origin of the name of this former town not ascertained.

Athens. Post office established May 28, 1884; moved to Thurston County January 29, 1885. Probably named for one of five places in the United States by this name or for Athens, Greece.

Bancroft. Peak population (1910), 742. Post office name changed from Portland September 30, 1889. Named in honor of George Bancroft, noted American historian. Sioux City and Nebraska Railway platted town October 20, 1880. Ford B. Barber donated land for the town but refused to have the village named for himself. Before the village was platted Indians called the area *Toe Nuga Zingha*, meaning Little Stopping Place. The John G. Neihardt Center, completed in 1976, honors Nebraska's Poet Laureate from 1921 until his death in 1973. It is a property of the Nebraska State Historical Society. Neihardt moved to Bancroft in 1901 and absorbed much of his knowledge of Native American culture while living there.

Beemer. Peak population (1980), 853. Post office name changed from Rock Creek September 29, 1884. Named by Congressman E. K. Valentine for A. D. Beemer, town founder, who built the site close to Rock Creek.

Bismarck. Census not available. Post office established March 7, 1881; discontinued

January 31, 1902. Former village named for German statesman, Prince Karl Otto Edward Leopold von Bismarck-Schonhausen (1815-98) by German settlers.

Buckau. Post office established January 6, 1873; discontinued May 30, 1883. Probably named for a city in Germany.

Catherine. Proposed town made county seat in October 1858 election. Never materialized and county seat moved to Dewitt.

Cloudy. Post office established June 3, 1870; discontinued May 20, 1884. Named in honor of Frank Cloudy, first postmaster.

Cottage Home. Post office established September 19, 1870; discontinued October 5, 1871. Named for the home of Hugh D. Petteplace, first postmaster.

Cuming. Post office established April 7, 1899; discontinued January 3, 1902. Named for the county.

Dead Timber. Located in Dodge County but was in Cuming County at the time the latter was formed.

Dewitt. Census not available. Post office established February 3, 1858; discontinued May 26, 1871. Incipient town lost county seat to West Point in October 1858 election. County seat located here a short time after Catherine abandoned in 1857.

Edwards. Prospective town laid out in 1884 between West Point and Wisner by A. D. Beemer and others.

Elmont. Post office established July 2, 1868; discontinued July 15, 1870. Origin of the name not learned.

Germanville. Census not available. Post office established June 27, 1898; discontinued January 31, 1902. Former village in the southern part of Cuming County named by German settlers.

Griffin. Post office established March 29, 1872; discontinued September 26, 1883. Probably named in honor of a local settler.

Lakeview. Post office established June 29, 1868; name changed to Wisner July 15, 1876. Probably named for a nearby lake. Name changed to Wisner with the coming of the railroad.

Longa Valley. Former community in Cuming County.

Manhattan. Paper town made county seat February 12, 1857. Before building could start, West Point was established and declared county seat. Probably named for a borough of New York City.

Monterey. Peak population (1890), 32. Post office established August 17, 1882; discontinued June 24, 1905. Former town probably named for Monterey, Mexico, site of Mexican War battle of Monterey (1846).

New Philadelphia. Name proposed for the present town of West Point but turned down.

North Cedar. Former community in early Cuming County.

Peterson. Post office name changed from Walnut Hill December 30, 1872; discontinued July 7, 1887. Named in honor of A. M. Peterson, first postmaster.

Plum Valley. Post office established September 19, 1870; discontinued April 21, 1875. Probably named for wild plum thickets in the vicinity.

Portland. Post office established November 21, 1879; name changed to Bancroft September 31, 1880. Probably named for places in Connecticut, Indiana, Maine, Michigan, or Oregon.

Rock Creek. Locality before the railroad came. Name changed to Beemer on September 29, 1884. Named for its location on Rock Creek.

St. Charles. Census not available. Post office established April 30, 1865; discontinued January 15, 1899. Former village named in honor of Charles Schueth, first postmaster.

Walnut Hill. Post office established October 10, 1871; name changed to Peterson December 30, 1872. Probably named for black walnut trees growing in area.

West Point. Peak population (2000), 3,660. Post office established March 29, 1858.

Named by settlers who thought of it as the western extreme of white settlement. First called New Philadelphia but the main part designated West Point. It won county seat election over Dewitt in October 1858. United States Land Office located here June 1869. Platted and surveyed by Niels Larsen on land owned by the founder John D. Neligh, who settled on the site in 1858. Neligh headed the Nebraska Settlement Association responsible for the settlement of West Point.

Wisner. Peak population (1930), 1,323. Post office name changed from Lakeview July 15, 1876. Named in honor of Samuel P. Wisner, vice president of the Sioux City and Pacific Railroad. Town originally owned by the Elkhorn Land and Town Lot Company. Surveyed by N. E. Farrell on July 26, 1871.

CUSTER COUNTY

Named in honor of Gen. George A. Custer (1839-76), killed at the battle on the Little Big Horn in 1876. Organization of the county approved and boundaries defined on February 17, 1877.

Abel. Former ranch locality five miles north of Oconto. Named for Anton Abel, one of the founders of Custer County.

Algernon. Post office established September 13, 1880; discontinued August 27, 1887. Post office named by Maj. C. S. Ellison, a Civil War veteran, for his favorite statesman, Algernon S. Paddock, former U.S. senator from Nebraska.

Anselmo. Peak population (1930), 472. Post office established November 17, 1886. Town honors Anselmo B. Smith, surveyor and civil engineer who platted towns for the Burlington Railroad and Lincoln Land Company.

Ansley. Peak population (1930), 817. Post office established April 20, 1886. Town named in honor of Eliza Ansley, sister of R. O. Phillips, president of the Lincoln Land Company, which platted the town. She invested a large sum of money in the community.

Aranda. Post office established June 15, 1891; discontinued December 22, 1892. Origin of the name not learned. First postmaster was Levi Curtis.

Argile. Post office established May 24, 1889; discontinued May 16, 1895. Origin of the name not learned. Named by a member of the S. P. Grote family.

Arnold. Peak population (1950), 936. Post office established April 18, 1877. Town named in honor of George Arnold, a member of the Arnold and Ritchie ranch firm.

Battle Bend. Post office established February 28, 1884; discontinued August 8, 1887. Probably named for a creek where an Indian battle took place.

Beechville. Post office established January 6, 1885; discontinued November 13, 1889. Named in honor of Mrs. T. A. Pickering, whose maiden name was Emma Beech.

Berwyn. Peak population (1910), 225. Post office name changed from Janesville December 21, 1886. Probably named for a railroad surveyor, a Mr. Berwyn. Town platted by Lincoln Land Company in 1886.

Broken Bow. Peak population (1980), 3,979. Post office established November 4, 1879. The name Broken Bow was suggested to postal authorities by Postmaster Wilson Hewett, whose two sons found a shoulder blade of a buffalo pierced by the steel head of an arrow. They also found a three-foot-long bow splintered and broken off in such a manner as to be unusable. Broken Bow was finally accepted after several other names had been rejected. In early decades the city was the center of conflict between cattlemen and homesteaders with fenced farms. Broken Bow became the county seat in a January 1883 election. A U.S. Land Office was once established here.

Burroak. Post office established January 6, 1908; discontinued October 31, 1922. Named by William Davis, first postmaster, for the creek along which grew oak trees. Burroak Church is in the vicinity.

Callaway. Peak population (1930), 840. Post office name changed from Grant August 2, 1886. Named in honor of S. R. Callaway, general manager of the Union Pacific Railroad.

Campville. Stage stop on Kearney-Black Hills Trail. Probably a sod house dwelling one mile northwest of present Anselmo.

Cliff. Post office established April 23, 1884; discontinued April 11, 1907. Named by postmaster Samuel High and John Shade for High's little daughter Cliff.

Climax. Post office established November 29, 1909; discontinued May 31, 1927. Named by Mrs. Mary T. Ewing, who owned the farm on which the post office was located.

Coburgh. Post office established December 21, 1885; discontinued April 4, 1904. Probably named for a city in Germany.

Comstock. Peak population (1930), 454. Post office established November 18, 1899. Named in honor of W. H. Comstock, store owner and early resident.

Cummings Park. Early community established on the eastern county line by James and Gilbert Cummings in 1879. The railroad bypassed the place, causing its decline.

Cumro. Peak population (1930), 21. Post office established December 21, 1885; discontinued 1943. Former hamlet named by Williams Edmunds for Cumro, Wales.

Custer. Peak population (1890), 130. Post office established October 10, 1871; changed to McKinley January 20, 1899. Former town named for the county by Frank Young. It was the second post office in Custer County.

Custer Center. Rural neighborhood between Broken Bow and Merna; location of school, Grange hall, and cemetery of same name.

Dale. Peak population (1890), 25. Post office established January 8, 1883; discontinued April 30, 1894. Former hamlet was to be named Daley for James Daley, first postmaster, who objected. The office was thereafter called Dale.

Delight. Post office name changed from Set Up September 23, 1880; name changed to Grant, April 29, 1886. Probably named for its pleasant location in Delight Township.

Doris. Post office established December 14, 1903; discontinued September 29, 1917. Named in honor of the daughter of Rufus Carr, a miller.

Douglas Grove. Post office established January 18, 1875; name changed to Wescott October 11, 1883. Named in honor of Ed Douglas, early homesteader. Post office probably located in a grove of trees.

Elm. Proposed town in Delight Township.

Elm Bridge. Name of Westerville before it became a post office.

Elton. Peak population (1880), 26. Post office established February 6, 1879; discontinued March 5, 1916. Former hamlet named by Mrs. C. Comstock for her home in Elton, New York.

Eri. Post office established February 16, 1880; discontinued June 25, 1886. Named in honor of the brother of Mrs. J. E. Ash, first postmistress.

Ernst. Former railroad station and community named for C. J. Ernst, an assistant treasurer of the Burlington Railroad.

Etna. Post office established March 3, 1885; discontinued September 30, 1921. Origin of the name not ascertained.

Eudell. Post office established March 9, 1883; discontinued August 6, 1900. Named in honor of Lester Eudell Gibson, first postmaster.

Finchville. Census not available. Post office established March 26, 1914; discontinued 1935. Former town named in honor of E. S. Finch, pioneer settler.

Gasmann Springs. Post office established April 18, 1877; discontinued December 7, 1877. Named in honor of James Gasmann of the T. D. Ranch.

Gates. Post office established May 5, 1884. Named in honor of S. R. Gates, first postmaster, who operated the post office in his store.

Gavin. Former railroad station named for A. B. Gavin, train dispatcher for the Burlington Railroad.

Genet. Post office established March 17, 1886; discontinued November 29, 1889. Origin of the name not learned. First postmaster was Robert Farley.

Georgetown. Peak population (1900), 65. Post office established November 12, 1877; discontinued October 31, 1922. Former town named after L. D. George, stockman and farmer.

Goodyear's Ranch. Former locality probably named for a settler having a sizeable ranch and shipping point.

Grant. Post office name changed from Delight April 29, 1886; name changed to Callaway August 2, 1886. Probably named in honor of Ulysses S. Grant, President of the United States and commander of the Union forces during the Civil War.

Green. Post office established January 11, 1886; discontinued September 24, 1903. Named in honor of Perley Green, its only postmaster.

Guilford. Post office established August 4, 1880; discontinued 1885. Schoolhouse in the vicinity called Guilford for the grandparents of Mrs. William Wheeler.

Harlan. Post office established February 6, 1855; discontinued January 29, 1889. Named in honor of Harlan Hewitt, first postmaster.

High. Post office established February 4, 1884; discontinued November 11, 1886. Former post office petitioned by T. Daggett. It was located on high tableland.

Highland. Stage stop on the Kearney-Black Hills Trail about three miles west of present Broken Bow.

Hinckley. Proposed name for Weissert. Postal authorities refused the name.

Hoosier. Post office established August 8, 1898; discontinued July 15, 1905. Named for the Hoosier state of Indiana, where many of the settlers had lived.

Huxley. Post office established April 17, 1879; discontinued February 25, 1927. Commemorates Thomas H. Huxley, noted English scientist. Named by J. M. Lowry, who admired Huxley.

Janesville. Post office established January 5, 1880; name changed to Berwyn December 21, 1886. Named by J. M. Armstrong for a city of Wisconsin, where he had lived.

Jefferson. Post office established December 13, 1882; discontinued June 25, 1886. Named in honor of Thomas Jefferson Butcher, father of photographer Solomon D. Butcher, first postmaster.

Keota. Post office established June 14, 1883; discontinued April 16, 1887. Named for Keota, Iowa.

Kingston. Post office established December 2, 1889; discontinued January 31, 1905. Name suggested by A. O. Leach in honor of Kingston, New York, his former home.

Klump. Post office established April 18, 1899; discontinued June 14, 1901. Probably named for postmistress Jane Parkinson Klump.

Lamore. Post office established March 6, 1878; discontinued February 16, 1883. Origin of the name not learned. First postmaster was Patrick Cox.

Lee Park. Post office moved from Valley County February 13, 1889; discontinued December 8, 1904. Named in honor of James Lee, early settler.

Lena. Post office moved from Blaine County June 14, 1884; discontinued February 18, 1888. Named in honor of Lena van Sickle by her father, James van Sickle, first postmaster.

Leonard. Post office established April 30, 1907; discontinued May 16, 1908. Named in honor of the Leonard family living in the vicinity.

Lillian. Census not available. Post office established May 14, 1883; discontinued 1934. Former town named in honor of Lillian Gohean, second daughter of Hugh Gohean, first postmaster.

Lodi. Post office established October 17, 1882; discontinued October 15, 1928. Named by settlers who came from Lodi, Wisconsin.

Lomax. Post office established September 26, 1889; discontinued November 30, 1921. Probably named for Harvard Lomax, early Wood River Valley homesteader.

Longwood. Post office established April 5, 1875; discontinued July 19, 1903. Origin of the name not learned.

Loyal. Post office established April 24, 1907; discontinued August 31, 1914. Named by William Schuck, first postmaster.

Lydia. Post office established December 14, 1885; discontinued April 2, 1887. Named in honor of Mrs. Lydia Keyes, first postmistress.

Magoon. Post office established March 9, 1885; discontinued January 29, 1889. Probably named in honor of Richard Magoon, first postmaster.

Manchester. Post office established July 15, 1879; discontinued August 16, 1882. Probably named for Manchester, England, or for one of the twenty-three Manchesters in the U.S. Principal cities with this name are in Connecticut, New Hampshire, and Ohio.

Marvin. Former station on the Burlington Railroad; probably named for a railroad official.

Mason City. Peak population (1920), 487. Post office established August 27, 1886. Lincoln Land Site Company named this town in honor of Judge O. P. Mason of Lincoln.

McKinley. Post office name changed from Custer January 20, 1899; discontinued September 30, 1918. Probably named in honor of William McKinley, president of the United States.

Merna. Peak population (1920), 553. Post office established March 2, 1880. Town platted by Lincoln Land Company and named in honor of the youngest daughter of Samuel Dunning, first postmaster.

Milburn. Peak population (1940), 24. Post office established December 1, 1887. Village named in honor of James Milburn, first postmaster.

Milldale. Peak population (1890), 25. Post office established September 28, 1883; discontinued October 31, 1928. Former town apparently named for a mill site on the South Loup River.

Milton. Former locality near Miller in Buffalo County. Origin of name not learned.

Myrtle. Post office established June 26, 1878; discontinued January 21, 1884. Named by Emery Safford for the daughter of Frank Lowery, a local resident.

Nea. Post office established October 11, 1882; discontinued February 18, 1884. Origin of the name not learned.

Nemo. Post office established May 12, 1911; discontinued June 30, 1924. Name coined from the first two letters of Nebraska and the abbreviation of Missouri by Mrs. C. D. Kellogg, first postmistress.

New Callaway. Short-lived townsite just west of Callaway, which came into being in 1887. The Union Pacific subsidiary, the Omaha and Republican Valley Railway, surveyed two rail lines toward Callaway via the South Loup and Wood River valleys. Citizens believed that Callaway would be bypassed, and organized the new town. When neither materialized, New Callaway faded. Three years later the Kearney and Black Hills Railway took over the Wood River Valley grade to build the line into Callaway. A feud ensued between the original town and the railroad addition, with Callaway the victor.

New Helena. Peak population (1900), 67. Post office established June 18, 1875; discontinued June 15, 1910. Former town named by C. R. Matthews for Helena, Virginia.

Noel. Post office established April 25, 1884; discontinued April 3, 1890. Named in honor of Arthur Noel Binger, first postmaster.

Obi. Post office established February 28, 1884; discontinued November 11, 1886. Said to be named by Armenian Christians who settled west of here.

Oconto. Peak population (1920), 272. Post office established May 10, 1880. Named for Oconto, Wisconsin. Of Menominee Indian origin, it means place of the pickerel. Town platted by Lincoln Land Company.

Olax. Peak population (1880), 25. Post office established March 26, 1880; discontinued October 8, 1883. Chosen by Frank Young from a list of names.

Ormsby. Former station on the Burlington Railroad probably named for a company official.

Ortello. Peak population (1890), 40. Post office established March 27, 1884; discontinued January 21, 1906. Former town named in honor of Grove Ortello Joyner, local settler. Town first called Ortello Grove.

Over. Post office established August 11, 1884; discontinued July 17, 1907. Origin of the name not learned.

Phillipsburg. Post office established May 8, 1882; discontinued April 15, 1915. Named for a Mr. Phillips, mail carrier.

Pilot. Post office established February 25, 1880; discontinued December 23, 1908. Named after a landmark for early travelers.

Pleasant Hill. Former locality on table land five or six miles northeast of Arnold.

Prairie Center. Rural neighborhood between Broken Bow and Merna.

Redfern. Post office established January 13, 1885; discontinued June 1, 1906. Named in honor of Charles W. Redfern, first postmaster.

Rest. Post office established November 28, 1890; discontinued August 14, 1906. Named for a mail carrier who stopped here to rest his horses.

Robville. Post office established February 24, 1881; discontinued September 1, 1881. Name coined from three letters of the surname of James Robertson, first postmaster, with ville (town).

Roten. Post office established May 26, 1884; discontinued April 27, 1892. Named in honor of High Roten, who had the post office in his home or for first postmaster Jacob Roten.

Round Grove. Post office established March 1, 1880; discontinued April 28, 1894. Named by first postmaster James Bingham for a grove of trees in a round formation.

Round Valley. Post office established January 2, 1880; discontinued 1936. Probably named by Postmaster John Taylor for a round valley formed by hills or by Norwegian settlers Nels and Severt Lee.

Ryno. Post office established December 16, 1884; discontinued May 25, 1904. Named by Postmaster James M. H. Knoor for Ryno, Pennsylvania.

Sargent. Peak population (1920), 1,078. Post office established July 23, 1879. The original Sargent, located one mile east of the present office, was named by Mrs. George Sherman, first postmistress, in remembrance of friends in Streeter, Illinois. In 1883, when Ezra P. Savage and Joseph W. Thomas founded their town nearby, Mrs. Sherman agreed to surrender the post office and permit its removal to the new locality on condition that the name remain Sargent. This suited the founders, because Savage wished to perpetuate the name of his uncle, George D. Sargent, a Davenport, Iowa, banker.

Scandia. Post office established February 6, 1879; discontinued October 15, 1904. Abbreviated form of the word Scandinavia.

Seneca. Census not available. Post office established February 6, 1879; discontinued August 28, 1882. Named by residents from Seneca, Wisconsin. The town was discontinued when the railroad built through nearby Westerville.

Set Up. Post office established August 30, 1880; name changed to Delight September 23, 1880. Let Up was the name sent to postal authorities, who in error returned the name of Set Up.

Somerford. Post office established June 29, 1883; discontinued March 31, 1910. Named by James Pierce, first postmaster, for a town in England.

South Loup. Stage stop on the Kearney-Black Hills Trail on the South Loup River.

Springville. Post office established May 21, 1886; discontinued January 14, 1889. Named for its characteristic location.

Stop. Post office established June 18, 1884; discontinued April 25, 1894. Origin of the name not learned.

Table. Post office established May 2, 1896; discontinued February 15, 1928. Named for the township in which it was located and for the high table land of the region.

Tallin. Post office established March 3, 1885; discontinued May 19, 1899. Named in honor of John Tallin, first postmaster.

Triumph. Post office established November 9, 1877; discontinued September 6, 1902. Named by postmaster Frederick Schreyer after winning a struggle with cowboys who had a timber claim. Located north of Callaway.

Tuckerville. Post office established October 22, 1888; discontinued March 15, 1916. Probably named for William H. Tucker, first postmaster or for Reginald Tucker, former county sheriff.

Tufford. Post office established April 18, 1877; discontinued March 4, 1903. Named for Isaiah Tufford, Civil War veteran from Maryland and homesteader.

Upton. Post office established December 22, 1890; discontinued May 12, 1903. Origin of the name is unknown.

Victoria. Name of the first settlement at Victoria Springs in Custer County. It did not have a post office.

Walworth. Census not available. Post office established December 16, 1884; discontinued November 15, 1928. Former town named for a Mr. Walworth, who owned a chain of lumber yards throughout Nebraska.

Wayne. Proposed town in Delight Township.

Weissert. Peak population (1950), 19. Post office established October 8, 1892; discontinued 1953. Name suggested by a Mr. Weiser, a postal employee, after Hinckleyville was rejected. The first post office and store was located one mile north and just east of the present location on the D. C. Konkel farm.

Wescott. Peak population (1890), 61. Post office name changed from Douglas Grove October 11, 1883; discontinued July 10, 1901. Former hamlet named for J. F. Wescott, who owned a ranch, store, and flour mill.

Westerville. Peak population (1930), 176. Post office established September 25, 1891. Named in honor of its first resident, James Westervelt, merchant. Postal authorities spelled the name Westerville.

West Union. Peak population (1900), 90. Post office established June 10, 1879; discontinued May 9, 1912. Former hamlet named for West Union, Iowa.

Wirt. Post office established June 10, 1879; discontinued May 9, 1912. Named in honor of the son of C. D. Smith, local settler.

Woods Park. Proposed town near Sargent named for Joseph A. Woods in 1874.

Woods Stage Ranch. Station on Black Hills Trail located on Dave Rankins ranch.

Yucca. Post office established March 3, 1885; discontinued February 12, 1889. Named for indigenous liliaceous plant yucca glauca, known as bear grass or Spanish bayonet.

Yucca Hill. Post office established October 3, 1906; discontinued August 31, 1917. Named for a hill covered with the yucca plant.

DAKOTA COUNTY

Named for the Dakota Sioux. Boundaries were defined by an act of the Legislature approved March 7, 1855; redefined January 26, 1856.

Beer Man Spur. Former railroad station on the Chicago, St. Paul, Minneapolis and Omaha Railroad.

Blyburg. Town did not last long enough for a post office identification. Platted by Colonel Plyel and named for John Bly, settler, on September 20, 1856.

Brady. Same as Brady's Crossing.

Brady's Crossing. Mail served from Jackson. Located one mile west and north of present Willis. Town named for an early settler, John Brady, centered around St. John's Catholic Church and general store. Town later moved one-fourth mile north near the North Western Railroad tracks. Name changed to Vista when shipments were confused with Brady's Island in Lincoln County.

Coburn. Former junction for two railroads—Chicago, St. Paul, Minneapolis and Omaha Railroad and the Burlington Railroad west of Dakota City.

Covington. Post office established March 29, 1858; annexed to South Sioux City May 1, 1893. Town originally called Harney City, then Newport, and finally Covington. Named for Covington, Kentucky, home of Judge Thomas L. Griffey, one of the town fathers. The Covington, Columbus and Black Hills Railroad was named for the town.

Crockwell. Paper town which never got beyond the platting stage. Probably named for Dr. J. D. M. Crockwell, early settler of Dakota County.

Dakota City. Peak population (2000), 1,821. Post office established January 28, 1856. County seat named for the county. The city played an important part in Nebraska history as a Missouri River port and site of the General Land Office until that agency moved to Niobrara in 1878. The Nebraska Territorial Court was held here. Dakota City Land Company platted and surveyed the townsite in 1856.

Deer Creek. Post office established September 17, 1859; discontinued September 15, 1860. Named for the creek on which it was located.

Elk Valley. Post office established April 13, 1871; discontinued January 13, 1896. Named for its location in a valley which once harbored elk.

Emerson. Peak population (1930), 883. Post office moved from Dixon County January 15, 1926. Originally in Dixon County. Portions of Emerson are still in Dixon and Thurston counties, with the main part in Dakota County. Town named for author Ralph Waldo Emerson.

Emmett. Post office established June 15, 1871; discontinued October 4, 1872. Origin of the name not learned. Location was on the Missouri River.

Farmington. Place listed in early Dakota County records.

Ferry. Station on the Burlington Railroad, now a part of South Sioux City.

Finnerty. Former station on the Burlington Railroad probably named for John Finnerty, early settler. It later became Willis Beach.

Floyd. Former station on the Chicago, St. Paul, Minneapolis and Omaha Railroad located near South Sioux City.

Fort Charles. Fort Carlos IV built by Spanish fur traders and occupied between 1795 and 1797 near present Homer.

Franklin. Proposed name for a town eventually called Jackson. The name could not be used because there already was a Franklin in the state.

Franklin City. Founded by Joseph T. Turner and John Feenan, but it never progressed beyond the platting stage.

Goodwin. Peak population (1940), 33. Post office established July 8, 1882; discontinued 1943. Former town named in honor of John C. Goodwin, a railroad official in 1882 when the town was established.

Greenwood. Post office established Sept. 29, 1859. Became Ponca Agency.

Harney City. Town platted by Sioux City Company in 1856, but on a site nearby, Newport was established. Later it became Covington. Probably named for Gen. William Harney.

Homer. Peak population (2000), 590. Post office changed from Omadi January 23, 1874. Town came into being after Omadi, one mile away, was washed out by floods. Named after Homer, Greek poet. Located on the former site of an Omaha Indian village, the town was started by John and Joseph Smith, brothers who had lived in the vicinity since 1856.

Hubbard. Peak population (1980, 2000), 234. Post office established January 19, 1881.

Named in honor of Judge Asahel W. Hubbard, first president of the Covington, Columbus and Black Hills Railroad. Dakota City Land Company platted town in 1880.

Jackson. Peak population (1900), 339. Post office name changed from O'Gorman December 14, 1865. Origin of the name not learned.

Laketon. A station on the Burlington Railroad located near Dakota City.

Lodi. Post office established July 14, 1870; discontinued February 1, 1875. Probably named for Lodi, New Jersey, or Lodi, Wisconsin.

Logan. Post office established July 16, 1858; discontinued March 24, 1860. Once a rival of Omadi, this former town boasted about twenty-five houses and several business establishments. Several buildings were moved to Dakota City after boom collapsed. Townsite lies beneath the Missouri River. Origin of the name not learned.

Millis. Also called Millis Beach.

Millis Beach. Formerly called Finnerty's, Millis Beach was armed for the Millis family. Charles Millis operated a store at Crystal Lake Beach, a resort on the horseshoe-shaped lake near Dakota City. The Missouri River floods of 1951 and 1952 filled the lake with silt and debris. Today most of the former lake area is a residential section.

Nacora. Census not available. Post office established April 22, 1882; discontinued 1945. Name of this former town derives from the Spanish nacio, which means "I am born." Before the post office was established, the place was called Simons Siding.

Newport. See note on Covington.

Northshore. Present community near South Sioux City.

O'Gorman. Post office name changed from St. Johns February 5, 1863; name changed to Jackson December 14, 1865. Origin of the name not learned.

Omadi. Post office established June 8, 1857; name changed to Homer January 23, 1874. Origin of the name not learned.

Oneida. Listed in Dakota County history of 1865.

Orshek. Station on the Burlington Railroad.

Pacific City. Early proposed town that never got beyond the platting stage.

Ponca City. Place listed in early Dakota County history.

Randolph. Another proposed town that never went beyond the platting stage.

Simons Siding. Former station on the Chicago and North Western Railroad before it became the town of Nacora.

Sioux. Post office established February 25, 1888; name changed to South Sioux City March 25, 1889. Named for the Sioux Indians.

South Sioux City. Peak population (2000), 11,925. Post office name changed from Sioux March 25, 1889. Town named for its location south of Sioux City, Iowa, across the Missouri River.

Stanton. Proposed town that was platted and finally annexed by South Sioux City.

St. Johns. Post office established March 10, 1857; name changed to O'Gorman February 5, 1863. Origin of the name not learned. First postmaster was John M. Hays. Platted by John Tracy, town vied for county seat with Dakota City.

St. Patrick. Listed in early Dakota County history.

Turner Grove. Post office established July 25, 1888; discontinued 1889. Origin of the name not learned.

Verona. Proposed town founded by Joseph Kerr and W. D. Roberts opposite the mouth of the Floyd River; never got beyond the platting stage.

Vista. Name changed from Brady's Crossing. Name said to have been selected because of picturesque hills and valleys surrounding it. A boxcar served as depot. Name changed to Willis in 1908 due to confusion with Vesta in Johnson County.

Willis. Mail served from Jackson. Name changed from Vista in 1908. Named for a Mr. Willis, president of the Chicago and North Western Railroad. When the North Western tore up the track in 1933, it left the elevator without transportation. James P. O'Neill, who owned the store and elevator, moved these enterprises one-half mile east and located on the Burlington Railroad.

Wood Park. Former station on the Burlington Railroad.

DAWES COUNTY

Named in honor of James W. Dawes (1844-1918), governor of Nebraska from 1883 to 1887. Boundaries of the county were defined by the Legislature and approved February 19, 1885. Previously part of Sioux County.

Antelope. Post office name changed from Wanatah April 27, 1898; discontinued December 30, 1916. Named for antelope in the vicinity.

Belmont. Peak population (1950), 60. Post office established November 9, 1889; discontinued 1957. Former town on the Burlington Railroad named for a railroad official.

Bordeaux. Peak population (1890), 150. Post office established May 8, 1884; discontinued August 7, 1896. Former town on the Burlington Railroad named after Bordeaux Creek. James Bordeaux, French trapper and trader, lived in the area in an earlier period.

Camp Canby. Temporary military camp used during the winter of 1876-77. Clay Dear's store was near this encampment.

Camp Custer. Temporary military camp in use during the winter of 1876-77 by the Fourth and Fifth Cavalry Regiments.

Camp Red Cloud Agency. Military post established March 5, 1874, near Red Cloud Agency; name changed to Camp Robinson March 29, 1874.

Camp Robinson. Name changed from Camp Red Cloud Agency March 29, 1874. Post office moved from Camp Red Cloud Agency February 14, 1877; post office changed to Fort Robinson September 9, 1879. See Fort Robinson.

Carney's Station. Former station on the Sidney and Black Hills Stage route. Also known as Big Cottonwood Creek.

Chadron. Peak population (1980), 5,993. Post office established August 2, 1880. County seat town named for fur trader Louis Chartran, who had charge of a trading post on Chadron Creek in the 1840s. Early Frenchmen from Missouri pronounced his name "Shattron," which was finally corrupted into "Chadron" by first permanent settlers in the county. Platted in 1885. Chadron Normal, founded in 1911, is today Chadron State College.

Coxville. Post office established December 23, 1885; discontinued May 12, 1888. Named in honor of John W. Cox, first postmaster.

Crawford. Peak population (1980), 1,315. Post office established February 27, 1891. Town named for Lt. Emmett Crawford (1844-86), stationed at Fort Robinson in the 1870s. The name of John Wallace "Captain Jack" Crawford (1847-1917), Indian fighter, scout, and poet, has sometimes been mistakenly associated with that of Crawford. Town began as tent city in 1886 on land of William E. Annin when Fremont, Elkhorn and Missouri Valley Railroad arrived.

Crow Butte. Post office established June 23, 1884; discontinued July 20, 1886. Named for a war party of Crow who took refuge on the butte after an 1849 fight with Sioux.

Dakota Junction. Station where line of Chicago and North Western Railroad branches toward South Dakota.

Dawes City. Post office established August 4, 1885; name changed to Whitney July 24, 1886. Named for the county, it was once a contender for county seat.

Dooley. Former station on the Burlington Railroad located north of Marsland.

Dunlap. Post office established February 11, 1888; discontinued 1935. Named by a Mr. Roberts, Union soldier in the Civil War, after an officer under whom he served (probably Brig. Gen. James Dunlap).

Earth Lodge. In this community the railroad station was known as Earth Lodge, while the post office was called Dawes City.

Esther. Post office established November 13, 1889; discontinued April 14, 1923. Origin of the name not learned. First postmaster was Alva McLaughlin.

Fort Robinson. Post office name changed from Camp Robinson September 9, 1879; discontinued 1953. Named in honor of Lt. Levi H. Robinson, killed west of Fort Laramie in battle against the Indians. Fort Robinson is principally known for the part it played during Indian unrest of the nineteenth century. It served as a training post during the Spanish-American War, World War I, and World War II. It also functioned as a remount depot, war dog training center, and prisoner of war camp. It was turned over to the U.S. Department of Agriculture on July 1, 1948. On May 23, 1955, the administration of certain areas of Fort Robinson passed by lease agreement to the University of Nebraska, State Game and Parks Commission, and the Nebraska State Historical Society for museum and recreational purposes. On October 24, 1962, title to certain areas was transferred to the state.

Hamilton. Post office established January 29, 1889; discontinued September 16, 1889. Possibly named for Captain Hamilton, an officer at Fort Robinson who later owned a ranch at nearby Soldier Creek.

Helper. Former station on the Burlington Railroad.

Horn. Former station on the Burlington Railroad located near Crawford.

Hough. Post office established February 5, 1892; discontinued 1934. Was to be named Huff, but there was an office within the state so named and Hough was accepted.

Huff. See Hough.

Hughes. Post office established September 5, 1884; discontinued August 4, 1885. Possibly named in honor of John S. Hughes, first postmaster.

Ida. Post office established September 21, 1894; discontinued April 30, 1912. Origin of the name not learned. First postmaster was A. Kraut.

Kendall. Post office established December 23, 1885; discontinued April 2, 1887. Named in honor of the Kendall family. Mrs. Christena Kendall was first postmistress.

Lawn. Post office established July 31, 1885; moved to Box Butte County August 20, 1886. Origin of the name not learned.

Leonard. Post office established September 20, 1886, discontinued January 12, 1888. Origin of the name not learned. First postmaster was Wayne Sullenberger.

Little White Clay Creek. Former station on the Sidney-Black Hills Stage route. Three miles south of present Crawford.

Little Cottonwood. Former station on the Sidney-Black Hills Stage route. Four miles north of present Crawford.

Longhorn. Post office established December 17, 1885; discontinued April 2, 1887. Probably named for Longhorn cattle which Texas cattlemen brought to this region.

Manchester. Post office established May 3, 1910; discontinued December 31, 1920. Possibly named in honor of William S. Manchester, first postmaster.

Marsland. Peak population (1910), 200. Post office established September 12, 1889. Village named in honor of Thomas Marsland of Lincoln, Nebraska, general freight agent of the Burlington Railroad.

O'Linn. Post office established September 15, 1884; discontinued January 12, 1885. Named in honor of Mrs. Fannie O'Linn, first postmistress.

Pepper Creek. Post office established April 17, 1913; discontinued May 14, 1921. Named for the creek near which post office was located.

Pine Ridge. Post office established March 11, 1911; discontinued 1947. Named for the ridge on which pine timber grew.

Red Cloud Agency. The first one was built in 1871 just west of the Wyoming-Nebraska line. In August 1873 it was moved to a location one and one-half miles east of future Fort Robinson and in October 1877 to Lyman County, South Dakota. Post office established

January 8, 1875; moved to Camp Robinson February 14, 1877. In 1878 the agency was moved to Pine Ridge, South Dakota.

Named for Oglala Chief Red Cloud.

Remington. Former station on the Burlington Railroad.

Running Water Station. Station on the Sidney-Black Hills stage and freight line located two miles west of Marsland.

Rutland. Post office established August 10, 1891; discontinued October 1, 1891. Former station on the Burlington Railroad probably named for Rutland, Massachusetts, or Rutland, Vermont.

Sarles. Post office established June 9, 1890; discontinued February 1, 1893. Named in honor of Ebenezer Sarles, first postmaster.

Sodtown. Name proposed for the Lawn post office.

Tableau. Post office established December 14, 1885; discontinued June 3, 1886. Named for a stone formation of figures which appeared as a tableau. French trappers were in this area at an earlier period.

Wanatah. Post office established September 6, 1887; name changed to Antelope April 27, 1898. Indian in origin. There is also a Wanatah in Indiana.

Wayside. Post office established December 18, 1906; discontinued 1956. Former post office and present station on the Chicago and North Western Railroad; probably named by railway of- ficials.

Whitney. Peak population (1930), 177. Post office name changed from Dawes City July 24, 1886. Town named in honor of Peter Whitney, land agent for the Pioneer Town Site Company when the North Western Railroad was built.

Wolfington. Post office established June 5, 1914; discontinued March 15, 1923. Possibly named in honor of James Wolfington, first postmaster.

DAWSON COUNTY

Named for John L. Dawson, U.S. congressman from Pennsylvania. County formed on June 26, 1871, by proclamation of Acting Governor William H. James. Boundaries were defined by the Legislature January 11, 1860, and redefined June 6, 1871.

Buffalo. Census not available. Post office established May 4, 1896; discontinued 1957. Former town named for its location on Buffalo Creek. Community centered around a Lutheran Church, school, and combined store-post office.

Buzzard's Roost. Union Pacific Railroad livestock loading siding, constructed by the Buzzard's Roost Ranch operated by John B. Colton, a California forty-niner. Named for buzzard roost in Buzzard's Roost Canyon. Located north of Eddyville.

Cantella. Post office established March 3, 1885; discontinued December 10, 1887. Origin of the name not learned.

Congdon. Post office established May 23, 1881; name changed to Eddyville November 12, 1890. Possibly named in honor of J. H. Congdon, general manager of the Union Pacific Railroad.

Coyote. Post office established July 30, 1877; discontinued October 31, 1877. Origin of the name not learned.

Cozad. Peak population (1980), 4,453. Post office established June 18, 1874; name changed to Gould June 15, 1881; name retained as Cozad October 23, 1885. Named in honor of its founder, John J. Cozad, head of a company of Ohio pioneers in 1873.

Darr. Peak population (1930), 45. Post office established December 19, 1902; discontinued May 31, 1923. Mail served from Cozad. Former town and present community and railroad station named in honor of George B. Darr, owner of townsite.

Dawson. Post office established May 7, 1871; name changed to Plum Creek April 20, 1872. Named for the county.

Dewey. Post office established August 12, 1904; discontinued February 28, 1905. Former post office and present railroad station probably commemorates Adm. George Dewey of Spanish-American War fame.

Dorrington. Post office established February 15, 1890; discontinued August 25, 1892. Origin of the name not learned.

Doss. Post office name changed from Potter October 2, 1882; discontinued March 12, 1904. Named after an African American ranch employee who carried mail from Overton.

Eddyville. Peak population (1910), 254. Post office name changed from Congdon November 12, 1890. Town named by officials of the Kearney and Black Hills Railroad for Eddyville, Iowa.

Esther. Former station on the Union Pacific Railroad.

Farnam. Peak population (1910), 462. Post office name changed from Keystone December 11, 1886. Named in honor of Henry W. Farnam, railroad builder and Burlington official. The first settlement made in 1883 by a Pennsylvania company. Town platted in summer of 1887.

Gothenburg. Peak population (2000), 3,619. Post office name changed from Gottenburgh July 16, 1883. Town and precinct named by E. G. West for Gothenburg, Sweden, where many immigrants had lived.

Gottenburgh. Post office established November 23, 1882; name changed to Gothenburg July 16, 1883. See Gothenburg.

Gould. Post office name changed from Cozad June 15, 1881; name changed back to Cozad October 23, 1885. Origin of the name not learned.

Gurnsey. Post office established March 3, 1884; discontinued February 16, 1905. Probably named in honor of Albert Gurnsey, first postmaster.

Hilton. Post office name changed from Pencie February 18, 1884; discontinued April 25, 1895. Origin of the name not learned.

Humpback. Post office established August 2, 1880; discontinued July 13, 1884. Probably named for a characteristic formation of hills.

Jewell. Post office name changed from Newport May 7, 1875; discontinued October 23, 1890. Possibly named in honor of Postmaster General Marshall Jewell.

Josselyn. Post office established March 25, 1898; discontinued May 24, 1900. Former town and railroad station on the Union Pacific named in honor of S. T. Josselyn, U.P. paymaster.

Jovian. Former station on the Union Pacific Railroad.

Keystone. Post office established September 5, 1881; name changed to Farnam December 11, 1886. Probably named for the Keystone State (Pennsylvania) or for a ranch by this name.

Leoti. Post office established November 21, 1896; discontinued January 5, 1897. Origin of the name not learned.

Level. Post office established June 18, 1884; discontinued April 29, 1904. Name is probably descriptive in origin.

Lexington. Peak population (2000), 10,011. Post office name changed from Plum Creek March 23, 1889. Named by citizen vote to commemorate the Battle of Lexington, Massachusetts, during the Revolutionary War. Lexington retained the county seat after the name change.

Markel. Former Union Pacific Railroad station probably named for Jacob Ely Markel, who established eating houses along the U.P. from Council Bluffs, Iowa, to Huntingdon, Oregon.

Meriden. Post office established February 21, 1890; discontinued August 25, 1892.

Possibly named for one of the six Meridens in the United States, the largest of which is Meriden, Connecticut.

Merom. Post office established September 20, 1883; discontinued June 26, 1896. Possibly named for a Biblical lake located north of Sea of Galilee, where Joshua fought the Canaanite kings.

Midway. No. 18 of the Pony Express stations in Nebraska, three miles south of the present town of Gothenburg on the Henry Williams ranch.

Mullahla's Station. Post Mullahla in maps of Nebraska Territory posts, 1865.

Myers. Post office established July 28, 1884; discontinued May 11, 1887. Possibly named in honor of Abraham Myers, first postmaster.

Newington. Post office established September 15, 1888; discontinued September 17, 1889. Origin of the name not learned.

Newport. Post office established August 11, 1874; name changed to Jewell May 7, 1875. Origin of the name has not been learned.

Overton. Peak population (2000), 646. Post office established June 3, 1873. The James M. Potter family made the first settlement here in 1873. Town named in honor of a government official in charge of men guarding workmen constructing the Union Pacific Railroad.

Pencie. Post office established July 11, 1881; name changed to Hilton February 18, 1884. Origin of the name not learned.

Plum Creek. Post office name changed from Dawson April 20, 1872; name changed to Lexington March 23, 1889. The first county seat takes its name from nearby Plum Creek. Early trading post.

Plum Creek Station. No. 16 of the Pony Express stations, located ten miles southeast of Lexington.

Potter. Post office established April 6, 1882; name changed to Doss October 2, 1882. Named in honor of Ira W. Potter, first postmaster.

Ringgold. Post office established December 13, 1880; discontinued January 25, 1893. Origin of the name not learned. A county in Iowa by this name.

Rugby. Prior name of Buzzard's Roost, livestock loading station. Rancher John B. Colton, of Irish descent, threatened to ship his cattle via the Burlington if the English sounding name was not changed. The Union Pacific changed the name to Buzzard's Roost.

Simonds. Former station on the Union Pacific Railroad.

Sumner. Peak population (1920), 345. First postmaster, Phillip J. Reser, was appointed August 6, 1889. Town named in honor of Senator Charles Sumner of Massachusetts, who advocated the abolition of slavery.

Trappers Grove. Post office established June 27, 1877; discontinued January 21, 1884. Possibly named for a grove of trees near a trapper's hut or for the place of his trapping operations.

Trued. Station on the Union Pacific Railroad.

Velte. Post office established September 17, 1885; discontinued January 25, 1893. Named in honor of Adam F. Velte, first postmaster.

Warren. Former station on the Union Pacific Railroad.

White Rabbit. Post office established January 2, 1880; discontinued April 6, 1894. Possibly named for a light-colored rabbit killed in the vicinity.

Willow. Post office established October 29, 1894; name changed to Willow Island February 2, 1906. See Willow Island.

Willow Island No. 1. Pony Express Station No. 17 and later an Overland Stage stop. Sometimes called Willow Bend, it was located about nine miles southeast of Cozad.

Willow Island No. 2. Peak population (1950), 85. Post office name changed from Willow February 2, 1906. First settler was Joseph Huffman, who located here in 1873. Named after a large island, ten miles long and one mile wide, in the Platte River south of town. Before being ravaged by prairie fires, the island was a wilderness of willow trees.

DEUEL COUNTY

Deuel County came into existence through election held in November 1888; it was organized in January 1889. Previously a part of Cheyenne County, it was named in honor of Harry Porter Deuel (1836-1914), pioneer citizen of Omaha. He was an official for a Missouri River transportation company, the Burlington Railroad, and the Union Pacific Railroad. Deuel County was divided in 1909, and the northern part became Garden County.

Barton. Station on the Union Pacific Railroad named in honor of Guy C. Barton of North Platte, Nebraska, a contractor for the railroad.

Big Springs. Peak population (1930), 595. Post office established February 13, 1861. Named for the springs which furnished water for settlers. Town platted by Union Pacific Railroad in November 1884. Big Springs vied with Froid and Chappell (the winner), for county seat in an election.

Chappell. Peak population (1950), 1,297. Post office established December 27, 1886. Named for Charles Henry Chappell, superintendent of the Union Pacific second division. A cornerstone of the Chappell Memorial Library and Art Gallery, made possible by Chappell's widow, Orianna Ward Chappell, was dedicated by the Masonic Grand Lodge of the State of Nebraska, September 1935, in his honor. J. B. and M. A. Carmichael platted the town in July 1884. Chappell won county seat election over Big Springs and Froid.

Day. Post office established April 26, 1890; discontinued January 27, 1903. Named in honor of E. M. Day, early settler and editor of a Big Springs paper.

East Barton. Present station on the Union Pacific Railroad.

Froid. Census not available. Post office established February 1, 1886; discontinued November 30, 1915. Former town named in honor of either Andre F. Froid, first postmaster, or Fred Froid, early settler. Froid vied for county seat with Big Springs and Chappell.

Nine Mile Station. No. 28 of the Pony Express stations in Nebraska, located two miles southeast of Chappell.

Ottman. Name changed to Perdu. Former railroad station named in honor of J. A. Ottman, general roadmaster of the Union Pacific Railroad.

Perdu. Former Union Pacific station name changed from Ottman. Probably named for a local rancher or railroad official.

Ralton. Former station on the Union Pacific Railroad. Probably named for a local rancher or railway official.

Weir. Former railroad station named either for Charles A. Weir, Union Pacific conductor, or for his father, James Weir, a construction worker on the Union Pacific Railroad.

DIXON COUNTY

County created and organized by act of the Legislature in December 1858. Previously part of Dakota County.

Activity. Post office established January 23, 1860; discontinued July 5, 1861. Probably named for the activity in the settlement.

Allen. Peak population (1930), 489. Post office established 1890. Town named in honor of Henry Allen, a homesteader who located here in 1870. Town eventually platted on his land.

Aoway Creek. Post office established October 10, 1879; discontinued January 3, 1882. Named for nearby Aoway Creek, derived from an Indian word.

Bow Creek. Probably a proposed town that never got beyond the platting stage. Named for nearby Bow Creek.

Concord. Peak population (1930), 263. Post office established July 13, 1858. Named for

Concord, Massachusetts, Revolutionary War battle site. Name suggested by Marvin Hughett, president of the Chicago, St. Paul, Minneapolis and Omaha Railroad.

Daily. Census not available. Post office name changed from Daily Branch February 13, 1895; discontinued August 29, 1900. Town named in honor of Pat Daily, early pioneer.

Daily Branch. Post office established June 23, 1874; name changed to Daily February 13, 1895. See Daily.

Dixon. Peak population (1920), 241. Post office established February 12, 1859. Named for the county.

Ellis. Post office established June 15, 1881; name changed to Emerson November 10, 1890. Possibly named in honor of Oliver J. Ellis, first postmaster.

Emerson. Peak population (1930), 883. Post office name changed from Ellis November 10, 1890. Commemorates the American author, Ralph Waldo Emerson. Original townsite platted in 1883.

Galena. Former locality named by a Mr. Crockwell and settled by people who probably came from Galena, Illinois. The site later became the town of Martinsburg.

Hawkeye. Post office established June 15, 1871; name changed to Waterbury July 2, 1890. Probably named for Iowa, the Hawkeye State.

Hazle. Post office established December 22, 1894; discontinued September 25, 1900. Named for nearby Hazle Creek. Origin of creek's name unknown.

Ionia. Peak population (1890), 65. Post office established February 23, 1860; discontinued October 10, 1900. Former village located on the Missouri River. It was eventually abandoned because of high flood waters. Its name may have come from the town of Ionia, Michigan, which was named for Ionia, Greece.

Justice. Post office established April 13, 1870; discontinued September 9, 1898. Probably named for an early settler.

Lime Creek. Post office established September 28, 1868; discontinued September 10, 1883. Named for a nearby creek, which probably had outcroppings of limestone.

Lime Grove. Peak population (1900), 25. Post office established May 2, 1883; discontinued November 1, 1902. Former hamlet probably named for a grove of trees near a limestone quarry.

Logan Grove. Post office established March 19, 1877; discontinued July 12, 1887. Origin of the name not learned.

Martinsburg. Peak population (1910), 291. Post office established May 30, 1880; discontinued 1968. Mail served from Ponca. Town named in honor of Jonathan Martin, early pioneer.

Maskell. Peak population (1920), 165. Post office established July 22, 1908. Town named in honor of A. H. Maskell, owner of land on which town was platted. Named by the St. Paul Town Site Company.

Newcastle. Peak population (1920), 500. Post office established June 29, 1864. Town named by Gustavus Smith, the first settler who built the first house in the area and referred to it as his new castle. There is also a Newcastle, England.

Norman. Place mentioned in early Dixon County history.

North Bend. Former locality mentioned as contender for county seat.

North Creek. Early locality in Dixon County.

Norway. Locality near Ponca in the 1890s.

Parkhill. Post office established June 23, 1874; discontinued January 1, 1882. Named in honor of William Park, first postmaster.

Ponca. Peak population (2000), 1,062. Post office established September 17, 1857. County seat named for Ponca Indians. One of the oldest towns in the state, it was platted in 1856 by Frank West and a Dr. Stough. Ponca won county seat in election with Ionia, Concord, and North Bend. It retained the administrative post in several other elections.

Powder Creek. Post office established April 5, 1875; discontinued January 31, 1876. Named for a nearby creek.

Silver Ridge. Post office established December 28, 1876; discontinued June 14, 1894. Origin of the name not learned.

South Creek. Post office established April 5, 1869; discontinued February 4, 1885. Named for a nearby creek.

Spring Bank. Post office established June 18, 1874; discontinued June 14, 1894. Origin of the name has not been ascertained.

Stebbins. Former station on the Burlington Railroad located six miles west of Waterbury. Possibly named for a railroad official.

St. Peter. Post office established April 30, 1896; moved to Cedar County June 25, 1901. Named in honor of Peter Abts, first postmaster.

Wakefield. Peak population (2000), 1,411. Post office established October 22, 1881. Named in honor of L. W. Wakefield, surveyor for the St. Paul and Sioux City Railroad between Emerson and Norfolk. Part of the town is in Wayne County.

Waterbury. Peak population (1930), 204. Post office changed from Hawkeye July 2, 1890. Town named for spring which supplied Burlington Railroad station with water. There is a city in Connecticut with this name.

DODGE COUNTY

Named in honor of U.S. Senator Augustus Caesar Dodge (1812-83) of Iowa, a supporter of the Kansas-Nebraska Bill. County was organized and its boundaries defined by the first Territorial Legislature. It was approved on March 6, 1855; redefined November 2, 1858; December 22, 1859; and reorganized January 13, 1860.

Albion. First name of Lincoln (later Timberville). Located one mile south of Ames in Platte Township.

Ames. Peak population (1950), 65. Post office established August 10, 1885. Town named in honor of Oakes Ames, official of the Union Pacific Railroad. Here were the yards of the Standard Cattle Company, where cattle were brought from western ranges to be fed before sale on the Omaha markets.

Bangs. Post office established September 29, 1891; discontinued July 14, 1900. Named in honor of Charles A. Bang, early settler who came from Denmark.

Bay State. Former locality and railroad station on the Union Pacific Railroad probably named by some resident from Massachusetts, the Bay State. Named for the Bay State Livestock Company, which had extensive holdings in the area.

Blacksmith's Point. Locality was never a post office, although it was a contender for county seat.

Chautauqua. Former station on the Union Pacific Railroad located near Fremont.

Clyde. Post office established March 26, 1896; discontinued July 30, 1903. Origin of the name not learned. Hugh Ganghen was first postmaster.

Crowell. Peak population (1940), 107. Post office name changed from Oak Springs May 6, 1872; discontinued 1965; mail served from Scribner. Town platted by Elkhorn and Town Lot Company and named in honor of a Mr. Crowell, who started the first grain elevator.

Dodge. Peak population (1980), 815. Post office established May 10, 1880. Town platted by the Pioneer Town Site Company in 1886 and named for the county.

East End. Former station on the Union Pacific Railroad located east of Fremont.

Elizabeth. Early locality in Dodge County.

Emerson. Post office established January 18, 1858; name changed to Wallace December 28, 1858. Possibly named for George Emerson, early pioneer of Dodge County.

Everett. Post office established April 16, 1870; discontinued December 8, 1906. Former post office was located in a small general store operated by Postmaster S. D. Pickard.

Franklin. Post office established February 3, 1858; discontinued November 25, 1864. Origin of the name not learned. First postmaster was George Burton.

Fredonia. Proposed town in early Dodge County history.

Fremont. Peak population (2000), 25,174. Post office established May 5, 1857. County seat named in honor of Gen. John C. Fremont (1813-90), explorer. The town site was surveyed by E. H. Barnard, and the first claim stake was driven by George Pinney in August 1856. Initial building was by the Fremont Town Association, an outgrowth of the original townsite company. Fremont was made county seat in election with Robbinsville and Blacksmith's Point in 1860. Midland Lutheran College was moved to Fremont from Atchison, Kansas, in 1919.

Galena. Post office established December 30, 1867; discontinued May 1, 1883. Former post office established by J. B. Robinson and S. B. Parks. Possibly named for Galena, Illinois, or for Galena, Missouri.

Glencoe. Peak population (1900), 46. Post office established April 13, 1871; discontinued February 7, 1896. Former hamlet said to be named for James Glen, first postmaster, who conducted a store while holding the office for twenty-one years. The community was settled by an Illinois colony in 1868 and 1869; most of the people were of Scottish parentage. There is a Glencoe in Cook County, Illinois, and a Glencoe in Scotland.

Golden State. Former community probably named by someone returning from California, the Golden State.

Hooper. Peak population (1920), 1,014. Post office established July 11, 1871. One source says town named in honor of Samuel Hooper of Boston, Massachusetts, member of Congress during the Civil War. The other source says town named in honor of Richard Hooper, homesteader who came from England.

Ihno. Post office established March 3, 1898; discontinued August 1, 1900. Named in honor of Ihno Harms on whose farm the post office was located.

Inglewood. Present community near Fremont.

Jalapa. Post office established January 18, 1859; discontinued July 11, 1870. Origin of the name has not been determined. There are cities in Guatemala and Mexico with this name.

Jamestown. Post office established April 13, 1871; discontinued September 9, 1901. Named after James Beemar and James C. Hanson. Post office was located on Hanson farm.

Ketchum. Former station on the Union Pacific Railroad located west of Fremont.

Latrobe. Proposed town that never got beyond the platting stage.

Leavitt. Company town owned by the Standard Beet Sugar Company's sugar beet processing plant. The town was named for Heyward D. Leavitt, company president and general manager.

Lewisburgh. Post office established February 3, 1858; discontinued January 25, 1865. Named in honor of Lewis D. Hunter, first postmaster.

Lily. Post office established April 1881; discontinued February 18, 1884. Origin of the name not learned. First postmaster was Patrick Cusick.

Lincoln. Post office established August 22, 1865; name changed to Timberville February 25, 1867. Commemorates President Abraham Lincoln. Name was relinquished when the state capital was named Lincoln.

Logan. Post office established January 25, 1869; discontinued November 15, 1878. Origin of the name not learned.

Manhattan. While never a post office, it contended for the Cuming County seat when part of that county.

Maple Creek. Post office established March 5, 1869; discontinued March 13, 1901. Named for a nearby creek. A Father Monroe kept the post office within his home.

Mapleville. Peak population (1890), 95. Post office established April 13, 1871; discontinued June 8, 1901.

Nickerson. Peak population (2000), 431. Post office established April 5, 1871. Named in honor of its founder, Frederick Nickerson.

North Bend. Peak population (1980), 1,368. Post office name changed from Wallace August 12, 1864. Named by S. S. Caldwell, M. S. Cotterell, and Union Pacific Railroad officials for the bend of the Platte River at its farthest point north. First steam mill in the county was located in the area.

Oak Springs. Post office established January 23, 1868; moved to Crowell May 6, 1872. Office was located on Cohee farm northeast of Crowell. Probably named for springs on a creek near oak timber.

Ogan. Post office established September 5, 1884; discontinued December 4, 1891. Possibly named for Granville Ogan, Civil War veteran and early settler.

Patrick. Station on the Union Pacific Railroad.

Pebble. Census not available. Post office name changed from Pebble Creek March 4, 1872; discontinued October 2, 1882. See Pebble Creek.

Pebble Creek. Post office established January 15, 1868; name changed to Pebble March 4, 1872. Named for white pebbles found in the creek by soldiers in 1859 during the Pawnee War. Town platted by J. B. and H. J. Robinson.

Pleasant Valley. Post office established May 6, 1872; discontinued October 12, 1903. Named for township in which the office was located. First post office was situated in a general store.

Purple Cane. Post office established April 10, 1872; discontinued July 31, 1902. Named for Purple Cane, first postmaster.

Rawhide. Former station on the Chicago and North Western Railroad named for a nearby creek.

Ridgeley. Census not available. Post office established April 13, 1871; discontinued July 31, 1902. Original of the name has not been learned.

Riverside. Probably a former station on the Union Pacific Railroad.

Robbinsville. Never had a post office but contended for the county seat with Blacksmith's Point and Fremont.

Sanberg. Former station on the Union Pacific Railroad.

Sandell. Former station on the Union Pacific Railroad.

Sandpit. Former station on the Union Pacific Railroad was probably a site of the sand and gravel industries along the Platte River.

Scribner. Peak population (1930), 1,059. Post office established August 19, 1874. Town named by John J. Blair, prominent railroad official, for Charles Scribner, founder of a large publishing house in New York City. An army air field was located here during World War II.

Snyder. Peak population (1930), 458. Post office established April 12, 1882. Town named for Conrad Schneider, first postmaster, on whose farm town was platted August 5, 1886. The spelling of his name was anglicized by postal authorities.

St. Vrain. Post office established January 16, 1860; discontinued prior to 1862. Probably located near a church and named for a saint in the religious order.

Summerville. Post office established September 9, 1898; discontinued December 4, 1900. Origin of the name has not been learned.

Sumner. Post office established July 11, 1875; discontinued July 5, 1877. Origin of the name has not been learned.

Swaburgh. Post office established May 2, 1872; discontinued April 1, 1901. Named for a settlement in northern Sweden. Founded by a colony led by Peter Saspur. Post office moved from section 14 to section 24 in 1888.

Timberville. Census not available. Post office name changed from Lincoln February 25,

1867; discontinued October 9, 1884. Town named for timber in the neighborhood and platted by John Farnsworth.

Troxel. Present station on the Union Pacific Railroad.

Uehling. Peak population (1930), 297. Post office established January 23, 1906. Town named in honor of Theodore Uehling, first postmaster, and platted on his land.

Wallace. Post office name changed from Emerson December 28, 1858; name changed to North Bend August 12, 1869. Wallace was the name of an Eastern philanthropist who offered to build a library in any town taking that name.

Webster. Post office established April 13, 1871; discontinued January 31, 1902. Origin of the name has not been learned. Post office was located in a general store.

West End. Former station on the Union Pacific Railroad located west of Fremont.

Winslow. Peak population (1920, 1930), 154. Post office established 1895. Origin of the name is unknown. Town platted by Sioux City and Ashland Development Company December 1, 1895.

DOUGLAS COUNTY

Named in honor of U.S. Senator Stephen A. Douglas (1813-61) from Illinois. County created in the fall of 1854 and approved by the Nebraska Territorial Legislature March 2, 1855.

Albright. Station for the Chicago, Rock Island and Pacific Railroad and the Burlington Railroad. Named for William G. Albright.

Allis. Former station on the Burlington Railroad.

Augur. Post office established August 26, 1869; name changed to Omaha Barracks December 20, 1869. Commemorates Gen. Christopher C. Augur, veteran of the Civil War and Indian campaigns and commander of the Department of the Platte.

Bennington. Peak population (2000), 937. Post office established January 30, 1888. Town named for Bennington, Vermont, and platted by the Pioneer Town Site Company in 1887.

Benson. Post office established May 6, 1891. Made a station of Omaha, 1914. Named for a member of the Erastus A. Benson family.

Benson Acres. Section of Omaha.

Benson Gardens. Section of Omaha.

Blakesly. Projected townsite that never went beyond platting and recording stage.

Boys Town. First known as Father Flanagan's Home, an institution for homeless boys. Father Flanagan and others purchased the 320 acres of land, also known as Overlook Farm. In 1936 it was incorporated as a village, which today occupies 1,500 acres and has about eight hundred boys with a boy mayor and six commissioners.

Briggs. Post office established April 13, 1892; discontinued March 15, 1913. Former town now a part of Omaha and named in honor of Judge Clinton Briggs, former mayor of Omaha and one of the incorporators of the Omaha and Southwestern Railroad.

Cabanne's Trading Post. This post was among the first settlements in present Nebraska and was on Ponca Creek in present Hummel Park. Founded by John Pierre Cabanne, it was operational by 1823 but the year of its founding is conjectural, possibly 1822. It was abandoned during the winter of 1838-39.

Camoak Park. Station on the Burlington Railroad,

Chicago. Post office established August 18, 1858; name changed to Douglas, May 7, 1872. Named for the precinct, which was probably named for Chicago, Illinois.

Childs. Early community established in 1856 by Charles Childs, who operated a sawmill and grist mill on Otoe Creek. Omaha has engulfed this site.

Cutler's Park. Temporary Mormon camp established before Winter Quarters was built.

Dale. Moved from Washington County and now a station on the Chicago and North Western Railroad.

Debolt. Post office established March 12, 1892; discontinued March 18, 1899. Origin of the name not learned.

Debolt Place. Station on the Chicago and North Western Railroad. Probably named for Debolt post office.

Deerfield. Post office established March 23, 1898; discontinued March 5, 1901. Said to be named for deer in nearby Seymour Park.

Dodge. Former station on the Chicago and North Western Railroad.

Douglas. Post office name changed from Chicago May 7, 1872; discontinued February 6, 1884. Named for the county.

Druid Hill. Former station on the Missouri Pacific Railroad.

Dryden. Probably a proposed town that never had a post office and which was eventually absorbed by Omaha.

Dundee. Present section of Omaha (annexed in 1915) and former station on the Chicago, Burlington and Quincy Railroad. Probably established in 1894 by Frank Underwood and named for Dundee, Scotland.

Dundee Place. Community or place annexed by Omaha.

Elk City. Peak population (1900), 78. Post office name changed from Gelston March 28, 1884; discontinued 1968. Mail served from Valley. Proposed name of Elkhorn City not adopted to avoid confusing the mail for Elkhorn eight miles distant.

Elkhorn. Peak population (2000), 6,062. Post office established January 31, 1857. Elkhorn or Elkhorn Station named for the Elkhorn River which empties into the Platte a short distance from town. Ta-ha-zouka (Elk's Horn) is probably an Omaha Indian word.

Elkhorn City. Early freighting and staging point to Fort Kearny in 1856. It later became the site of Elk City.

Elkhorn Junction. Community and former railroad station on the Chicago and North Western Railroad in Florence Precinct.

Florence. Census not available. Post office name changed from Winter Quarters March 14, 1855; made a station of Omaha, 1919. Florence was established on the Mormon site of Winter Quarters and platted by James Mitchell (1811-60), member of the Council of the first Territorial Legislature. Mitchell named the town in honor of Florence Kilbourne, a niece of his wife.

Fort Omaha. Post office name changed from Omaha Barracks July 26, 1876; discontinued September 5, 1896. Mail served from Omaha. This military post served the Seventh Corps area. The post was abandoned in 1896 but was reactivated several times.

Fowler. Post office established March 18, 1886; discontinued November 11, 1895. Origin of the name not learned.

Foxley. Former station on the Union Pacific Railroad.

Gelston. Post office established February 6, 1864; name changed to Elk City March 28, 1884. Possibly named for George W. Gelston, early settler.

Gibson. Station on the Burlington Railroad.

Green Meadows. Section of Omaha.

Gunderson's Crossing. Former railroad station.

Hayes. Post office established April 26, 1887; discontinued July 12, 1888. Origin of the name has not been learned.

Homestead. Former community which eventually became a part of Omaha.

Inco. Station on the Union Pacific Railroad.

Ireland's Mill. This early community on Big Papillion Creek included a grist mill, store, and blacksmith shop.

Irish. Former railroad station.

Iron Bluffs. Place mentioned in early Douglas County history.

Irvington. Peak population (1960), 150. Post office established July 2, 1877; made a station of Omaha in 1967. One source says town named for Irvington, New York, by a Mr. Brewster, who owned the townsite. Another source says town named by Frank Hibbard, a resident.

King Lake. Section near Valley.

Lander. Post office established April 29, 1872; discontinued December 22, 1874. Possibly named in honor of Postmaster Jacob Overlander, using only the last six letters of his name.

Lane. Station on the Union Pacific Railroad possibly named for C. J. Lane, freight agent.

Lawn. Former station on the Union Pacific Railroad.

Lee Valley. Section of Omaha.

Little Papillion. Probably a community in the early 1880s.

Mascot. Probably a former railroad station.

McCandless. Probably a former railroad station.

Melrose. Probably another proposed town that never went beyond the platting stage.

Mercer. Station on the Union Pacific Railroad named for a member of the Mercer family of Omaha.

Millard. Peak population (1970), 7,263. Post office established February 1, 1871; made a station of Omaha in 1968. Named for Ezra Millard, who platted the town.

Millers. Former station on the Missouri Pacific Railroad.

Mount Michael. Post office established, 1955; made a station of Elkhorn in 1957. Monastery located near Elkhorn.

Moval. Station on the Union Pacific Railroad.

Nasco. Station on the Union Pacific Railroad.

North Omaha. Section of Omaha.

Oakchatam. Section of Omaha.

Old Mill. Section of Omaha.

Omaha. Peak population (2000), 390,007. Post office name changed from Omaha City July 7, 1865. Founded by William D. Brown, Dr. Enos Lowe, Jesse Lowe, Jesse Williams, and Joseph H. D. Street in late 1853 and early 1854. Attractively located, Omaha's name was suggested by Jesse Lowe after a nearby Indian tribe. The Council Bluffs and Nebraska Ferry Company also figured in locating the city: After a treaty with the Omaha Indians was secured, plans could be made for building the city. The first Territorial Legislature for Nebraska met in Omaha, January 16, 1855. The first capitol, considered too small after its completion in January 1858, was replaced by the second capitol (1858), which served until Nebraska became a state in 1867. Omaha has always been the county seat and had a United States Land Office, established in March 1857. Often called the crossroads of the nation, Omaha played an important part in the expansion of the West by serving as an outfitting point and trading center for overland immigrants. Creighton University, founded in 1878 by the Jesuit Fathers, was named for Edward Creighton. Omaha Municipal University, founded in 1931, became the University of Nebraska at Omaha in 1968.

Omaha Barracks. Post office name changed from Augur December 20, 1869; name changed to Fort Omaha July 26, 1876. See Fort Omaha.

Omaha City. Post office established May 5, 1854; name changed to Omaha July 7, 1865. See Omaha.

Omaha Heights. Former section annexed by Omaha.

Oriental City. Proposed townsite that eventually became a part of Omaha.

Pappio. Probably the name of Irvington before a post office was established.

Parkvale. Census not available. Post office established January 5, 1885; discontinued August 3, 1887. Name of this former town probably descriptive.

Pawnee. Probably an early settlement in Douglas County history.

Platteau. Proposed town in early Douglas County history.

Platte Valley. Name of Valley before a post office was established.

Porterville. Proposed town that probably never got beyond the platting stage.

Pratoulowski. Proposed town site that eventually became part of Omaha.

Primrose. Post office established December 5, 1864; discontinued December 8, 1870. Origin of the name not learned.

Ralston. Peak population (2000), 6,314. Post office established October 25, 1909; made a station of Omaha 1967. Town named in honor of a Mr. Ralston, prominent businessman.

Regency. Section of Omaha.

Roanoke. Section of Omaha.

Rockbrook. Section of Omaha.

Sander. Former railroad station.

Saratoga. Post office established September 17, 1857; discontinued March 24, 1858. Possibly named for the famous spa in New York state. Located between Omaha and Florence.

Sarpy. Former station on the Union Pacific Railroad named for Peter Sarpy, whose name was also given to Sarpy County.

Seymour. Station on the Union Pacific Railroad.

Seymour Park. Station on the Missouri Pacific Railroad.

Sherman Barracks. Name of Omaha Barracks prior to December 20, 1869.

South Cut. Station on the Chicago and North Western Railroad.

South Omaha. Post office established September 22, 1884. South Omaha grew up around area packing plants and continued as an autonomous municipality until 1915, when it was annexed by Omaha.

South Platte. Post office established Dec. 21, 1855.

Summer Hill. Post office established March 4, 1879; discontinued 1892. Origin of name not learned.

Sunnyslope. Section of Omaha.

Thurston. Former railroad station.

Tomahawk Hills. Section of Omaha.

Underwood Hills. Section of Omaha.

Usher. Former railroad section.

Valley. Peak population (2000), 1,788. Post office established January 29, 1869. In 1867 John Sanders named this town Platte Sanders after himself. Later the name was changed to Platte Valley. When incorporated, Platte was accidentally omitted, and the town became Valley, although it is still located in Platte Valley precinct. Railway officials called this place Valley Station. It was the first station on the Union Pacific Railroad in the Platte Valley; later the name was shortened to Valley.

Venice. Peak population (1960), 25. Mail served from nearby Waterloo.

Walnut Hill. Post office established November 23, 1886; discontinued August 3, 1887. Probably named for nearby black walnut trees.

Waterloo. Peak population (1960), 516. Post office established April 10, 1871. Town named by officials of the Union Pacific Railroad for a battlefield in Belgium. There is also a Waterloo, Iowa.

Weco. Former station on the Union Pacific Railroad.

West Lawn. Former station on Chicago and North Western Railroad.

Westside. Possibly a former railroad station.

Winter Quarters. Post office established March 24, 1854; changed to Florence March 14, 1855. From 1846 to 1848 Winter Quarters, established by Brigham Young, served as a stopover for the Mormons enroute to the Salt Lake Basin in Utah. Inadequately prepared for the harsh winter, many immigrants lost their lives. A cemetery and monument now mark the place.

Woody. Section of Omaha.

Yossems Paradise Valley. Section of Omaha.

DUNDY COUNTY

Named in honor of Judge Elmer S. Dundy (1830-96) of the U.S. Circuit Court, who was prominent in Nebraska politics. County created by legislative enactment February 27, 1873.

Allston. Peak population (1890), 15. Post office established February 29, 1888; discontinued December 16, 1907. Former hamlet intended to honor David Rollston. The name was too similar to Ralston, Douglas County, and postal authorities used the name Allston. Charles W. Towle and John Hildebrand set aside a forty-acre tract for town lots in 1887. Town vied unsuccessfully for county seat.

Arakan. *Dundy County History* lists Arakan as a post office from April 1879 to February 22, 1880, on star route from Culbertson, Nebraska; Jake Haigler listed as postmaster. Located on Haigler Ranch.

Benkelman. Peak population (1950), 1,512. Post office name changed from Collinsville June 29, 1885. County seat town named in honor of J. G. Benkelman, stockraiser, by Burlington Railroad officials.

Burntwood City. After railroad bypassed this platted town, it was abandoned.

Callison. Post office established July 3, 1896; discontinued May 29, 1905. Probably named in honor of Callison C. Richards, a settler.

Calvert. Census not available. Post office established February 18, 1886; discontinued July 31, 1911. Former town probably named for Lincoln, Nebraska, resident Thomas E. Calvert, superintendent of the Burlington Railroad.

Circle Ranch. The Leavenworth Pikes Peak Stage Line entered Dundy County at this location.

Colfer. Former station on the Burlington Railroad named in honor of Thomas Colfer, an attorney from McCook, Nebraska.

Collinsville. Post office established December 6, 1880; name changed to Benkelman June 29, 1885. Named in honor of Moses Collins, a settler.

Connor's 25 Ranch. The town of Collinsville was probably built on part of this ranch.

Crab Island. Former church and school community located one mile north of Callison, which existed about 1898. Grasshopper invasion, drought, and religious differences brought about its downfall.

Doane. Station on the Burlington Railroad. Named in honor of Thomas Doane, superintendent of the Burlington system.

Dundy Centre. Town proposed for a county seat by homesteader Samuel Shinner, who wanted the site on his farm in the center of the county. Shinner surveyed lots to start a boom in 1887. Benkelman, however, won the county seat following an election, and Dundy Centre disappeared.

Elmer. Said to be a post office before Collinsville and operated on a star route from Culbertson from 1878 to 1880. Mrs. Elmer Miller listed as first postmistress. Site was probably on Conner's 25 Ranch or Elmer Miller Ranch.

Haigler. Peak population (1930), 535. Post office established October 5, 1882. Town named in honor of Jacob Haigler, ranchman.

Hancock. Post office established June 26, 1888; discontinued June 30, 1911. Probably named for Gen. Winfield Scott Hancock, Union Army officer in the Civil War and presidential candidate in 1880.

Hiawatha. Peak population (1930), 31. Post office name changed from Neel October 10, 1889; discontinued 1933. Former town named for Hiawatha Academy under the Rev.

Herbert Mott and erected by the Society of Friends. Henry Wadsworth Longfellow popularized the name with his poem "Hiawatha." There is a Hiawatha, Kansas.

Hoover. Former community sometimes called Pink Prairie and named for Nebraska Master Farmer William E. Hoover.

Ives. Post office established December 30, 1887; name changed to Parks December 19, 1888. Named for D. O. Ives, manager of Oak Cattle Company on upper Rock Creek, sometimes known as Rock Creek Ranch.

Jacobs. Post office established February 13, 1886; discontinued July 25, 1888. Named in honor of Postmaster Joshua R. Jacobs.

Kaw. Post office established June 15, 1908; discontinued August 15, 1916. Probably named for the Kaw Indians of Kansas.

Lamont. Post office established August 11, 1893; discontinued 1935. Probably commemorates Daniel Scott Lamont, secretary of war under President Grover Cleveland.

Lux. Census not available. Post office name changed from Norton April 15, 1909; discontinued June 15, 1918. Named by Inspector A. F. Rice from an Indian word meaning light. The town was to be named for Postmaster George West, but he refused to allow it.

Max. Peak population (1960), 150. Post office established March 28, 1881. Town named in honor of Max Monvoisin, French-Canadian settler, first postmaster, and businessman.

Neel. Post office established February 10, 1886; name changed to Hiawatha October 10, 1889. Named in honor of James Neel, first postmaster.

Norton. Post office established May 9, 1906; name changed to Lux April 15, 1909. Named in honor of Monroe L. Norton, first postmaster. Name was changed to avoid confusing railroad shipments to Norton, Kansas.

Ough. Peak population (1890), 25. Post office established February 13, 1886; discontinued January 31, 1912. Town named in honor of John Ough, first postmaster and for brothers William, James, and Henry.

Parks. Census not available. Post office name changed from Ives December 19, 1888. Former town probably named for Col. S. B. Parks of the U.S. Survey of 1867.

Pink Prairie. Former church community in the Hoover area.

Republican Forks. Name attached to the Elmer, Collinsville, Benkelman area prior to 1875.

Rollwitz. Post office established June 23, 1902; discontinued November 30, 1918. Probably named in honor of Adolph Rollwitz, Kinkaid homesteader and rancher.

Rosewater. Post office established June 30, 1892; discontinued July 25, 1894. Origin of the name not learned. Edward Rosewater was mayor of Omaha when the office was established.

Sanborn. Census not available. Post office established March 21, 1906; discontinued May 15, 1926. Former town on the Burlington Railroad named in honor of J. E. Sanborn, homesteader on land where the town was platted. He later became a Burlington engineer.

Sandwich. Post office established May 13, 1886; discontinued April 14, 1887. Named for Sandwich, Massachusetts, or for the location; it was "sandwiched" between the Parsons Ranch and the Circle Ranch.

Union. Community center, school house, and voting place in Hoover Precinct, sometimes called Hoover.

FILLMORE COUNTY

Named in honor of Millard Fillmore (1800-74), U.S. president from 1850 to 1853. County established and boundaries defined by an act of the Legislature on January 26, 1856, and formerly organized in 1871. On March 15, 1871, Acting Governor William H. James decreed April 21, 1871, as the date of election for county officers.

Ada. Present locality in Fillmore County.

Alpine. Post office established December 8, 1874; discontinued March 25, 1881. Named for its site on a high elevation in the area.

Belle Prairie. Post office established December 28, 1871; name changed to Strang April 29, 1886. Named for the precinct which was said to be named for a girl called Belle.

Bixby. Community and station on the Burlington Railroad. Named for brother of a depot agent at Lushton, Nebraska. The location was formerly Lyman.

Bryant. Post office established March 23, 1874; name changed to Momence June 26, 1874. Named for the precinct in which it was located.

Burress. Peak population (1900), 25. Post office established November 11, 1887; discontinued December 2, 1901. Mail served from Fairmont. Town named in honor of J. Q Burress, homesteader of the land where town was located. Station on the Burlington Railroad.

Buxton. Former station on the Burlington Railroad and the railroad name for the town of Sawyer. Probably named for a railroad official.

Carlisle. Peak population (1910), 1931. Post office established November 21, 1891; discontinued October 15, 1920. Former town named in honor of John G. Carlisle, secretary of the treasury in the cabinet of President Grover Cleveland.

Dudley. Post office established December 2, 1880; discontinued December 17, 1892. Origin of the name not learned. First postmaster was Benjamin Morgan.

East Strang Junction. Junction for two branches of the Burlington Railroad.

Eden. Post office established April 27, 1872; discontinued April 2, 1887. Origin of the name not learned. First postmaster was Francis H. Beach. Office located in the sod house of Mr. and Mrs. Henry Davis.

Empire. Peak population (1870), 25. Post office established April 5, 1871; discontinued October 16, 1874. Former town probably named for the Empire State of New York.

Eva. Post office established April 10, 1873; discontinued April 14, 1874. Origin of the name not learned. First postmaster was John S. Beardsley.

Exeter. Peak population (1930), 941. Post office name changed from Woodward December 18, 1871. Name suggested by a family from Exeter, New Hampshire. It also fit the alphabetical naming of towns along the Burlington Railroad.

Fairmont. Peak population (1910), 921. Post office name changed from Hesperia January 26, 1872. Named because of the fine surroundings and somewhat elevated position. The name fit the alphabetical naming of towns by the Burlington Railroad.

Fillmore. Census not available. Post office established January 31, 1871; discontinued January 30, 1879. Former town named for the county which declined after railroad bypassed it five miles away.

Gazelle. Post office moved from Thayer County February 18, 1879; discontinued January 10, 1884. See Gazelle, Thayer County.

Geneva. Peak population (1980), 2,400. Post office established April 19, 1871. Emma McCalla named this county seat town for Geneva, Illinois. Miss McCalla was a daughter of Col. J. A. McCalla, owner of the farm on which the town was built.

Glengarry. Post office established September 12, 1870; discontinued December 1, 1884. Post office named for the precinct which was named for the Glengarry Valley in Scotland or for a woolen cap worn by Scottish Highlanders. First postmaster was Duncan McLeod.

Grafton. Peak population (1910), 353. Post office name changed from Prairo October 7, 1872. Named for Grafton, Massachusetts, by Burlington Railroad after their town of the same name in Clay County failed.

Henry. Site proposed for the first county seat by county commissioners at a meeting in 1872. Town was platted. Name changed to Geneva.

Hesperia. Post office established June 29, 1871; name changed to Fairmont January 26, 1872. Origin of the name is unknown, but word means "the region of the west" in Greek.

Lisbon. Station and elevator siding on the Burlington Railroad.

Lyman. Post office established December 15, 1888; discontinued February 25, 1892. Origin of the name not learned.

Manleyville. Peak population (1870), 25. Post office established January 26, 1874; discontinued April 28, 1875. Town named in honor of A. J. Manley, who platted it.

Martland. Peak population (1940), 52. Post office established February 14, 1889; discontinued 1953. Word was perhaps coined from the first name of Martin Danielsen, landowner.

Milligan. Peak population (1930), 422. Post office established November 23, 1887. Named in honor of a Mr. Milligan, an official of the Kansas City and Omaha Railroad.

Momence. Post office name changed from Bryant June 26, 1874; discontinued April 2, 1887. Probably named for Momence, Illinois.

Ohiowa. Peak population (1920), 433. Post office established December 8, 1870. Name coined from Ohio and Iowa because settlers came in almost equal numbers from the two states.

Prairo. Post office established September 17, 1871; name changed to Grafton October 7, 1872. Probably named for the Latin word "prairo," meaning prairie.

Sawyer. Post office established January 18, 1888; discontinued April 29, 1922. Town named in honor of Simeon Sawyer, oldest settler in the vicinity.

Shickley. Peak population (1910), 429. Post office established April 18, 1886. Named for Fillmore Shickley, railroad official.

Shrule. Post office established November 12, 1877; discontinued November 18, 1881. Probably named for Shrule, Mayo County, Ireland. First postmaster was Patrick McTygue.

Sioux Valley. Early community in Fillmore County named for the Sioux Indians.

Spearville. Post office established November 8, 1875; discontinued October 23, 1876. Named for Erastus Spear, a settler.

Strang. Peak population (1890), 269. Post office name changed from Belle Prairie April 29, 1886. Town named in honor of A. L. Strang, resident who presented the citizens with a windmill for a town pump.

Turkey Creek. Post office established March 28, 1872; discontinued February 21, 1890. Named for the creek, which was named for wild turkeys found along its stream.

Walnut Creek. Post office established April 29, 1872; discontinued September 25, 1878. Named for the creek along which black walnut trees grew.

Walters. Former station and elevator siding on the Chicago and North Western Railroad. Once the railroad station name for Carlisle.

West Blue. Post office established April 7, 1871; discontinued September 1, 1873. Named for its location on the West Blue River.

Woodward. Post office established April 13, 1871; name changed to Exeter. Named in honor of Warren Woodward, first postmaster, who had the office at his homestead.

FRANKLIN COUNTY

Named in honor of American statesman Benjamin Franklin (1706-90). County was established February 16, 1867, and organized by an act of the Legislature in 1871.

Alpine. Post office name changed from Sand Hill May 9, 1884; discontinued February 1, 1887. Probably named for moderate elevation of the locality.

Amazon. Post office name changed from North Franklin May 7, 1875; name changed to Campbell January 22, 1887. Presumably named for the Amazon River in South America.

Ashgrove. Post office established February 15, 1875; discontinued April 15, 1901. Named for a grove of ash trees.

Atlee. Post office established March 8, 1880; name changed to Upland January 31, 1887. Origin of the name unknown. First postmaster was Perry Parker.

Bloomington. Peak population (1910), 554. Post office name changed from Brooklyn March 14, 1873. Probably named for Bloomington, Illinois, by a company from Plattsmouth, Nebraska. Bloomington lost a bid for county seat to Franklin City July 27, 1872; won county seat in 1874 election. Retained county seat until Franklin won it in 1920. The United States Land Office moved here from Lowell, Nebraska, in 1874.

Brooklyn. Post office established December 18, 1871; name changed to Bloomington March 14, 1873. Presumably named for Brooklyn, New York.

Campbell. Peak population (1910), 573. Post office name changed from Amazon January 22, 1887. Possibly named for a Mr. Campbell of the townsite company. However, Alexander Campbell was assistant superintendent of the Burlington and Missouri River Railroad when the line was under construction.

Camp Cameron. Temporary military post located about two miles above the mouth of Turkey Creek in the summer of 1871.

Clyde. Post office established April 30, 1880; discontinued September 14, 1883. Origin of the name has not been learned. First postmaster was Martin Hollenbeck.

Franklin. Peak population (1950), 1,602. Post office established September 15, 1879. County seat town named for the county. In 1920 Franklin won the county seat from Bloomington. Franklin Academy, a Congregational school, was founded in 1881. It was closed in 1922 and the buildings made a part of the town of Franklin.

Franklin City. Post office established September 15, 1871; moved to Franklin September 15, 1879. Original location a few miles from present town of Franklin. Franklin City founded by Republican Land Claim Association of Omaha in November 1870. There is no record of the plat being filed because the buildings were moved after the present town of Franklin was founded.

Grant. Town proposed by an African American colony in June 1871 on Lovely Creek. It failed to materialize.

Hancock. Post office established November 18, 1881; discontinued August 22, 1883. Origin of the name is unknown, but eleven states have places called Hancock, most of which honor John Hancock of Revolutionary War fame.

Hildreth. Peak population (1920), 453. Post office name changed from West Salem January 22, 1887. Named in honor of Carson Hildreth, who owned the land on which the town was platted.

Leota. Post office established May 5, 1881; discontinued March 9, 1885. Origin of the name not learned. First postmaster was John L. Cook.

Lexington. Post office established June 8, 1883; discontinued December 9, 1885. Probably named for one of three places in Kentucky, Massachusetts, or Missouri.

Locust. Post office established February 4, 1884; discontinued February 5, 1891. Probably named for a species of locust trees or for the devastating locust which ruined crops.

Long Den. Six miles southwest of Franklin, 1870s and 1880s.

Macon. Peak population (1930), 126. Post office established January 24, 1873. Town named for Macon, Georgia, by a former resident.

Marion. Post office established August 11, 1874; discontinued July 28, 1879. Origin of the name not learned. First postmaster was David Eastwood.

Moline. Post office established November 10, 1875; discontinued July 1, 1895. Presumably named for Moline, Illinois.

Moscow. This locality was shown as the first Franklin County settlement by G. W. and C. B. Colton and Company's 1881 Atlas.

Naponee. Peak population (1950), 291. Post office established March 22, 1872. Named for Naponee, Canada.

North Franklin. Post office established June 11, 1873; name changed to Amazon May 7, 1875. Named for its location a few miles north of Franklin.

Orange. Post office established February 25, 1880; discontinued September 8, 1888. Probably named for the Osage orange hedge tree used for fencing before the advent of barbed wire.

Osage. Former locality probably named for the Osage orange tree or for the Osage Indians.

Perth. Former railroad station probably named by railroad officials for a local settler or for Perth, Scotland. Located near Naponee.

Riverton. Peak population (1920), 399. Post office established September 27, 1871. Named for its site on the Republican River or for Riverton, Iowa.

Rush. Post office name changed from Stockton May 13, 1880; discontinued February 15, 1895. Origin of the name not known. First postmaster was Eli Gowdy.

Russia Town. Locality settled by Russian Germans, just west of Campbell.

Sad Corners. Community established in the early 1880s.

Sand Hill. Post office established November 20, 1878; name changed to Alpine May 9, 1889. Named for a hill which was sandy in appearance.

Sherwood. Post office established September 28, 1883; discontinued July 26, 1893. Named for Orrin Sherwood, first postmaster.

Stockton. Post office established March 17, 1873; name changed to Rush May 13, 1880. Origin of the name not learned, though R. E. Stockton, settler and Civil War veteran, lived in the county. First postmaster was Lewis Everly.

Upland. Peak population (1920), 433. Post office name changed from Atlee January 31, 1887. Town located on a high elevation.

Waterloo. Founded by the Plattsmouth Land Company in May 1871 near Franklin City. It never attained a post office because there was already another Waterloo in the state.

West Salem. Post office established April 17, 1878; name changed to Hildreth January 22, 1887. Named for its location west of Salem township.

FRONTIER COUNTY

Named for its geographic location in a frontier region of sparse settlement. County organized January 17, 1872.

Afton. Post office established October 14, 1874; discontinued May 29, 1893. Probably named for Afton, Iowa.

Bartonville. Post office established August 10, 1885; discontinued March 20, 1886. Named for Robert A. Barton, first postmaster.

Centerpoint. Census not available. Post office established February 18, 1901; discontinued February 28, 1919. Former town named for its location in the center of the township.

Colebank. Post office established May 8, 1909; discontinued May 31, 1910. Probably named for C. C. Colebank, who established and operated a store.

Cupid. Post office established August 10, 1885; discontinued January 31, 1889. Probably named for a betrothed couple or for the Roman god of love.

Curtis. Peak population (1970, 1,166). Post office established April 11, 1877. Town named for a trapper called Curtis who settled at the mouth of the creek also named for him. Town platted by the Lincoln Land Company.

Earl. Post office established August 22, 1884; discontinued March 31, 1916. Named for Earl Childs, son of Postmaster E. S. Childs, owner of a store and post office.

Equality. Post office established August 19, 1875; discontinued October 2, 1882.

Probably named for President Abraham Lincoln's pronouncements concerning slavery during the Civil War. There is also an Equality, Illinois.

Essex. Post office established April 1, 1896; moved to Gosper County January 31, 1906. Settled by English immigrants who probably came from Essex town or county in England.

Eustis. Peak population (2000), 464. Post office name changed from Somerset September 4, 1886. The Lincoln Land Company purchased the townsite and named it in honor of P. S. Eustis, passenger agent for the Burlington Railroad.

Fandon. Post office established April 28, 1887; discontinued September 7, 1899. Probably named for Fandon, New York.

Freedom. Post office established February 10, 1886; discontinued October 27, 1887. Probably named by a Union Civil War veteran who recalled the liberation of the slaves.

Havana. Post office established August 5, 1899; discontinued January 5, 1918. Probably named for Havana, Cuba, famous during the Spanish-American War.

Hopewell. Post office established February 1886; discontinued April 16, 1887. Probably named for a Hopewell, one of five such towns in America.

Hunt. Post office established June 8, 1905; discontinued January 31, 1916. Named for Isaac Hunt, first postmaster, who had the office in conjunction with his store.

Kingston. Station on the Burlington Railroad. Located near Eustis and Nebraska's largest silica mine.

Knowles. Post office established April 25, 1884; discontinued April 19, 1886. Named in honor of Charles H. Knowles, first postmaster.

Laird. Post office established February 24, 1881; name changed to Maywood August 1, 1881. Named in honor of James Laird, early settler. Name changed because of connection of trails and merchandise for Laird, Colorado, which was on the same railroad line.

Long. Post office established May 26, 1884; discontinued December 28, 1887. Probably named for a homesteader.

Maywood. Peak population (1920), 533. Post office name changed from Laird August 1, 1881. Named for May Wood, daughter of Mr. and Mrs. Israel Wood, original owners of the townsite. Town platted by Lincoln Land Company after Wood sold the land to Harry Phillips.

Moody. Post office established February 10, 1886; discontinued April 29, 1886. Origin of the name not learned.

Moorefield. Post office established June 10, 1886. Town first called Moore's Field for a Mr. Moore, original owner of townsite.

Norris. Post office moved from Hayes County June 20, 1907; moved to Hayes County November 15, 1927. See Norris, Hayes County.

Orafino. Post office established February 16, 1880; discontinued 1953. One source says named by H. C. Rogers for iron pyrites found in Mitchell Creek. Orafino, in Spanish, means fine ore. Another source suggests that the name derives from Orfin, a Swedish town, and was proposed by surveyor Nels Deulor.

Osborn. Post office established September 30, 1879; discontinued December 31, 1913. Named in honor of David Osborn, first postmaster.

Quick. Post office established January 26, 1887; discontinued 1945. Named in honor of M. W. Quick, first postmaster.

Rimmer. Community in the 1890s.

Russell. Post office established March 26, 1883; discontinued September 8, 1899. Probably named in honor of James F. Russell, early settler.

Somerset. Post office established September 5, 1884; name changed to Eustis September 4, 1886. Probably named for one of the eleven places in the U.S. called Somerset or for a county in England.

St. Ann. Post office established September 15, 1903; discontinued 1944. Presumably named for nearby St. Ann Church. There was a store adjacent to the church.

Steuben. Post office established February 5, 1885; discontinued November 2, 1887. Reason for the name not learned, but it is German in origin.

Stockville. Peak population (1900), 269. Post office established August 19, 1873. Town was made county seat when county organized. Staked out by W. L. McClary, Stockville was named by Samuel Watts, early settler, for the surrounding ranch country.

Stowe. Post office established July 24, 1878; discontinued July 19, 1893. Probably named for Harriet Beecher Stowe, author of *Uncle Tom's Cabin*.

Thornburg. Post office moved from Hayes County September 21, 1888; moved to Hayes County September 21, 1924. Probably named for Thornburg, Iowa.

Zimmer. Post office established March 15, 1888; discontinued December 24, 1898. Named in honor of Peter J. Zimmer, first postmaster.

FURNAS COUNTY

Named in honor of Robert W. Furnas (1824-1905), governor of Nebraska from 1873 to 1875. The county was organized and its boundaries defined February 27, 1873.

Arapahoe. Peak population (1950), 1,226. Post office established April 25, 1872. Named for the Arapahoe Indians. An exploring party from Plattsmouth, Nebraska, headed by Capt. E. B. Murphy, founded the town July 18, 1871. Arapahoe lost county seat in election with Beaver City on October 14, 1873.

Beaver City. Peak population (1920), 1,103. Post office established January 15, 1873. Named for its location on Beaver Creek. In early days there were beaver in the stream. Beaver City won county seat in election with Arapahoe on October 14, 1873.

Buffalo. Named for buffalo, which roamed the plains in early days.

Burton's Bend. Post office established August 27, 1872; name changed to Holbrook. Named in honor of J. B. Burton, early settler who platted the town.

Cambridge. Peak population (1950), 1,352. Post office name changed from Medicine Creek August 3, 1880. Hiram Doing entered a homestead claim in 1871 on the present townsite of Cambridge and built a house near Medicine Creek. In 1876 he sold it to J. A. Pickle, who in January of 1877 built a saw and grist mill on the west bank of the creek. Pickle surveyed a townsite in 1878 and laid out a town, which he wanted to call Northwood. Residents referred to it as Pickletown. Other suggested names were Scratchpot City and Lickskillet. The post office remained at Medicine Creek. With the building of the Republican Valley Railroad May 23, 1880, W. E. Babcock met railroad officials at Oxford, who suggested the name Cambridge, probably for Cambridge University in England or the town in Massachusetts. Pickle became the first postmaster.

Carisbrooke. Post office established April 10, 1873. Name changed to Stamford December 6, 1887. Named for Carisbrooke, village on the English Isle of Wight.

Coldwater. Post office established August 19, 1880; discontinued April 9, 1888. Named for Coldwater, Minnesota, by a resident.

Dudgeon. Post office established June 23, 1881; discontinued August 23, 1881. Probably named for J. A. Dudgeon, early settler and Civil War veteran.

Edison. Peak population (1910), 334. Post office established February 27, 1880. Village named for Eddie Rohr, son of Robert H. Rohr, storekeeper and postmaster.

Gilltown. Post office established March 28, 1882; discontinued May 14, 1883. Probably named for James Gill, first postmaster.

Grandview. Post office established May 3, 1880. Name changed to Oxford February 15, 1881. Named for its wonderful view. Ten states have places with this name.

Hendley. Peak population (1910), 238. Post office name changed from Lynden February 18, 1888. Town named in honor of a Mr. Hendley, local settler.

Holbrook. Peak population (1930), 488. Post office name changed from Burton's

Bend March 16, 1881. Town named in honor of a Mr. Holbrook, official of the Burlington Railroad.

Hollinger. Census not available. Post office established January 4, 1905; discontinued 1945. Former town and present railroad station probably named for E. A. Hollinger, a local settler.

Judson. Post office established September 19, 1873; discontinued December 18, 1874. Probably named in honor of Samuel Judd, first postmaster.

Lynden. Post office established April 25, 1873; name changed to Hendley February 18, 1888. Named for the precinct and established by I. S. Meyers.

Medicine Creek. Post office established September 16, 1873. Name changed to Cambridge August 3, 1880. Named for the creek on which it was located.

Midway. Post office established May 19, 1873; discontinued November 7, 1878. Named for its location midway between two other post offices.

New Era. Post office established June 3, 1872; discontinued April 27, 1881. Named by Theodore Phillips, a local settler.

Northwood. Proposed name for Cambridge.

Oram. Post office established October 1, 1883; discontinued May 13, 1886. Origin of the name not learned.

Oxford. Peak population (1950), 1,270. Post office name changed from Grandview February 15, 1881. Probably named by Burlington Railroad officials for Oxford University, England.

Pickletown. See Cambridge.

Precept. Post office established February 26, 1877; discontinued July 21, 1906. Probably named for the word precept in the Bible or for other locations named Precept.

Rexford. Post office established May 3, 1881; discontinued February 4, 1888. Probably named in honor of Jacob Rexford, first postmaster.

Richmond. Post office established October 8, 1872; discontinued April 4, 1877. Named by Henry Brown, who came from Richmond, Illinois, and built a mill.

Rockton. Post office established June 18, 1874; discontinued April 2, 1887. Probably named for a nearby rocky area. Places in Illinois and Pennsylvania have this name.

Scratchpot City. Name proposed for Cambridge.

Sett. Post office established August 4, 1880; discontinued April 21, 1901. Probably named for George Sett Johnson, early settler.

Sherman. Post office established March 28, 1881; discontinued June 27, 1893. Probably named for Gen. William Tecumseh Sherman of Civil War fame.

Spring Green. Post office established May 27, 1873; discontinued February 28, 1905. Probably named in the spring when vegetation was green. There is a Spring Green, Wisconsin.

Vincent. Post office established August 23, 1880; discontinued November 29, 1887. Origin of the name not learned. Vinceus Schwap was first postmaster.

Whitney. Post office established March 12, 1877; moved to Red Willow County August 1, 1879. Probably named for B. F. Whitney, early settler and county officer.

Wild Turkey. Post office established April 18, 1873. Name changed to Wilsonville December 16, 1873. Named for the wild turkey then found along the creeks.

Wilmot. Post office established October 31, 1877. Moved to Norton County, Kansas, August 28, 1882. Named by John Gamble, first postmaster, for a friend, Wilmot Champion.

Wilsonville. Peak population (1930), 489. Post office name changed from Wild Turkey, December 16, 1873. Named in honor of L. M. and Carlos Wilson brothers, merchants and stockmen.

Yeager. Post office established February 11, 1899; discontinued July 12, 1899. Named in honor of Amon Yeager, postmaster.

GAGE COUNTY

Gage County was established and its boundaries redefined by an act of the Legislature approved March 16, 1855; reestablished and redefined January 26, 1856. The county was named after William D. Gage (1803-55), Methodist minister and chaplain of the first Territorial Legislature. He was one of the commissioners appointed to locate the Gage County seat.

Adams. Peak population (1910), 674. Post office established December 12, 1872. Named in honor of John O. Adams, early settler. Town was built with the coming of the Atchison and Nebraska Railroad.

Aurich. Post office established May 1, 1896; discontinued July 28, 1898. Probably named for a district in Prussia by settlers who formerly lived there.

Austin. Post office established November 5, 1858; discontinued April 14, 1864. Town was established while in old Clay County. This former post office named for Edward C. Austin. Located near present town of Pickrell. Its identity was lost when Beatrice was founded.

Baden. Post office established June 15, 1869. Name changed to Clatonia September 21, 1874. Early German settlers named post office for a German location.

Badger. Station on the Union Pacific Railroad located near Barneston.

Barkey. Post office established October 17, 1876; discontinued August 13, 1884. Named in honor of Enos Barkey, early settler and Civil War veteran who homesteaded here in 1873.

Barneston. Peak population (1890), 300. Post office changed from Oto Agency July 19, 1880. Named in honor of Francis M. Barnes, member of original townsite company. Barnes owned an early trading post on the Oto Indian reservation. After the tribe's removal to Oklahoma, he opened another store for the accommodation of land seekers and early settlers. Town platted May 17, 1884.

Bear Creek. Post office established February 8, 1877. Name changed to Hanover December 17, 1879. Named for the creek on which it is located.

Beatrice. Peak population (1890), 13,836. Post office established July 16, 1857. Named in honor of Julia Beatrice Kinney, eldest daughter of Judge J. F. Kinney. Beatrice won county seat in election with Blue Springs in 1859. City founded July 4, 1857, and incorporated October 29, 1858. The town grew when a mill was set up on the Big Blue River by Fordyce Roper in July 1857.

Blaine. Post office established May 14, 1876; discontinued September 19, 1878. Probably named for James G. Blaine, U.S. senator from Maine and presidential candidate in 1884.

Blue Springs. Peak population (1890), 963. Post office established February 15, 1859. Located on the Blue River and named for the springs feeding the river.

In July 1857 James H. Johnson, Jacob Puff, Martin Elliot, and his sons, and Henry Elliott and their families settled on the public domain and with government surveyors projected a townsite. Their plans failed, and the endeavor was abandoned. Reuyl Noyes and Joseph Chambers, returning from Pike's Peak, took up the claim again, and attempted to divert travel from the Oregon Trail at Ash Point, Kansas. A toll bridge was built across the Blue River in 1859 by the founders. The town was platted by Solon M. Hazen. William Ticknor erected a dam and mill in 1868. Town vied for the county seat with Beatrice in 1859.

Bluff City. One of the earliest settlements recorded in Gage County.

Bonn. Post office established August 11, 1874; discontinued April 28, 1881. Named for a city in Germany.

Caldwell. Post office established March 3, 1873; name changed to Hoag August 10, 1885. Townsite platted by Lincoln Land Company from Boston, Massachusetts, in April 1872. Robinson and Howard erected a grist mill one-half mile below Caldwell on the Blue River.

Cedar Bend. Post office established February 9, 1877; discontinued October 15, 1883. Named for a bend on Cedar Creek where cedar trees grow. A schoolhouse by this name and a farmhouse post office were nearby. Located northwest of Filley.

Charleston. Post office established November 7, 1877; moved to Odell October 21, 1880. Located one mile from present town of Odell. William La Gorgue surveyed and platted Charleston on his farm on the south side of Big Indian Creek. After the coming of the railroad, which missed the townsite, the buildings were moved to Odell.

Chicago. Early proposed townsite in Gage County.

Clatonia. Peak population (1990), 296. Post office name changed from Baden September 21, 1874. Named for Clatonia Creek, derived from old Clay County through which the creek flowed. Henry Albert and J. H. Steinmeyer, town proprietors, surveyed and platted it in 1892.

Cortland. Peak population (2000), 488. Post office established February 20, 1884. First called Galesburg after Alfred Gale, owner of the townsite. Postal authorities turned down the name. After the advent of the railroad, the town became Courtland, after Courtland, New York. The spelling was finally changed to Cortland.

Cottage Hill. Post office established September 14, 1874; discontinued October 8, 1883. Located at the farm home of Lucius Filley. Named for the farm residence of Elijah Filley and situated southwest of the present town of Filley.

Cropsey. Post office established December 14, 1869; discontinued April 1, 1902. Located in extreme northeastern Gage County and named after a local settler who had a mill on the creek nearby.

Crossing. Former station on the Union Pacific Railroad.

Danville. Early settlement in Gage County.

Davis Quarry. Locality in Gage County.

Dennison. Post office of this name established in Gage County April 28, 1860; discontinued September 17, 1860. Perhaps named after Oto Indian Agent William Wallace Dennison. May have been former Hewarts post office renamed Dennison.

Dover. Post office established March 20, 1878; discontinued January 4, 1882. Origin of the name has not been learned. There are eighteen places in the United States with this name, as well as several in England.

Dry Creek. Post office established May 13, 1868; discontinued September 30, 1869. Named for the creek on which it is located.

Ellis. Peak population (1900), 180. Post office established June 21, 1887; made a station of Beatrice in 1951. Named for John R. Ellis, Beatrice banker, when the town was built upon the completion of the Rock Island Railroad.

Favors. Post office established October 3, 1882; discontinued March 30, 1883. Named in honor of Sheriff P. M. Favors of Gage County.

Filley. Peak population (1890), 301. Post office established July 10, 1883. Town named for founder Elijah Filley. Birthplace of the first Farmers Alliance in Nebraska.

Floral. Post office name changed from Townsend August 28, 1882; discontinued August 5, 1884. Former post office was to be named for Postmaster John Flowers, but because there already was a Flowers post office, the related word Floral was used.

Freeman. Post office established March 28, 1881; discontinued September 8, 1903. Named in honor of Daniel Freeman, first homesteader under Homestead Act of 1862, who filed his claim in Gage County.

Gasco. Station for the natural gas installation north of Beatrice.

Grandview. Post office name changed from Howard October 16, 1901; discontinued May 19, 1902. Named for its descriptive location.

Greer. Post office established January 4, 1880; discontinued February 27, 1882. Named in honor of George R. Greer, first postmaster.

Hamilton. Post office established January 28, 1890; discontinued June 20, 1899. Probably named for a local settler. Located east of Rockford.

Hanover. Post office name changed from Bear Creek December 17, 1879; discontinued April 15, 1903. Named for a city and province in Germany where many of the settlers had formerly lived. Located northwest of Filley.

Hewarts. Post office established October 19, 1858; discontinued April 28, 1860, when name changed to Dennison.

Hoag. Peak population (1900), 88. Post office name changed from Caldwell August 10, 1885; discontinued 1935. Former town and present railroad station named in honor of a Mr. Hoagland, who owned the townsite.

Holmesville. Peak population (1930), 274. Post office name changed from Shaw October 18, 1880. Named in honor of Morgan L. Holmes, founder and first postmaster. Most of the stone used in the first state capitol in Lincoln (1868) was quarried nearby. J H. Steinmeyer and sons completed a dam and hydroelectric power and lighting plant on the Big Blue River in 1911 to furnish nearby towns with electric power.

Hooker. Post office established June 7, 1866; discontinued June 13, 1884. Named by Postmaster John Hillman for a local settler.

Howard. Post office established June 27, 1901; name changed to Grandview October 16, 1901. Origin of the name not learned. First postmaster was J. B. Brethower.

Kam. Post office established December 2, 1873; discontinued November 25, 1884. Origin of the name has not been learned.

Kinney. Census not available. Post office established March 27, 1909; discontinued February 15, 1927. Former hamlet named in honor of Samuel A. Kinney, on whose farm the site was established.

Krider. Station on the Burlington Railroad. Located near Wymore.

Lanham. Peak population (1910), 250. Post office name changed from Morton June 8, 1886; made a rural station of Odell 1958. Named for an official of the Burlington Railroad. Part of the town is in Kansas; most is in Nebraska.

Laona. Post office established June 21, 1867; moved to Adams March 1, 1880. Origin of name not learned. First postmaster was John Lyons.

Leland. Early settlement in Gage County.

Lemon. Early settlement in Gage County.

Liberty. Peak population (1890), 469. Post office established January 22, 1869. When the Burlington Railroad was built near this early post office the town was named Liberty.

Littlejohn. Post office established January 4, 1882; discontinued April 14, 1884. Named in honor of William Littlejohn, early settler who came here in 1869.

Mellroy. Post office established March 15, 1877; discontinued May 29, 1888. Coined word for two sons of two area settlers: Mell Gale and Roy Tinklepaugh. There was a schoolhouse with the same name. Located north of Filley.

Meserveville. Post office established March 28, 1879; discontinued May 25, 1887. Named in honor of Joseph M. Meserve, early settler.

Morton. Post office established October 20, 1884; name changed to Lanham June 8, 1886. Origin of the name not learned; it was changed to avoid confusion with Norton, Kansas, mail.

Odell. Peak population (1890), 500. Post office name changed from Charleston October 21, 1880. Named in honor of Legrand Odell, friend of J. D. Meyers of Chicago, Illinois, who had a half-interest in the site. Town located on old Oto Indian reservation and platted September 21, 1880, by Anselmo Smith for Lincoln Land Company. Odell was induced to come West by Meyers and went into business soon after the railroad was established.

Otoe Agency. Post office established July 8, 1867; name changed to Barneston July 19, 1880. Named for the Oto Indians, the agency served the Oto reservation.

Paris. Post office established May 13, 1868; discontinued January 21, 1869. Probably named for Paris, France.

Pickrell. Peak population (1910), 250. Post office established February 21, 1884. Town named in honor of two brothers, William and Watson Pickrell.

Putman. Post office established October 3, 1882; discontinued July 30, 1884. Former post office and present railroad station named for N. B. Putman, chief locomotive engineer on the Burlington Railroad.

Reserve. Post office established May 7, 1879; discontinued October 11, 1881. Probably named for nearby Oto Indian reservation. Store and church community founded by Upson family.

Rockford. Peak population (1900), 80. Post office established March 8, 1886. Village founded by William Girl. Named for rock quarries near Mud Creek. Post office discontinued 1957. Mail served from Beatrice.

Roperville. Post office established January 24, 1870; discontinued March 27, 1878. Named in honor of Joseph Roper, early settler.

Shaw. Post office established December 15, 1879; name changed to Holmesville October 18, 1880. Probably named for Samuel Shaw, first postmaster.

Sicily. Post office established January 22, 1878; discontinued January 4, 1882. Former post office and railroad station named for the township, earlier named for an early settler.

Silver. Post office established July 13, 1876; discontinued September 22, 1884. Named in honor of Henry H. Silver, first postmaster and a member of the Nebraska Legislature.

Stevens Creek. Locality mentioned in Gage County history. Named for Orrin Stevens.

Stone. Former station on the Union Pacific Railroad. Located near Holmesville.

Taylor. Locality mentioned in early Gage County history.

Townsend. Post office established November 22, 1878; name changed to Floral August 28, 1882. Named in honor of William Townsend, early settler.

Union Center. Never a post office; located near Liberty and Wymore. Nearby are a school and store.

Virginia. Peak population (1900), 243. Post office established August 30, 1887. Named in honor of a daughter of Mr. and Mrs. Ford Lewis. Lewis was instrumental in platting the town and inducing the Chicago, Rock Island and Pacific and the Kansas City and Northwestern (subsidiary of the Missouri Pacific) to enter the town. This was the terminus for the Kansas City and Northwestern, which was discontinued in the 1920s. Dalbey Pond west of town furnished water for the railroad.

West Barneston. Locality west of Barneston which was later annexed.

Whitesville. Never a post office but designated as the first county seat of Gage County. It is doubtful that any buildings were erected. Located near present town of Holmesville. Limestone used for the first capitol came from a nearby quarry.

Wildcat. Post office established March 8, 1872; discontinued August 29, 1872. Named by a Dr. Tibbets for a nearby creek.

Wymore. Peak population (1900), 2,626. Post office established October 7, 1881. Named for Samuel Wymore, early settler. Wymore gave the Burlington Railroad land as an inducement to build here. Became headquarters for Wymore Division of Burlington. Roundhouse located here.

GARDEN COUNTY

John T. Twiford and William Twiford, Oshkosh realtors, suggested the name. They thought the area would develop into the "garden spot of the west." County divided from northern Deuel County in election held November 2, 1909.

Cormick. Former station on the Union Pacific Railroad.

Dewey. Post office established April 27, 1900; name changed to Moffitt November 23, 1900. Probably commemorates Adm. George Dewey of Spanish American War fame.

Edward. Post office established February 5, 1909; moved to Arthur County May 1, 1915. Named in honor of Edward Fiesterman, first postmaster.

Fort Grattan. Army sod fort located near Ash Hollow; established in September 1855 and abandoned in the spring of 1856. Named in honor of Lt. John L. Grattan, whose entire command was killed near Fort Laramie by Indians in 1854.

Garden. Post office established August 19, 1910; discontinued September 30, 1912. Named for the county.

Goodland. Post office established June 3, 1913; discontinued May 13, 1922. Probably named for the soil in the region. There is also a Goodland, Kansas.

Hartman. Post office established August 12, 1889; discontinued October 6, 1899. Named in honor of Sebastian Hartman, first postmaster, who had the post office in his store on Lost Creek.

Hewett. Post office established December 19, 1910; discontinued August 15, 1913. Possibly named in honor of James Hewett, early settler.

Hillsdale. Post office established February 15, 1911; discontinued July 31, 1912. Describes geographical features of the land.

Hutchison. Post office established August 12, 1889; discontinued July 31, 1913. Possibly named in honor of Oswin Hutchison, first postmaster.

Kowanda. Post office established March 22, 1888; discontinued December 31, 1921. Named for a Czech settler in the vicinity.

Lakeview. Post office established March 25, 1912; discontinued November 30, 1915. Probably named for its site near a lake.

Lewellen. Peak population (1940), 532. Post office moved from Keith County December 4, 1891. Town platted by D. C. Hooper and others in 1906. See Lewellen, Keith County.

Lisco. Peak population (1940), 219. Post office established July 26, 1909. Named in honor of Reuben Lisco, who platted the town and opened a store and post office. The railroad station of Lisco had previously been in Morrill County. Lisco was once sheriff of Deuel County and helped establish the Rush Creek Land and Livestock Company.

Lutherville. Former station on the Union Pacific Railroad named by railway for Luther Kountze. Located on site of old Ramsey post office.

Lyon. Former community east of Oshkosh on an irrigation canal.

Lytle. Former station on the Union Pacific Railroad.

Moffitt. Post office name changed from Dewey November 23, 1900; discontinued March 25, 1907. Named in honor of Edith Moffitt, first postmistress.

Mumper. Post office established April 14, 1896; discontinued 1945. Named in honor of Anna Mumper, first postmistress and homesteader. Located at the Crescent Ranch owned by Boyd Rice.

Orlando. Post office established September 3, 1891; discontinued February 28, 1930. Name suggested by Ada Jackelt, office patron. Located at the Samuel and Charles Avery ranch. Origin of the name not known. There is also an Orlando, Florida.

Oshkosh. Peak population (1950), 1,124. Post office established May 24, 1886. Named for Oshkosh, Wisconsin, by former residents Henry G. Gumaer and Alfred W. Gumaer. With Herbert W. Potter and John Robinson, they established the Oshkosh Land Company. Became county seat on organization of county in 1909.

Pawlet. Post office established May 24, 1915; discontinued December 31, 1920. Origin of the name not learned. There is also a Pawlet, Vermont.

Penn. Present community and former station on the Union Pacific Railroad probably named for a local settler or railroad official.

Rackett. Post office established September 13, 1910; discontinued 1945. Named by Devashers family for their former home of Rackett, Kentucky.

Ramsey. Post office established December 22, 1887; discontinued June 16, 1893. Named in honor of Alfred Ramsey, pioneer rancher.

Ruthton. On Union Pacific line 1.5 miles east of Lewellen.

Sowser. Former station on the Union Pacific Railroad located near Lewellen.

Sterbins. Post office established July 31, 1913; discontinued January 15, 16. Possibly named in honor of Tacy Sterbins, first postmaster.

Thelma. Post office established May 28, 1912; discontinued May 15, 1915. Origin of the name has not been learned. First postmistress was Maria J. Peerson.

Tippetts. Post office established September 30, 1912; discontinued October 14, 1916. Named either for Lottie Tippetts, first post mistress, or for Bert Tippetts, a settler.

Velma. Post office established April 22, 1914; moved to Arthur County May 14, 1917. Named in honor of Velma Redlinger, daughter of Henry Redlinger, first postmaster.

Warren. Post office established April 10, 1912; discontinued September 30, 1921. Probably named for Warren County, Iowa. First postmaster was Caleb W. Gault.

GARFIELD COUNTY

Named in honor of James A. Garfield (1831-81), U.S. president in 1881. County was formed from western part of Wheeler County by vote on November 8, 1881, but did not complete its initial organization until ordered to do so by the governor in 1884.

Ballagh. Post office established February 18, 1890; discontinued 1934. Named in honor of its first settler, Robert A. Ballagh.

Blake. Post office established February 6, 1902; discontinued 1934. Named in honor of Blake Mayer, business partner on the ranch of Leonard B. Fenner, first postmaster.

Bluff City. Projected town that never consisted of more than a store built in a dugout in 1879.

Burwell. Peak population (1960), 1,425. Post office established January 21, 1884. County seat town platted by Frank Webster on his farm in 1883 and first called Webster's Town. Name changed to honor Ada Burwell, fiancee of Webster's brother. Town grew near a post office called The Forks. Town was the terminus of the Burlington Railroad branch from Palmer.

Carson. Post office established August 11, 1913; moved to Holt County March 15, 1916. Probably named for a Mr. Carson, neighbor of Norman Johnson, a local settler.

Deverre. Post office established January 4, 1905; discontinued 1934. Named in honor of Deverre Cass, local settler.

Dumas. Census not available. Post office established March 17, 1905; discontinued 1935. Former town commemorates the French author, Alexandre Dumas.

Easton. Post office established March 13, 1901; discontinued July 15, 1905. Named by Postmaster Joseph Warren for Easton, Illinois.

Erina. Post office established September 3, 1880; discontinued June 30, 1921. Proposed name was Erin, but there was already a post office named Erin. The letter "a" was added to change the sound. Community settled by Irish immigrants.

The Forks. Peak population (1870), 25. Post office established July 9, 1875; discontinued January 21, 1884. Named for the forks of the North Loup River and the Calamus River. First county seat of Garfield County. Abandoned after railroad built to nearby Burwell.

Gables. Census not available. Post office established February 2, 1909; discontinued May 15, 1929. Former town named for the post office building which had a high gabled roof.

Jones Trading Post. Settlement in early county history.

Jordan. Post office established March 24, 1884; discontinued February 13, 1894. Origin of the name not learned.

Key. Post office established August 26, 1905; discontinued February 28, 1915. Named in honor of F. L. Key, local settler.

Kim. Post office established December 22, 1885; rescinded June 21, 1886. Origin of the name not learned. First postmaster was Elias Carter.

Rosedale. Post office established January 26, 1907; discontinued July 31, 1917. Former post office in Rose Valley named for wild roses growing in the region.

Sheridan. Peak population (1890), 12. Post office established February 11, 1885; moved to Wheeler County April 6, 1891. Former town commemorates Gen. Philip H. Sheridan of Civil War fame.

Webster's Town. Name changed to Burwell when post office was established. Named after Frank Webster, donor of land to the town.

Willow Springs. Peak population (1890), 25. Post office established June 22, 1880; discontinued October 1, 1892. Seat of the former Wheeler area of Garfield County, Willow Springs lost county seat to Burwell. Named for springs located near willow trees.

GOSPER COUNTY

Named in honor of John J. Gosper (1842-1913), secretary of state of Nebraska. County organized August 29, 1873. Organization was legalized and the boundaries defined by an act approved March 2, 1881.

Arbuta. Post office established September 4, 1883; discontinued January 16, 1893. Origin of the name not learned.

Ceryl. Post office established October 4, 1880; discontinued August 31, 1904. Named in honor of Dr. Ceryl J. Laurent, first postmaster.

Cora. Post office established September 11, 1883; moved to Dawson County October 22, 1883. Origin of the name unknown. First postmaster was Alfred Price.

Daviesville. Peak population (1890), 65. Post office established March 19, 1874; discontinued July 21, 1887. Former town named in honor of John Davies, first county judge of Gosper County. It became first county seat November 26, 1873. A courthouse was never built, and records were kept by officials in their homes. Daviesville lost county seat election to Homerville in August 1882.

Elwood. Peak population (2000), 761. Post office name changed from Mick November 16, 1885. One source says this county seat named for Elwood Thomas, homesteader, by A. B. Smith, townsite builder. Another source says town named for Elwood Calvert, for forty years chief engineer and later superintendent of the Burlington Railroad. Elwood won county seat in bitter election with Homerville in 1888. County seat removal made in 1889 with most Homerville buildings moved to Elwood.

Essex. Post office established December 14, 1892; moved to Frontier County September 22, 1894. Origin of the name not learned. Probably named for an English location.

Gosper. Census not available. Post office established May 4, 1880; discontinued May 2, 1906. Former town named for the county.

Highland. Post office established January 12, 1885; discontinued October 27, 1887. Description for an elevated area.

Hillier. Post office established August 31, 1883; discontinued February 12, 1884. Origin of the name unknown.

Homerville. Census not available. Post office name changed from Vaughn November 23, 1883; changed to Milton January 11, 1890. Former county seat named in honor of Homer Walt, who donated land for the town and courthouse. Homerville won county seat over Daviesville and another rival in August 1882. Burlington Railroad bypassed the town in favor of Elwood, which won county seat from Homerville in bitter election of 1888.

Johnson's Ranch. Post office established December 3, 1878; discontinued January 23, 1882. Named in honor of Elijah D. Johnson, first postmaster, on whose ranch the post office was established.

Judson. Post office established December 30, 1874; discontinued August 28, 1876. Origin of the name unknown. First postmaster was Orin Judd.

Mick. Post office established June 10, 1884; name changed to Elwood November 16, 1885. Origin of the name not learned.

Milton. Post office name changed from Homerville January 11, 1890; discontinued July 23, 1901. Origin of the name not learned. First postmaster was John R. Lord.

Smithfield. Peak population (1920), 229. Post office established May 23, 1891. Village named in honor of E. B. Smith. With the coming of the railroad, the town was platted in Smith's field on a quarter section of land.

Tracyville. Post office established February 27, 1880; discontinued May 14, 1886. Named for either John Tracy, early settler, or Otis Tracy, first postmaster.

Union Ridge. Post office established June 3, 1879; discontinued January 26, 1887. Probably named by a Union Civil War veteran living in the area.

Vaughn. Post office name changed from Vaughn's Ranch September 20, 1880; changed to Homerville November 23, 1883. See note below.

Vaughn's Ranch. Post office established February 2, 1877; name changed to Vaughn September 20, 1880. Named for Benjamin and Enoch Vaughn, early settlers.

GRANT COUNTY

Named in honor of Ulysses S. Grant (1822-85), U.S. president from 1869 to 1877, and a Union Army commander during the Civil War. County created by legislative enactment March 31, 1887.

Abby. Post office established July 19, 1888; moved to Hooker County October 30, 1891. Probably named in honor of Abby Chamberlain, daughter of first postmaster.

Ashby. Peak population (1950), 175. Post office established February 5, 1908. Town named for Ashby, Massachusetts, by railroad officials, or for Col. W. H. Ashby of Beatrice, Nebraska, who had land interests here.

Benewa. Post office established November 6, 1919; discontinued August 15, 1929. Named in honor of C. L. Benewa, rancher and merchant.

Duluth. Former station on the Burlington Railroad named by company officials after Duluth, Minnesota.

Elva. Post office established July 5, 1911; discontinued October 31, 1919. Named in honor of the daughter of Mrs. R. L. Farnsworth, first postmistress.

Fetterman. Post office established September 30, 1916; discontinued May 15, 1918. Named in honor of Col. Fetterman, attorney at law and homesteader.

Hyannis. Peak population (1940), 449. Post office established April 25, 1888. County seat town named for Hyannis, Massachusetts, by railroad officials. Some citizens wanted town named for John S. Dellinger, owner of site. Hyannis won county seat in bitter election with Whitman in 1887.

Lucky Valley. Post office established April 17, 1911; discontinued October 15, 1920. Named for its "fortunate" location by Postmaster C. H. Currier, early homesteader.

Sandcut. Siding on the Burlington Railroad named for a grade made through a sand hill. Located west of Ashby.

Seabrooke. Post office established January 24, 1910; discontinued October 31, 1910. Named in honor of Joseph W. Seabrooke, first postmaster.

Soda Lake. Probably a locality in the northern part of the county.

Vervine. Post office established November 1, 1916; discontinued 1933. Named by a Rev. Pruitt, homesteader. He claimed vervine (vervain) is a flower or herb mentioned in the Bible.

Weir. Post office established November 30, 1887; discontinued June 25, 1889. Origin of the name of this former post office and railroad station is unknown. After discontinuance of the post office, the railroad station was moved to Hooker County.

Whitman. Peak population (1950), 150. Post office established September 6, 1887. Named for Whitman, Massachusetts, by Burlington Railroad officials. County seat upon organization of the county was lost in election with Hyannis in 1887.

GREELEY COUNTY

Named in honor of Horace Greeley (1811-72), American journalist and political leader. County was organized and the boundaries defined by an act of the Legislature March 1, 1871.

Acme. Post office established August 10, 1885; discontinued October 9, 1891. Considered a perfect location for town.

Belfast. Post office established February 17, 1908; discontinued April 30, 1909. Named for Belfast, Ireland, by Irish immigrants.

Brayton. Peak population (1910 and 1930), 75. Post office established February 15, 1888; discontinued 1945. Former town probably named for a railroad official and established by the Lincoln Land Company. There is also a Brayton, Iowa.

Chase. Post office established January 16, 1880; discontinued June 23, 1886. Origin of the name has not been learned.

Davis Creek. Post office established October 1, 1878; name changed to Howard July 11, 1879. Probably named for a local settler.

El Dorado. Post office established March 14, 1876; discontinued January 17, 1881. El Dorado, Spanish for the gilded one, was chosen for unknown reason.

Ellsworth. Post office established July 11, 1879; discontinued December 3, 1883. Probably named for one of the nine Ellsworths in the U.S.

Enfield. Post office established June 14, 1882; discontinued April 16, 1894. Probably named for Enfield, Iowa.

Floss. Post office established March 28, 1881; discontinued August 27, 1887. Origin of the name not learned.

Greeley. Peak population (1920), 919. Post office name changed from Spading August 16, 1887. Railroad and corporate name is Greeley Center. Named for its location in the center of the county. Founded by George Fox, who owned the land. Greeley won county seat in elections with Scotia and O'Connor in 1890.

Greeley Center. See Greeley.

Halifax. Post office established September 23, 1875; name changed to Spalding May 20, 1881. Named for Halifax, Vermont, by N. S. Worden, who formerly lived there.

Homestead. Post office established July 18, 1904; discontinued February 18, 1916. Post office derived name from its location in Homestead Precinct.

Horace. Peak population (1910), 47. Post office established April 8, 1890; discontinued 1943. Former hamlet named in honor of Horace Greeley, editor of the *New York Tribune*.

Howard. Post office name changed from Davis Creek July 11, 1879; discontinued in 1880. Origin of the name not learned.

Jacksonville. Post office established July 24, 1878; moved to O'Connor January 13, 1880. Named in honor of Charles Jackson, early settler.

Lamartine. Post office established April 17, 1873; discontinued May 13, 1881. Origin of the name of this frontier town not learned. Lamartine was awarded the county seat but lost it in an election with Scotia November 15, 1873.

Leo Valley. Post office established March 15, 1880; discontinued October 15, 1920. Origin of the name not learned.

O'Connor. Peak population (1880), 149. Post office established January 13, 1880; discontinued June 22, 1904. Former town named in honor of Omaha Bishop James O'Connor, who established this Catholic community with Irish immigrants from Massachusetts. O'Connor lost bid for county seat in election of 1890. Town gradually dwindled when railroad bypassed it in favor of Greeley.

Parnell. Post office established September 27, 1881; discontinued June 15, 1915. Named for the precinct which, in turn, was named in honor of Charles S. Parnell, Irish home rule leader, by Irish settlers.

Scotia. Peak population (1920), 559. Post office established December 19, 1873. First post office was at the farm home of Postmaster Samuel Scott, who named it for his native Scotland. When the town of Scotia was built in 1876, two and one-half miles away, the name was retained. The first grist mill in the county was built in 1880 one and one-half miles from present Scotia. Scotia won the county seat from Lamartine in election of November 1874 but lost it to Greeley Center in election of 1890. The vacant courthouse became the Scotia Normal and Business University for a few years. A spur of the Union Pacific Railroad was built to Scotia in 1883.

Scotia Junction. About one and one-half miles southwest of Scotia. Probably the site of the county's first grist mills.

Spading. Post office established October 9, 1885; name changed to Greeley August 16, 1887. Origin of name not learned.

Spalding. Peak population (1920), 878. Post office established May 20, 1881. Town was established on Cedar River and named in honor of Bishop John L. Spalding, president of the Irish Catholic Association that founded the town.

Summit. Post office established June 4, 1879; discontinued November 3, 1889. Named for the hill or divide on which it was located.

Tracy. Former community in Greeley County.

Troy. Post office established December 8, 1879; discontinued December 31, 1904. Probably named for Troy, New York.

Velda. Present community in Greeley County.

Wolbach. Peak population (1920), 589. Post office established April 27, 1888. Town named in honor of S. N. Wolbach of Grand Island, Nebraska. Wolbach had land interests in the area, including the townsite.

HALL COUNTY

Named in honor of Augustus Hall (1814-61), chief justice of Nebraska Territory in 1858 and a former congressman from Iowa. County was organized and the boundaries defined by an act of the Legislature approved November 4, 1858. Boundaries were redefined February 1, 1864, and again on March 1, 1871.

Abbott. Peak population (1930), 50. Post office established March 16, 1887; discontinued 1937. Former town and present railroad station named in honor of Othman Ali Abbott of Grand Island, first lieutenant governor of Nebraska, elected in the fall of 1876.

Albaville. Post office established October 30, 1866; discontinued August 12, 1868. Stage stop on the Omaha and Fort Kearny Trail.

Alda. Peak population (1970), 956. Post office established September 7, 1871. First settlement made in the vicinity in May 1859. Before a post office was established, the place was called Pawnee. Renamed Alda for the first white child born there, the daughter of a section foreman.

Belt Line Crossing. Former station on the St. Joseph and Grand Island branch of Union Pacific Railroad; 2.2 miles from Grand Island.

Berwick. Post office name changed from Zurich May 3, 1881; discontinued April 29, 1887. Probably named in honor of a local settler.

Bluff Center. Four miles southwest of Cairo. Rural school district and baseball team, ca. 1910-60, had same name.

Burkett. Post office name changed from Home, May 28, 1906; discontinued June 30, 1930. Named for state legislator E. J. Burkett, a lawyer from Lincoln. Soldiers and Sailors Home located here.

Cairo. Peak population (2000), 790. Post office established November 17, 1886. Named by the Lincoln Land Company, presumably for Cairo, Egypt. Some of the town streets have Egyptian names.

Cameron. Post office name changed from Northfield December 10, 1875; discontinued April 23, 1903. Probably named in honor of a local settler.

Carey. Station on the Union Pacific Railroad between Grand Island and St. Libory; 2.5 miles from Grand Island.

Coplant. Station on both the Union Pacific and Burlington Railroads. Named for the Cornhusker Ordnance Plant of World War II.

Doniphan. Peak population (2000), 763. Post office name changed from Orchard October 21, 1879. Town named in honor of Col. John Doniphan of St. Joseph, Missouri. Doniphan was an attorney for the St. Joseph & Western Railroad.

Easton. Post office name changed from Runnelsburgh January 28, 1885; discontinued December 20, 1886. Origin of the name has not been learned. There is also an Easton, Pennsylvania.

Fort Independence. Fort established in 1864 south of the William Stolley home as protection against Indian attacks. The log structure was 24 feet square, with 25 loopholes, and was banked with sod for defense against flaming arrows. The fort's 80-foot-long underground stable accommodated an entire company and its horses. Fort Independence probably served the area until the mid-1860s.

Grand Island. Peak population (2000), 42,940. Post office name changed from Grand Island Station, 1873. Name changed to Grand Island when the city was incorporated and moved to new location. Named after a large island in the Platte River, known as La Grande Ile by French trappers. Laid out by the Union Pacific Railroad in 1866, it was settled in 1857-58 by a group from Davenport, Iowa, consisting mostly of German settlers. Grand Island was made county seat when the county was established. Cornhusker Ordnance Plant was located here during World War II. Grand Island College was founded in 1892 and merged in 1931 with a Baptist College at Sioux Falls, South Dakota.

Grand Island City. Post office established April 8, 1858; discontinued January 11, 1869. Separate office from Grand Island. Stage stop on the Omaha and Fort Kearny Trail.

Grand Island Station. Post office established November 1, 1866, changed to Grand Island, 1873. See Grand Island.

Haspur. Former station on the St. Joseph and Grand Island branch of the Union Pacific Railroad, 8.6 miles from Grand Island between that city and Doniphan.

Home. Post office established June 8, 1903; name changed to Burkett May 28, 1906. Name shortened from Soldiers Home.

Junctionville. Post office established August 22, 1865; discontinued October 1866; reestablished December 3, 1872; discontinued December 19, 1873. This place at the junction of the Ox Bow Main Trail and the Nebraska City-Fort Kearny Cutoff was established in 1864 by W. J. Burger and his wife Martha. They returned to Plattsmouth during the Indian raids but came back to Junctionville a few years later. First postmaster was John P. Brown.

Kuester's Lake. A residential community east of Grand Island. Lake made at former sandpit.

Lamb's. Former stage stop on the Omaha and Fort Kearny Trail. Named for Squire Lamb, who operated the stage station.

Loyola. Post office name changed from Rundlett May 14, 1883; discontinued December 21, 1886. Possibly named for one of several towns in other states named Loyola.

Marengo. Probably named for a Marengo in Illinois, Indiana, Iowa, Ohio, or Wisconsin.

Martinville. Early settlement in Hall County, originally part of Adams County. Named in honor of George Martin. Frequently called Martinsville.

McDonald's Track. On Burlington Railroad. Served McDonald Ranch several miles northwest of Grand Island.

Mendotte. Early settlement started by David Croker seven miles west of Grand Island.

Northfield. Post office established February 2, 1875; name changed to Cameron December 10, 1875. Possibly named for one of several other locations called Northfield.

Orchard. Post office established August 11, 1874; name changed to Doniphan October 21, 1879. Named by Barton Easley for an orchard in the area.

Ovina. Post office established December 8, 1920; discontinued April 6, 1923. The name of this former post office on the Burlington Railroad may relate to the Latin word for sheep.

Parkview. Former community annexed by Grand Island.

Pawnee. Early locality named for Pawnee Indians. The name was not accepted for a post office due to confusion with mail bound for Pawnee City, Nebraska. Alda was selected.

Power. Station on the Burlington Railroad.

Prairie City. Early proposed town to be located on Prairie Creek.

River. Between Haspur and Westwood on the St. Joseph and Grand Island branch of Union Pacific Railroad; 6.4 miles from Grand Island. Frequently called Rivers.

Rosedale. Community established during the 1940s.

Rundlett. Post office established September 20, 1878; name changed to Loyola May 14, 1883. Named in honor of Thomas P. Rundlett, first postmaster.

Runelsburg. Post office established October 30, 1876; name changed to Easton January 28, 1885. Named in honor of Vitales S. Runnel, who had the general store, grist mill, and post office.

Schauppsville. Town established by John G. Schaupp, who operated a grist mill here in 1880. There is no record that it became a post office.

Schimmer. Former station on the St. Joseph and Grand Island branch of Union Pacific Railroad; 4.2 miles from Grand Island. Possibly named for Martin Schimmer, early settler.

Spencer. Census not available. Post office established July 12, 1878; discontinued April 9, 1884. Former town named in honor of George J. Spencer, first postmaster.

Taylor's Spur. Former station on the Burlington Railroad. Probably named for the Taylor Ranch.

Traill Spur. Possibly named for D. J. Traill, railroad ticket and passenger agent. (Name has two ll's.)

Underwood. Peak population (1890), 32. Post office established January 16, 1885; discontinued May 23, 1902. Named in honor of Cleantha A. Underwood, first postmistress. Post office was located on the farm of B. J. Underwood before the town was platted.

Westwood. Station on the St. Joseph and Grand Island branch of Union Pacific Railroad between River and Grand Island.

White Cloud. Stage stop on the Omaha and Fort Kearny Trail. Probably named for Chief White Cloud of the Iowa Indians, a peace conciliator.

Wood River. Peak population (2000), 1,204. Post office established August 3, 1868.

Named after the Wood River on which it is located. First platted in 1869 but did not exist at its present site until 1871.

Wood River Farm. Stage station on the Omaha and Fort Kearny Trail.

Zurich. Post office established August 19, 1873; name changed to Berwick May 3, 1881. Probably named for Zurich, Switzerland.

HAMILTON COUNTY

Named in honor of Alexander Hamilton (1757-1804), secretary of the treasury in U.S. President George Washington's Cabinet. Boundaries of the county were defined by an act approved February 16, 1867.

Alvin. Post office name changed from Hamilton January 10, 1876; discontinued February 23, 1888. Origin of the name not learned. First postmaster was Benjamin Abbott.

Aurora. Peak population (2000), 4,225. Post office name changed from Spafford's Grove May 2, 1872. Name suggested by David Stone, early settler, as a compliment to his wife, a native of Aurora, Illinois. Robert Miller cast the deciding vote to determine the name. Aurora was made county seat in bitter election with Orville City in January 1876.

Avon. Post office established August 19, 1875; name changed to Marquette December 2, 1881. Origin of the name not learned. Thirteen states have places called Avon.

Briggs Ranch. Stop on the Old Fort Kearny Trail, sometimes known as Pikes Peak Trail.

Bromfield. Post office name changed from Lerton February 25, 1887; name changed to Giltner September 14, 1895. Origin of the name not learned. Town platted in 1886.

Buckeye. Post office established December 14, 1876; discontinued April 7, 1884. Probably named for Ohio, the Buckeye State. The state tree of Ohio is the buckeye.

Bunker Hill. Post office established June 14, 1876; discontinued December 22, 1881. Probably named for Bunker Hill, Massachusetts, site of the Revolutionary War's first major battle on June 17, 1775.

Case. Post office established February 15, 1883; discontinued February 18, 1887. Probably named in honor of Thomas Case, first postmaster.

Cedar Valley. Post office established June 23, 1874; discontinued April 6, 1880. Probably named for nearby cedar trees.

Curry. Former community probably named for G. W. Curry, miller of Aurora.

Deep Well Ranch. Stopping place for early day freighters, well-known for its deep well. Established by John Harris and Alfred Blue.

Farmers Valley. Post office established August 26, 1869; name changed to Farmvale November 3, 1894. Name agreed upon by local farmers.

Farmvale. Post office name changed from Farmer's Valley November 3, 1894; discontinued December 1, 1895. See Farmer's Valley.

Giltner. Peak population (1910), 550. Post office name changed from Bromfield September 14, 1895. Named in honor of the Rev. Henry M. Giltner, Presbyterian minister and early Nebraska missionary.

Glover. Post office established April 17, 1879; discontinued February 24, 1880. Named for an early settler. Probably named for T. H. Glover or William Glover, early settlers.

Hamilton. Post office established February 18, 1874; name changed to Alvin January 10, 1876. Named for the county.

Hampton. Peak population (1920), 457. Post office established February 18, 1880. Probably named for Hampton, Iowa.

Hordville. Census not available. Post office name changed from Stark October 25, 1907. Named in honor of T. B. Hord, pioneer cattleman and landowner. Townsite owned by the Swedish Lutheran Church and platted by Town Site Company of Stromsburg.

Huntington. Railroad name for Bromfield.

Kronborg. Community east of Marquette.

Leonard. Post office established January 12, 1880; discontinued December 7, 1885. Origin of the name not learned. First postmaster was William Garlicke.

Lerton. Post office name changed from Linden May 7, 1875; name changed to Bromfield February 25, 1887. Origin of the name not learned.

Lincoln Valley. Post office established November 12, 1872; name changed to St. Joe November 12, 1878. Origin of the name is unknown. Post office was located at the farm home of Charles Tompkins.

Linden. Post office established January 23, 1874; name changed to Lerton May 7, 1875. Origin of the name not learned.

Marquette. Peak population (1930), 308. Post office name changed from Avon December 2, 1881. Named in honor of Thomas M. Marquette of Lincoln, Nebraska, general attorney for the Burlington Railroad. Town platted by Lincoln Land Company in 1882.

Millspaw Ranch. The first ranch in Hamilton County and stop for freighters, established in 1861 on Beaver Creek on the trail from Nebraska City to Fort Kearny. It was named for David Millspaw.

Miramichi. Post office established February 20, 1874; discontinued November 27, 1877. Origin of the name not learned.

Murphy. Post office established April 2, 1912; discontinued 1943. Mail served from Phillips. Origin of the name not learned.

Orville City. Post office name changed from Verona December 4, 1872; discontinued January 29, 1880. Former town named in honor of Orville Wescott, son of J. D. Wescott, first postmaster and county clerk. First courthouse established here in May of 1872 but lost to Aurora after election in January 1876. Town soon lost its identity and the site later became the Hamilton County Poor Farm.

Otis. Post office established October 29, 1873; discontinued April 6, 1889. Probably named for early settler J. W. Otis. First postmaster was Stephen K. Butler.

Overland. Station on the Burlington Railroad.

Penn. Post office established April 16, 1895; probably discontinued 1896. Origin of the name not learned.

Phillips. Peaks population (1980), 405. Post office name changed from Phillips Station April 16, 1895. See Phillips Station.

Phillips Station. Post office established May 28, 1884; name changed to Phillips April 16, 1895. Town named in honor of R. O. Phillips, locator of townsites for the Lincoln Land Company.

Prairie Camp. Relay stage station on the Overland Trail located six miles west of Millspaw Ranch.

Primrose. Post office established September 5, 1881; discontinued November 27, 1882. Origin of the name not learned.

Rock. Post office established January 9, 1879; discontinued October 3, 1881. Origin of the name is unknown.

Sandburg. Former locality in Hamilton County.

Seaton. Post office established March 17, 1884; discontinued February 17, 1887. Named in honor of Robert Seaton, first postmaster.

Shiloh. Post office established May 17, 1876; discontinued May 11, 1889. Probably named by a Civil War veteran who participated in the Civil War battle at Shiloh, Tennessee.

Spafford's Grove. Post office established April 5, 1871; name changed to Aurora May 2, 1872. Named in honor of Silvester W. Spafford, first postmaster.

Stark. Post office established October 21, 1887; name changed to Hordville October 2, 1907. Named in honor of a local settler.

St. Joe. Peak population (1880), 32. Post office name changed from Lincoln Valley

November 12, 1878; discontinued October 23, 1885. Platted by Joe Skelton and named St. Joe by the residents. Town buildings moved to Phillips when the railroad bypassed St. Joe.

Stockham. Peak population (1920), 239. Post office established July 5, 1876, made a rural station of Aurora in 1968. Named in honor of Joseph Stockham, a member of the town board of trustees.

Traill. Burlington Railroad station. Possibly named for D. J. Traill, railroad ticket and passenger agent. (Name contains two ll's.)

Verona. Post office established December 14, 1870; name changed to Orville City December 4, 1872. Named for Verona, Wisconsin. Robert Lamont was first postmaster.

Williamsport. Post office established May 2, 1872; moved to Hampton in December 1879. Named in honor of William Hiatt, son of George W. Hiatt, first postmaster.

HARLAN COUNTY

Separated from Lincoln County by an act of the Legislature approved June 3, 1871. Named for a nephew of U.S. Senator James Harlan of Iowa. The nephew was once a revenue collector who lived near Republican City, Nebraska.

Alma. Peak population (1950), 1,768. Post office name changed from Alma City on August 21, 1873. County seat named in honor of a daughter of N. P. Cook. Townsite selected by Mark Coad, N. P. Cook, and Thomas Murrin, members of the Cheyenne Colony, in the spring of 1871.

Alma City. Post office established July 14, 1871; name changed to Alma August 21, 1873. See Alma.

Bainbridge. Post office established April 14, 1873; name changed to Huntley December 10, 1888. Origin of the name is unknown. There are places in Georgia, Maryland, New York, Ohio, and Pennsylvania with this name.

Cannonville. Post office established October 17, 1882; discontinued May 18, 1891. Probably named in honor of either J. C. F. Cannon, Civil War veteran and early settler, or for Robert Cannon, first postmaster. Post office established June 7, 1906; discontinued October 15, 1915. Former town and station on the Burlington Railroad, probably named for E. G. Carter, railroad official.

Carter. Census not available. Post office established June 7, 1906; discontinued October 15, 1915. Former town and station on the Burlington Railroad. Probably named for E. G. Carter, railroad official.

Cudahy. Former station on the Burlington Railroad. Probably named for the Cudahy meat-packing family of Chicago, Illinois.

Eva. Post office established June 2, 1882; discontinued September 22, 1887. Origin of name is unknown. First postmaster was Frank W. Stevens.

Everson. Former station on the Burlington Railroad probably named for the Everson family living in the vicinity.

Freewater. Post office established March 8, 1875; discontinued April 2, 1887. The post office was named for the free water given by John Elliott, 1874 settler from New York. Nothing remains of the ranch, church, and post office once known as Freewater.

Garber. Post office established October 12, 1874; discontinued September 3, 1878. Named in honor of Silas Garber, governor of Nebraska (1875-79).

Graft. Post office established September 29, 1874; discontinued August 2, 1886. Named in honor of the Graft family, pioneers of Harlan County.

Grandview. Post office established August 11, 1874; moved to Furnas County May 3, 1880. Named for its location.

Harlan. Post office established August 19, 1873; discontinued September 21, 1873. Named for the county.

Huntley. Peak population (1910), 250. Post office name changed from Bainbridge December 10, 1888. Town named in honor of a Mr. Huntley, official of the Kansas City and Omaha Railroad.

Lewisburgh. Post office established March 4, 1879; discontinued December 7, 1885. Named in honor of Lewis Rifenburgh, who established a mill and townsite on Prairie Dog Creek.

Mascot. Peak population (1950), 55. Post office established August 27, 1886; discontinued February 19, 1892. Mail served from Oxford. Originally named Rouse, it was changed because there was another Rouse, Nebraska. Both named by Burlington Railroad officials.

Maywood. Post office established August 4, 1882; discontinued February 28, 1883. Probably named for Maywood, Illinois.

Melrose. Post office established January 6, 1873; name changed to Orleans March 2, 1878. Origin of the name not learned.

Midway. Post office established September 2, 1879; discontinued February 9, 1880. Named for its site between two post offices.

Napoleon. The first townsite in what is now Harlan County, selected by Victor Vifquain in 1870 and then abandoned. Although no buildings were ever erected at the site, it received several votes in a later election for county seat.

Orleans. Peak population (1930), 984. Post office name changed from Melrose March 2, 1878. Probably named for Orleans, Massachusetts. Town platted by D. N. Smith, well-known site locator, for Burlington Railroad.

Oxford Junction. Division point for two branches of the Burlington Railroad.

Pleasant Ridge. Post office established March 6, 1876; discontinued July 21, 1887. Named for its pleasing location.

Prairie Dog. Post office established May 6, 1875; discontinued July 26, 1875. Named for its location on Prairie Dog Creek, named for its numerous prairie dog villages.

Ragan. Peak population (1920), 222. Post office established August 29, 1887. Town probably named in honor of a railroad official of the Chicago, Kansas City and Omaha Railroad.

Republican City. Peak population (1950), 580. Post office established February 6, 1872. Named for its location on the Republican River, so named because it flowed through the lands of the Republican band of the Pawnee tribe.

Rouse. See Mascot.

Sappa. Post office established November 15, 1886; discontinued July 28, 1903. Named for the precinct, which was probably named for a local settler.

Scandinavia. Post office established June 18, 1874; discontinued February 17, 1888. Applies to the countries of Denmark, Norway, and Sweden. First postmaster was Gustav Hanson.

Spring Grove. Post office established September 12, 1877; discontinued June 14, 1882. Probably named for a spring located in a grove of trees.

Spring Hill. Post office established September 20, 1878; discontinued April 9, 1880. Name describes its location.

Stamford. Peak population (1920), 302. Post office established December 6, 1887. Originally called Carisbrooke and located in Furnas County. With the coming of the railroad, the Lincoln Land Company relocated the town in Harlan County. Probably named for Stamford, Connecticut.

Stratton's Store. Early county settlement surrounding a store owned by a Mr. Stratton.

Washington. Post office established September 4, 1882; discontinued March 26, 1884. Probably named in honor of President George Washington.

Watson. Post office established May 8, 1872; discontinued June 30, 1880. Named in honor of a local settler.

HAYES COUNTY

Created by legislative enactment February 19, 1877. Named in honor of Rutherford B. Hayes (1822-93), U.S. president from 1877 to 1881.

Cactus. Post office established July 25, 1890; discontinued June 19, 1895. Named for desert cactus growing in the region.

Carrico. Post office established July 13, 1896; discontinued May 15, 1914. Probably named for a local settler.

Catherine. Post office moved from Chase County August 7, 1891; moved to Chase County September 3, 1896. See Catherine, Chase County.

Eddy. Post office established October 18, 1888; discontinued March 15, 1912. Origin of the name not learned. First postmaster was Harvey Harman.

Elmer. Post office established December 8, 1887; discontinued June 8, 1895. Origin of the name is unknown. First postmaster was Andrew McCutchen.

Estelle. Post office established October 31, 1881; discontinued December 19, 1891. Origin of the name not determined. Estelle lost in county seat election with Hayes Center January 10, 1885.

Galena. Post office established September 24, 1886; discontinued April 29, 1916. Probably named for Galena, Illinois, or for Galena, Kansas, both lead mining centers. Galena is natural lead sulfide.

Hamlet. Peak population (1940), 220. Post office name changed from Hudson October 31, 1904. Name changed because another post office within the state was called Hudson. The new name chosen by the residents signified a small town.

Hayes Center. Peak population (1950), 361. Post office established July 10, 1885. Named for the county. Hayes Center won county seat in election with La Forest and Estelle January 10, 1885. Located in the center of the county.

Highland. Post office established April 26, 1888; discontinued May 15, 1903. Named for its high elevation.

Hope. Post office established February 16, 1888; discontinued May 11, 1905. Origin of the name not learned.

Hudson. Post office established February 21, 1890; name changed to Hamlet October 31, 1904. Origin of the name not learned.

La Forest. Post office established December 16, 1884; moved to Hayes Center July 10, 1885. First county seat, named in honor of La Forest Dyer, first postmaster. Buildings were moved to Hayes Center, which won county seat away from La Forest in election.

Lucille. Post office established April 26, 1890; discontinued January 26, 1904. Origin of the name not determined. First postmaster was Alfred Plunkett.

Marengo. Post office established May 23, 1891; discontinued 1935. Probably named for a Marengo in Illinois, Indiana, Iowa, Ohio, or Wisconsin.

McNaughton. Post office established February 15, 1881; discontinued July 11, 1883. Origin of the name has not been learned.

Morris. Post office established August 4, 1898; discontinued January 12, 1903. Origin of the name not learned.

Norris. Post office established December 5, 1904; moved to Frontier County June 20, 1907; moved from Frontier County November 15, 1927; discontinued 1928. Named in honor of Nebraska Senator George W. Norris (1861-1944).

Rain. Post office established December 18, 1894; discontinued December 31, 1919. Named during dry season when religious and other organizations held meetings to pray for rain. C. B. French, minister of the Church of Christ and the first postmaster, suggested Rain to remind patrons of the devastating drouth.

Robert. Post office established February 26, 1901; discontinued February 15, 1930.

Strickland. Post office established August 16, 1887; discontinued May 31, 1926. Origin of the name not learned.

Sullivan. Post office established May 12, 1891; discontinued July 26, 1893. Probably named in honor of Patrick E. Sullivan, first postmaster.

Thornburg. Post office established July 8, 1881; moved to Frontier County September 21, 1888; moved from Frontier County September 21, 1924; discontinued December 15, 1924. Named for the precinct. Origin of the name is unknown.

White. Census not available. Post office established December 29, 1904; discontinued 1939. Former hamlet named in honor of Arthur White, early homesteader.

HITCHCOCK COUNTY

Named in honor of Phineas Warrener Hitchcock (1831-81), United States senator from Nebraska at the time of the county's organization in 1873. Its boundaries were defined by an act approved February 27, 1873.

Beverly. Peak population (1910 and 1940), 35. Post office established June 23, 1881; discontinued 1945. Former village on the Burlington Railroad named for Beverly, Massachusetts, and platted in 1887.

Blackwood. Post office established December 16, 1884; discontinued June 13, 1893. Named for its location on Blackwood Creek.

Cornell. Post office established June 14, 1880; discontinued October 15, 1920. Origin of the name not learned. Precinct has the same name.

Cove. Post office established July 30, 1900; rescinded October 27, 1900. Named for a characteristic feature of the land along a creek.

Culbertson. Peak population (1940), 815. Post office established September 10, 1873. Named in honor of Alexander Culbertson, well-known Indian agent and fur trader. Culbertson was made county seat upon formation of the county August 30, 1873, but lost it in election with Trenton in 1894.

Dike. Post office established July 25, 1888; discontinued September 7, 1898. Origin of the name not learned.

Driftwood. Post office established February 12, 1880; discontinued May 26, 1888. Named for its site on Driftwood Creek.

Frontier. Post office established February 18, 1879; name changed to Stratton July 22, 1881. Named for its frontier location or for its proximity to Frontier County.

Meeker. Former station on the Burlington Railroad. One source says named for C. H. Meeker of McCook, Nebraska. Another says named for Charles W. Meeker of Imperial, by Ed Flynn, a friend of Burlington Railroad division superintendent at McCook.

Palisade. Peak population (1940), 799. Post office established February 25, 1880. Named by Samuel True because of the irregular terrain resembling palisades in the vicinity.

Poe. Former station on the Burlington Railroad named by company officials.

Rill. Post office established July 25, 1888; discontinued December 812, 1893. Former station on the Burlington Railroad.

Rupert. Former station on the Burlington Railroad. Located near Trenton.

Scudder. Post office established July 19, 1892; discontinued April 16, 1894. Origin of the name not learned.

Stratton. Peak population (1930), 660. Post office name changed from Frontier July 22, 1881. Town, named in honor of a Mrs. Stratton, one of the first settlers, was platted in 1883.

Trail. Post office established February 27, 1880; discontinued May 9, 1881. Probably named for the Texas-Ogallala cattle trail that passed nearby.

Trail City. Probably on the site of Trenton before a post office was established.

Trenton. Peak population (1950), 1,299. Post office established December 8, 1884. Named for Trenton, New Jersey, it won county seat in 1894 election with Culbertson.

HOLT COUNTY

Named in honor of Joseph Holt (1807-94) of Kentucky, postmaster-general and secretary of war in President James Buchanan's Cabinet. Later he served as judge advocate of the U.S. Army under President Abraham Lincoln. County boundaries were defined by an act of the Legislature approved January 9, 1862.

Agee. Post office established November 23, 1882; discontinued 1934. Named in honor of A. W. Agee, lieutenant governor of Nebraska (1883-84).

Amelia. Peak population (1910, 1920, 1930), 75. Post office established August 31, 1885. Town named in honor of Amelia A. Bliss. Platted by A. M. Anderson.

Angora Station. Station on the Chicago and North Western Railroad. Probably named for Angora sheep.

Anncar. Post office established June 18, 1900; discontinued November 14, 1931. Name is a combination of the first and middle names of Mrs. Anna Carroll O'Neill, at whose home the office was established. Use of the name of Carroll denied because there was already a Carroll, Nebraska.

Apple Creek. Post office established July 15, 1879; name changed to Omarel May 23, 1883. Named for apple trees growing along a creek. A store, hotel, and blacksmith shop were here when office was established.

Atkinson. Peak population (1980), 1,521. Post office established June 7, 1878. Town named for Col. John Atkinson of Detroit, Michigan, who owned land in the vicinity.

Badger. Post office established February 25, 1890; discontinued May 25, 1903. Named for the numerous badgers in the area.

Belknap. Post office established October 10, 1883; discontinued May 11, 1888. Named in honor of Lafayette Belknap, first postmaster.

Biscuit. Post office established March 17, 1906; discontinued January 6, 1908.

Blackbird. Post office established September 15, 1879; discontinued October 15, 1928. Possibly named for Chief Blackbird of the Omaha tribe.

Bliss. Post office moved from Wheeler County April 23, 1888; discontinued 1941. See Bliss, Wheeler County.

Brewer. Post office established October 1, 1879; discontinued February 14, 1881. See Brewer, Keya Paha County, where this office was later re-established.

Brodie. Census not available. Post office established June 13, 1892; discontinued September 24, 1907. Named in honor of a local settler.

Burton Creek. Post office established September 4, 1879; discontinued December 9, 1879. Named for a nearby creek.

Cache Creek. Post office established September 4, 1879; discontinued August 21, 1885. Named for a creek in the vicinity, where a cache of furs hidden by a trapper may have been found by another party.

Carson. Post office moved from Garfield County March 15, 1916; discontinued probably 1918. See Carson, Garfield County.

Catalpa. Post office established July 28, 1884; discontinued 1934. Named for catalpa trees growing in the area.

Cedar. Post office established August 1, 1912; discontinued November 30, 1921. Possibly named for cedar trees growing in the vicinity.

Celia. Post office established June 26, 1882; discontinued November 30, 1914. Origin of the name not learned. First postmaster was George M. Harker.

Chambers. Peak population (1960), 396. Post office established April 25, 1884. Town named in honor of B. F. Chambers, registrar of the U.S. Land Office at Niobrara, by W. D. Matthews, well-known frontier editor. R. C. Wray owned most of the town lots, once a part of his homestead. He built the store which included the first post office.

Chelsea. Post office established July 11, 1878; discontinued September 21, 1900. Named for Chelsea, Massachusetts.

Cleveland. Post office established March 20, 1879; discontinued August 21, 1895. Named in honor of Lyman Cleveland, first postmaster. A store and flour mill were located in this community.

Clifton. Post office name changed from Clifton Grove April 7, 1886; discontinued June 19, 1888. See Clifton Grove.

Clifton Grove. Post office established October 20, 1879; name changed to Clifton April 7, 1886. Origin of the name not learned. A blacksmith shop and a wagon shop were in this community.

Conley. Post office established April 25, 1884; discontinued May 11, 1888. Named for the precinct. Origin of name is unknown.

Deloit. Peak population (1890), 260. Post office established September 8, 1879; discontinued December 16, 1905. Former village named for Deloit, Iowa.

Dewey. Post office established October 1, 1898; discontinued December 4, 1902. Probably named in honor of Adm. George Dewey, Spanish-American War hero who in 1898 successfully led the U.S. Naval flotilla into Manila Bay in the Philippines and destroyed the Spanish fleet.

Disney. Post office established December 8, 1904; discontinued March 15, 1911. Origin of the name has not been ascertained.

Dorsey. Peak population (1950), 45. Post office name changed from Mineral July 18, 1892; discontinued 1957. Former village named in honor of Nebraska Congressman George W. Dorsey (1885-91).

Dustin. Census not available. Post office established November 9, 1883; discontinued 1957. Former village probably named in honor of William Dustin, first postmaster.

Eagle. The Millkamper Mill was located at this early settlement.

Emmet. Peak population (1910), 150. Post office established June 7, 1880. Town named in honor of Irish patriot Robert Emmet (1778-1803).

Emporia. Post office established December 8, 1890; discontinued August 5, 1902. Probably named for Emporia, Kansas.

Ewing. Peak population (1950), 705. Post office name changed from Ford April 10, 1884. Named in honor of James Ewing of Knoxville, Tennessee, who built a log house one and one-half miles below the present village of Ewing in 1871. Town platted by Pioneer Town Site Company.

Ferndale. Post office established February 23, 1882; discontinued April 6, 1888. Probably named for Ferndale, Michigan.

Ford. Post office established January 22, 1874; name changed to Ewing April 10, 1884. Named for a local settler. First post office in Holt County.

Frickel. Early settlement shown on Holt County map.

Gillespie. Post office established May 14, 1883; discontinued September 3, 1883. Possibly named in honor of B. S. Gillespie, former county sheriff and surveyor.

Grand Rapids. Peak population (1890), 57. Post office established May 27, 1879; discontinued January 21, 1907. Former village named for the rapids in the Niobrara River.

Gravel Pit. Locally descriptive name for a station on the Chicago and North Western Railroad.

Greeley. Post office established March 21, 1881; name changed to Phoenix March 19, 1887. Named in honor of Peter Greeley, owner of a store, blacksmith shop, and wagon shop. Name was changed when another office in the state was named Greeley.

Green Valley. Census not available. Post office established February 12, 1886; discontinued July 30, 1910. Former village named for the precinct. Name is locally descriptive.

Hainesville. Census not available. Post office established September 4, 1879; discontinued March 8, 1907. Former village named in honor of S. S. Haines, who made the first settlement here with D. S. Ludwig in February 1879.

Harold. Post office established July 16, 1886; discontinued September 5, 1912. Origin of the name not learned. First postmaster was Frank Smith.

Harriet. Post office established June 14, 1883; discontinued September 4, 1883. Origin of the name not learned. First postmaster was William H. Bice.

Hart. Post office established December 12, 1879; discontinued September 19, 1881. Possibly named in honor of William Hart, first postmaster.

Haypoint. Named for hay-shipping station on the Burlington Railroad.

Hollman. Post office established May 1, 1886; discontinued October 11, 1895. Origin of the name not learned.

Holt Creek. Post office established August 21, 1901; discontinued January 8, 1902. Named for the creek on which it was located.

Inez. Post office established September 24, 1886; discontinued March 30, 1930. Origin of the name not learned.

Ingells. Post office established September 25, 1896; discontinued July 30, 1910. Probably named in honor of John C. Ingles, first postmaster. The name was misspelled as Ingells.

Inman. Peak population (1920), 315. Post office changed from Inman's Grove September 16, 1881. Town named in honor of W. H. Inman, pioneer storekeeper and Holt County settler. Yorktown was once suggested as a name.

Inman's Grove. Post office established June 11, 1877; name changed to Inman September 16, 1881. See Inman.

Josie. Post office established August 22, 1881; discontinued 1943. Named for the precinct. First postmaster was John J. McCafferty.

Joy. Post office established March 10, 1886; discontinued 1934. Named by patrons to express their feelings over the prospect of having a post office.

Keya Paha. Post office established August 21, 1877; discontinued February 11, 1888. Located at the mouth of the Keya Paha River. H. Day and J. S. Axtell established a settlement in January 1877 with a store and sawmill. See Keya Paha County.

Knievels Corner. Present community in Holt County.

Kola. Post office established December 28, 1906; discontinued 1935. Named for a homesteader's child.

Krugman. Former locality.

Lake City. Former community in Holt County.

Lambert. Post office established September 8, 1880; discontinued February 11, 1891. Named for a local settler.

Laska. Former locality.

Laura. Post office established March 20, 1881; discontinued August 2, 1883. Named in honor of the wife of Postmaster J. A. Estep.

Lavinia. Post office established June 11, 1877; discontinued July 24, 1889. Named in honor of Lavinia Smith, wife of J. L. Smith and the first woman in the settlement.

Leonie. Post office established February 7, 1879; discontinued March 13, 1913. Named in honor of the wife of I. R. Smith, first postmaster.

Little. Post office established June 29, 1881; discontinued August 15, 1913. Named in honor of L. B. Little, early settler.

Lucerne. Post office established April 20, 1908; discontinued November 30, 1910. Named for Lucerne, Switzerland.

Maple Grove. Post office established March 29, 1909; discontinued 1914. Named for a grove of maple trees.

Martha. Post office established April 15, 1904; discontinued 1934. Named in honor of Martha Rollin Porter, pioneer and mother-in-law of the first postmaster.

Matthews. Post office established January 31, 1887; discontinued April 25, 1888. Possibly named in honor of W. D. Matthews, early settler.

McCaffery. Post office established February 8, 1899; discontinued December 3, 1901. Probably named in honor of Joseph McCaffery, first postmaster.

Meek. Census not available. Post office established September 10, 1899; discontinued 1934. Former town named in honor of Samuel Meek, at one time an area butter maker.

Middlebranch. Peak population (1950), 60. Post office moved from Knox County June 19, 1882; discontinued 1954. See Middlebranch, Knox County.

Midway. Rural community located near O'Neill.

Mineola. Post office established September 8, 1880; discontinued February 28, 1913. Possibly named for Mineola, New York, or Mineola, Iowa.

Mineral. Name of Dorsey before a post office was established.

Moore. Post office established July 17, 1884; discontinued July 24, 1889. Probably named in honor of Frederick Moore, first postmaster.

Norwood. Post office established March 30, 1905; discontinued July 31, 1919. Origin of name not learned. There is also a Norwood, Ohio.

Omarel. Post office name changed from Apple Creek, May 23, 1883; discontinued October 6, 1884. Origin of the name not learned.

O'Neill. Peak population (1980), 4,049. Post office name changed from O'Neill City October 24, 1883. Named in honor of John J. O'Neill, founder of this Irish colony from Scranton, Pennsylvania. "General" O'Neill, a Union Army veteran, was involved in the Fenian invasion of Canada in the late 1860s. O'Neill was platted by Thomas I. Atwood, and won county seat in election with Paddock in 1879. It served as a supply point for the Black Hills gold rush and was an important cattle town.

O'Neill City. Post office name changed from Rockford March 10, 1875; name changed to O'Neill October 24, 1883. See O'Neill.

Opportunity. Census not available. Post office established November 21, 1910; discontinued 1943. Founders of this former town thought they would "take an opportunity to make good" if they started a store and post office on an area ranch.

Paddock. Census not available. Post office name changed from Troy June 21, 1875; discontinued 1934. Former town named by an admirer in honor of U.S. Senator Algernon S. Paddock of Nebraska (1875-81). Paddock, second county seat, won first election from Twin Lakes in 1876 but lost county seat designation to O'Neill in election of November 1879.

Page. Peak population (1920), 608. Post office established March 13, 1890. Named for the Page family, which homesteaded here. When the railroad was built, townsite was partially on the Page land. Mrs. Selinda Page was first postmistress. Town platted by Pacific Town Site Company.

Parker. Post office established May 18, 1882; discontinued March 31, 1890. Possibly named in honor of James Parker, first postmaster.

Perryville. Former locality.

Phoenix. Post office name changed from Greeley March 19, 1887; discontinued January 26, 1888. Probably inspired by the legendary phoenix bird in Egyptian mythology.

Pumpkin Center. Former locality.

Ray. Peak population (1890), 65. Post office established November 29, 1880; discontinued October 15, 1921. Former hamlet named for the oldest son of Mr. and Mrs. M. T. Hoxie.

Redbird. Peak population (1950), 55. Post office established September 14, 1875; discontinued August 5, 1887. Mail served from Lynch. Present community named for nearby Redbird Creek, probably named for the cardinal or redbird.

Richmond. Post office established February 4, 1884; discontinued November 25, 1890. Probably named for one of the sixteen places in the U.S. called Richmond.

Riverside. Post office established August 20, 1884; discontinued May 16, 1893. Probably named for its location on the Niobrara River.

Rock Falls. Former locality.

Rockford. Post office established June 10, 1874; name changed to O'Neill City March 10, 1875. Possibly named for C. B. Rockford, early settler.

Rome. Post office established September 27, 1886; discontinued July 25, 1888. Probably named for Rome, Georgia, or Rome, New York.

Ross. Post office established June 19, 1882; discontinued January 22, 1883. Probably named in honor of James W. Ross, first postmaster.

Saratoga. Post office established October 20, 1879; discontinued January 14, 1910. Named after the precinct, which was probably named for the Revolutionary War battle of Saratoga, New York (1776). Peter Greeley opened a store here in 1880.

Scottville. Post office established May 10, 1882; discontinued November 15, 1915. Named in honor of Barrett Scott, pioneer who later was elected treasurer of Holt County.

Shamrock. Post office established March 19, 1886; discontinued December 3, 1888. Named by Irish settlers for the Irish shamrock.

Sizer. Post office established May 13, 1884; discontinued October 3, 1894. Possibly named in honor of Pemben Sizer, first postmaster.

Slocum. Post office established May 29, 1886; discontinued October 12, 1903. Named in honor of a local settler.

Southside. Post office established December 13, 1882; discontinued January 12, 1888. Named for its location south of some particular site.

Stafford. Census not available. Post office established May 2, 1888; discontinued 1939. Mail probably served from Inman. Town named in honor of Michael Stafford, roadmaster of the Fremont, Elkhorn and Missouri Valley Railroad, now the Chicago and North Western.

Stanley. Former community in Holt County.

Star. Census not available. Post office established July 7, 1882; discontinued 1956. C. E. Downey of O'Neill suggested the name for this former village and post office. Downey reports that he selected the name because it was short and familiar.

Steele Creek. Former community listed on maps in Holt County.

Stuart. Peak population (1960, 1970), 794. Post office established April 8, 1880. Named in honor of Peter Stuart, early settler who owned land on which the town was located.

Swan. Post office established December 2, 1886; discontinued January 15, 1923. Named after nearby Swan Lake, with its oblong body and long neck.

Thompson. Post office moved from Wheeler County November 20, 1885; discontinued November 19, 1887. See Thompson, Wheeler County.

Thorn. Post office established June 30, 1904; discontinued October 13, 1905. Origin of the name not learned.

Tonawanda. Post office established April 12, 1904; discontinued January 31, 1929. Probably named for Tonawanda, New York. Iroquois Indian word meaning swift water.

Tonic. Census not available. Post office established April 2, 1892; discontinued January 31, 1914. Origin of the name of this former village is unknown.

Troy. Name of a community before Paddock post office established.

Turner. Post office established July 14, 1881; discontinued February 28, 1914. Named by William Knollkampire in honor of a Mr. Turner, his partner in operation of a grist mill.

Twing. Post office established May 25, 1882; discontinued February 16, 1888. Probably named in honor of Samuel Twing, first postmaster.

Twin Lakes. First county seat of Holt County, located in the home of H. W. Haines in 1873. Twin Lakes lost the county seat in 1876 to Paddock. No record of a post office here.

Walker. Post office moved from Wheeler County February 4, 1884; discontinued January 26, 1885. See Walker, Wheeler County.

Winfield. Post office established August 23, 1880; discontinued November 20, 1881. Origin of the name not learned.

HOOKER COUNTY

Named in honor of Gen. Joseph Hooker (1814-79), Union Army commander in Civil War. County created by legislative enactment March 29, 1889.

Abby. Post office moved from Grant County October 30, 1891; discontinued April 16, 1894. See Abby, Grant County.

Crescent. Post office established January 5, 1911; discontinued October 31, 1911. Probably named for a cattle ranch or for a cattle brand.

Donald. Post office established May 10, 1907; discontinued August 15, 1922. Office named in honor of Roderick Donald, first postmaster, or for the son of Richard McKinney.

Dunwell. Post office established January 27, 1909; discontinued 1934. Coined name honors two men, William Dunbar and Frank Wells, who established the post office.

Eclipse. Post office established February 27, 1905; discontinued September 25, 1923. Name selected by ranchers at the home of A. J. Gragg. Probably derived from an eclipse of the sun or moon.

Hecla. Post office established November 30, 1887; discontinued May 29, 1908. Former post office on the Burlington Railroad probably named by railroad officials for Iceland volcano. There is also a Hecla, South Dakota.

Kelso. Station on the Burlington Railroad.

Moore. Post office established August 6, 1924; discontinued 1934. Named in honor of local ranchman C. T. Moore.

Mullen. Peak population (1960), 811. Post office established April 24, 1889. Town named by Burlington Railroad officials for an area railroad contractor.

Weir. Former station, previously across the Thomas County line, on the Burlington Railroad.

HOWARD COUNTY

Organized and boundaries defined by an act of the Legislature approved March 1, 1871, and again organized by an act approved March 28, 1871. Named in honor of Gen. Oliver Otis Howard (1830-1909), Union officer during the Civil War and commander in Indian Wars. It is sometimes stated that the county was named after Howard Paul, son of an early settler.

Athens. Name first suggested for the present town of St. Paul, but there already was a Nebraska post office named Athens.

Boelus. Peak population (1900), 289. Post office established February 1, 1886. Named for Belus, a small river in Palestine described by the Roman author Pliny as rising at the foot of Mt. Carmel and falling into the sea near Ptolemais (Acre).

Brass Spur. Former station on the Burlington Railroad located near Cushing.

Brooks. Post office established June 15, 1881; discontinued March 19, 1886. Origin of name not learned.

Canada Hill. Rural neighborhood just northeast of Farwell.

Cascade. Post office established October 30, 1879; discontinued July 13, 1886. Probably named for a small waterfall on a nearby creek.

Chojnice. Rural Polish community northwest of Farwell led by Father Anthony Klawiter (Klaviter), a Polish Catholic priest from Pittsburgh, Pennsylvania. Chojnice commemorates a city in northern Poland. Also called Choynice, Paplin, or rarely Mt. Carmel for Our Lady of Mt. Carmel Catholic Church, established in 1882. A Catholic parochial school and convent were established on nearby Turkey Creek.

Clarendon. Rural neighborhood between the Loup Forks, 1872.

Cotesfield. Peak population (1920), 214. Post office established December 1, 1871. Named in honor of a Miss Coates who, with Gen. Christopher C. Augur and his daughter, visited the vicinity as guests of Captain Munson.

Cushing. Peak population (1930), 126. Post office established September 5, 1887. Named in honor of James Cushing, early settler. Post office discontinued 1968. Mail served from St. Paul.

Dannebrog. Peak population (1920), 436. Post office established March 5, 1872. Named for Danish flag and suggested by the Danish Land and Homestead Colony of Milwaukee, Wisconsin, which settled here in May 1871. Town platted by Mr. and Mrs. Lars Hannibal.

Dannevirke. Census not available. Post office established February 16, 1880; discontinued December 21, 1903. Named by Danish settlers for ancient wall built by Danes to stop German aggression.

Davis Creek. Post office established July 11, 1879; discontinued October 5, 1879. Located on Davis Creek, which was probably named for a local settler.

Devries. Former station on the Burlington Railroad. Origin of name not learned.

Dublin. Former station on the Union Pacific Railroad probably named for Dublin, Ireland.

Elba. Peak population (1910), 302. Post office established April 24, 1883. The railroad company named this town for a curve in its grade south of town shaped like an "elbow."

Fardale. Post office established January 5, 1876; discontinued September 27, 1880. Origin of the name not learned.

Farwell. Peak population (1930), 248. Post office name changed from Posen December 9, 1889. The original name of the town, Posen, was selected by Polish settlers. Because of a disagreement concerning nationality, the name was changed by petition to Farwell, which suggested the Danish word for good-bye, or "good-bye, Posen."

Funston. Post office established January 29, 1902; discontinued October 8, 1906. Origin of the name not learned.

Gage Valley. Post office established July 11, 1871; discontinued March 14, 1883. Named in honor of Alonzo Gage, early settler.

Glasgow. Post office established November 4, 1879; discontinued June 23, 1886. Probably named for Glasgow, Scotland, by an early settler.

Grantville. Post office established May 13, 1875; name changed to St. Libory May 16, 1878. Probably named in honor of President Ulysses S. Grant (1869-77).

Howard City. Corporate name for Boelus.

Kelso. Post office established December 14, 1873; discontinued April 14, 1894. Named for Kelso, Scotland. Former station on the Burlington Railroad.

Kenyon Spur. Former station on the Union Pacific Railroad located near Boelus.

Loup Fork. Post office established November 4, 1875; discontinued March 20, 1886. Named for a fork, or branch, of the Loup River.

Midway. Station on the Burlington Railroad named for its location midway between Farwell and St. Paul.

Mound. Post office established October 2, 1882; discontinued October 3, 1890. Origin of the name not learned.

Nowy Poznan. Most commonly called New Poznan or Poznan. Site of St. Anthony of

Padua Catholic Church and Polish colony of 1877, two miles southwest of Farwell. Church was moved into Farwell in 1925.

Nysted. Peak population (1890), 65. Post office established April 12, 1883; discontinued September 30, 1918. Mail served from Dannebrog. Former town and present community named for a Danish city where most of the residents once lived.

Paplin. Same location as Polander post office of 1887.

Polander. Post office established August 12, 1887; discontinued December 4, 1891. Named for Polish settlers in the area. More commonly known as Chojnice or Paplin.

Posen. Post office established December 17, 1887; name changed to Farwell December 9, 1889. Town named for a Polish province, where many of the settlers had resided.

Slavonia. Former locality, site of the first Catholic church in Howard County.

St. Libory. Peak population (1960), 175. Post office name changed from Grantville May 16, 1878. Town named for St. Libory, Illinois, where some of the settlers once lived.

St. Paul. Peak population (2000), 2,218. Post office established July 12, 1871. First settlement made by J. N. and N. J. Paul in the spring of 1871, and the town was laid out October 10, 1871. N. J. Paul suggested the name Athens, which postal authorities returned because of another, Athens post office in Nebraska. Senator Phineas W. Hitchcock then proposed St. Paul for the Paul brothers. St. Paul was made county seat upon formation of the county.

Tynerville. Post office established June 30, 1879; discontinued August 27, 1887. Origin of the name not learned.

Warsaw. Post office established September 14, 1873; discontinued November 25, 1885. Named by Polish immigrants for a Canadian town Warsaw, after Polish capital.

West Posen. Competing addition to Farwell platted in 1888.

Winsor. Some settlers preferred this name for Posen.

Wola. Post office established April 16, 1880; discontinued June 6, 1883. Probably named for Wola, Poland, former home of many of the settlers.

JEFFERSON COUNTY

Named in honor of Thomas Jefferson (1743-1826), U.S. president from 1801 to 1809. Jefferson County was first organized in 1864 after an election at Big Sandy. In 1867 the Territorial Legislature combined it with Jones County on the west. In 1871 another legislative act dissolved the two counties and the eastern part (Jones County) was named Jefferson. Jefferson County was attached to Gage County for judicial purposes between 1857 and 1864.

Antelope. Post office established March 25, 1868; name changed to Jefferson February 23, 1872. Named for antelope which once roamed this area.

Big Sandy. Pony Express Station No. 4 in Nebraska and an important home station. The Nebraska City road joined the Oregon Trail a short distance west of Big Sandy. Located three miles west of present Alexandria.

Big Sandy. Post office established January 10, 1865; name changed to Meridian August 5, 1870. Town named for nearby Big Sandy Creek. First town to be surveyed and platted (1868) in Jefferson County.

Bower. Peak population (1870), 25. Founder was Lewis C. Bower of Ohio, who settled in the area in 1870. Post office name changed from Bowerville January 26, 1872; discontinued January 14, 1901. See Bowerville.

Bowerville. Post office established April 18, 1870; name changed to Bower January 26, 1872. Named in honor of a local settler.

Buckley. Post office established May 7, 1888; name changed to Thompson March 9, 1892. Origin of the name not learned.

Caroline. Post office established April 18, 1870; discontinued April 24, 1872. Origin of the name not learned. Frederick Elwood was first postmaster.

Clayton. Station on the Union Pacific Railroad.

Cub Creek. Post office established April 18, 1870. Name changed to Plymouth April 24, 1872. Named for a nearby rock.

Daniel's Ranch. Post office established July 13, 1858; discontinued January 10, 1865, when name changed to Big Sandy. Named in honor of Daniel C. Patterson, who had the post office on his ranch.

Daykin. Peak population (1910), 220. Post office established August 22, 1887. Town named in honor of John Daykin, who owned the land on which the town was platted.

Diller. Peak population (1910), 506. Post office established April 5, 1880. Town named in honor of William H. Diller, early settler.

East Meridian. Former locality named for location east of the town of Meridian.

Endicott. Peak population (1890), 256. Post office established October 13, 1880. Town commemorates William E. Endicott, secretary of war in President Grover Cleveland's Cabinet.

Fairbury. Peak population (1960), 5,572. Post office established February 8, 1869. County seat, platted by Woodford G. McDowell and James B. Mattingly, was named by the former for his home in Fairbury, Illinois. A Russian-German colony was established on 27,000 acres of railroad land nearby. Fairbury was made county seat in election with Meridian in 1871.

Fort Helvey. Early fort established to protect the settlers from Indians. Frank, Thomas, and Jasper Helvey, early settlers in Jefferson County, suffered through Indian raids. Fort Helvey may have been located at one of their ranches.

Freeport. Settlement founded in 1867 across the Little Blue River from Jenkins' Mill (later Steele City). Settlers moved across the river after a flood in September of 1869. When the railroad arrived about 1872-73 Freeport ceased to exist.

Georgetown. Post office established May 16, 1870; discontinued March 13, 1871. Origin of the name not learned.

Gladstone. Peak population (1920), 105. Post office established August 17, 1887. Town named by M. A. Law, attorney of the Chicago, Rock Island and Pacific Railroad, for English statesman William E. Gladstone.

Grayson's. Name given Virginia City when the Overland Stage Lines and Wells Fargo took over on April 15, 1861.

Harbine. Peak population (1900), 242. Post office established June 21, 1887. Town named for Col. Thomas Harbine of Fairbury.

Hedrix. Station on the Union Pacific Railroad possibly named for Charles Edward Hedrix, former superintendent of the St. Joseph and Grand Island Railroad.

Helvey. Peak population (1930), 126. Post office established June 24, 1892; discontinued 1939. Town, located eight miles north and four miles west of Fairbury, was named in honor of Thomas Helvey, Jefferson County settler who located in the vicinity March 25, 1859.

Hughes. Station on the Chicago, Rock Island and Pacific Railroad, possibly named for Wallace T. Hughes, former attorney of the railroad.

Jansen. Peak population (1910), 308. Post office established February 25, 1887. Town named in honor of a Mennonite emigrant from Russia, Peter Jansen, who owned the townsite. Jansen was a state legislator (1899, 1911).

Jefferson. Post office name changed from Antelope February 23, 1872; discontinued June 1, 1874. Named for the county.

Jenkins' Mill. Post office name changed from Rock Creek October 24, 1867. Name changed to Steele City October 29, 1872. Named in honor of David C. Jenkins, first area settler, who had a toll bridge near the post office.

Kesterson. Post office established April 12, 1883; discontinued October 14, 1891. Named in honor of John C. Kesterson of Fairbury, early freighter on the Overland Trail.

Lemonville. Former locality in Overland Trail days.

Little Blue. Post office established December 6, 1861; discontinued August 25, 1873. Named for its location near this creek.

Little Sandy. Post office established February 14, 1870; discontinued August 25, 1873. Office located near Little Sandy Creek.

Marks' Mill. Former locality during Overland Trail days. Possibly named for the Rev. Ives Marks of Rose Creek.

Marysburgh. Post office established June 4, 1879; discontinued April 7, 1881. Origin of the name not learned.

Meridian. Peak population (1880), 50. Post office name changed from Big Sandy August 5, 1870; discontinued November 8, 1883. Town was made county seat upon formation of Jefferson County. Named for its location on the 6th principal meridian. Meridian lost county seat to Fairbury in election of 1871.

Oak Grove. Post office established February 14, 1861; discontinued October 30, 1866. Named for oak timber in the vicinity.

Plymouth. Peak population (1980), 506. Post office name changed from Cub Creek April 24, 1872. D. E. Jones, a Congregational minister and land agent for the Burlington Railroad, led a small group which located a site for a colony that would follow the ideals of the Pilgrims who founded Plymouth, Massachusetts. Settlers came from eastern states and Germany.

Powell. Peak population (1890), 300. Post office established May 2, 1883. Town named by the Nebraska Land and Town Company in honor of James D. Powell, Reuben Powell, and the Powell family, early settlers locating here in 1865.

Reynolds. Peak population (1890), 271. Post office name changed from Rose Creek September 27, 1880. Town named for the father of a Mr. Reynolds, contractor for the Burlington Railroad.

Rock Creek. Pony Express Station No. 2 in Nebraska. Located six miles southeast of Fairbury. Site of the shooting of David C. McCanles by James B. "Wild Bill" Hickok. It is now a state historical park operated by the Nebraska Game and Parks Commission.

Rock Creek. Post office established August 22, 1865; name changed to Jenkins' Mill October 24, 1867. Probably named for the Pony Express station near Rock Creek.

Rock House. Pony Express Station No. 1 in Nebraska, sometimes known as Otoe Station. Located in Jefferson County at its juncture with Kansas border and Gage County line, near the present town of Steele City.

Rose Creek. Post office established June 23, 1872; name changed to Reynolds September 27, 1880. Named for a nearby creek named for a Mr. Rose, local minister. Also called Rose Creek City.

Rudy. Union Pacific point established northwest of Steele City in 1952 for U.P. personnel. It was named for Rudy Grieshaber, clerk for C. E. Hedrix, superintendent of the St. Joseph and Grand Island Railroad, and later a trainmaster's clerk at Marysville, Kansas.

Shea. Post office established October 12, 1912; discontinued June 15, 1916. Abandoned town originally platted four miles west of present town of Diller on the O. F. Willems farm in 1907. Former "whistle stop" on the Burlington Railroad.

Slocumb. Post office established May 3, 1881; discontinued September 5, 1881. Origin of the name not learned.

Steelburg. Post office name changed from Steele City October 3, 1894; name changed back to Steele City February 20, 1896. See Steele City.

Steele City. Peak population (1890), 390. Post office name changed from Jenkins' Mill October 29, 1872; name changed to Steelburg October 3, 1894. Name changed from

Steelburg February 20, 1896. Town named by the Nebraska Land and Town Company in honor of Dudley M. Steele, president of the St. Joseph and Denver City Railroad.

Thompson. Peak population (1940), 56. Post office name changed from Buckley March 9, 1892; discontinued 1968. Named in honor of Isaac N. Thompson, pioneer settler who owned the townsite.

Virginia City. Pony Express Station No. 3 in Nebraska, four miles west of the present city of Fairbury.

Watt's Mill. Settlement during the Overland Trail days in Nebraska.

Whiskey Run. Another name for Pony Express station at Virginia City.

JOHNSON COUNTY

Named in honor of Col. Richard M. Johnson (1781-1850) of Kentucky, U. S. vice president from 1837 to 1841. County boundaries were defined by an act of the Legislature approved March 2, 1855. In 1857 Tecumseh was designated the official seat of justice, and the first regular election was held.

Albany. Never a post office but an early locality in Johnson County.

Bryson. Post office established June 7, 1866; name changed to Sterling March 16, 1870. Named in honor of a Mr. Bryson.

Butler. Post office established July 14, 1868; discontinued February 15, 1871. Probably named for J. H. Butler, an early settler killed by Indians.

Charleston. Community which never had a post office.

Cook. Peak population (1910), 387. Post office name changed from Spring Creek June 19, 1888. Named in honor of Andrew Cook, area landowner, by his son John William Cook. Platted during the coming of the railroads.

Crab Orchard. Peak population (1920), 278. Post office established April 26, 1864. Original town of Crab Orchard was about one mile west of the present site. Named for a crab apple orchard located on the townsite.

El Dorado. Probably another proposed town that never got beyond the platting stage.

Elk Creek. Peak population (1900), 347. Post office established April 12, 1872. Creek named for elk once seen nearby. Town named after the creek.

Ernst. Post office established in June 1890; discontinued September 27, 1890. Origin of the name is unknown.

Graf. Peak population (1910), 150. Post office established April 28, 1890. Named in honor of Lewis A. Graf, who donated the townsite.

Helena. Census not available. Post office established January 8, 1866; discontinued March 21, 1891. Platted and surveyed by W. L. Dunlap. This former town lost its identity when bypassed by the railroad. Origin of the name is unknown.

Kingston. Post office established July 24, 1858; discontinued September 16, 1862. Origin of the name not learned but probably for one of twenty-two places in the U.S. so identified.

Latrobe. Post office established July 7, 1863; discontinued April 10, 1884. Origin of the name not learned. There is also a Latrobe, Pennsylvania.

Lexington. Early Johnson County locality.

Loganville. Probably a proposed town that never got beyond the platting stage.

Otoe Mission. Post office established September 17, 1857; name changed to Stewards March 12, 1858. Probably named for an Oto Indian mission.

Smartville. Post office established September 29, 1879; name changed to St. Mary February 28, 1908. Named for the Smart brothers who kept a general store. Name changed when St. Mary's parochial school was built.

Spring Creek. Post office established August 26, 1868; name changed to Cook June 19, 1888. Named for the creek on which it was located.

Sterling. Peak population (1920), 804. Post office name changed from Bryson March 16, 1870. Town named by John Mann, one of its first settlers, who came from Sterling, Illinois.

Stewards. Post office name changed from Otoe Mission March 12, 1858; discontinued October 19, 1858. Origin of the name has not been learned.

St. Mary. Peak population (1910), 100. Post office name changed from Smartville February 28, 1908. Named after a Catholic church in the community.

Tecumseh. Peak population (1940), 2,104. Post office established January 29, 1857. Before a post office was established, the town was called Frances, for the wife of Col. Richard Johnson for whom the county was named. A year later the name was changed to honor the Shawnee leader, Tecumseh, killed in battle by Colonel Johnson in 1813. Platted by John Maulden in 1856 and made county seat by legislative act February 13, 1857.

Turkey Creek. Post office moved from Pawnee County August 22, 1860; discontinued July 27, 1861. Named for creek on which it was located.

Vesta. Peak population (1930), 252. Post office established September 7, 1858. Named by William H. Strong, first postmaster, for a school pupil of his in Massachusetts.

Weston. Proposed town that never went beyond the platting stage.

Woolseyville. Post office established April 13, 1871; discontinued March 25, 1872. Named in honor of Wright Woolsey, first postmaster.

KEARNEY COUNTY

Named for Fort Kearny, which commemorated Maj. Gen. Stephen Watts Kearny (1794-1848). County organized and the boundaries defined by an act approved January 10, 1860.

Axtell. Peak population (1990), 707. Post office established January 14, 1884. Named in honor of a passenger train engineer on the Burlington Railroad. Swedish settlement known for its many windmills.

Blaineville. Post office established February 25, 1880, discontinued July 1, 1895. Probably named for James Blaine (1830-93), secretary of state under President Rutherford B. Hayes.

Carpenterville. Post office established April 21, 1875; discontinued October 5, 1875. Named in honor of Thomas Carpenter, first postmaster.

Centoria. Post office established April 14, 1875; discontinued April 5, 1878. Name was probably coined because the town is geographically near the center of the U.S. Name suggested by Moses H. Sydenham, first postmaster. There was a fanciful movement at the time to place the U.S. capital here.

Central City. Locality platted two miles west of Fort Kearny by a company from St. Joseph, Missouri, which included Colonel Scott, a Mr. Pfoutts, and Alex Constant. Named for its central location. Site later became Kearney City.

Christena. Post office established May 23, 1879; discontinued April 2, 1887. Named for a queen of Sweden by a Scandinavian colony which settled here.

Dobytown. See Kearney City.

Dogtown. Name of Valley City before a post office was established. Named for an area prairie dog village.

Eaton. Post office established January 26, 1874; discontinued January 2, 1879. Origin of the name has not been learned.

Folsomdale. Post office established September 23, 1886; discontinued December 24, 1890. Origin of the name has not been learned.

Fort Childs. After the first Fort Kearny was moved from Otoe County in 1848, the new army post was named for Col. Thomas Childs, father-in-law of engineer Lt. Daniel P. Woodbury. Colonel Childs participated in the battle of Monterrey during the Mexican War. A few months later the post name was changed to Fort Kearny.

Fort Kearny. Name changed from Fort Childs. Honors Maj. Gen. Stephen Watts Kearny (1794-1848), commander in the War of 1812 and in the Mexican War California campaign. Fort Kearny moved from Otoe County in 1848 and relocated on the Platte River. It protected from the Indians the settlers in Nebraska, the travelers on the California and Oregon Trails, and the construction workers on the Union Pacific Railroad. Fort Kearny was abandoned in 1871. Today the site is a state historical park operated by the Nebraska Game and Parks Commission.

Fort Kearny. This was Pony Express Station No. 13 in Nebraska.

Fredericksburg. Post office established May 10, 1876; discontinued January 5, 1887. Community settled by Danes, probably named for former king of Denmark.

Graveldale. Station on the Union Pacific Railroad probably named for gravel pits nearby.

Harmony. Post office established July 19, 1880; discontinued September 14, 1895. Named for the sentiments of the patrons.

Heartwell. Peak population (1930), 182. Post office established January 14, 1884. Town named in honor of James B. Heartwell of Hastings. Town settled by Scotch and Irish.

Junctionville. Name proposed for Valley City before a post office was established.

Kearney City. Post office established July 5, 1861; discontinued June 15, 1871. Former town derived its name from nearby Fort Kearny. First courthouse was established here; however, it lost the county seat to Lowell in election June 17, 1872. Also called "Dobytown," Kearney City was at one time the principal outfitting point west of the Missouri River. Several buildings in the area were of adobe construction, hence the nickname.

Kearney Station. This was Pony Express Station No. 12 in Nebraska, located one and one-half miles northeast of Lowell.

Keefer. Former station on the Burlington Railroad.

Keene. Peak population (1940), 102. Post office established May 10, 1871; discontinued 1945. Mail served from Axtell. Village named for a workman who lived there.

Koller. Station on the Union Pacific Railroad.

Latrobe. A post office when in Johnson County, but when removed to Kearney County the office was withdrawn.

Lowell. Peak population (1880), 300. Post office established February 5, 1872; discontinued 1943. Mail served from Gibbon. Named in honor of poet James Russell Lowell (1819-91). Lowell won county seat from Kearney City June 17, 1872, but lost it to Minden in an election November 11, 1876. U.S. Land Office located here from 1872 to 1874. Town dwindled in population after land office was removed.

May. Post office established March 15, 1877; discontinued February 4, 1888. Origin of the name not learned. First postmaster was Daniel Emil.

Minden. Peak population (2000), 2,964. Post office established July 13, 1876. Fred Bredemier, first postmaster, named the town after his home of Minden, Germany. The townsite was selected in December 1876 by five men who conceived the idea of forming a town while working in a broom corn field in September 1875. Each bought a quarter section at the center of the county. Joe Hull, originator of the idea, paid the Union Pacific Railroad $3.50 an acre. Minden won county seat in election with Lowell on November 11, 1876.

Mirage. Post office established June 18, 1875; discontinued February 4, 1884.

Motala. Station on the Burlington Railroad located near Minden.

Newark. Peak population (1880), 125. Post office established October 22, 1879; discontinued 1954. First settlement in this vicinity made by A. J. Lindbeck in May 1877. A. E. Touzalin, general manager of the Burlington Railroad, suggested the name Newark.

Norman. Peak population (1920), 127. Post office established September 7, 1887. Town named in honor of John and Carl Norman, who owned the eighty acres on which town was built.

Osco. Post office established June 21, 1875; discontinued March 15, 1901. Possibly named for Osco, Illinois, or by Danish settlers for a place in Denmark.

Park. Post office established July 13, 1876; discontinued April 6, 1880. Origin of the name has not been learned.

Reservation. Post office established April 9, 1878; discontinued June 27, 1878. Probably named for its closeness to the Fort Kearny military reservation.

Snowflake. Post office established January 19, 1881; discontinued February 28, 1884. Possibly named for a snowfall.

Valley City. Census not available. Post office established August 7, 1862; discontinued May 31, 1867. Former town named for its location in the Platte River Valley. Platted by John Lott and Amos Hook. A stopping point for the Overland stages two miles from Lowell.

Walker's Ranch. Stopping point for stages on divide road to Republican Valley. Named for Charles Walker, the owner of the ranch.

Wilcox. Peak population (1910), 382. Post office established November 30, 1886. Town named in honor of Henry Wilcox, one of its founders.

Zyba. Post office established August 10, 1880; discontinued February 16, 1888. Possibly named for a local settler.

KEITH COUNTY

Named in honor of Morrill C. Keith of North Platte. Keith was the grandfather of Keith Neville (1884-1959), governor of Nebraska from 1917 to 1919. Boundaries were defined by an act approved February 27, 1873. County was organized on May 3, 1873.

Alkali. Post office established December 6, 1883; name changed to Paxton December 22, 1885. Named for the alkaline content of the soil.

Alkali Lake. Nebraska Pony Express Station No. 25. It is not definitely located, but supposedly two miles southwest of Paxton. A Dr. Clark in 1860 called it Pikes Peak Station.

Belmar. Census not available. Post office established April 2, 1910; discontinued 1941. Origin of the name of this former town not learned. There is also a Belmar, New Jersey.

Bertha. Census not available. Post office established August 5, 1901; discontinued 1933. Former town named in honor of Bertha Matthews, daughter of Francis Matthews, first postmaster.

Bevier. Former station on the Union Pacific Railroad.

Bosler. Former station on the Union Pacific Railroad located west of Ogallala. Probably named for the Bosler brothers of the Ogallala Cattle Company.

Broganville. Station on the Union Pacific Railroad.

Brule. Peak population (1970), 423. Post office established August 27, 1886. Founded by Major and Mrs. I. R. Burton, this town was named for the Brule Sioux Indians.

Camp Ogallala. This U.S. Army outpost was a one-company tent detachment near the railroad station at Ogallala. Its signal service in Nebraska was the protection of stage lines and stations on the Union Pacific Railroad serving the Platte Valley.

Diamond Springs. Nebraska Pony Express Station No. 27 located one mile west of Brule.

Georgetown. This name was given by the Public Relations Department of the Tri-County project to the town which housed workers and construction headquarters at the George P. Kingsley Dam site north of Ogallala. Because many Georges figured in the construction, it is not really known for whom the town was named. These men all contributed to its building: Senator George W. Norris; George Kingsley, in whose honor Kingsley Dam was named; George E. Johnson, chief engineer and general manager of Tri-County; George Carter, Tri-County resident engineer in charge of the dam construction; George Youmans, engineer for Morris-Knudsen; and George P. Leonard, superintendent for Minneapolis Dredging Company-Martin Wunderlich Company, firms building the dam and control structures. Several hundred people lived here at the peak of construction, many of them in trailers. Active in late 1930s, it was abandoned and the site was inundated in 1941 by North Platte River waters which formed Lake McConaughy.

Gill's. Relay station and Pony Express Station No. 26 in Nebraska. It was also the point of the Texas Trail crossing of the 1870s. Sometimes called Sand Hill. The exact site is unknown, but is thought to have been one and one-half miles south of the present Ogallala.

Glenrose. Post office established March 13, 1911; moved to Arthur County May 25, 1916. Locally descriptive name for wild roses growing in a valley.

Irvine. Post office established January 11, 1886; discontinued November 13, 1889. Origin of the name has not been learned.

Keystone. Peak population (1910), 150. Post office established April 25, 1891. W. A. Paxton, early cattle owner, used the keystone brand, and owned the Keystone Ranch. When the town was platted, it took the same name.

Kingsley. Station on the Union Pacific Railroad, probably named in honor of George P. Kingsley, responsible for Kingsley Dam being built on the Platte River.

Korty. Station on the Union Pacific Railroad named in honor of Louis Henry Korty of Omaha, superintendent of the telegraph division for the railway. He was a pioneer in the introduction of the telephone in the West.

La Ruhe. Post office established December 21, 1885; discontinued April 29, 1886. Probably named in honor of William S. Ruhe, first postmaster. How "la" originated is not known.

Lemoyne. Peak population (1960), 90. Post office established 1882. Town named in honor of Lemoyne Jacobs, rancher who donated right-of-way land to the Union Pacific Railroad.

Lewellen. Post office established July 7, 1887; moved to Garden County December 4, 1891. Named in honor of Frank Lewellen, early settler.

Lynden. Post office established October 11, 1902; discontinued December 12, 1902. Origin of the name not learned.

Martin. Station on the Union Pacific Railroad located near Lemoyne.

McGeath. Former station on the Union Pacific Railroad.

Nevens. Union Pacific Railroad station.

Ogallala. Peak population (1980), 5,638. Post office established July 11, 1873. This county seat derives its name from the Oglala band of the Lakota Sioux Indians. Ogallala developed as a cattle shipping point on the Union Pacific Railroad. The town was also a destination of trail drives from Texas. Herds began arriving in 1867 and continued until about 1885.

Oren. Post office established August 13, 1906; discontinued January 31, 1919. Presumably named in honor of Oren F. Chesbro, first postmaster, or for his son, Oren Chesbro.

Paxton. Peak population (2000), 614. Post office name changed from Alkali December 22, 1885. Town named in honor of W. A. Paxton of Omaha, who had cattle interests in the vicinity.

Pickard. Post office established January 11, 1886; discontinued July 6, 1896. Possibly named in honor of William Pickard, first postmaster.

Plano. Former station on the Union Pacific Railroad.

Roscoe. Census not available. Post office established, 1909. A station on the Union Pacific Railroad established in 1868. Town platted in 1909. Origin of the name not learned. Post office discontinued 1977. Mail served from Paxton.

Ruthton. Station on the Union Pacific Railroad.

Sarben. Peak population (1950), 100. Post office established July 29, 1910. Town named for the first six letters of Nebraska in reverse order. Post office discontinued 1973. Mail served from Paxton.

Tredway. Post office established March 23, 1906; discontinued August 13, 1906. Origin of the name not learned.

Triangle. Post office established July 10, 1906; discontinued September 30, 1910. Possibly named for the Triangle Ranch or for a cattle brand.

Tyghe. Post office established August 25, 1885; discontinued October 27, 1887. Origin of the name not learned.

Zella. Post office established February 18, 1910; moved to Arthur County June 1, 1915. Named in honor of the wife of Edmund Stone, first postmaster.

KEYA PAHA COUNTY

Created by legislative enactment November 4, 1884. Previously part of Brown County and prior to that, of Holt County. Named for the Keya Paha River in the northeastern part of the county. River's name derived from the Sioux title of a hill: ke'-ya, turtle; pa-ha', hill; wa-kpi', river—or Turtle Hill River.

Adrian. Census not available. Post office established September 25, 1884; discontinued November 2, 1886. Former town probably named for a local settler. There are places in eleven states with this name.

Brewer. Peak population (1890), 20. Post office established February 15, 1881; discontinued April 29, 1887. Former town named by Postmistress Elsy E. Kuhn for her father, a Mr. Brewer.

Brockman. Post office name changed from McClean, 1884; name changed to Brocksburg November 22, 1899. See Brocksburg.

Brocksburg. Peak population (1910), 60. Post office name changed from Brockman November 22, 1899; discontinued 1957. Mail served from Jamison. Former town originally called Brockman. Postal authorities changed name to Brocksburg. Town named in honor of Henry Brockman, early settler.

Burton. Peak population (1940), 104. Post office established June 5, 1884. Named in honor of George W. Burton, general merchant, when the county was first settled. Burton vied with Springview for county seat March 24, 1885, and lost bitter election. Post office discontinued 1973. Mail served from Springview.

Carns. Census not available. Post office name changed from Elm Grove December 15, 1879; discontinued 1943. Named by postal authorities, probably in honor of Lt. Gov. Edmund Crawford Carns.

Carrie. Post office established June 4, 1884; discontinued August 5, 1884. Probably named for Carrie Muncil, second postmaster.

Cedarville. Post office established April 6, 1891; discontinued March 5, 1896. Probably named for the cedar trees growing in the vicinity.

Darnall. Peak population (1890), 10. Post office established August 22, 1884; discontinued October 24, 1891. Former town named in honor of Daniel Darnall, first postmaster, who had the office in his home.

Elders. Post office established August 22, 1884; discontinued March 10, 1886. Origin of the name not learned.

Elm Grove. Because the name Carns had been used elsewhere, Elm Grove was selected.

Enterprise. Census not available. Post office established July 10, 1884; discontinued September 30, 1928. Former town named by the settlers for their own energetic ways.

Gouldale. Listed as a locality but never recorded as a post office.

Ira. Post office established February 8, 1904; rescinded June 13, 1904. Origin of the name not learned.

Jamison. Peak population (1950), 200. Post office established June 9, 1903. Town named in honor of S. P. Jamison, founder and one-time sheriff of Boyd County. Post office discontinued 1973. Mail served from Newport.

Lattin. Post office established May 8, 1884; discontinued December 14, 1892. Named in honor of William H. Lattin, first postmaster.

Lomo. Peak population (1890), 38. Post office established May 8, 1882; discontinued May 18, 1895. Origin of the name of this former town is unknown. In Spanish, it means "back" or "spine," or "a ridge between two furrows."

Lutes. Peak population (1890), 40. Post office established June 17, 1884; discontinued January 13, 1906. Former town named in honor of John Lutes, first postmaster.

Marlbank. Census not available. Post office established February 5, 1885; discontinued August 29, 1917. Former town named by Ellen G. Phelps but for what person or place is unknown.

McClean. Post office established October 10, 1881; name changed to Brockman 1884. Probably named for Frank McLain, local settler. It was misspelled McClean.

McGuire. Listed as a locality but never recorded as a post office.

Meadville. Peak population (1950), 29. Post office established October 29, 1883; discontinued 1960. Former town named in honor of Merrit I. Mead, first postmaster.

Mills. Peak population (1900), 58. Post office established September 1, 1885. Town named for a grist mill once operated here.

Munt. Peak population (1890), 12. Post office established October 9, 1882; discontinued March 21, 1896. Former town named in honor of James Munt, first postmaster.

Nesbit. Post office established August 27, 1885; discontinued April 8, 1887. Named in honor of Robert W. Nesbit, first postmaster.

Norden. Peak population (1930 and 1940), 176. Post office established August 5, 1884. A Mr. Bastedo, the first settler, named this town after his former German home near the North Sea. Post office made a rural branch of Springview 1974.

Pekin. Post office established February 1, 1886; discontinued January 10, 1901. Probably named for Pekin, Illinois.

Penbrook. Post office moved from Cherry County October 3, 1892; moved back to Cherry County February 13, 1898. Origin of the name not learned.

Pinecamp. Census not available. Post office established March 2, 1885; discontinued 1935.

Rimrock. Post office established February 20, 1886; discontinued March 11, 1886. Named for a nearby rock formation.

Riverview. Census not available. Post office established June 13, 1912; discontinued 1956. Former village named for its view of the Niobrara River.

Sanford. Post office established February 5, 1885; discontinued June 10, 1891. Named in honor of Dan Sanford, first postmaster.

Simpson. Census not available. Post office established May 8, 1882; discontinued June 30, 1925. Former town named in honor of Henry J. Simpson, first postmaster, who also homesteaded here in 1880.

Springview. Peak population (1940), 347. Post office established July 21, 1885. County seat said to be named for a spring near the town square.

Stephenson. Census not available. Post office established October 17, 1884; discontinued March 31, 1890. Former hamlet named in honor of William J. Stephenson, first postmaster.

Tiffany. Locality sometimes listed as a post office, but according to U.S. Post Office Directory, it never was one. Site later became the Enterprise post office. Named in honor of J. N. Tiffany, who came from Pennsylvania.

KIMBALL COUNTY

Named in honor of Thomas L. Kimball (1831-99), vice president and general manager of the Union Pacific Railroad. County was organized in 1888. Kimball was formed from Cheyenne County by vote November 6, 1888.

Adams. Former railroad station named for Adam Ames, official of the Union Pacific Railroad, but name changed to honor his brother Oliver. There was some confusion in freight addressed to Adams in Gage County, Nebraska.

Adrel. Post office established March 12, 1907; discontinued May 21, 1907. Origin of the name not ascertained. Anton Gwartney was first postmaster.

Antelopeville. Post office established July 27, 1882; name changed to Kimball October 23, 1885. Named for antelope in the vicinity. Name changed to Kimball to avoid confusion with another Antelopeville in the state.

Beacon. Post office name changed from Parker May 1, 1913; discontinued August 14, 1915. Named by Fred Overton, postmaster, because one could see many miles away from this point.

Bennett. Former Union Pacific station named for James Gordon Bennett of the *New York Herald* or for a Colonel Bennett, superintendent of the Pullman Palace Car Company. Located east of Kimball.

Bethel. Post office established February 27, 1905; discontinued June 14, 1924. Named after a local sod church, dedicated by a pioneer minister for Bethel in Palestine. It means "house of God."

Bushnell. Peak population (1930), 341. Post office name changed from Orkney May 18, 1895. Named in honor of Cornelius Bushnell, civil engineer on the Union Pacific.

Crossbar. Post office established April 16, 1908; discontinued November 30, 1912. Named for cattle brand used by Elmer Johnson on whose ranch the post office was located.

Dix. Peak population (1960), 420. Post office established March 4, 1887. Town in the Lodgepole Valley named for Dixon, Illinois. Because there already was an office named Dixon, postal authorities shortened the word to Dix. Townsite was on land owned by Margaret Robertson, who came from Dixon, Illinois. An alternate explanation is that the town was named for Dr. John A. Dix, employed by the Union Pacific Railroad. Town platted by C. T. Robertson. Dix lost county seat to Kimball on January 22, 1889.

Dye. Post office moved from Cheyenne County June 5, 1913; discontinued January 30, 1923. Named in honor of Lydia Dye, first postmistress.

Field. Former station on the Union Pacific Railroad.

Gifford. Post office established March 31, 1911; discontinued July 31, 1918. Named in honor of William Gifford, homesteader of the land where this former office was located.

Hodges. Post office established April 18, 1912; discontinued May 14, 1921. Named in honor of Earl R. Hodges, first postmaster.

Jacinto. Station was on the Union Pacific Railroad near Dix. In Spanish it means a flower, a hyacinth. Named by J. O. Brinkerhoff, general manager of the Union Pacific Railroad.

Kaufman. Post office established February 24, 1911; discontinued December 1, 1915. Named in honor of Cora B. Kauffman, first postmistress.

Kimball. Peak population (1960), 4,384. Post office name changed from Antelopeville October 23, 1885. City honors Thomas L. Kimball, vice president and general manager of the Union Pacific Railroad. Kimball made county seat in selection wlth Dix January 22, 1889. At one time it was the southern terminus of the stage route that passed through the Wildcat Range to Gering on the North Platte River.

Oliver. Union Pacific station named in honor of Oliver Ames, contractor and builder on the Union Pacific Railroad.

Orkney. Post office established September 22, 1886; name changed to Bushnell May 18,

1895. Town probably named for a local settler, a railroad official, or for the Orkney Islands of Great Britain.

Owasco. Station on the Union Pacific Railroad named because it was opposite the Circle Arrow Ranch; "O" represents the circle and "co" represents the company. Located east of Kimball.

Parker. Post office established May 21, 1907; name changed to Beacon May 1, 1913. Named in honor of Harold H. Parker, first postmaster.

Smeed. Union Pacific Railroad station named for an Irish foreman on a horse ranch owned by the Creighton interests of Omaha. Located southwest of Bushnell.

Troy. Post office established May 3, 1911; discontinued November 15, 1919. Named in honor of Link Troy, first postmaster.

KNOX COUNTY

Named in honor of Maj. Gen. Henry Knox (1750-1806) but originally called L'Eau Qui Court. Renamed Knox by the Legislature at the request of Representative David Quimby on February 21, 1873. County was established and its boundaries defined by an act approved February 10, 1857, and redefined January 13, 1860.

Addison. Post office established October 21, 1880; discontinued August 13, 1904. Origin of the name not learned. There are places in nine other states with this name.

Anawan. Post office established February 1, 1882; discontinued March 11, 1882. Name may have been coined from two proper first names.

Armstrong. Post office established June 6, 1880; discontinued August 31, 1911. Named in honor of J. L. Armstrong, first to make a land claim with the U.S. Land Office here.

Arthur. Post office established February 15, 1883; discontinued December 8, 1887. Possibly named in honor of President Chester A. Arthur (1881-85).

Bazile Mills. Peak population (1900), 175. Post office established January 10, 1879; discontinued 1951. Mail served from Creighton. Town built on Bazile Creek, for which it was named. Creek probably named for Bazeilles, Ardennes, France, by French settlers. A grist mill and the first woolen mill in the state were established here.

Bloomfield. Peak population (1940), 1,467. Post office established October 16, 1890. Town named in honor of Bloomfield Dyer, who once owned the land on which the town is now located.

Blyville. Peak population (1900), 61. Post office established January 26, 1874; discontinued August 8, 1898. Former village said to be named in honor of George W. Bly, early settler.

Bohemian. Locality listed in Rand McNally Atlas of 1882.

Bonhomme City. Post office established June 4, 1854; discontinued October 3, 1861. Office was reestablished later across the Missouri River in South Dakota. Name is French in origin.

Breckenridge. Post office established May 2, 1857; discontinued May 2, 1859. Possibly named in honor of John Breckenridge (1821-75), U.S. vice president from 1857 to 1861.

Center. Peak population (1920), 198. Post office name changed from Plum Valley January 17, 1902. County seat named for its location in the center of the county. It was founded to end a forty-year dispute among four county seat claimants—Niobrara, Bloomfield, Creighton, and Verdigre. A survey established the geographical center of the county in a cornfield; each of two owners agreed to contribute twenty acres to the new county seat. The site was platted in 1901 by James Lovell. The courthouse, also founded in 1909, was replaced in 1934.

Christmanville. Post office established May 29, 1882; discontinued December 13, 1882. Possibly named in honor of Walter Christman, former postmaster.

Cline. Post office established November 23, 1882; discontinued January 7, 1884. Possibly named in honor of Samuel Cline, first postmaster.

Coker. Post office established June 27, 1890; discontinued May 22, 1891. Origin of the name has not been learned.

Creighton. Peak population (1970), 1,461. Post office established August 21, 1871. One source says town named by a Mr. Bruce in honor of John A. Creighton of Omaha, founder of the John A. Creighton Medical College at Creighton University. Another source says John and Matt Wagoner, also of Omaha, were involved in naming the place. Town platted by Pioneer Town Site Company.

Crockett. Post office established July 30, 1890; discontinued February 1, 1892. Possibly named in honor of Charles Crockett, first postmaster.

Crofton. Peak population (1980), 948. Post office established June 18, 1893. One source reports J. T. Pierce named the town after Crofton Court, a place he owned in England. He spent time and money in bringing the railroad to town. According to another source, a Mr. Pierce came to America after the Civil War and bought land for an Englishman named Crofton. When the site was platted, Pierce named the town for the British owner, who never visited the U.S.

Croy's Grove. Locality listed in early Knox County history just north of Blyville.

Dobson's Landing. Former community named in honor of D. B. Dobson, early settler. Located on the Missouri River.

Dolphin. Post office established August 27, 1886; name changed to Halestown April 1, 1890. Named in honor of John Dolphin, first postmaster.

Dressen. Post office established June 11, 1890; discontinued June 18, 1891. Named in honor of Peter Dressen, first postmaster.

Dukeville. Post office established December 8, 1875; discontinued August 31, 1911. Named after Herko Amenzo "Duke" Koster, area pioneer who carried the mail to and from Dukeville in the 1870s.

Floyd. Post office established August 10, 1885; name changed to Loyd October 20, 1885. Origin of the name not learned. First postmaster was Leroy Middlekauf.

Fort Mitchell. This was the first Fort Mitchell established before Nebraska became a territory. It was founded at the junction of the Niobrara and Missouri rivers as a trading post in 1833 by Narcisse LeClerc and named for D. D. Mitchell, then an official of the American Fur Company and later superintendent of Indian Affairs at St. Louis. He later participated in the Indian Treaty Council of 1851 at the mouth of Horse Creek in what is now Scotts Bluff County.

Frankfort. Post office established December 24, 1859; discontinued October 20, 1899. This Indian trading post founded by S. Loeber in 1856 was named in honor of Frankfort, Germany. Town was eventually disbanded after severe floods.

Grimton. Locality on Middle Branch Creek named for homesteaders Henry and Catherine Bowers Grimm, who came to Nebraska in 1872.

Halestown. Post office name changed from Dolphin April 1, 1890; discontinued January 12, 1895. Origin of the name not learned.

Herrick. Post office established April 17, 1877; discontinued November 3, 1905. Named in honor of Charles Herrick, a local settler.

Jelen. Census not available. Post office established February 8, 1904; discontinued January 31, 1916. Former town named in honor of Anton Jelen, first postmaster, who maintained the post office in his store.

Kemma. Post office established February 20, 1870; discontinued October 5, 1894. Name is probably Swedish in origin.

Knoxville. Post office established June 20, 1879; discontinued 1931. Named by William Darnell for his former home of Knoxville, Illinois.

LeBlanc. Post office established March 4, 1902; discontinued November 30, 1912. Named in honor of G. A. LeBlanc, merchant and first postmaster.

Lindy. Peak population (1960), 45. Mail served from Bloomfield. Community probably named in honor of Charles Lindbergh, aviator who made the first non-stop flight from New York to Paris in 1927. Founded by George Tews.

Loyd. Post office name changed from Floyd October 20, 1885; discontinued April 14, 1892. Origin of the name not learned.

Lucerne. Former locality probably named for Lucerne, Switzerland.

Manning. Post office established January 14, 1886; discontinued December 31, 1909. Origin of the name not learned.

Mansfield. Projected townsite named after Mansfield, Ohio, by homesteader George W. Quimby.

Mars. Post office established March 17, 1886; discontinued December 31, 1909. Origin of the name has not been learned.

Middlebranch. Post office established February 20, 1879; moved to Holt County June 19, 1882. Probably named for the middle branch of the Verdigris Creek.

Midland. Locality in early county history.

Millerboro. Peak population (1890), 65. Post office established June 28, 1874; discontinued May 31, 1904. Former village named in honor of Capt. J. M. Miller, first settler.

Morgan. Post office established December 30, 1890; discontinued March 13, 1896. Origin of the name not learned.

Morrilville. Post office established April 2, 1883; discontinued May 7, 1904. Possibly named in honor of Holman McMorrill, first postmaster. One "l" left off the name, as well as the "Mc," probably to shorten it.

Niobrara. Peak population (1930), 761. Post office established August 12, 1859. Named after the Niobrara River, it is situated at its confluence with the Missouri River. Omaha and Ponca Indians named the Niobrara—"running water." The county seat, located here by an act of the Legislature approved February 14, 1877, was moved to Center about 1901.

Orient. Post office established April 25, 1884; discontinued July 20, 1890. Probably named for Asiatic countries or for one of eight places in the U.S. with this name.

Peoria. Post office established November 9, 1883; discontinued August 3, 1893. Probably named for Peoria, Illinois.

Pishelville. Peak population (1910), 42. Post office name changed from Running Water August 11, 1872; discontinued January 15, 1927. Former town named in honor of Anton Pischel, early Czech settler, town founder, and first postmaster. The "c" was omitted in final spelling.

Plum Valley. Post office established April 30, 1875; name changed to Center January 17, 1902. Named for wild plum thickets.

Reidsville. Census not available. Post office established June 10, 1872; discontinued February 6, 1880. Former village named for Charles Reid, first postmaster.

Richling. Post office name changed from Verdigris Bridge September 2, 1890; discontinued May 24, 1895. Probably named in honor of Lorenzo Richling, first postmaster.

Roudeu. Post office established January 20, 1882; discontinued November 11, 1882. Named in honor of Ole Roudeu, first postmaster.

Running Water. Post office established, 1858; name changed to Pishelville August 11, 1872. Indian name for the Niobrara River.

Ruth. Post office established September 18, 1902; discontinued June 15, 1913. Origin of the name not learned.

Santee. Peak population (1980), 388. Post office established September 9, 1865; discontinued 1956. Mail served from Niobrara. Town named for the Santee Sioux. It centered around the Santee mission and normal training school that operated until 1928.

Secret Grove. Listed as a locality five miles southwest of Blyville.

Shylock. Post office established April 24, 1860; discontinued July 27, 1863. Origin of the name not learned.

Sparta. Post office established February 12, 1880; discontinued October 31, 1912. Probably named for Sparta, Illinois, or for Sparta, Wisconsin. Name itself derived from the ancient Greek city.

Sweden. Post office established, 1872; discontinued November 1, 1886. Named by Swedish settlers for their native country.

Talbot. Post office established November 7, 1882; discontinued November 23, 1884. Probably named in honor of Richard C. Talbot, first postmaster.

Tewsville. Tewsville grew up around a general store operated by Fritz Tews, brother of Lindy founder George Tews. In 1928 a dance hall (now gone) was built there. The Tews store burned in 1944.

Thorson. Post office established June 13, 1884; name changed to Wausa November 24, 1890. Named in honor of Theodore Thorson, first postmaster.

Trudell. Post office established October 9, 1906; discontinued October 4, 1907. Origin of the name not learned.

Vasa. Former name of Wausa. Changed from Thorson in 1885.

Venus. Peak population (1890), 32. Post office established August 9, 1880; discontinued 1960. Mail served from Orchard. Community named by Sylvanus Whitmore for the beauty of the countryside.

Verdel. Peak population (1910, 1920), 162. Post office established August 5, 1895. Named for daughter of the town's founder, G. A. LeBlanc, also postmaster of the town of LeBlanc.

Verdigre. Peak population (1930), 618. Post office name changed from Verdigris Valley June 20, 1884. Town named after Verdigris Creek. The name, French in origin, refers to a green or greenish-blue pigment made from copper acetate, once used as a dye.

Verdigris Bridge. Post office established, 1879; name changed to Richling September 2, 1890. See Verdigre.

Verdigris Valley. Post office established June 18, 1874; name changed to Verdigre June 20, 1884. See Verdigre.

Wall's Mill. Post office established June 3, 1879; discontinued January 15, 1880. Possibly named in honor of Nancy M. Wall, first postmistress.

Walnut. Census not available. Post office established September 22, 1894; discontinued 1956. Former town named for nearby black walnut trees.

Walnut Grove. Post office established January 11, 1875; discontinued July 6, 1882. Named for a grove of walnut trees.

Watson. Post office established February 5, 1892; discontinued September 7, 1905. Named in honor of Douglas Watson, first postmaster.

Wausa. Peak population (1930), 754. Post office name changed from Vasa November 24, 1890. Two Lutheran ministers, Foglelstrom and Torell, named the town for Gustavus Vasa, first Protestant king of Sweden. The spelling of Wausa, a combination of the king's name and the letters "U.S.A," was adopted to conform with the pronunciation of the name.

Weigand. Post office established February 20, 1883; discontinued January 25, 1906. Probably named in honor of Mr. and Mrs. Leonard Weigand. Mrs. Weigand was first postmistress.

Welch. Post office established April 25, 1875; discontinued July 26, 1883. Origin of the name has not been learned.

Winnetoon. Peak population (1910), 220. Post office established September 22, 1891. Town named by W. F. Fitch, railroad official, after a farm in Dane County, Wisconsin, owned by Nathan Deane.

LANCASTER COUNTY

Named after the town and county of Lancaster in Pennsylvania, from Lancaster County, England. Boundaries were defined by an act of the Legislature approved March 6, 1855. County was reestablished and its boundaries redefined January 26, 1856.

Agnew. Peak population (1910), 60. Post office established August 17, 1886. Village named in honor of William James Agnew, a railroad contractor and later conductor on the Union Pacific Railroad.

Aldo Junction. It was established in 1983 by Missouri Pacific and Union Pacific where their branch lines crossed south of Lincoln as interchange trackage to facilitate Crete Mills flour shipments to West Coast. Named for Aldo Hoffmeier, traffic manager of Crete Mills.

Arbor. Post office established October 2, 1894; discontinued June 21, 1900. Named by Joy Morton, son of J. Sterling Morton, who inspired Arbor Day. Arbor Lodge, the Morton home, is a state historical park in Nebraska City.

Arnold Heights. Suburb northwest of Lincoln, site of former Lincoln Army Air Field (1942-45) and Lincoln Air Force Base (1952-66). See Huskerville.

Asylum. Post office established March 16, 1880; discontinued June 14, 1910. Location near the state asylum.

Athens. Post office established February 12, 1889; name changed to University Place July 30, 1889. Probably named for one of fifteen Athenses in the U.S.

Bedford. A proposed town that never got beyond promotion stage.

Belmont. Suburb of Lincoln located on an elevation north of that city. Probably named for one of eighteen Belmonts in the U.S. A federal land grant issued in 1868 for a proposed Baptist community did not produce an actual settlement. The Episcopal Church opened the Worthington Military Academy in the Belmont area in 1892, but the school was destroyed by an explosion in 1898. It was not until the Lincoln Air Force Base was activated in 1952 that the area was substantially developed.

Bennet. Peak population (2000), 570. Post office name changed from Bennett's Station February 18, 1880. When the Midland Pacific Railroad was built through here in 1871, the town was surveyed and platted. Named in honor of John Bennett, resident and railway official. Sometime during the early 1880s a "t" was dropped from the name to form the present spelling with one "t."

Bennett's Station. Post office name changed from Rebecca March 2, 1871; name changed to Bennett (later Bennet) February 18, 1880. See Bennet.

Berks. Census not available. Post office established April 29, 1898; discontinued May 15, 1912. Present station on the Burlington Railroad and former town named by railroad officials for Berks County, Pennsylvania. Another source says town named for a resident named Berks.

Bethany. Post office established December 6, 1890. Bethany has been a section of Lincoln since 1926. J. Z. Briscoe of Lincoln, later of Bethany, was one of the town founders. He selected "Bethany" because the Biblical Bethany, Palestine, a suburb of Jerusalem, was an educational center of the Jews. Bethany, a suburb of Lincoln and also an educational center, was settled by the Disciples of Christ, who founded Cotner College. Incorporated name of Bethany is Bethany Heights.

Bethany Heights. Suburb of Lincoln. See Bethany.

Buda. Post office established September 2, 1870; discontinued November 14, 1872. Origin of the name not learned.

Burnham. Post office established July 11, 1899; discontinued January 4, 1910. Former post office and present railroad station named in honor of S. W. Burnham, landowner. Frank Burnham was first postmaster. On the Burlington southwest of Lincoln.

Camp Creek. Post office established November 13, 1866; name changed to Waverly December 8, 1870. Named for nearby Camp Creek.

Carlos. Station on the Missouri Pacific Railroad.

Centreville. Post office established October 8, 1865; name changed to Sprague November 24, 1888. Named for its central location.

Cheney. Peak population (1940), 149. Post office established September 28, 1876; discontinued 1943. Mail served from Lincoln. Railroad station was known as Cheyney's. Town named in honor of a Mr. Cheney, first settler in the township.

Chester. One of the first settlements in Lancaster County and the first designated county seat.

Clayton. The designated county seat in old Clay County.

Cobb. Former station southwest of Lincoln on the Burlington Railroad. Named in honor of an early landowner.

College View. Post office established March 3, 1891; established as a station of Lincoln, 1931. So named because it is the home of Union College founded by Seventh-Day Adventists. Its elevation gives a view of the surrounding area.

Crounse. Post office established April 29, 1873; discontinued October 24, 1901. Possibly named in honor of Governor Lorenzo Crounse, associate justice of the Nebraska Supreme Court at the time the post office was established.

Cushman. Former station on the Burlington Railroad.

Davey. Peak population (1970), 163. Post office established February 1, 1887. Named to honor Michael Davey, on whose land part of the town was platted by Western Town Lot Company in 1886.

Denton. Peak population (2000), 189. Post office established May 1, 1877. Named in honor of Daniel M. Denton on whose land the town was built.

Douglas. Proposed town on Salt Creek to which the Territorial Legislature voted on January 5, 1857, to move the capital. The bill was vetoed by Territorial Governor Mark W. Izard.

Dunn. Post office established March 27, 1884; discontinued February 20, 1888. Presumably named in honor of William H. Dunn, first postmaster.

Emerald. Peak population (1890), 100. Post office established January 22, 1884; discontinued 1945. Mail served from Lincoln. Named by settlers who described this location as the most beautiful green spot in the country.

Enterprise. Post office established July 6, 1871; discontinued April 7, 1876. Probably named by enterprising settlers who wanted their locality to prosper.

Firth. Peak population (2000), 564. Post office established December 6, 1872. Town named in honor of Superintendent Frank R. Firth of the Atchison and Nebraska Railroad, later the Chicago, Burlington and Quincy line.

Garrat. Former station on the Union Pacific Railroad.

Gregory's Basin. Post office established May 28, 1863; discontinued April 12, 1871. Possibly named in honor of John S. Gregory, Jr., first postmaster.

Hallam. Peak population (1990), 309. Post office established July 10, 1893. Town platted by Kansas Town and Land Company in 1892 and probably named for Hallau, Switzerland.

Hanlon. Station on the Union Pacific Railroad near Roca.

Havelock. Post office name changed from Newton December 31, 1890. Made a station of Lincoln. Suburb of Lincoln named in honor of Sir Henry Havelock (1785-1857), English general and hero of the siege of Lucknow, India.

Hawthorne. Former community in Lancaster County.

Hickman. Peak population (2000), 1,084. Post office name changed from South Pass December 4, 1872. Named in honor of C. H. Hickman, who platted the town in 1872.

Highland. Former name of Berks before a post office was established. The railroad retained the name Highland.

Highland Park. Former station on the Burlington Railroad.

116

Hobson. Station on the Burlington Railroad.

Holland. Peak population (1960), 110. Post office established May 20, 1873. Town named by settlers for European nation.

Huskerville. Huskerville was built around the Lincoln Army Air Field during World War II. After the war, the base's barracks were used as housing for returning soldiers and their families. It was closed shortly after a 1952 polio outbreak. A housing development is now located on the site. See Arnold Heights.

Hyersville. Post office name changed from Nobesville April 29, 1887; discontinued November 25, 1889. Named in honor of Reuben Hyers.

Ivanhoe. Post office established February 15, 1881; discontinued September 18, 1891. Presumably named for the hero of Sir Walter Scott's novel *Ivanhoe*.

Jamaica. Station on the Union Pacific Railroad in Yankee Hill Precinct. Probably named for Jamaica, New York.

Kramer. Peak population (1930), 133. Post office established January 15, 1889; discontinued 1955. Mail served from Crete. Town named in honor of a Mr. Kramer, donor of land for the townsite.

Lancaster. Post office established January 18, 1854; name changed to Lincoln February 25, 1868. Town named for county and platted in 1864 by Elder John M. Young, the Rev. Peter Schamp, Dr. J. McKesson, Luke Lavender, and Jacob Dawson. Elder Young formed the Lancaster Seminary Association for the Methodist colony here. Lancaster was made county seat in 1864 with the first court session held at the Jacob Dawson cabin. County previously connected with Cass County for judicial purposes. Lancaster settled with prospects of a salt company being formed there.

Lancaster. Post office established March 1892; discontinued January 14, 1910. Former post office and present station on the Burlington Railroad south of Lincoln.

Lincoln. Population (2000), 225,581. Post office name changed from Lancaster February 25, 1868. Nebraska's capital city named in honor of President Abraham Lincoln (1809-65). Senator J. N. H. Patrick of Omaha suggested the name. Another faction had wanted the capital called Douglas. The capital-finding committee included Governor David Butler, State Auditor John J. Gillespie, and Secretary of State Thomas P. Kennard. They met August 26, 1867, at home of William T. Donovan, early settler of the area, and filed for the incorporation of the capital August 26, 1867, and for the incorporation of the State Historical and Library Association the same day. The University of Nebraska was founded on February 16, 1869. Nebraska has had three capitol buildings in Lincoln. The first was completed in 1869, the second in 1888; both were razed. Ground was broken April 15, 1922, for the present capitol, completed in 1932. It is considered an outstanding example of modern architecture, with a 400-foot granite tower topped by a 32.5-foot bronze statue of the Sower, symbolizing Nebraska's agriculture. Lincoln was made county seat in transition from Lancaster February 12, 1869.

Lincoln Air Force Base. Lincoln Army Air Field (1942-45) was reactivated in 1952 by the Strategic Air Command as the Lincoln Air Force Base. Base was closed in 1966. See also Lincoln Army Air Field, Arnold Heights, and Huskerville.

Lincoln Army Air Field. Opened in 1942 on former Lincoln Municipal Airport property and leased to the U.S. Army by the city. It was closed in December of 1945.

Linpark. Station on the Union Pacific Railroad.

Little Salt. Former station on the Union Pacific Railroad.

Loyal Hill. Post office established March 4, 1874; discontinued August 19, 1885. Possibly named by patrons of the post office.

Malcolm. Peak population (2000), 413. Post office established November 19, 1874. Named for Malcolm A. Showers, who owned land on which it was laid out in 1877.

Margaretta. Early settlement possibly named in honor of the wife of Governor Lorenzo Crounse.

Martell. Peak population (1950), 104. Post office established December 27, 1894. Town named by R. J. Greene, A. G. Beeson, and H. M. Bushnell of Lincoln, who bought the land and laid out the townsite. Possibly named in honor of Charles Martel, king of the Franks (689-741).

Mayville. Post office established April 2, 1872; discontinued April 6, 1874. Origin of the name not learned. First postmaster was W. W. Carder.

McFarland. Post office established August 11, 1874; discontinued December 3, 1878. Named in honor of a local settler.

Middle Creek. Post office established April 24, 1868; discontinued August 2, 1869. Named for a creek on which the post office was located.

Millville. Post office name changed from Sod Hill March 17, 1874; discontinued December 12, 1876. Probably named for an area grist mill.

Newton. Former name of Havelock before a post office was established.

Nobesville. Post office name changed from Penitentiary August 4, 1880; name changed to Hyersville April 29, 1887. Named for C. J. Nobes, penitentiary warden.

Normal. Post office established August 25, 1892; discontinued January 31, 1930. Site of the Lincoln Normal School, for which town was named. The school no longer exists and the town has become a part of Lincoln.

Olathe. Early settlement on Salt Creek fifteen miles south of Lincoln; founded by John D. Prey and sons in old Clay County. Olathe quarries were near present Roca. Proposed town never developed.

Olive Branch. Post office established November 13, 1866; discontinued February 12, 1889. Office probably named for the people's hope for a peaceful community. There is also an Olive Branch, Illinois.

Opequon. Post office established November 16, 1869; discontinued April 12, 1870. Name is probably Indian in origin. Places with the same Tuscarora Indian name founded in Jefferson County, West Virginia, and Frederick County, Virginia.

Orient. Locality mentioned in early county history.

Orlando. Post office established February 6, 1878; name changed to Raymond May 15, 1880. Origin of the name not learned. There is also an Orlando, Florida.

Panama. Peak population (2000), 253. Post office established December 20, 1869. Probably named for the Isthmus of Panama. Precinct has the same name. There are five other U.S. towns with the same name.

Paris. Early locality in Lancaster County.

Park. Post office established December 14, 1870; discontinued August 11, 1873. Origin of the name not learned.

Peck's Grove. Station on the Missouri Pacific Railroad named in honor of Philetus Peck, landowner and planter of a grove of trees.

Pella. Peak population (1900), 18. Post office established August 24, 1883; discontinued July 14, 1903. Former hamlet founded by Dutch settlers from Pella, Iowa. Location was in southeastern part of county.

Penitentiary. Post office established July 2, 1879; name changed to Nobesville August 4, 1880. Named for the Nebraska State Penitentiary, whose postal service it handled.

Prairie Home. Peak population (1930, 1940), 126. Post office established October 3, 1872. Town named by a Mr. Waite, first depot agent on the Chicago, Rock Island and Pacific Railroad. Post office discontinued in 1968.

Princeton. Census not available. Post office established April 30, 1886; made a rural station of Lincoln in 1958. Village probably named for Princeton, New Jersey.

Raymond. Peak population (1920), 249. Post office name changed from Orlando May 15, 1880. Town named in honor of I. M. Raymond, senior member of the firm of Raymond Brothers and Clark, wholesale grocers of Lincoln.

Rebecca. Post office established August 26, 1868; name changed to Bennett's Station March 2, 1871. Origin of the name not learned. First postmaster was John Staley.

Roca. Peak population (2000), 220. Post office established May 18, 1876. When the town was platted in 1876, the citizens wished to choose a name which would suggest the chief industry in the area, stone quarrying. Roca is the Spanish word for stone.

Rock Creek. Post office established April 25, 1872; discontinued March 24, 1876. Named for a nearby creek.

Rokeby. Peak population (1900), 100. Post office established September 22, 1894; discontinued May 22, 1919. Former village and station on the Chicago, Rock Island and Pacific Railroad, probably named for Sir Walter Scott's Poem, "Rokeby."

Saline City. Founded by Wescott Field at the crossing of Salt Creek. It was intended as a stop on the Steam Wagon Road from Nebraska City to Fort Kearny. The present state hospital is situated nearby.

Salt Basin. Early settlement founded by John Prey, who pre-empted a claim here in 1857. The inhabitants wanted the state capital to be located in the vicinity.

Salt Creek. Locality mentioned in early county history.

Saltillo. Census not available. Post office established March 27, 1865; discontinued January 7, 1906. Town was founded in 1862. Possibly named for Saltillo, Mexico. Platt vacated 1997.

Shirley's Station. Post office established September 25, 1863; discontinued November 25, 1865. Possibly named in honor of William Shirley, first postmaster.

Silver. A proposed name for a post office, May 1886.

Sod Hill. Post office established April 25, 1872; name changed to Millville March 17, 1874. Possibly named by someone taking sod from a hill to build a sod house.

South Pass. Post office established April 8, 1869; name changed to Hickman December 4, 1872. Probably named for its location near the crest of a watershed or divide.

Sprague. Peak population (1980), 168. Post office name changed from Centreville November 24, 1888. Town surveyed on the Missouri Pacific Railroad in 1888 and named by a Mr. Sprague.

Stevens Creek. Post office established April 30, 1868; discontinued June 17, 1870. Named for a nearby creek, in turn named for a local settler.

Stircus Creek. Locality established in the early 1880s.

Stockwell. Locality in early county history.

Strickland Mills. Locality in early county history.

Summit. Former station on the Burlington Railroad in South Pass Precinct.

Tipton. Post office established April 27, 1869; discontinued April 22, 1873. Probably named in honor of a local settler.

University Place. Post office name changed from Athens July 30, 1889; made a station of Lincoln June 15, 1907. Town named for Nebraska Wesleyan University located here.

Wagner's. Probably a former railroad station north of Lincoln.

Walton. Peak population (1940), 152. Post office established December 13, 1880. Town named in honor of A. Walton, who homesteaded nearby.

Waverly. Peak population (2000), 2,448. Post office name changed from Camp Creek December 8, 1870. Named for Sir Walter Scott's historical novel *Waverly*. Streets are named for characters in the book.

Welch. Stop on Table Rock and Columbus line between Saltillo and Lancaster, probably in vicinity of state penitentiary.

West Lincoln. Peak population (1960), 507. Post office established February 15, 1880; discontinued September 7, 1901. Mail served from Lincoln. Named for its location west of Lincoln.

West Oak. Former station on the Union Pacific Railroad. Probably named for the burr oak timber in the area.

Woodlawn. Peak population (1880), 100. Post office established August 11, 1874; discontinued April 20, 1891. Mail served from Lincoln. Town named for the precinct; locally descriptive term.

Yankee Hill. Former community vied for county seat with Lancaster.

LINCOLN COUNTY

Named in honor of Abraham Lincoln (1809-65), U.S. president from 1861 to 1865. Previously known as Shorter County, organized and boundaries defined by an act of the Legislature January 7, 1860. Legislature approved name change from Shorter to Lincoln County on December 11, 1861.

Arna. Census not available. Post office established June 26, 1905; discontinued March 15, 1912. Former village derives its name from a village in the Grecian archipelago.

Beck. Station on the Union Pacific Railroad.

Bignell. Census not available. Post office established January 8, 1908; discontinued 1934. Former town named in honor of E. C. Bignell of Lincoln, superintendent of the Burlington Railroad.

Birdwood. Post office established April 3, 1888; discontinued May 18, 1896. Named for nearby Birdwood Creek along which grew birdwood or indigo shrubs.

Brady. Peak population (1940), 450. Post office name changed from Brady Island May 4, 1894. See Brady Island.

Brady Island. Post office established December 21, 1875; name changed to Brady May 4, 1894. Village platted by G. D. and Mabel Matherson January 28, 1889. Named for a Mr. Brady, first settler.

Buchanan. Post office established January 11, 1886; discontinued March 21, 1903. Named in honor of Butler Buchanan, first postmaster.

Burnham. Post office established August 4, 1885; discontinued April 26, 1887. Probably named in honor of Leavitt Burnham of Omaha, land commissioner of the Union Pacific Railroad.

Camp Sergeant. A small military outpost at North Platte, established during the construction of the Union Pacific Railroad to protect rail line stations and workers from the Indians.

Coker. Station on the Union Pacific Railroad.

Cold Springs. Nebraska Pony Express Station No. 22 in Nebraska. Located on Box Elder Creek two miles south and one mile west of the present city of North Platte.

Cold Water. Former locality.

Cottonwood. Post office established April 17, 1860; name changed to Cottonwood Falls October 19, 1860. Named for area cottonwood trees.

Cottonwood Falls. Post office name changed from Cottonwood October 19, 1860; name changed to Cottonwood Springs January 8, 1861.

Cottonwood Springs. Nebraska Pony Express Station No. 21, located on the east side of Cottonwood Creek. It was one mile southeast of present Fort McPherson National Cemetery. Sometimes known as the McDonald Ranch, it also served as an overland stage station. Two brothers, Ike and Nelson Boyer, operated a trading post here in 1858.

Cottonwood Springs. Post office name changed from Cottonwood Falls January 8, 1861; discontinued April 11, 1895. First county records were kept at Cottonwood Springs, which served as county seat until the Union Pacific Railroad and the town of North Platte were established. Records were then transferred November 12, 1867.

Dansey's. Nebraska Pony Express Station No. 24. Located two miles south and four miles west of the present town of Sutherland. Sometimes called Elkhorn or Halfway House.

Deer Creek. Locality mentioned in early Lincoln County history.

Delay. Post office established January 11, 1886; discontinued December 16, 1886. Named in honor of John Delay, first postmaster.

Denmark. Post office established December 7, 1900; discontinued March 15, 1912. Former community settled chiefly by Danish immigrants and named for their native country.

Dexter. Station on the Union Pacific Railroad near Sutherland.

Dickens. Census not available. Post office established March 20, 1888. Town named in honor of Charles Dickens (1812-70), the noted English author.

Echo. Post office established April 30, 1895; discontinued July 9, 1908. Name probably selected because it was a short, pleasant word.

Elizabeth. Post office established May 13, 1887; discontinued March 17, 1899. Origin of the name not learned. First postmaster was Acton Orr.

Eureka. Post office established July 8, 1873; discontinued October 26, 1874. Greek name meaning "I have found it."

Fairview. Post office established September 10, 1885; discontinued June 19, 1908. Name is locally descriptive.

Forks. Post office established September 9, 1901; moved to McPherson County August 11, 1908. Named because of its location on a fork of East and West Birchwood creeks.

Fort Cottonwood. Originally named Fort McKean in 1863, this military post became Fort Cottonwood in May 1864. Two years later its name was changed to Fort McPherson.

Fort McKean. Military post established in 1863 and named in honor of Maj. Thomas J. McKean. Sometimes known as Cantonment McKean.

Fort McPherson. This military post underwent two name changes (see above) before it was named Fort McPherson in 1866 for Maj. Gen. James B. McPherson, killed in the Civil War. Cavalry stationed here played an important part in guarding wayfarers on the Oregon-California trail and protecting cattle ranches. The fort was in continuous use until 1880, when it was abandoned. The graveyard adjoining it became a national cemetery in 1873. Men and women of the armed forces—and their dependents—who have served since the mid-nineteenth century are buried here. It still accepts interments.

Fox Creek. Post office established April 15, 1878; discontinued January 31, 1884. Named for a nearby creek.

Fremont Springs. Nebraska Pony Express Station No. 23, located one and one-half miles from present town of Hershey. Sometimes referred to as Buffalo Ranch, it was named for Gen. John C. Fremont.

Gannett. Former station named in honor of Joseph W. Gannett of Omaha, auditor of the Union Pacific Railroad.

Garfield. Post office established June 13, 1884; discontinued October 14, 1916. Probably commemorates President James Garfield (1831-81).

Gaslin. Post office established February 17, 1881; discontinued June 14, 1890. Named in honor of Judge William Gaslin, noted western jurist.

Gilmans. Nebraska Pony Express Station No. 19, located in southwest Lincoln County.

Glenburne. Former station on the Union Pacific Railroad located west of Sutherland.

Hatton. Post office established January 27, 1882; name changed to Vroman January 22, 1887. Origin of the name not learned.

Hershey. Peak population (1980), 633. Post office name changed from O'Fallons January 14, 1890. Town named in honor of J. H. Hershey, early rancher, landowner, and business partner of William Paxton.

Hindrey. Former station on the Union Pacific Railroad located west of Brady.

Ingham. Peak population (1950), 80. Post office established January 10, 1898; discontinued 1953. Former village named for a Mr. Ingham, then traveling through the country.

Josephine. Post office established April 30, 1908; discontinued June 19, 1908. Origin of the name not learned.

Keeler. Post office established December 16, 1884; discontinued April 29, 1890. Probably named in honor of Elisha Keeler, first postmaster.

Keith. Station on the Union Pacific Railroad situated west of Maxwell.

Kilmer. Post office established September 3, 1884; discontinued September 15, 1915. Probably named in honor of Robert Kilmer, first postmaster.

Leslie. Post office established May 29, 1890; discontinued January 27, 1892. Origin of the name not ascertained.

Linn. Post office established February 8, 1908. Origin of the name not learned.

Machette's. Nebraska Pony Express Station No. 20, located on the Williams Upper 96 Ranch. It was four miles east of Fort McPherson.

Maxwell. Peak population (1940), 480. Post office name changed from McPherson May 15, 1882. Town's name said to be a variation of "Mac's well," kept by John "Mac" McCullough at Fort McPherson.

McPherson. Post office established December 31, 1867; name changed to Maxwell May 15, 1882. Named for nearby Fort McPherson.

Medicine. Post office established January 8, 1883; discontinued November 9, 1887. Named for nearby Medicine Creek.

Midway. Post office established May 19, 1865; discontinued February 13, 1867; probably named for its location in the county.

Myrtle. Peak population (1910), 110. Post office established August 27, 1886; discontinued May 31, 1914. Former town named in honor of Myrtle Brink, a young lady who lived in the vicinity.

Napoleon. Post office established November 13, 1871; discontinued January 3, 1873. Probably named for Napoleon Bonaparte, renowned general and emperor of the French.

Nichols. Post office established February 8, 1884; discontinued November 2, 1889. Former post office and railroad station named in honor of Peter J. Nichols, general superintendent of the Nebraska division of the Union Pacific Railroad.

North Platte. Peak population (1980), 24,479. Post office established February 13, 1867. County seat laid out for the Union Pacific Railroad by Gen. C. M. Dodge in 1866. Situated on the North Platte River. County seat records transferred from Cottonwood Springs November 12, 1867.

O'Fallons. Post office established December 6, 1883; name changed to Hershey January 14, 1890. This junction point on the Union Pacific Railroad received its name from a nearby bluff named for a hunter reportedly killed in the area, a man who sold liquor to Indians here, or for Benjamin O'Fallon of St. Louis.

O'Fallons. Post office established March 19, 1859; post office discontinued April 9, 1864. A trading post and stage station just southwest of present Sutherland.

O'Fallon's Bluff. Post office established March 19, 1859; discontinued April 9, 1864. A trading post and stage station just southwest of present Sutherland, this was considered one of the most formidable barriers on the trail. First postmaster was Isaac Hockaday. See O'Fallons.

Pallas. Former station on the Union Pacific Railroad near North Platte.

Pawnee. Post office established March 24, 1854; discontinued July 1, 1857. Site of this former post office later became a station on the Union Pacific Railroad; also called Pawnee. Named for the Pawnee Indians.

Peckham. Post office established March 2, 1881; discontinued October 20, 1896. Mail served from Gothenburg. Named for only postmaster, Joshua Peckham. The building which housed the post office was built from timber from the barracks at discontinued Fort McPherson. Also acquired from the fort was the army post office letter box, which was donated by its owner, Mrs. Golda V. Peckham Suttie of Omaha, to the U.S. Post Office at its request. Later it was acquired by the Smithsonian Institution.

Seeley. Post office established July 29, 1892; discontinued October 3, 1894. Probably named in honor of John S. Seeley, first postmaster.

Silas. Post office established March 16, 1886; discontinued August 16, 1887. Named in honor of Silas Clark, first postmaster.

Somerset. Post office established December 9, 1887; discontinued 1945. Former post office and station on the Burlington Railroad. Probably named for Somerset, Massachusetts.

Spannuth. Post office established February 11, 1885; discontinued July 15, 1909. Possibly named in honor of Fred C. Spannuth, first postmaster.

Spear. Post office established May 25, 1909; discontinued June 30, 1913. Probably named in honor of William T. Spear, first postmaster.

Spuds. Post office established November 20, 1895; discontinued June 17, 1902. Probably named for a harvested field of potatoes ("spuds").

Sunshine. Post office established January 11, 1886; discontinued October 29, 1892. Named either for Sunshine Ranch or for the sunshiny weather when names were proposed.

Sutherland. Peak population (1980), 1,238. Post office established March 9, 1892. Town named for a Mr. Sutherland, Union Pacific Railroad official.

Turner. Former station on the Union Pacific Railroad located near Dickens.

Van Wyck. Post office established August 18, 1886; discontinued March 4, 1887. Possibly named in honor of United States Senator Charles H. Van Wyck (1881-87).

Varner. Station on the Union Pacific Railroad.

Vroman. Post office name changed from Hatton January 22, 1887; discontinued January 28, 1903. Former post office and railroad station on the Union Pacific Railroad named in honor of William Vroman, a resident.

Wallace. Peak population (1930), 406. Post office established December 20, 1887. The Lincoln Land Company laid out the town, and the company's manager named it in honor of his son-in-law.

Warren. Former station on the Union Pacific Railroad. Probably named for Union Gen. G. K. Warren, who explored the Sand Hills in 1850s.

Watts. Post office established January 11, 1886; discontinued January 16, 1908. Possibly named in honor of Samuel F. Watts of Stockville, surveyor.

Wellfleet. Peak population (1950), 310. Post office established September 6, 1887. Town named for Wellfleet, Massachusetts.

Whitaker. Former station on the Union Pacific Railroad.

Whittier. Post office established December 22, 1884; discontinued January 7, 1900. Probably named in honor of John Greenleaf Whittier, noted American poet.

Willard. Post office established November 20, 1890; discontinued June 30, 1922. Origin of the name not learned. First postmaster was William A. Gregg.

Willow Bend. Former locality.

LOGAN COUNTY

Named in honor of John A. Logan (1826-86), Union general. Its boundaries were defined by an act of the Legislature approved February 24, 1885.

Augustus. Post office established February 1, 1886; discontinued August 27, 1886. Named in honor of Augustus Bolten, first postmaster.

Dorp. Post office established November 23, 1882; discontinued February 28, 1901. Post office named by Franklin R. Hogeboom, first postmaster. Name probably German in origin.

Ford. Post office established April 18, 1907; discontinued August 31, 1913. Named in honor of "Bud" Ford, first postmaster at whose ranch home the post office was located.

Gandy. Peak population (1890), 300. Post office established January 14, 1886. Named in honor of James Gandy, former Broken Bow resident who promised Logan County he would build a courthouse if they would name the town after him. Gandy won county seat from Logan in election July 25, 1885. A special courthouse election held May 2, 1929, was contested by Stapleton, which finally was awarded the county seat on February 24, 1930. Gandy declined in population after railroad bypassed the town. Post office discontinued 1977. Mail served from Stapleton.

Gandy Station. Station on the Union Pacific Railroad located north of Gandy.

Gem. Post office established May 22, 1912; discontinued February 15, 1923. Name suggested by Postmaster C. T. Johnson, who owned the land on which post office was located.

Hoagland. Census not available. Post office established July 15, 1912; discontinued 1945. Former village named in honor of W. V. Hoagland, North Platte attorney who homesteaded the land on which village was platted.

Kirsch. Post office established May 28, 1910; discontinued September 15, 1915. Named in honor of F. J. Kirsch, first postmaster.

Logan. Census not available. Post office established December 22, 1884; discontinued 1953. Former hamlet named for county.

Nesbit. Post office established February 8, 1890; moved to McPherson County December 8, 1902. Origin of the name not learned.

Ranger. Post office established February 11, 1914; discontinued February 15, 1918. Named by postal patrons and by Homer Shattuck. Reason for name not learned.

Shidler. Post office moved from Thomas County September 15, 1915; discontinued after removal to Logan County in 1916. Named in honor of Richard Shidler, first postmaster.

Stapleton. Peak population (1930), 431. Post office established June 8, 1912. Named in honor of C. Stapleton by Henry O'Neill, a partner of the townsite promoter who offered to give a donation to the town. Stapleton won county seat election from Gandy May 2, 1929. It became the Union Pacific terminus of the railroad from Kearney in 1913.

Wagner. Post office established November 19, 1906; discontinued July 15, 1919. Named in honor of Frederick Wagner, on whose ranch the post office was located.

LOUP COUNTY

The original Loup County (called Taylor) was created by legislative enactment March 6, 1855. The present Loup County, named in honor of the Pawnee Loup or the Loup River, was constituted in 1883.

Almeria. Peak population (1900), 63. Post office established August 3, 1884. One source says the town was named after a former sweetheart of founder Wesley Strohl. Lost county seat election to Taylor on July 23, 1883.

Butka. Post office established February 10, 1886; moved to Brown County April 24, 1897. Named in honor of Frank Butka, first postmaster.

Calamus. Post office established January 18, 1908; discontinued August 31, 1917. Named for the Calamus River on which it was located. Calamus is a Sioux word meaning "food of the muskrat."

Clarks Point. Platted as a town but expired before a post office was established. Origin of the name is unknown. Location was between Almeria and Taylor.

Cooleyton. Post office established December 14, 1885; discontinued February 13, 1908. Named in honor of Mr. and Mrs. Ashley B. Cooley, homesteaders who emigrated from Iowa.

Crane. Post office established September 28, 1885; discontinued April 2, 1887. Named in honor of Morgan Crane, first postmaster.

Ferguson. Post office established March 10, 1902; discontinued September 30, 1929. Named in honor of an early Scotch immigrant called Ferguson.

Fort Rodney. Named for Rodney P. Alger, a homesteader on whose place a temporary garrison was established. Settlers formed this small post and remained several weeks when advised to do so by Capt. Samuel Munson.

Fox. Post office established June 1, 1914; discontinued December 31, 1920. Probably named in honor of Burton C. Fox, first postmaster.

Gracie. Post office established March 17, 1905; moved to Rock County 1915. Named in honor of a daughter of Dick Ray, first postmaster.

Harrop. Post office established October 24, 1912; discontinued 1932. Named in honor of John Harrop, Kinkaid settler and first postmaster.

Kent. Census not available. Post office established September 19, 1876; discontinued May 31, 1907. Former town said to have been named for Kent, England, birthplace of a settler. Kent was the first county seat of Loup County. The town declined in population after the town of Taylor was made county seat.

Moulton. Post office established August 24, 1883; discontinued 1943. Named in honor of Levi M. Moulton, Civil War veteran and homesteader who was instrumental in securing the post office.

Munson. Post office established 1879; moved to Taylor January 2, 1880. Named in honor of Capt. Samuel Munson of Fort Hartsuff.

Nunda. Post office established September 5, 1884; discontinued December 11, 1889. Named for one of the three Nunda brothers who lived in the locality.

Ovitt. Post office established January 23, 1911; discontinued 1943. Named in honor of Mrs. Laura R. Ovitt, first postmistress.

Pawnee. Once designated as the county seat, Pawnee never got beyond the embryo stage.

Prime. Post office established September 6, 1890: discontinued August 31, 1899. Origin of the name not learned.

Sioux Creek. This place featured the Farmers' Hotel, a stopping place or tavern for travelers of the North Loup valley in the 1880s.

Strohl. Post office established July 8, 1880; discontinued April 8, 1887. Named in honor of an early settler.

Taylor. Peak population (1930), 349. Post office established January 2, 1880. Joseph Rusho is remembered as the "Father of Taylor." He gave several lots and buildings to the county and town, including the courthouse block, public square, and park which adjoined his homestead. Rusho named the town to honor Edward H. Taylor, a pioneer friend. Robert Harvey of Grand Island surveyed and platted the town in October 1883. Rusho had formerly lived in the vicinity of Fort Hartsuff. Taylor won county seat in election with Almeria July 23, 1883.

Valleyview. Post office established September 30, 1914; discontinued 1939. Former post office located at an elevation which gave a view for several miles overlooking a valley. Name suggested by Walter Hesselgesser.

MADISON COUNTY

One source says county named for James Madison (1751-1836), U.S. president from 1809 to 1817. Another source says named by German settlers formerly of Madison County, Wisconsin. County was organized December 1867. Established by an act of the Legislature approved January 26, 1856, and redefined by an act approved March 3, 1873.

Battle Creek. Peak population (2000), 1,158. Post office established July 27, 1870. The Pioneer Town Site Company platted the town and named it after a nearby stream where a skirmish between the militia and Pawnee Indians took place. Battle Creek vied for county seat in election of 1875.

Blakely. Post office established February 25, 1880; discontinued June 21, 1899. Named to honor a Mr. Blakely, first settler and blacksmith shop owner.

Burnett. Post office name changed from Ogden January 20, 1880; name changed to Tilden August 8, 1887, to honor a Mr. Burnett, first superintendent of the Sioux City and Pacific Railroad. Became Tilden because mail was mistakenly sent to Bennet, Nebraska.

Chloe. Post office established March 4, 1882; discontinued January 6, 1886. Named for a school district by Scandinavian settlers.

Clarion. Post office established April 4, 1872; discontinued October 23, 1899. Possibly named for Clarion County, Pennsylvania, by a Mr. Riegle.

Deer Creek. Post office established December 11, 1870; name changed to Meadow Grove November 2, 1899. Named for a nearby creek.

Dry Creek. Post office established March 28, 1872; discontinued November 20, 1888. Named for an area creek, often dry.

Dunlap. Post office established February 11, 1888; discontinued 1889. Origin of the name not learned.

Emerick. Census not available. Post office established May 24, 1873; discontinued December 31, 1920. Former village named in honor of John Emerick, pioneer.

Enola. Census not available. Post office established January 22, 1906; discontinued December 31, 1909. Town named for founder T. J. Malone (spelled backwards with the "m" eliminated). This device prevented confusion with another Malone in the state.

Fairview. A former locality recorded in the Rand McNally Atlas of 1882.

Gates. Post office established May 24, 1873; discontinued October 12, 1875. Origin of the name not learned.

Glenaro. Post office established December 21, 1874; discontinued August 7, 1876. Possibly this word was coined from two names.

Hale. Post office established January 30, 1888; discontinued October 27, 1897. Possibly named for a local settler.

Hiram. Post office name changed from Munson June 2, 1887; name changed to Warnerville June 11, 1887. Origin of the name not learned.

Hope. Former station on the Chicago, St. Paul, Minneapolis and Omaha Railroad. Named in honor of H. C. Hope, superintendent of telegraph. Located near Norfolk.

Kalamazoo. Post office established June 23, 1874; discontinued August 24, 1904. Named in honor of Kalamazoo, Michigan.

Kent Siding. Former station on the Chicago and North Western Railroad.

Madison. Peak population (2000), 2,367. Post office established December 23, 1869. One source says town named for the county. Another source believes town named for Herman Madison Barnes, son of Frank Barnes, a homesteader in the fall of 1868. Town founded by a German colony of twenty from Wisconsin. Madison won county seat election over Norfolk and Battle Creek in 1875.

Marrietta. Post office established November 18, 1873; discontinued May 20, 1881. Origin of the name not learned. First postmaster was Caleb Alberry.

Meadow Grove. Peak population (1930), 483. Post office name changed from Deer Creek November 2, 1889. Named for a grove of trees near a meadow.

Munson. Post office established January 12, 1880; name changed to Hiram June 2, 1887. Origin of the name not learned.

Newman Grove. Peak population (1920), 1,260. Post office established June 23, 1874. Named for a grove of cottonwood trees on land belonging to Newman Warren.

Norfolk. Peak population (2000), 23,516. Post office established June 9, 1868. Col. Charles P. Mathewson, one of its founders, told the following story concerning the origin of the name Norfolk: When it was time to petition authorities for a post office, "Nor'fork," a contraction of North Fork, was agreed upon because the town was located on the north fork of the Elkhorn River. The petition was accepted, but postal authorities spelled the name Norfolk, assuming petitioners had misspelled the name. Norfolk lost the county seat election of 1875. According to Frank W. Barnes, a Mr. Wagner submitted a petition to postal authorities with the name Nordfolk. A department clerk at Washington interpreted the name as Norfolk.

Ogden. Post office moved from Boone County April 8, 1878; name changed to Burnett January 20, 1880. Origin of the name not learned.

Parry. Post office established October 15, 1872; discontinued May 6, 1873. Origin of the name not learned. First postmaster was Henry Franklin.

Plum Grove. Post office established April 5, 1872; discontinued October 1, 1873. Possibly named for its location near a wild plum thicket.

South Norfolk. Junction point for two railroad lines on the Chicago and North Western.

Spring Valley. Post office established March 21, 1872; discontinued December 19, 1873. A descriptive term.

Tilden. Peak population (1930), 1,106. Post office name changed from Burnett August 8, 1887. Commemorates Samuel L. Tilden (1814-86) of New York state, lawyer and statesman.

Union Valley. Post office established July 3, 1872; discontinued February 15, 1875. Possibly named by a local settler who served as a soldier in the Union Army during the Civil War.

Warnerville. Peak population (1910), 67. Post office name changed from Hiram June 11, 1887; discontinued November 30, 1917. Former town named in honor of H. Warner, settler who operated a store and elevator for many years.

Warren. Post office established December 26, 1871; discontinued August 18, 1890. Origin of the name not learned. First postmaster was Eri Pulman.

Yellow Banks. Post office established June 14, 1877; discontinued December 19, 1879. Probably named for yellow clay banks along a stream near the post office.

McPHERSON COUNTY

Named in honor of James B. McPherson (1828-64), Union general during the Civil War. County organized in 1890.

Brighton. Post office established February 19, 1910; discontinued September 15, 1916. Named in honor of the Brighton family who homesteaded in this locality.

Chandler. Post office established November 5, 1909; discontinued July 31, 1926. Named in honor of Mrs. S. L. Chandler, who lived in the vicinity.

Flats. Census not available. Post office established January 15, 1909. Mrs. Dana Lombard and two sons homesteaded land three miles from this town, in a broad valley known as Lombard Flats. Later the post office was established at the Lombard home, and the office became known as Flats. Post office discontinued 1973. Mail served from Sutherland.

Forks. Census not available. Post office moved from Lincoln County August 11, 1908; discontinued January 19, 1919. Former town named for its location at the forks of East and West Birdwood creeks.

Lamo. This place shown on early maps, but there is no record of its ever being platted.

Largo. Post office established May 22, 1891; discontinued January 19, 1893. Origin of the name not learned.

Lemley. Post office established January 24, 1891; discontinued October 30, 1907. Named in honor of the infant son of George L. Brooks, first postmaster.

Lilac. Post office established April 25, 1891; discontinued 1936. Name selected by postal authorities from a number of names submitted. Named for a small lilac bush in the yard of the family who wished to establish the office.

Mayflower. Post office established February 3, 1906; discontinued 1920. Named in honor of May E. Mooney, first postmistress. Her first name was combined with the word "flower."

McPherson. Post office established August 12, 1889; discontinued April 26, 1894. Named for the county.

Nesbit. Post office moved from Logan County December 8, 1902; discontinued November 29, 1922. Origin of the name is unknown.

Ney. Post office established February 27, 1907; discontinued October 31, 1913. Origin of the name not learned.

Noark. Post office established June 17, 1914; discontinued July 31, 1916. Origin of the name not revealed.

Omega. Census not available. Post office established February 29, 1888; discontinued 1960. Former hamlet named after a biblical reference to Alpha and Omega, the beginning and the end (Revelations). The place was at the end of a star mail route.

Ringgold. Post office established December 1, 1910; discontinued 1968. See Ringgold, Dawson County.

Summit. Post office moved from Thomas County January 10, 1923; discontinued 1935. See Summit, Thomas County.

Thune. Post office established March 28, 1924; discontinued 1953. Named by first postmaster Daniel V. Platt for Dora Thune, who lived in the vicinity.

Tryon. Peak population (1950), 150. Post office established January 19, 1893. Authorities and old residents differ as to the naming of this county seat. Some say it was named for William Tryon, a colonial governor of America (1725-88). Others say it was named by Judge William Neville of North Platte. Still others say that it came from a statement by Mrs. Jay Smith, who declared, "Let's keep trying (tryon) to have a town."

Turnip. Post office established November 15, 1910; discontinued September 15, 1911. Probably named for a patch of turnips.

Valyrang. Post office established June 3, 1907; discontinued 1932. This former post office was established at the home of Mrs. Lou Hurd, who submitted the name "Valley Rang" to postal authorities. They shortened it to Valyrang.

MERRICK COUNTY

Named in honor of Elvira Merrick (Mrs. Henry W. DePuy). The county was established and its boundaries defined by an act of the Legislature approved November 4, 1858. The bill to establish Merrick County and to locate the county seat at Elvira was introduced by Representative Henry W. DePuy of Dodge County.

Adamston. Post office established August 25, 1885; discontinued May 11, 1886. Named in honor of Charles W. Adams, first postmaster. The last three letters were added because there already was an Adams within the state.

Amity. Post office established November 7, 1879; discontinued July 13, 1888. Probably named for Amity Presbyterian Church, established by German settlers.

Archer. Peak population (1930), 151. Post office established November 11, 1887. Town named in honor of Robert T. Archer, pioneer.

Bethel. Post office established July 23, 1879; discontinued July 5, 1883. Probably named for a church or religious group. Bethel means a hallowed spot or house of God.

Brass. Former station on the Union Pacific Railroad.

Brewer's Ranch. Post office established August 8, 1864; discontinued 1869. Named in honor of Probate Judge James G. Brewer, settler.

Bryant's Grove. Post office established September 4, 1879; discontinued December 7, 1880. Named in honor of Homer Bryant, first postmaster.

Burlingame. Post office established December 31, 1872; discontinued June 22, 1888. Possibly named in honor of George M. Burlingame, first postmaster.

Cattaragus. Townsite platted by Ed L. Peet in 1886 several miles northwest of Clarks.

Central City. Peak population (1980), 3,063. Post office name changed from Lone Tree April 26, 1875, upon a petition of the citizens. This county seat is named because of its location in the central part of the state. Nebraska Central College was founded by the Quakers in 1898 and was continued until the 1940s.

Chapman. Peak population (1970), 371. Post office established December 28, 1868. Town named in honor of a Mr. Chapman, roadmaster on the Union Pacific Railroad, by John Donovan, the local section foreman.

Clarks. Peak population (1910), 605. Post office name changed from Clarksville June 15, 1880. Town named in honor of Silas Henry Clark of Omaha, general manager of the Union Pacific Railroad.

Clarksville. Post office established February 26, 1869; name changed to Clarks June 15, 1880.

Conrad. Post office established May 3, 1881; discontinued May 9, 1882. Commemorates the maiden name of Mrs. Charles W. Adams.

Elkdale. Post office name changed from Silver Glen June 23, 1874; moved to Gage Valley, Howard County, July 14, 1874. Origin of the name not learned.

Elvira. Platted November 4, 1858, this county seat did not last long enough for a post office to be established. Named in honor of Mrs. Elvira Merrick DePuy.

Farmersville. Post office established August 19, 1875; discontinued March 8, 1881. Probably named for the farmers who formed the nucleus of post office patrons.

Gardiner Station. Post office established June 30, 1884; moved to Platte County July 31, 1884. Post office and railroad station on the Union Pacific Railroad moved across the Platte County line.

Gulfoil. Station on Union Pacific Railroad.

Havens. Post office established June 24, 1919; discontinued 1935. Former post office and present station on the Union Pacific Railroad, probably named for Charles Best Havens, superintendent of railroad bridges.

Heber. Station on the Union Pacific Railroad located near Central City.

Hord. Former station on the Union Pacific Railroad may have been a grain elevator or cattle feeding station operated by T. B. Hord in 1884.

Junction Ranch. Stage stop on the Omaha and Fort Kearny Trail during the early 1860s.

Kilgravel. Burlington Railroad station.

Lester. Post office established February 19, 1878; name changed to Merrick January 14, 1880. Origin of the name has not been learned. The first postmaster was John Knapp.

Lockwood. Peak population (1890), 26. Post office established November 17, 1874; discontinued July 24, 1890. Former town probably named in honor of a Union Pacific Railroad official.

Lone Tree. Post office established June 10, 1867; name changed to Central City April 26, 1875. Town named for the Lone Tree Ranch. In time it became one of the "20-mile" stopping places for Overland Stage coaches. A lone cottonwood tree became a landmark for travellers.

Mentzer. Post office established November 26, 1879; discontinued August 27, 1886. Origin of the name not learned.

Merrick. Post office name changed from Lester January 14, 1880; discontinued July 13, 1888. Named for the county.

Paddock. Station on the Union Pacific Railroad named for a company official.

Palmer. Peak population (1990), 753. Post office name changed from Vick November 2, 1887. Town named in honor of an official of the Burlington Railroad.

Prairie Creek. Post office established August 19, 1875; discontinued March 8, 1880. Named for nearby Prairie Creek.

Shoemaker Point. Post office established December 29, 1863; discontinued January 4, 1865. First post office established in the county; named in honor of Jesse Shoemaker, a settler.

Silver Creek. Peak population (1990), 625. Post office established April 4, 1877. Town named for a nearby creek.

Silver Glen. Post office established January 17, 1865; name changed to Elkdale June 23, 1874. Descriptive designation for the locality.

Sunrise. Census not available. Post office established June 19, 1899; discontinued November 17, 1906. Former town named for its view of the sunrise.

Thummel. Former station on the Union Pacific Railroad.

Vayden. Burlington Railroad station.

Vick. Post office established May 14, 1883; name changed to Palmer November 2, 1887. Origin of the name not learned.

Worms. Census not available. Post office established October 20, 1897; discontinued December 5, 1901. Former town probably named for Worms, Rhein-Hessen, Germany.

MORRILL COUNTY

Named in honor of Charles Henry Morrill (1843-1928), regent of the University of Nebraska. Originally a part of Cheyenne County, it was established at the general election November 3, 1908, and proclaimed by Governor George L. Sheldon, November 12, 1908.

Alden. Station on the Burlington Railroad located southeast of Bridgeport.

Angora. Peak population (1950), 80. Post office name changed from Antelope Hill September 21, 1901. Supposedly named by railroad officials, possibly for Angora in Anatolia, Asia Minor.

Antelope Hill. Post office name changed to Angora September 21, 1901. Probably named for antelope seen on the slopes of hills in the area.

Atkins. Station on the Burlington Railroad. Possibly named in honor of Col. Auburn Wayland Atkins, who helped establish the first irrigation ditch in the county.

Bayard. Peak population (1980), 1,435. Post office established April 21, 1888. Town named by Millard and Jay Senteny for their former home of Bayard, Iowa.

Becker. Station on the Burlington Railroad located near Bayard.

Beet. Former station on the Union Pacific Railroad.

Bonner. Station on the Burlington Railroad located near Lightner.

Bridgeport. Peak population (1980), 1,668. Post office established March 9, 1900. This town was made county seat upon formation of the county. Name is derived from bridge over the Platte River erected by Henry Tefft Clarke in 1876 to facilitate travel from Sidney to the Black Hills during the gold rush.

Broadwater. Peak population (1930), 367. Post office established May 25, 1909. Town named in honor of General Broadwater by his friend A. L. Mohler, president of the Union Pacific Railroad.

Camp Clarke. Post office established June 16, 1876; discontinued March 20, 1901. Named in honor of Henry Tefft Clarke, Jr., a Bellevue engineer who built the bridge across the North Platte River at this point.

Chimney Rock. Post office established February 28, 1913; discontinued June 30, 1922. Probably established on an old Pony Express station site. A visitors center near the rock is operated by the Nebraska State Historical Society.

Chimney Rock. This was Pony Express Station No. 34 in Nebraska. It was named by overland travellers for the familiar landmark along the Oregon Trail.

Clark's Station. See Camp Clark.

Cleman. Post office established September 25, 1896; discontinued June 15, 1914. Ranch post office named in honor of John Kleman, first postmaster. Postal authorities spelled the name with a "c" instead of a "k."

Colyer. Post office established September 22, 1908; moved to Garden County May 15, 1919. Named in honor of Mrs Nannie J. Colyer, first postmistress.

Courthouse Rock. This was Pony Express Station No. 33 in Nebraska. Named for historic Courthouse Rock, one of a series of familiar landmarks for early overland trail travelers.

Craft. Possibly a station on the Union Pacific Railroad.

Cyrus. Post office established August 14, 1896; discontinued December 31, 1922. Possibly named in honor of Cyrus Johnson, settler.

De Graw. Station on the Burlington Railroad. George De Graw was a prominent ranchman.

Eastwood. Post office established March 29, 1907; discontinued May 15, 1917. Named for the precinct in which it was located.

Finley. Former station on the Union Pacific Railroad located east of Broadwater.

Goodstreak. Post office established February 15, 1911; discontinued November 30, 1915. Named by a Dr. Worth, pioneer physician and homesteader. He reported to friends that surface fuel was abundant and that he had found a "good streak."

Greenwood Station. This stage station and inn on the Sidney-Black Hills Trail was located on the Morrill and Cheyenne County borders.

Guthrie. Former station on the Burlington Railroad named in honor of S. L. Guthrie.

Hayne's Station. Stage station and inn on the Sidney-Black Hills Trail situated on Redwillow Creek, four miles west of Angora.

Hickory. Post office established July 25, 1913; discontinued 1932. Origin of the name not learned. First postmaster was Samuel Hickman.

Irving. Post office established December 19, 1898; discontinued April 30, 1909. Named in honor of Frank Irving, settler.

Kelley. Former station on the Union Pacific Railroad. Probably named in honor of Judge W. R. Kelley.

Kemp. Station on the Burlington Railroad.

Kuhn. Former station on the Union Pacific Railroad named for the senior member of Kuhn, Loeb and Company.

Lightner. Post office established October 2, 1909; discontinued February 28, 1911. Former post office and present railroad station named in honor of Bonus Lightner, first postmaster.

Lisco. This place established a short time in Morrill County before its removal just across the line into Garden County. See Lisco, Garden County.

Lynn. Post office established October 18, 1910; discontinued July 31, 1923. Name suggested by J. L. Johnson either for a relative or a friend.

Midway. Post office established August 12, 1889; discontinued March 9, 1896. Named for being located midway between two places.

Mohler. Station on the Union Pacific Railroad possibly named for A. L. Mohler, former president of the line.

Mud Springs. This was Pony Express Station No. 32 in Nebraska. Location was twelve miles southeast of the present town of Bridgeport.

Northport. Peak population (1960), 125. Post office established June 1, 1910. The town derives its name from its location on the north side of the Platte River. Post office discontinued 1975. Mail served from Bridgeport.

Perrin. Station on the Burlington Railroad.

Piper. Station on the Burlington Railroad.

Prinz. Station on the Burlington Railroad.

Pumpkin Creek Station. Stage station on the Sidney-Black Hills Trail located about two miles west of Court House Rock.

Redington. Peak population (1940), 31. Post office established January 11, 1884; discontinued 1963. Town commemorates famous Indian fighter Henry V. Redington. The region was part of his patrol area in the 1870s and 1880s. Redington was an important trading center near the scenic Wildcat and South Ranges. Today the site is known as Morrill County's ghost town.

Redwillow Station. Stage station on the Sidney-Black Hills Trail.

Riley. Former station on the Union Pacific Railroad.

Schermerhorn. Station on the Union Pacific Railroad.

Silverthorn. Post office established January 15, 1892; discontinued December 30, 1916. Origin of the name not learned.

Simla. Post office established September 10, 1900; discontinued January 30, 1915. Former railroad station and former post office located on the site of a Pony Express station. Simla named by Burlington Railroad officials for a province in India. There is a station by the same name in Colorado.

Towers. Station on the Union Pacific Railroad.

Vance. Former station on the Burlington Railroad north of Northport.

Vockery. Former station on the Union Pacific Railroad.

Wellsville. Post office established December 16, 1886; discontinued November 15, 1890. Origin of the name not learned.

Yockey. Post office established November 15, 1920; discontinued September 15, 1923. Possibly named in honor of Vera Yockey, county superintendent of schools.

NANCE COUNTY

Named in honor of Albinus Nance (1848-1911), governor of Nebraska from 1879 to 1882. County originated February 4, 1879. The boundaries were defined by an act of the Legislature approved February 13, 1879.

Belgrade. Peak population (1920), 493. Post office name changed from Myra May 7, 1883. Town named by James Main for Belgrade, Serbia, because its location on a hill resembled the locale of the Serbian city overlooking the Danube and Sava rivers.

Cedar Rapids. Location with a post office moved to Fullerton in 1879.

Cedar River. Post office established June 7, 1880; discontinued 1881. Named for the nearby Cedar River.

Fullerton. Peak population (1940), 1,707. Post office established December 8, 1879. Town named in honor of Randall Fuller, one of the earliest settlers. He was instrumental in securing the county seat and donated the land on which it was built March 1, 1881.

Genoa. Peak population (1910), 1,376. Post office established July 13, 1858. Town named by Mormons who lived here briefly in 1857 before journeying to Utah.

Glenwood. Post office established January 20, 1879; discontinued May 5, 1891. Probably named for one of the nineteen places in the United States called Glenwood.

Kent. Former station on the Union Pacific Railroad named for the Kent Cattle Company.

Lone Tree. Post office established September 4, 1879; discontinued August 31, 1885. Probably named for an area landmark.

Merchiston. Station on the Union Pacific Railroad possibly named for Merchiston, Scotland.

Myra. Post office established May 16, 1879; name changed to Belgrade May 7, 1883. Origin of the name not learned. First postmaster was Charles Harris.

North Star. Post office established December 21, 1901; discontinued October 29, 1902. Probably named for Polaris (North Star) in the constellation Ursa Minor (Little Dipper).

Olive. Post office established July 10, 1884; discontinued September 19, 1904. Origin of the name not learned. First postmaster was Thomas McIntyre.

Omro. Post office established September 12, 1884; discontinued April 8, 1887. Probably named for Omro, Wisconsin.

Redwing. Post office established April 17, 1879; discontinued September 7, 1894. Possibly named for Redwing, Minnesota, or for an Indian warrior.

Tekonsha. Post office established January 27, 1879; discontinued November 4, 1885. Probably named for the Pottawatomi Indian leader or for a town in Michigan named in his honor.

Timber Creek. Early settlement in Nance County.

Westgard. Post office established December 9, 1879; discontinued May 19, 1888. Said to be named by a settler for a place in Norway.

Woodville. Post office established April 23, 1913; discontinued February 15, 1919. Proably named for its location in a wooded area.

NEMAHA COUNTY

Named for the Nemaha River. Nemaha is derived from the Oto Indian word "nimaha" for miry water: ni, water; maha, miry. County boundaries were defined by an act of the Legislature approved March 7, 1855; redefined January 26, 1856, and November 1, 1858. Formerly part of Forney County.

Aspinwall. Post office established November 29, 1865; discontinued December 14, 1903. Town probably named for Aspinwall, Iowa.

Auburn. Peak population (1970), 3,650. Post office established February 1, 1886. Town named for Auburn, New York, by Charles D. Nixon. Auburn won county seat in election with Brownville in 1883.

Bedford. Post office name changed from Sherman April 27, 1880; name changed to Howe February 13, 1882. Named for the precinct in which it was located. Twelve states have places called Bedford.

Bracken. Post office established January 12, 1897; discontinued October 26, 1907. Possibly named for E. P. Bracken, former roadmaster of the Burlington Railroad of the Wymore division.

Bratton. Post office established March 10, 1870; name changed to Eden January 7, 1897. Probably named for George W. Bratton, early settler and former county treasurer.

Brock. Peak population (1900), 543. Post office name changed from Podunk February 13, 1882. Town said to be named by railroad officials of the Chicago, Burlington and Quincy line for the superintendent of this division.

Brownville. Peak population (1880), 1,309. Post office established January 16, 1855. Named in honor of Richard Brown who, with B. B. Frazer, owned the townsite and planned and platted the original town in April 1856. County seat, located here upon organization of the county, lost by election to Auburn. This was an early port on the Missouri River before the advent of the railroad.

Calvert. Post office established October 3, 1881; name changed to South Auburn June 8, 1882. Probably named for a local settler or railroad official.

Carson. Post office established February 7, 1882; discontinued May 31, 1883. Possibly named for John L. Carson of the Lincoln Land Company.

Clifton. Post office established February 24, 1868; discontinued May 29, 1883. Named for the surrounding rocky hills and cliffs.

Dayton. Post office established December 1856; name changed to Howard November 11, 1867. Probably named for Dayton, Ohio.

Eddy's Switch. A former station on the Brownville, Fort Kearny and Pacific Railroad and the Burlington Railroad.

Eden. Post office name changed from Bratton January 7, 1897; discontinued November 26, 1901. Reason for name not learned.

Febing. Peak population (1890), 200. Post office established June 21, 1871; discontinued May 28, 1894. Origin of the name of this former town not learned.

Frederick. Proposed town that never developed beyond the platting stage.

Glenrock. Peak population (1900), 120. Post office established August 23, 1859; discontinued 1930. Former town named by Irvin Bristol for its location in a valley near stone quarries.

Golden Spring. Probably another proposed town that never got beyond the recording stage.

Grant. Post office name changed from Morrallton November 1, 1864; discontinued July 27, 1882. Probably named for Gen. Ulysses Grant, commander of the Union Army during the Civil War.

Hillsdale. Census not available. Post office established August 26, 1868; discontinued March 30, 1891. Former town named for its site west of St. Deroin. Platted June 15, 1876.

Howard. Post office established November 11, 1867; name changed to Podunk May 15, 1880. Origin of the name not learned. First postmaster was Jonathan Higgins.

Howe. Peak population (1900), 248. Post office name changed from Bedford February 13, 1882. Made a rural station of Auburn, 1963. Town named in honor of Maj. Church Howe, American consul at Palermo, Italy, and at Sheffield, England. His former home was near the town.

Johnson. Peak population (1900), 352. Post office established February 25, 1873. Named for founder Julius A. Johnson, official of the Brownville and Fort Kearny Railroad. Town platted by Lincoln Land Company.

Julian. Peak population (1900), 206. Post office established December 31, 1882. The first post office was established at a farm house one mile from the present town of Julian. Named in honor of Julian Bahaud, who owned several farms in the area.

Lafayette. Probably another proposed town that never got beyond the recording stage.

Little York. Probably another proposed town that never advanced beyond the recording stage.

Locust Grove. Post office established February 13, 1868; discontinued February 2, 1869. Probably named for honey locust trees growing in the region. A schoolhouse in the area is called Locust Grove.

London. Census not available. Post office established September 2, 1867; discontinued September 16, 1895. Former town possibly named by Robert Heap, who once lived in London, England.

McCandless. An elevator siding operated by A. R. McCandless and Sons.

Minerva. Another proposed town that never got beyond the recording stage.

Morrallton. Census not available. Post office established July 15, 1854; name changed to Grant November 1, 1864. Former port on the Missouri River named in honor of Horatio Morrall, first postmaster.

Mount Vernon. Post office established January 8, 1857; name changed to Peru October 9, 1867. Probably named for the home of President George Washington, located in Virginia on the Potomac River.

Nemaha. Peak population (1880), 475. Post office established April 1, 1856. Town named for the county and river. Probably called Nemaha City at one time.

North Auburn. Post office name changed from Sheridan June 8, 1882; annexed to Auburn May 28, 1899.

Pebble Creek. Probably another embryo town that never got beyond the platting stage.

Peru. Peak population (1970), 1,380. Post office name changed from Mount Vernon October 9, 1867. Named by early settlers who came here from Peru, Illinois. Mount Vernon Academy, a Methodist institution founded in 1861, became Peru State Normal in 1867 by legislative enactment. It is today Peru State College.

Podunk. Post office name changed from Howard May 15, 1880; name changed to Brock February 13, 1882. Probably whimsically called Podunk because of lack of a suitable name. This name used informally to characterize a small, unimportant, isolated community.

Popens. Post office established June 15, 1865; discontinued April 26, 1866. Probably named in honor of a local settler.

Rohrs. Census not available. Post office established October 8, 1917; discontinued 1945. Town possibly named in honor of a local settler.

Rosefield. Another proposed town that never went beyond the platting stage.

San Francisco. This town, platted by Captain Holland and others from St. Louis, Missouri, failed to materialize. Located between Nemaha City and Aspinwall on Missouri River.

Sheridan. Post office established August 21, 1867; name changed to North Auburn June 8, 1882. Probably named in honor of Phil Sheridan, Union general.

Sherman. Post office established March 22, 1866; name changed to Bedford April 27, 1880. Probably named in honor of William Sherman, Union general.

Sonora. Another proposed town that never grew beyond the platting stage. Probably named for Sonora, Mexico, or for the famous gold mining town of the California gold rush.

South Auburn. Post office name changed from Calvert June 8, 1882; annexed to Auburn May 28, 1899.

St. Deroin. Census not available. Post office established March 23, 1854; discontinued April 15, 1910. This former town, one of the oldest in Nebraska, was washed away by a Missouri River flood in 1911. Named in honor of Joseph Deroin, who owned the land on which the town was built.

Stein. Proposed town that never advanced beyond the recording stage.

St. Frederick. Census not available. Post office established October 19, 1857; discontinued May 26, 1879. Name is probably Germanic in origin.

St. George. Another embryo town that never progressed beyond the recording stage.

Willowdale. Post office established October 5, 1878; discontinued March 20, 1891. Probably named for Its locatlon near a small valley where numerous willow trees grew.

Wing. Place recorded on maps of Nemaha County.

Wood Siding. Former station on the Burlington Railroad located near Peru.

NUCKOLLS COUNTY

Named in honor of Stephen F. Nuckolls (1825-79), prominent Nebraska statesman and pioneer. Boundaries of the county were defined by an act of the Legislature approved January 13, 1860. The county was organized June 27, 1871.

Abdal. Post office established July 19, 1893; discontinued April 1, 1902. Former village on the Missouri Pacific Railroad. The name is Arabic, meaning a good or religious man.

Alechol. Post office established July 19, 1893; discontinued April 8, 1902.

Angus. Peak population (1900), 118. Post office name changed from Ox Bow December 6, 1886. Town platted by the Lincoln Land Company and named in honor of J. B. Angus, official of the Burlington Railroad. Post office discontinued 1977. Mail served from Nelson.

Arnsburg. Post office established November 8, 1887; discontinued July 16, 1889. Named for a town in Germany.

Baird. Post office established September 5, 1881; name changed to Beulah March 3, 1885. Possibly named in honor of Henry Baird, settler, or Robert M. Baird, first postmaster.

Beachamville. Post office established April 12, 1875; name changed to St. Stephen February 9, 1881. Named in honor of James S. Beacham, first postmaster.

Beulah. Post office name changed from Baird March 3, 1885; discontinued June 9, 1886. Origin of the name has not been learned. First postmaster was Charles Childress.

Bostwick. Peak population (1920), 157. Post office name changed from Irving November 20, 1885. Named for the precinct, which was named for an official of the Burlington Railroad. Post office discontinued 1970. Mail served from Superior.

Cadams. Peak population (1930), 101. Post office established November 11, 1897; discontinued 1941. Former town was to be named Adams, for C. Adams, a banker of Superior, but there was already a post office in the state so named. Postal authorities added the first initial of his name to Adams, thus coining Cadams. The Pioneer Town Site Company platted the town.

Coy. Post office established February 10, 1900; name changed to Sedan September 25, 1906. Origin of the name not learned.

Delphi. Former station on the Missouri Pacific Railroad located near Rosemont.

Elkton. Post office established December 18, 1871; discontinued October 11, 1886. Named by the first settlers in the area. Elkton vied for county seat in 1872.

Elora. Post office established January 20, 1882; discontinued July 24, 1891. Daniel Kenny and J. Warren Keifer, Jr. took the word Elora out of a post office directory. Probably named for Elora, Tennessee; another source says Elora, Ontario, Canada.

Hardy. Peak population (1910), 496. Post office name changed from Spring Valley June 17, 1880. Town probably named for an official of the Burlington Railroad.

Henrietta. Post office established February 13, 1871; name changed to Ruskin June 23, 1887. Origin of the name not learned. First postmaster was Thomas B. Johnson.

Irving. Post office established August 10, 1885; name changed to Bostwick November 20, 1885. Named in honor of William Irving, superintendent of the Burlington Railroad when the town was established.

Keithleys. Former station on the Missouri Pacific Railroad.

Lawrence. Peak population (1920, 1930), 528. Post office established February 7, 1887. Town named for an official of the Burlington Railroad.

Mill Spur. Former locality and railroad station.

Mount Clare. Peak population (1920), 131. Post office established February 20, 1889; discontinued 1945. This former town and railroad station on the Missouri Pacific Railroad received its name from two sources. Mount was derived from the town's location on a ridge between the Blue and Republican rivers. Clare was taken from the name of Capt. Clare Adams of Omaha, an official in the Land, Loan and Town Site Company that promoted the town.

Nelson. Peak population (1900, 1910), 978. Post office established January 26, 1874. Town named in honor of Horatio Nelson Wheeler of Peoria, Illinois. An election for county seat, (involving Vernon, Elkton, and Nelson) was held in October 1872. Nelson was favored because of its central location in the county. Another election was held July 30, 1889, between Nelson and Superior, with Nelson retaining the county seat.

Nora. Peak population (1920), 130. Post office established May 14, 1878. The post office established on a farm owned by a Mr. Whiting three fourths of a mile from the present townsite. Whiting, when requested to name the new office, scanned a postal directory and suggested Nora (also in Illinois), which was approved. When the town was built, the post office was moved to the new site.

Oak. Peak population (1910), 237. Post office established June 23, 1874. Town named for nearby oak trees.

Oak Grove Station. This was Pony Express Station No. 7 in Nebraska, one and one-fourth miles from the present town of Oak. C. E. Comstock owned the Oak Grove Ranch. In 1864 the neighborhood was attacked by Sioux Indians.

Ox Bow. Post office established October 30, 1873; name changed to Angus December 6, 1886. Probably named for the U-shaped river bend where only a neck of land remained between two channels of the stream. There was a large flour mill on the stream.

Rosa. Former station on the Chicago and North Western Railroad.

Ruskin. Peak population (1920), 360. Post office name changed from Henrietta June 23, 1887. Commemorates English author John Ruskin (1819-1900). The town was the terminus for the Chicago, Rock Island and Pacific Railroad from Horton, Kansas.

Schell. Post office established June 25, 1883; discontinued February 7, 1887. Named in honor of Joseph T. Schell, first postmaster.

Sedan. Peak population (1950), 35. Post office name changed from Coy September 25, 1906; discontinued 1953. Mail served from Edgar. Town probably named for a city in France.

Smyrna. Peak population (1900), 58. Post office established February 18, 1887; discontinued January 31, 1913. One source says named for a seaport in Asia Minor. However, there are eight places in the United States having this name.

Spring Valley. Post office established March 15, 1875; name changed to Hardy June 17, 1880. Probably named for a spring in the valley where the office was located.

Stateline. Former railroad station located on the Kansas-Nebraska border.

St. Stephen. Peak population (1880), 18. Post office name changed from Beachamville February 9, 1881; discontinued April 2, 1887. Former hamlet probably named for a local church.

Superior. Peak population (1950), 3,227. Post office established October 23, 1872. Town named for the superior quality of the land in the vicinity compared with other land along the railroad grade.

Valley Home. Former station on the Missouri Pacific Railroad. Located near Superior.

Vernon. Contended for county seat in election with Elkton and Nelson in 1872 but probably did not last long enough for a post office to be established. Reason for name not learned.

Warwick Spur. Former station on the Burlington Railroad.

OTOE COUNTY

Named for the Oto tribe. The boundaries were defined by an act of the Legislature, approved March 2, 1855, and redefined by an act approved January 26, 1856.

Arlington. Post office established February 26, 1875; discontinued April 5, 1876. Origin of the name not learned.

Askotope. Place mentioned in the Session Laws of Nebraska. Probably a proposed townsite.

Aucoria. Post office established December 11, 1858; name changed to Colona April 27, 1860. Origin of the name not learned.

Avondale. Post office established February 19, 1885; discontinued June 14, 1889. Probably named for one of the eight places in the United States called Avondale, which probably adopted the name from England.

Barney. Former station on the Burlington Railroad located eleven miles south of Nebraska City.

Belmont. Proposed townsite which eventually became part of Nebraska City.

Bennett's Ferry. Post office established January 28, 1856; name changed to Otoe City April 20, 1857. Named in honor of a Mr. Bennett who operated a ferry across the Missouri River to Iowa.

Berlin. Post office established 1882; name changed to Otoe October 18, 1918. One source says town named for Berlin, Germany, and another for E. D. Berlin, Civil War veteran and Otoe County pioneer.

Brooklyn. Early settlement said to rival Old Wyoming as a Missouri River port.

Burr. Peak population (1920), 133. Post office name changed from Burr Oak September 3, 1888. See Burr Oak.

Burr Oak. Post office established July 15, 1869; name changed to Burr September 3, 1888. Town derived its name from a grove of burr oak trees. Name changed to Burr to avoid confusion with Burr Oak, Kansas.

California City. Proposed town that never got beyond the platting and recording stage.

Cambridge. Proposed town in early Otoe County that never got beyond the platting and recording stage.

Camp Creek. Post office established April 21, 1875; discontinued January 13, 1879. Named for the creek on which post office was located.

Cio. Railroad station name for the town of Delta.

Colona. Post office name changed from Aucoria April 27, 1860; discontinued February 11, 1861. Origin of the name not learned.

Condit. Projected town that never got beyond the platting and recording stage.

Crete Junction. A junction for two railroads.

Delaware. Former station on the Midland Pacific Railroad located east of Dunbar.

Delaware City. Post office established February 24, 1858; discontinued June 23, 1858. Probably named for the state of Delaware or for Delaware, Ohio.

Delta. Post office established June 26, 1882; name changed to Lorton November 6, 1894. Town probably named for a small delta on the Missouri River.

Dennison. Proposed name for Dunbar.

Douglas. Peak population (1910), 305. Post office name changed from Hendricks October 29, 1888. One source says a Mr. Douglas owned the eighty acres which included the present townsite. Another source thinks that Simpson McKibben married a Miss Douglas and the town adopted her maiden name. First postmaster was George M. Douglas.

Dover. Post office established September 28, 1885; discontinued July 19, 1901. Probably named for one of eighteen places in the United States with this name. They were probably named for Dover, England.

Dresden. Post office established September 3, 1873; discontinued May 13, 1887. Probably named for Dresden, Germany. Post office site on the old location of the town of Old Wyoming.

Dunbar. Peak population (1940), 336. Post office name changed from Wilson April 2, 1874. Named in honor of Thomas Dunbar, oldest resident in the community. Town platted by Midland Pacific Railroad.

Edgar. Probably another proposed town that did not go beyond the platting and recording stage.

Ela. Post office established May 24, 1872; discontinued March 26, 1878. Origin of the name not learned. First postmaster was William K. Ehlers.

Elberon. Station on the Burlington Railroad located near El Dorado. Another proposed town that never got beyond the platting and recording stage.

Elmwood City. Proposed town that eventually became part of Nebraska City.

Emerson. Proposed town that never got beyond the recording and platting stage.

Erie. Proposed town that never materialized after the recording and platting stage.

Faires. Proposed town that never progressed beyond the recording stage.

Farmersville. Post office name changed from Woodville July 29, 1862; discontinued January 15, 1863. Named for the farming community.

Fort Kearny. Post office established, 1847; discontinued 1849. U.S. Army fort established in 1846. It was a log blockhouse on a hill overlooking the Missouri River near present Nebraska City. When it became evident that the area was outside the general stream of overland travel, the fort was moved west on the Platte River near the present city of Kearney. (Town and fort spelled differently.)

Frankfort. Place mentioned in early Otoe County history.

Greggsport. This early settlement in Otoe County eventually became part of Nebraska City.

Groveland. Proposed town that never got beyond the platting and recording stage.

Hamilton. Post office established January 29, 1854; discontinued October 12, 1858. Origin of the name not learned.

Hendricks. Post office established February 28, 1863; name changed to Douglas October 29, 1888. Named for a local settler.

Iola. Post office established May 6, 1872; name changed to Victoria March 5, 1874. Origin of the name not learned. First postmaster was Joseph Young.

Kearney City. Post office established May 23, 1856; discontinued April 6, 1857. Named for the former Fort Kearny by John Boulware.

Knoxville. Proposed town that never advanced beyond the recording and platting stage.

Lorton. Peak population (1900), 290. Post office name changed from Delta November 6, 1894. In 1881 Delta was platted on the present townsite of Lorton. Later when the Missouri Pacific Railroad passed through, it objected because there was a Delta, Kansas. The railroad called the spot Cio, while the post office remained Delta. To prevent confusion, citizens chose Lorton for both station and post office, honoring Robert Lorton, in the 1890s a wholesale grocer in Nebraska City who called on Cio merchants.

Marietta. Proposed town filed for recording in October 1856.

McWilliams. Former name of Tangeman before it became a railroad station.

Minersville. Census not available. Post office name changed from Otoe City December 21, 1874; discontinued February 15, 1923. Former town named for the coal deposits found nearby.

Nebraska City. Peak population (1890), 11,941. Post office name changed from Table Creek March 14, 1855. Nebraska City named for the state of Nebraska. Most of the ground now embraced by the city was previously occupied by the original Fort Kearny. John Boulware, John B. Boulware, Hiram P. Downs, Stephen F. Nuckolls, Allen A. Bradford, and others had their share in making this city. Charles W. Pierce surveyed and staked it off, and construction began July 10, 1854. The city was incorporated January 26, 1856. Nebraska City retained the county seat after its name change from Table Creek. At first a trading post, it became a famous river port, as well as the starting point for overland freighters and emigrants heading west. Arbor Lodge, the home of Arbor Day founder J. Sterling Morton, is a state historical park operated by the Nebraska Game and Parks Commission.

Nesuma. Proposed town that never got beyond the platting and recording stage. Location was to be one mile southeast of the present town of Unadilla.

North Branch. Post office established April 5, 1871; discontinued January 26, 1877.

North Nebraska City. Suburb of Nebraska City.

Northville. Proposed town that never got beyond the recording and platting stage.

Nursery Hill. Post office established March 13, 1863; name changed to Syracuse March 6, 1872. Probably named for a sizeable acreage of nursery stock.

Old Wyoming. Post office established November 21, 1856; discontinued prior to 1868. A mail depot and stage route point for the Pioneer Stage Company between St. Joseph, MIssouri, and Omaha. It was also a steamboat port on the Missouri River and outfitting station for Mormons moving westward.

Olson. Place mentioned in early Otoe County history.

Osage. Post office established July 19, 1871; discontinued June 2, 1890. Probably named for the Osage Indians.

Otoe. Peak population (1940), 298. Post office name changed from Berlin October 18, 1918. Town named for the county.

Otoe City. Post office name changed from Bennett's Ferry April 20, 1857; name changed to Minersville December 21, 1874. Named for the county.

Paisley. Census not available. Post office established January 26, 1869; discontinued September 17, 1872. Origin of the name not learned.

Palmyra. Peak population (2000), 546. Post office established June 20, 1862. The Rev. John W. Taggert founded the town, which was platted on his homestead. His daughter, Mrs. Jeanette Taggert White, named the place after the ancient city of Palmyra, Asia Minor.

Paul. Peak population (1910, 1920, 1930), 75. Post office established May 20, 1884; discontinued 1955. Mail served from Nebraska City. The townsite was platted on land owned by Paulinus Kuwitzky, who wished the town to be named for him. A compromise was reached by using the first four letters of his Christian name.

Prairie City. This early settlement became part of Nebraska City.

Saltville. Proposed town that never got beyond the recording and platting stage.

Solon. Post office established March 23, 1868; discontinued July 17, 1888. Reason for the name not learned.

South Nebraska City. Settlement founded about 1855 and annexed to Nebraska City December 31, 1857.

South Syracuse. Locality in early Otoe County.

Spring Grove City. Place mentioned in early Otoe County history.

St. Charles. Proposed town filed and recorded January 30, 1858. site was one mile south and one mile west of present town of Lorton.

St. Peters. This proposed addition to Wyoming was to be platted by Thomas Asking, but it never got beyond the recording stage.

Summerville. Proposed town on the Missouri River filed and recorded July 25, 1857; it never got beyond the promotion stage.

Summit. Place mentioned in early Otoe County history.

Sunnyside. Proposed town that never developed beyond the recording and platting stage. Location was to be two miles south of Nebraska City.

Swift. Census not available. Post office established April 24, 1883; discontinued May 28, 1895. Origin of the name of this former town has not been ascertained.

Syracuse. Peak population (2000), 1,762. Post office name changed from Nursery Hill March 6, 1872. Town named after the precinct, which was named for Syracuse, New York, former home of George Warner, settler.

Table Creek. Post office established December 20, 1853; name changed to Nebraska City March 14, 1855. Located on creek with the same name. Table Creek was first county seat of Otoe County.

Talbot. Former station on the Midland Pacific Railroad located just west of Nebraska City.

Talmage. Peak population (1920), 525. Post office established April 27, 1882. Town platted by Clark Puffer in 1881 and named by him in honor of Dewitt Talmage, division superintendent of the newly constructed Missouri Pacific Railroad. Later Talmage became one of the foremost Presbyterian clergymen in the United States.

Tangeman. Station on the Missouri Pacific Railroad.

Turlington. Post office established February 8, 1881; discontinued November 18, 1901. Named for nineteenth century inventor and entrepreneur Turlington Harvey of Chicago.

Unadilla. Peak population (2000), 342. Post office established April 4, 1872. Town named by I. N. White for his former home, Unadilla, New York. Unadilla, an Iroquois Indian word, means place of meeting.

Victoria. Post office name changed from Iola March 5, 1874; discontinued February 8, 1893. Probably named for the popular queen then ruling England.

Wilson. Post office established May 16, 1866; name changed to Dunbar April 2, 1874. Probably named in honor of Thomas Wilson, first postmaster.

Woodville. Post office established November 21, 1856; name changed to Farmersville Juiy 29, 1862. Probably named in honor of the Rev. Joel M. Wood, member of Nebraska's first territorial legislature. The place later became part of the Greggsport addition to Nebraska City.

Worcester. Place mentioned in early Otoe County history.

WX Siding. Station on the Missouri Pacific Railroad.

Wyoming. Post office established, 1887; discontinued 1928. Present railroad station and former town named after Wyoming, Pennsylvania. Located near the site of Old Wyoming.

Xenia. Place mentioned in early Otoe County history.

PAWNEE COUNTY

Named after the Pawnee tribe. The boundaries were defined by an act of the Legislature approved March 6, 1855; January 25, 1856; and reapproved January 8, 1862.

Appleton. Former station on the Burlington Railroad. Located north of Table Rock.

Armour. Peak population (1910, 1920, 1930), 100. Former station on the Kansas City and Northwestern Railroad. Post office established February 21, 1890; discontinued 1935. Former town started by J. M. Cravens after 1893. Post office had been established previously near the village. Some authorities believed town named for Armour, Chicago meat packer. Others believe named for director of the KC&NW.

Bookwalter. Peak population (1910), 56. Post office established February 25, 1890; discontinued August 30, 1919. Named in honor of J. W. Bookwalter, who formerly owned the land on which the town was located. Station on the Kansas City and Northwestern Railroad.

Burchard. Peak population (1910), 315. Post office name changed from Tip's Branch January 3, 1882. Founded by Lincoln Land Company in 1881. Named in honor of a local minister named Burchard.

Butler. This locality eventually became the Violet post office. Named in honor of David Butler, Nebraska's first governor (1867-71).

Calla. Post office established April 15, 1870; discontinued June 13, 1876. Origin of the name not learned.

Cincinnati. Post office established November 24, 1869; name changed to Dubois December 16, 1886. Named for Cincinnati, Ohio, by Christian Bobst, pioneer who formed a company to settle the area.

Dubois. Peak population (1910), 339. Post office name changed from Cincinnati December 16, 1886. Named in honor of a Mr. Dubois, chief engineer of the first railroad built through the town. John Mallory and G. W. Miner gave the right-of-way.

Fairview. Post office established May 12, 1860; discontinued October 4, 1861. Name is descriptive.

Gartner. Locality established two miles north of Mayberry and named for a settler. Name changed after the railroad entered the area.

Jacksonville. Place mentioned in early Pawnee County history.

Lewiston. Peak population (1930), 168. Post office established August 19, 1887. Named in honor of Virginia Lewis, daughter of Mr. and Mrs. Ford Lewis, who owned the land on which the town was platted.

Linton. Post office established January 24, 1863; discontinued August 15, 1874. Origin of the name unknown. There is also a Linton, Indiana.

Mayberry. Peak population (1910), 125. Post office name changed from Newhome June 26, 1884; discontinued 1935. This hamlet uas originally located one and one-half miles from present site. It was moved with the coming of the Rock Island Railroad. Named in honor of Charles N. Mayberry, pioneer.

Mission. Peak population (1900), 62. Post office established October 3, 1870; discontinued December 11, 1900. Former town on Mission Creek. The stream named in honor of the Presbyterian Church mission to the Oto Indians.

Newhome. Post office established April 5, 1871; name changed to Mayberry June 26, 1884. Origin of the name not learned.

Pawnee City. Peak population (1900), 1,969. Post office established June 2, 1858. County seat town named for the county. Surveyed by Joseph J. Lebo in 1857. Railroad name for Pawnee.

Pleasant Valley. Post office established August 28, 1863; discontinued January 11, 1869. Named for the pleasant surroundings.

Shaffer. Post office established November 1, 1897; discontinued July 10, 1900. Named in honor of Alexander D. Shaffer, first postmaster.

Steinauer. Peak population (1910), 248. Post office established November 18, 1874. Named in honor of Joseph A. Steinauer, first postmaster and pioneer who located here in 1856.

Table Rock. Peak population (1900), 852. Post office established December 9, 1856. Derives its name from a large table rock situated on high land near the village; who named it, and when, is not known. Platted by Table Rock Town Company in 1855. Actual settlement began in 1857.

Tate. Peak population (1910), 100. Post office established December 9, 1891; discontinued October 15, 1920. Station on the Kansas City and Northwestern Railroad and declined with discontinuance of the railroad. Named for KC&NW director.

Tip's Branch. Named for the creek on which it was located.

Turkey Creek. Post office established January 29, 1857; moved to Johnson County August 22, 1860. Named for the creek on which it was located.

Violet. Peak population (1900), 27. Post office established February 5, 1885; discontinued 1936. Former town named in honor of daughter of David Butler, first governor of Nebraska (1867-71).

West Branch. Post office established April 5, 1871; discontinued January 17, 1881. Named for the creek on which it was located.

Wolf Creek. Post office established February 18, 1880; discontinued November 11, 1886. Named for the creek on which it was located.

PERKINS COUNTY

Named in 1888 in honor of Charles E. Perkins (1840-1907), president of the Chicago, Burlington and Quincy Railway system. First settlement of the county began in 1885. Local tradition maintains that the county was named after Joseph Perkins, resident of Grant. Perkins County was formed from Keith County by vote November 8, 1887.

Brandon. Peak population (1950), 35. Post office established March 18, 1890. Town probably named in honor of a railroad official on the Burlington Railroad or for Brandon, Ohio. Post office made a rural station of Grant in 1963.

Chris Creek. Locality in Perkins County.

Cummings. In honor of W. H. Cummings, name first considered for town of Grainton; however, there was already a Cummings in the state.

Elliston. Post office established August 27, 1886; name changed to Madrid October 31, 1887. Probably named for a local settler.

Elsie. Peak population (1930), 262. Post office established September 6, 1887. Town said to be named for a daughter of Charles E. Perkins, president of the Burlington Railroad. Another source says named for a daughter of Joseph Perkins, a Grant merchant.

Flint. Post office established February 11, 1889; discontinued June 13, 1891. Origin of the name is unknown. There is also a Flint, Michigan.

Grainton. Peak population (1930), 139. Post office established March 16, 1918. Probably named for the great amount of grain shipped by the railroad from this point.

Grant. Peak population (1980), 1,270. Post office established May 11, 1886. County seat named in honor of President Ulysses S. Grant. Town first built three-fourths of a mile from present site. Grant won county seat in election with Madrid and Lisbon.

Lisbon. Census not available. Post office established October 27, 1887; discontinued May 28, 1891. Origin of the name not learned. Probably named for Lisbon, Portugal.

Madrid. Peak population (1930), 449. Post office name changed from Elliston October 3, 1887. Platted by the Lincoln Land Company and named after Madrid, Spain. Vied for county seat with Grant and Lisbon.

Pearl. Post office moved from Chase County May 9, 1900; discontinued May 15, 1914. Origin of the name not learned. First postmaster was Henry Waggoneer.

Perkins. Post office established April 6, 1889; discontinued January 8, 1890. Named for the county.

Phebe. Post office established February 1, 1886; discontinued August 31, 1914. Named in honor of Mrs. Phoebe Jack, first postmistress. The "o" omitted by postal authorities.

Trail City. Former name of Elliston before post office established. Now the town of Madrid. A Mr. McKenzie located a bank here and called the embryo city Trail City.

Venango. Peak population (1930), 287. Post office established December 3, 1887. Town probably named for Venango, Pennsylvania.

Yankee. Post office established September 23, 1886; discontinued January 12, 1888. Probably named to express the sentiments of a Union soldier.

PHELPS COUNTY

Organized and boundaries defined by legislative act approved February 11, 1873. Named in honor of William Phelps, a settler in this part of Nebraska. Phelps was a native of New York state and for many years was a steamboat captain on the Missouri River.

Aaelson. Established February 27, 1880.

Atlanta. Peak population (1920), 258. Post office established September 12, 1884. Probably named for Atlanta, Georgia, or Atlanta, Illinois.

Axelson. Post office established February 27, 1880; discontinued June 10, 1886. Named in honor of Andrew Axelson, first postmaster.

Bertrand. Peak population (2000), 786. Post office name changed from Whitewater July 10, 1885. Town named in honor of an official of the Burlington Railroad. It was organized in December 1885.

Clarence. Post office established November 14, 1879; discontinued April 21, 1884. Origin of the name not learned. First postmaster was Charles S. Dodge.

Clyde. Burlington Railroad station.

Denman. Post office name changed from Phelps March 30, 1895; discontinued October 28, 1899. Origin of the name not learned.

Frank. Post office established April 3, 1883; name changed to Romeyn October 7, 1889. Named in honor of William Frank, Sr., first postmaster. The name was changed because of its similarity to names of other offices within the state.

Fraser. Post office established September 11, 1883; discontinued October 29, 1892. Named in honor of John Fraser, first postmaster.

Funk. Census not available. Post office established January 28, 1888. Town named in honor of Philip C. Funk, early pioneer and Civil War veteran.

Garden. Pony Express Station No. 15 in Nebraska. It was located about six miles southwest of Elm Creek, Buffalo County, the exact location unknown. Some authorities say it was on the Biddleman Ranch; others speak of the Shakespear, or some referred to it as the Craig station.

Haydon. Post office established June 4, 1884; discontinued November 19, 1892. Origin of the name not learned.

Highland. Post office established July 24, 1879; discontinued August 9, 1883. Name denotes its superior elevation.

Holcomb. Post office established May 4, 1896; discontinued March 11, 1903. This former office may have been named for a local settler, but some authorities say it honored Silas A. Holcomb, first Populist governor of Nebraska (1895-99).

Holdrege. Peak population (2000), 5,636. Post office established November 9, 1883. County seat named in honor of George W. Holdrege, master builder and later superintendent of the Burlington Railroad. Holdrege won the county seat in special election with Phelps Center November 11, 1884.

Hopeville. Post office established April 8, 1864; discontinued September 22, 1864. This historic ranch and stage station eighteen miles west of Fort Kearny was run by Postmaster Moses Sydenham and his brother.

Hudson. Post office established August 11, 1874; discontinued May 10, 1875. Origin of the name not learned.

Industry. Post office established July 24, 1878; discontinued January 29, 1885. Probably so named because the people hoped to attract industry. There is also an Industry, Illinois.

Integrity. Post office established December 7, 1879; discontinued February 12, 1884. Named for the honesty and uprightness of the community's people.

Lake. Post office established May 27, 1879; discontinued April 2, 1887. Probably named for a small lake in the vicinity.

Loomis. Peak population (1980), 447. Post office established January 21, 1886. Town named in honor of N. H. Loomis, who was associated with the Burlington Railroad.

Lute. Former locality named in honor of A. T. Lute, early settler.

O'Kane. Post office established January 31, 1883; discontinued March 31, 1886. Named in honor of James O'Kane, first postmaster.

Oscar. Post office established August 15, 1878; discontinued June 15, 1888. Origin of the name not learned. First postmaster was Andrew J. Olson.

Phelps. Post office name changed from Phelps Center October 3, 1877; name changed to Denman March 30, 1895. See Phelps Center.

Phelps Center. Census not available. Post office established November 4, 1876; name changed to Phelps October 3, 1877. Former town named for the county. Phelps Center was made second county seat November 4, 1879. The county seat, here for five years, was moved by an election to Holdrege November 11, 1884. Town declined after railroad bypassed it in favor of Holdrege.

Plum Creek. Post office established October 4, 1861; discontinued March 16, 1868. Site of Plum Creek Massacre of whites by Indians, August 7, 1864.

Rock Falls. Census not available. Post office established September 10, 1874; discontinued June 6, 1894. Former town probably named for the rocky falls of a nearby creek.

Romeyn. Post office name changed from Frank October 7, 1889; discontinued June 23, 1902. Name chosen without reference to any person or place.

Sacramento. Peak population (1890), 195. Post office established February 4, 1879; discontinued April 2, 1887. Former town named for Sacramento, California.

Sherwood. Post office established June 9, 1875; discontinued December 11, 1877. Probably named in honor of a settler.

Urbana. Post office established February 9, 1885; discontinued November 4, 1889. Probably named for either Urbana, Illinois, or Urbana, Ohio.

Wac. Station on the Burlington Railroad.

Westmark. Post office established June 7, 1880; discontinued January 12, 1903. One source says the town named after a sod pile which was a landmark on a west section of land.

Whitewater. Post office established November 14, 1879; name changed to Bertrand July 10, 1885. Named by settlers from Whitewater, Wisconsin.

Williamsburg. Census not available. Post office established August 28, 1878; discontinued December 15, 1904. Named in honor of William Dilworth, son of C. J. Dilworth, Nebraska attorney general. Williamsburg, at first the county seat, lost that designation in an election with Phelps Center in 1879.

PIERCE COUNTY

Named for Franklin Pierce (1804-69), U.S. president from 1853 to 1857. The original Pierce County was one of eight counties created by proclamation by Acting Territorial Governor Thomas Cuming in 1854. Pierce County reappeared as a county name in 1856 when the Territorial Legislature created a large county which included the area of the present Pierce.

Birch. Post office established February 12, 1885; discontinued May 31, 1903. Named in honor of Frank H. Birch, first postmaster.

Bishop. Post office established January 26, 1885; discontinued August 27, 1886. Named in honor of William E. Bishop, who established the office and was first postmaster.

Breslau. Peak population (1950), 45. Post office established May 3, 1911; discontinued 1935. Former hamlet named for Breslau, Germany. The community had a large German settlement.

Colbergen. Post office established February 9, 1880; discontinued March 31, 1904. First settlement made here in 1872 and probably named for a place in Germany.

Crystal Lake. Early locality in Pierce County.

Foster. Peak population (1920), 140. Post office name changed from Moorehouse May 4, 1886. Named in honor of George and Caroline Foster, who conveyed all property rights to the land and town.

Hadar. Census not available. Post office established May 19, 1880. Hadar community was a well defined district before the town was established June 26, 1883; Hader in German means a wordy argument. The name (with the change of an "e" to "a") recalls the squabble between two German settlers over the selection of the town name.

Hunton. This place existed in name only in early county history.

Joseph. Locality in Pierce County during the 1940s.

Lucas Siding. Former station on the Chicago and North Western Railroad named in honor of R. S. Lucas, early pioneer, Pierce County judge, and newspaper editor.

Marrowville. An earlier name proposed for the town of McLean.

McLean. Post office established January 15, 1900. Town named for McLean, Ohio, or for Donald McLean, official of the Pacific Short Line Railroad.

Moorehouse. Post office established January 26, 1886; name changed to Foster March 4, 1886. Named for a Mr. Moorehouse, station agent for the Chicago and North Western Railroad when the only buildings were a section house, watering tank, and loading platform.

Osmond. Peak population (1970), 883. Post office established June 23, 1890. Village named in honor of a Mr. Osmond, official of the Burlington Railroad. Town platted by James Brisfield, civil engineer for the Pacific Short Line Town Site Company, May 5, 1890.

Pierce. Peak population (2000), 1,774. Post office established October 3, 1870. The county seat was located at Pierce at the first election July 26, 1870. City named for the county—after President Franklin Pierce. The first settlement was made in 1870, and J. H. Brown built the first house on Willow Creek. It served as hotel, post office, and courthouse as well. Town platted May 4, 1871.

Plainview. Peak population (1980), 1,483. Post office name changed from Roseville January 26, 1874. Name was changed to Plainview because some resentful settlers felt Roseville gave too much prominence to one family. Postman Christian Lerum, who had recently lived in Plainview, Minnesota, was present at a town board meeting when the argument over the city name again erupted. Tired of endless controversy, those in attendance unanimously accepted Lerum's suggestion that Plainview be permanently adopted.

Roseview. An early locality in Pierce County.

Roseville. Post office established December 26, 1871. Changed to Plainview January 26, 1874. Named for first postmaster Charles Rose.

Shannon. Name earlier proposed for the town of McLean, before a post office was established.

Warren. Early locality in Mills Precinct.

West Randolph. Part of the town of Randolph, Cedar County, extending into Pierce County.

Willowdale. Locality which later became Colbergen.

PLATTE COUNTY

Named for the Platte River, the name of which means "flat" in French and is a translation by French explorers or missionaries of Nebraska, the Omaha Indian name. The county was first called Loup. Platte County was formed by territorial enactment January 26, 1856, and included the eastern half of the present county. The western half of the present county was Monroe County, with the town of Monroe the county seat. Monroe County was absorbed by voter approval into Platte County in 1859. The boundaries were redefined by an act approved December 22, 1859. Colfax County was formed by legislative enactment February 15, 1869, from the part that originally had been Dodge County.

Arcala. Town laid out on farm of G. C. Barnum. The town company built a cabin for Joseph Wolf to live in, in order to hold the site. Arcala did not exist long enough to have a post office established.

Barnum Ranch. Named for Guy C. Barnum whose ranch was an emigrant rest stop. Located near Columbus.

Bedford. Place was staked out as a townsite in 1857 near the townsite of Columbus. Unlike its neighbor, Bedford never got beyond the platting stage.

Behlen. This station on the Union Pacific Railroad is the site of the Behlen Manufacturing plant.

Boheet. Post office established November 23, 1882; discontinued January 14, 1905. Name said to be a Pawnee Indian word, meaning "to stop."

Brookfield. Proposed town which never got beyond the recording stage. Named for the Brooks family.

Bunker Hill. Rural neighborhood once located near St. Edward, Boone County.

Burrows. Town platted by the Union Land Company July 25, 1889. Before it secured a post office, the name was changed to Tarnov. Burrows township and town named for James Burrows.

Cayuga. Former station on the Union Pacific Railroad, probably named for Cayuga, New York. The word is Indian.

Cherry Grove. Proposed town that never got beyond the platting stage in early county history.

Cherry Hill. Post office established June 17, 1869; name changed to Duncan January 2, 1880. Name is descriptive.

Cleveland. This town, founded outside Columbus, never existed long enough to secure a post office.

Columbus. Peak population (2000), 20,971. Post office established in 1856. The Columbus Company, composed of former residents of Columbus, Ohio, laid out the townsite in the summer of 1856. Columbus was made county seat.

Cone. Post office established September 10, 1883; name changed to Palestine November 6, 1883. Origin of the name not learned.

Cornlea. Peak population (1930), 105. Post office established June 1, 1887. Name compounded of "corn" and "lea" and means cornland or land of corn. Named by Welsh settlers and platted by Western Town Lot Company.

Creston. Peak population (1920), 381. Post office established April 12, 1875. Town named for its location atop a hill from which the waters flowed east to the Elkhorn River and west to the Platte.

Dorrance. Post office name changed from Lost Creek September 10, 1885; name changed to Oconee April 8, 1887. Named in honor of W. H. Dorrance, division superintendent of the Union Pacific Railroad but changed so as not to conflict with mails and freight to Dorrance, Kansas.

Duncan. Peak population (2000), 359. Post office name changed from Cherry Hill January 2, 1880. Town named for a Mr. Duncan, conductor on the Union Pacific. Town was to be called Jackson until it was discovered that a Dakota County town was already named Jackson.

Eagle Island. Former stage stop on the Western Stage Lines from Omaha to Fort Kearny.

Eldorado. Post office established April 1, 1859.

Farrall. Post office established October 15, 1872; discontinued July 29, 1884. Possibly named in honor of Thomas Farrall, first postmaster.

Galley's Ranch. Emigrant rest stop.

Galva. Swedish settlement in northwest Platte County. Probably named for Galva, Illinois.

Gardiner. Station on the Union Pacific Railroad. See Gardiner Station.

Gardiner Station. Post office moved from Merrick County July 31, 1884; discontinued 1887. When the post office was discontinued, the place became a station on the Union Pacific Railroad. Probably named for Joseph Gardiner, first postmaster.

Gleason. Post office established May 27, 1873; discontinued March 22, 1880. Named for Patrick Gleason, first postmaster.

Gould City. This railroad terminal, proposed by the Omaha, Niobrara and Black Hills Railroad near the center of Platte County, was never completed.

Grand Prairie. Post office established September 20, 1878; discontinued January 18, 1881. Named for Grand Prairie Township, formerly called Sterns Prairie. A faction opposed the former name, and Grand Prairie was accepted as a compromise name.

Granville. Former community located in Granville Precinct.

Gruetli. Rural neighborhood and church named by Swiss settlers for a Swiss location. Pronounced "Greet-lee."

Grunewald. Former locality in Humphrey Township established on the Columbus-Norfolk Stage Road in the early 1870s.

Hill Siding. This former siding and stock yard on the Chicago and North Western

Railroad near Creston was used when car loads were too heavy to make the steep grade in one haul.

Humphrey. Peak population (1920), 870. Post office established August 28, 1871. Town named by Postmistress Mrs. Nancy Leach (later Wanzer) for her former home of Humphrey, New York. The present Humphrey is about three miles from the site of the original post office.

Jackson. Railroad name for Cherry Hill Station given by Elisha Atkins and E. H Rollins, officials of the Union Pacific Railroad.

Keatskatoos. Post office established August 22, 1873; name changed to Norwich July 14, 1882. Post office established August 22, 1873. Name is a Pawnee Indian word for the Platte River. The name of Indian trader L. W. Platt seemed similar to the Indians, and they named him and the store Keatskatoos.

La Loup. Early proposed town that never got beyond the platting stage.

Lindsay. Peak population (1920), 490. Post office established December 14, 1874. Town named by John Walker, early settler, for Lindsay, Ontario, Canada.

Long Branch. This rural store and service station, once called Lusche's, is now a tavern named for the Long Branch Saloon on the former TV series "Gunsmoke."

Looking Glass. Post office established December 2, 1873; discontinued May 7, 1904. Named for nearby Looking Glass Valley.

Lost Creek. Post office established May 27, 1879; name changed to Dorrance September 10, 1885. Town named for an area creek, which, during dry times, would appear and disappear at intervals.

Matson. Post office established July 5, 1882; discontinued July 25, 1892. Possibly named for first postmistress Mathilda Matson, for Alfred Matson, or for early landowner William Matson.

Mesopotamia. Former locality.

Metz. Post office established January 14, 1876; discontinued August 14, 1885. Probably named for Metz, France.

Millville. Former locality in northern Platte County.

Monroe. Peak population (1920, 1990), 309. Post office established May 3, 1858. Leander Gerrard of Columbus named the town for President James Monroe. Gerrard and his brother, E. A. Gerrard, founded the town. At that time, he later recalled, no place in the United States had been named for President Monroe. Present town not on original site.

Moorman. Station on the Union Pacific Railroad.

Nebo. Post office established August 27, 1875; discontinued December 4, 1875. Probably named for Nebo, the mountain in the Holy Land where Moses died. There is also a Nebo, Illinois.

Neboville. Post office established October 4, 1880; discontinued October 6, 1903. Office established a few years after the first post office of Nebo had been discontinued.

Norwich. Post office name changed from Keatskatoos, July 14, 1882; discontinued January 9, 1883. Probably named for a city in Connecticut, New York, Ohio, or Vermont.

Oconee. Peak population (1910, 1920, 1930), 71. Post office name changed from Dorrance April 8, 1887; discontinued April 29, 1916. F. A. Baldwin suggested Oconee because the name was unlike that of any other post office in Nebraska or the surrounding states. The name was accepted by postal authorities and the railroad. Thought to have been named for Oconee, Shelby County, Illinois. Word is Indian in origin.

Okay. Post office established June 9, 1881; discontinued April 6, 1894. Post office named by W. J. Thurston. Many early post office names were rejected because they duplicated others already in use. The name Okay was accepted because of its uniqueness.

Oldenbusch. Post office established September 7, 1899; discontinued May 31, 1904. Name is derived from the first part of Oldenberg, Germany, and the last part of the surname of a Mr. Hellbusch.

Palestine. Post office name changed from Cone November 6, 1883; discontinued October 7, 1903. Probably named for the country of Palestine; Palestine, Illinois; or Palestine, Ohio.

Palestine Valley. Post office established March 8, 1878; discontinued October 7, 1903. See above on Palestine.

Parkersburgh. Early projected town that never advanced beyond the platting stage.

Pawnee. Early projected town that never got beyond the platting stage. Probably was located on the present site of Columbus when the county was known as Loup.

Peck. Former station on the Union Pacific Railroad. Located near Humphrey.

Platte Center. Peak population (1930), 525. Post office established December 8, 1879. Town platted by Omaha, Niobrara and Black Hills Railroad January 22, 1880. Named for its location in center of county.

Postville. Peak population (1900), 14. Post office name changed from Wolf October 17, 1878; discontinued September 10, 1902. Former hamlet possibly named for Alfred M. Post, who resided in Platte County and served six years as a judge on the Nebraska Supreme Court.

Prairie Hill. Post office established February 11, 1879; discontinued October 22, 1879. Descriptively named for its location.

President. Post office established June 30, 1882; discontinued March 18, 1898. Probably named during a presidential election. The name Arthur was submitted during the presidential campaign of Chester Arthur. Another post office named Arthur already existed and the name of President was submitted.

Rosenburg. Post office established July 23, 1901; discontinued May 9, 1904. Probably named for Rosenborg, Denmark, by Danish settlers. Postal authorities used the spelling Rosenburg.

Sheldonville. Station on the Union Pacific Railroad probably named in honor of Addison E. Sheldon, Nebraska legislator and historian.

Springville. Short-lived locality inhabited by a splinter sect of Mormons.

St. Anthony. Post office established February 11, 1879; discontinued April 6, 1880. Locality and former post office was situated two and one-half miles south of Tarnov. St. Anthony was centered around a Catholic church by that name, based presumably on a religious society founded by Father Sebastian Zubilla in 1878. Church was on the farm of Peter Peff.

St. Bernard. Census not available. Post office established February 11, 1879; discontinued March 17, 1906. This former town, located in a German settlement, was platted by R. L. Rossiter, county surveyor, in June 1878. The Franciscan Brotherhood owned a section of the land on which they erected a school and church. Bernard Schroeder built a hotel on his adjoining land. The town was then named in honor of Schroeder's patron saint.

Stearns Prairie. Post office established December 1, 1871; discontinued August 27, 1878. Probably named for Orson E. Stearns, who operated a halfway point inn on Grand Prairie, called Stearns Prairie. Stearns was first postmaster.

St. Mary. Post office established March 5, 1878; discontinued April 26, 1882. Named for a Catholic church settlement founded by priests from Omaha. Location was four and one-half miles southeast of Humphrey.

Tarnov. Peak population (1920), 128. Post office name changed from Burrows July 24, 1891. Town platted by Union Land Company July 25, 1889. It was settled by Polish immigrants and named for Tarnov, Galicia, a province in Poland. Made a community post office of Humphrey 1977.

Timber Hill. Locality near Hill Siding which perpetuated a rural school name. Original name may refer to area timber used by the railroad.

Tracy Valley. Name still used for a community along Tracy Creek. May be derived from Madison County, in which most of the creek is located.

Wagners Lake. Present community near Columbus.

Walker. Post office established April 16, 1873; discontinued October 23, 1874. Possibly named for Irishman John Walker, who migrated from Ontario Province, Canada.

Warrack. Place mentioned in Platte County history. Former station east of Columbus.

Wattsville. Probably a community in early Platte County history.

West Chicago. Western Platte County locality with a general store, now a tavern.

West Hill. Post office established August 19, 1875; discontinued June 9, 1900. Named by serviceman Hiram Eley, postmaster, for West Hill, England.

Wolf. Post office established August 19, 1873; name changed to Postville October 17, 1878. Named for Wolf family.

Woodburn. Post office established October 23, 1878; discontinued September 14, 1904. Origin of the name not learned. There is also a Woodburn, Iowa.

Woodville. Census not available. Post office established June 18, 1874; discontinued May 4, 1920. Named for the precinct in which it is located.

Yankee. Former locality in Platte County.

Zigzag. Locality probably named for zigzag route of the Columbus-Genoa road, in the vicinity or near former site of Keatskatoos.

POLK COUNTY

Named in honor of James K. Polk (1795-1849), U.S. president from 1845 to 1849. Polk County was organized during an election held August 6, 1870. Its boundaries were defined and established by an act of the Legislature approved January 26, 1856. Previously part of Butler County.

Arcade. Name of Shelby before a post office was established. Name turned down by postal authorities because it would conflict with mails for Arcadia, Nebraska.

Belleville. Post office established April 3, 1873; discontinued July 24, 1875. Probably named in honor of James Bell, first postmaster.

Beulah. Post office established February 25, 1889; discontinued September 15, 1904. Origin of the name not learned. First postmaster was Henry Lohr.

Conkling. Post office established May 27, 1879; discontinued January 3, 1882. Probably named in honor of John Conkling, Civil War veteran and county pioneer.

Cyclone. Post office established March 16, 1874; name changed to Shelby August 4, 1880. Probably named for a tornado that struck about the time the office was started. Located near the community of Arcade.

Durant. Station on the Union Pacific Railroad just west of Stromsburg. Probably named in honor of Thomas Durant, one-time vice president of the Union Pacific.

Economy. Post office established March 17, 1875; discontinued February 1, 1876. Origin of the name not learned. There is also an Economy, Indiana.

Edna. Former locality existing during the early 1880s.

Glade. Post office established March 17, 1882; discontinued October 2, 1882. Origin of the name is unknown.

Laclede. Post office established December 2, 1890; discontinued April 16, 1894. Origin of the name not learned. There are towns in Illinois and Missouri by this name.

Mahlon. Post office established May 16, 1895; discontinued December 21, 1901. Named in honor of the son of Mr. and Mrs. James Bonner. Bonner was first postmaster.

Osceola. Peak population (1920), 1,209. Post office established July 21, 1871. County seat named for Osceola, Seminole Indian leader in Florida. Town was three miles southeast of present site, to which it was moved in 1871. First courthouse was burned January 1, 1881.

Pleasant Home. Post office established November 11, 1872; moved to York County November 15, 1877. Name describes the sentiments of postal patrons toward this community.

Polk. Peak population (1920), 561. Post office established November 16, 1906. Named for the county.

Prairie. Early settlement in Polk County.

Redville. Post office name changed from Seberger July 16, 1873; discontinued July 14, 1877. Coined from the name of the first postmaster, David Redpath.

Rochon. Post office established July 30, 1900; discontinued July 16, 1903. Probably named for Belle Rochon, first postmistress, or for Ben Rochon, resident.

Seberger. Post office established February 24, 1873; name changed to Redville July 16, 1873. Named in honor of Frank Seberger, first postmaster.

Shank. Post office established December 15, 1885; discontinued June 21, 1886. Named in honor of a local settler.

Shelby. Peak population (1980), 724. Post office changed from Cyclone August 4, 1880. Town named in honor of a Mr. Shelby, former official of the Union Pacific Railroad.

Stromsburg. Peak population (1890), 1,400. Post office established November 11, 1872. Founded by Lewis Headstrom, member of the townsite company of Galva, Illinois. Settled by Swedish immigrants. One source says town named for Stromsburg, a suburb of Stockholm, Sweden. Another source attributes it to the last part of Headstrom's name. Stromsburg contended with Osceola in a 1916 election for the county courthouse location.

Swedehome. Post office established July 20, 1883; discontinued June 28, 1902. Named for Swedish settlers. Swedehome was first spelled Swede Home. Community now consists of a Swedish Lutheran church and a few residents.

Thornton. Post office established August 1874; discontinued June 14, 1895. Origin of the name not learned. There are places in eleven states with this name.

Wayland. Post office established February 10, 1873; discontinued November 12, 1901. Name selected by Mrs. Sarah Locke. There are post offices in seven states called Wayland.

RED WILLOW COUNTY

Named for Red Willow Creek. The term is a mistranslation of the Sioux word Chan shasha Wakpala, literally, Red Dogwood Creek. This shrub was abundant along the stream. Boundaries were defined by an act of the Legislature and approved February 27, 1873.

Addenda. Place shown in early county atlas as a community.

Banksville. Peak population (1910), 19. Post office established February 10, 1886; discontinued September 30, 1907. Named in honor of Edward Banks, former sheriff of Red Willow County.

Bartley. Peak population (1910), 511. Post office established July 29, 1886. Named in honor of the Rev. Allen Bartley, Methodist Episcopal minister who homesteaded the land on which the town was platted in July 1886. A Methodist school, Mallalieu College, was operated here for a few terms before it was abandoned.

Billingsville. Proposed town that never went beyond the platting stage in early county history.

Bondville. Peak population (1890), 12. Post office established March 13, 1882; discontinued December 6, 1887. Former village named in honor of William Bond, first postmaster.

Boxelder. Post office established September 30, 1879; discontinued June 15, 1911. Named for the many box elder trees in the locality.

Campbell. Formerly called Perry.

Camp Redwillow. Temporary army post established in summer of 1872.

Canby. Post office established June 23, 1874; discontinued August 20, 1875. Origin of the name not learned.

Coon Creek. Early settlement named for the stream on which it was located. Creek named for numerous raccoon trapped along its banks.

Danbury. Peak population (1930), 321. Post office established December 24, 1873. Name changed to Danbury Station January 13, 1888; name changed back to Danbury April 16, 1888. Town named by Postmaster George Gilbert for his former home of Danbury, Connecticut.

Danbury Station. See note on Danbury.

Fairview. Post office established July 2, 1879; name changed to McCook June 14, 1882. Name descriptive of its location.

Hamburgh. Post office established November 24, 1879; discontinued January 18, 1888. Probably for Germanic spelling of Hamburg, Germany.

Indianola. Peak population (1930), 815. Post office established June 25, 1873. Town named by I. Starbuck for Indianola, Iowa, his former home. Platted by the Republican Valley Land Association and surveyed by D. N. Smith in May 1873. Indianola was made county seat on the county's establishment but lost the title in election with McCook, April 1896.

Lebanon. Peak population (1930), 262. Post office established September 12, 1873. Named for the cedars of Lebanon mentioned in the Bible, by a Mr. Bradbury, first postmaster. Railroad station known as Lebanon Station.

Luray. Post office established June 23, 1884; discontinued September 21, 1886. Probably named for a region in Virginia.

Marion. Peak population (1930), 252. Post office established January 14, 1902. Named by Burlington Railroad officials in honor of Marion Powell, who owned a large tract of land and was prominent in the town's livestock and feed business.

McCook. Peak population (1980), 8,404. Post office name changed from Fairview June 14, 1882. Named in honor of Alexander McDowell McCook, Union general in the Civil War. City platted by the Lincoln Land Company. Won county seat election against Indianola April 15, 1896. McCook was a division point for Burlington Railroad. The former home of U.S. Senator George W. Norris is now a property of the Nebraska State Historical Society.

Narcissus. Post office established November 14, 1879; discontinued July 26, 1880. Possibly named for a flower. Narcissus was also a character in Greek mythology.

Perry. Station on the Burlington Railroad named for W. S. Perry, superintendent of bridges on the McCook Division. Station was first called Campbell.

Redwillow. Peak population (1890), 105. Post office established April 22, 1872; discontinued August 31, 1912. Former town named for the county.

Shippee. Peak population (1930), 14. Post office established February 10, 1913; discontinued 1934. Present railroad station and former town named for Leonard Shippee, first postmaster and early resident.

Silver Creek. Post office established May 5, 1876; discontinued March 12, 1877. Named for the creek on which it was located.

Sloughton. Post office established March 24, 1880; discontinued February 5, 1886. Named in honor of a local settler.

Tyrone. Post office established May 4, 1881; discontinued May 5, 1902. Origin of the name is unknown. There is also a Tyrone, Ireland, and Tyrone, Pennsylvania.

Vailton. Post office established March 29, 1881; discontinued August 17, 1900. Origin of the name not learned.

Valley Grange. Post office established September 29, 1873; discontinued February 4, 1884. Probably named for a Grange hall in the valley. The National Grange, a farmers' organization, was active in Nebraska during this period.

Van Wyck. Post office established March 28, 1881; discontinued April 6, 1883. Probably named in honor of Charles H. Van Wyck, United States senator.

Whitney. Post office moved from Furnas County August 1, 1879; discontinued December 23, 1884. See Whitney, Furnas County.

Willow Grove. Post office established June 25, 1879; discontinued August 28, 1882. Named for a grove of willow trees near the post office.

RICHARDSON COUNTY

Named in honor of William Richardson (1811-75) of Illinois, territorial governor of Nebraska in 1858. County was temporarily organized by a proclamation of Acting Governor Thomas B. Cuming, dated November 23, 1854; it was organized and boundaries were defined by an act approved March 7, 1855. Boundaries were redefined by an act approved January 26, 1856.

Arago. Peak population (1870), 364. Post office established July 14, 1862; discontinued December 14, 1903. This former town founded by German settlers from Buffalo, New York, and named in honor of French astronomer and natural philosopher Dominique Francois Arago (1786-1853). A famous port on the Missouri River, Arago engaged in extensive river commerce in the early period. It was moved five miles west of its original site to avoid floods.

Archer. Peak population (1860), 25. Post office established February 4, 1856; discontinued July 1, 1865. This former town was made the first county seat of Richardson County but lost it by election to Salem in 1857. Named in honor of Robert T. Archer, founder and first sheriff of Richardson County.

Athens. Post office established November 26, 1860; discontinued November 4, 1881. Origin of the name not learned. Fifteen states have places called Athens, some of which are named for Athens, Greece.

Barada. Peak population (1900), 147. Post office established October 25, 1877; made a rural station of Falls City in 1963. Town named in honor of French-Omaha Indian Antoine Barada, the son of Count Michael Barada.

Bluffton. The name was assigned to the railroad station, while the post office was called Sac. Both names were changed when the town became Preston.

Breckenridge. Another proposed town that never got beyond the platting stage. Staked out on a farm belonging to Isaac Clark.

Chasta. Post office established October 4, 1857; discontinued October 8, 1859. Origin of the name not learned.

Cottage Grove. Census not available. Post office established June 18, 1879; discontinued December 12, 1883. Former village was located two miles northwest of the present town of Verdon. Cottage Grove declined after railroad built through Verdon.

Davison. Former station located between Humboldt and Salem on the Burlington Railroad.

Dawson. Peak population (1940), 394. Post office name changed from Dawson's Mill March 11, 1882. See note below on Dawson's Mill.

Dawson's Mill. Post office name changed from Noraville August 26, 1868; name changed to Dawson March 11, 1882. Town named in honor of Joshua Dawson, settler who built a flour and feed mill in the vicinity in 1868. Legal name of town is Noraville although never adopted as post office name.

Dorrington. Post office established April 30, 1880; name changed to Stella January 9, 1882. Possibly named in honor of David Dorrington, Richardson County settler.

Elkton. Post office established July 3, 1862; discontinued December 26, 1875. Post office was located at the home of Postmaster Greenburg Patterson. Origin of the name not learned.

Elmore. Post office established July 3, 1862; discontinued October 27, 1882. Origin of the name not learned.

Falls City. Peak population (1950), 6,203. Post office established February 24, 1857. Name taken from the falls of the Nemaha River nearby. City formed in 1856 by the Falls City Town Association led by John A. Burbank and others. Falls City secured county seat in election with Salem in 1860.

Fargo. Census not available. Post office established May 11, 1895; discontinued February 15, 1913. Former town, located on the old site of Arago, named after the Wells Fargo Express Company.

Flowerdale. Post office established August 16, 1871; discontinued October 27, 1882. Former post office located at the home and store of H. D. Weaver.

Forney. Post office established February 14, 1857; discontinued March 14, 1858. Probably named for the former county of Forney, which honored either William or Christian Forney, early settlers.

Franklin. Peak population (1860), 237. This former town, listed in Session Laws of Nebraska and in A. E. Sheldon's *Nebraska, the Land and the People*, was probably an early river port. However, the town was short-lived because no post office is recorded at this location. Named in honor of Franklin Ferguson.

Freeling. This former station located north of Falls City on the Missouri Pacific Railroad, was named in honor of a local settler.

Geer. Post office name changed from Wells Mills April 9, 1884; discontinued November 3, 1886. Possibly named for John Geer or C. H. Geer, early settlers.

Geneva. Post office established February 26, 1858; discontinued August 20, 1862. Probably named for Geneva, Switzerland, by a settler.

Genou. Another proposed town that never got beyond the platting stage.

Gibraltar. This former station on the Burlington Railroad was located near the Kansas border.

Highland. Post office established August 10, 1869; discontinued September 29, 1870. Named for the characteristic features of the land.

Homond. Post office established July 3, 1862. It may never have operated.

Humboldt. Peak population (1930), 1,433. Post office established January 11, 1861. According to one source, this town was named by O. J. Tinker, its founder and an admirer of Baron Friedrich Alexander von Humboldt. Others say town named by Edward P. Tinker, son of O. J. Tinker, for Humboldt, Tennessee.

Iowa Ford Mills. Place recorded in Rand McNally Atlas of 1882.

Long Branch. Post office established July 25, 1861; discontinued June 29, 1872. Named for a creek in the locality. Site was four miles northwest of Humboldt.

Merles Ranch. Established July 3, 1862. Name changed to Well's Mills March 19, 1867.

Middleburgh. Post office established July 13, 1858; discontinued March 26, 1901. Location of office was southwest of Salem.

Miles Ranch. Post office established July 13, 1858. Name changed to Wells Mills March 19, 1867. Named in honor of Stephen Mills, settler and mail contractor of stage lines from Independence, Missouri, to Salt Lake City, Utah. Located four miles southwest of Dawson.

Monond. Post office established July 3, 1862; discontinued August 21, 1869. Probably named for a region in Germany or Switzerland. Post office was located at residence of Thomas Rothenberger.

Monterey. Post office established February 8, 1858; discontinued October 5, 1873. Platted as a town by Nathan Meyers but post office located in a log house. Thought to have been named by a Mexican War veteran for Monterrey, Mexico.

Munson. Locality recorded in Richardson County history.

Nemaha. Post office established February 26, 1855; name changed to St. Stephens September 17, 1855. Named for the river near which the post office was located.

Nemaha Falls. Post office established April 1, 1858; discontinued July 27, 1859.

Named for the falls on the Nemaha River located two miles southwest of present site of Falls City. A mill was erected here by L. H. Springfield in 1853.

Nims. Former locality probably named for either Mrs. Betsy V. Nims or Reuel Nims, early settlers.

Nohart. Post office established October 10, 1860; discontinued May 29, 1888. Named for a leader of the Iowa Indian tribe.

Noraville. Legal name for the town of Dawson. Railroad name for Dawson at an earlier date.

Padonia. Locality mentioned in early county history.

Pawneeville. Locality or proposed townsite mentioned in early Richardson County history.

Peora. Proposed town that never got beyond the platting stage. Located on farm of James Hanley near present town of Verdon.

Porter. Post office established April 20, 1880; discontinued December 6, 1880. Possibly named for Adm. David Dixon Porter, Union naval officer in the Civil War.

Poteet. Post office established December 13, 1880; discontinued August 13, 1883. Probably named for Ben Poteet, early settler.

Preston. Peak population (1890), 150. Post office name changed from Sac June 23, 1881. Name for town suggested by James C. Eatough, storekeeper, for his former home of Preston, England. Post office made a rural branch of Falls City in 1974.

Rulo. Peak population (1900), 877. Post office established February 13, 1857. Named in honor of Charles Rouleau and located on land belonging to his wife. Postal authorities spelled name Rulo instead of Rouleau. This was an important town on the Missouri River before the advent of the railroad.

Sac. Post office established July 29, 1874; name changed to Preston June 23, 1881. Named in honor of the Sac and Fox Indians, who had land in this region.

Salem. Peak population (1860), 694. Post office established January 4, 1856. Town platted by Justus C. Lincoln, relative of President Abraham Lincoln, and named for Salem, Illinois. Thomas Hare and J. W. Roberts also participated in the platting of the town. The county seat was won in election with Archer in 1857 and then lost in election with Falls City in 1860.

Shasta. Place mentioned in Richardson County history as a post office, but postal records do not list it.

Shubert. Peak population (1940), 404. Post office established February 18, 1884. Town named in honor of Henry Shubert, early settler.

Spezer. Peak population (1860), 394. Origin of the name not learned. Port on the Missouri River, but U.S. Postal Directory does not list it as an office.

Springfield. Projected townsite that failed to materialize. Platted by Johnson Sharp and James Trammel in 1856.

Stella. Peak population (1900), 498. Post office name changed from Dorrington January 9, 1882. Town named in honor of Stella Clark, daughter of Mr. and Mrs. J. W. Clark, who owned the land on which townsite is located.

Strausville. Census not available. Post office established July 10, 1899; discontinued July 31, 1912. Former town named in honor of Gustave Strauss, owner of the land on which the town was built.

St. Stephens. Peak population (1860) 404. Post office name changed from Nemaha September 17, 1855; discontinued December 9, 1868. This former town, located in a Catholic community, honors Stephen Story, first postmaster. Town at one time a port on the Missouri River.

Stumps Station. Former stage station whose site was later occupied by the post office of Williamsville. Named in honor of Alf Stumps.

Tynan. Station on the Missouri Pacific Railroad located near Stella.

Verdon. Peak population (1910), 406. Post office established March 4, 1882. Town platted by Mr. and Mrs. John A. Hall. Named by the Missouri Pacific Railroad.

Wells Mill. Post office name changed from Miles Ranch March 19, 1867; name changed to Geer April 9, 1884. Probably named in honor of a settler who had a mill at this site.

West Archer. A townsite platted by William Maddox. It never got beyond the platting stage.

Williamsville. Post office established April 23, 1867, discontinued May 5, 1879. Named in honor of Professor F. M. Williams, first county school superintendent. German community centered around a Lutheran church.

Winnebago. Former locality named for the Winnebago Indian tribe, which at one time occupied a tract of land in the northeast part of the county. Winnebago Creek is in Arago township. The townsite was platted on land belonging to Joseph Piquoit; it never developed into a town.

Yancton. Peak population (1858), 200. Post office established February 2, 1858; discontinued October 8, 1859. Former town thought to have been named for the Yankton Indian tribe. Town probably was abandoned because of high water from the Missouri River at flood stage.

ROCK COUNTY

Named for its rocky soil. County was formed from part of Brown County by vote November 6, 1888.

Aksarben. Post office established October 30, 1919; discontinued June 30, 1921. Name is Nebraska spelled backwards. A. A. Robinson was only postmaster.

Bassett. Peak population (1950), 1,066. Post office established January 27, 1882. Town named in honor of J. W. Bassett, a ranchman who drove the first herd of cattle into this section in 1871. Bassett was made county seat November 5, 1889.

Best. Name of the community until a post office was established and called Horsefoot. Named after William A. Best.

Buell. Post office established October 9, 1906; discontinued January 11, 1908. Named in honor of Benjamin F. Buell, only postmaster.

Butka. Post office moved from Loup County April 3, 1894; discontinued September 15, 1933. Named in honor of Frank Butka, first postmaster.

Capay. Post office established December 7, 1887. Origin of the name not determined.

Carlin. First postmaster, William Goldner, took office February 12, 1907. It was closed November 13 of that year.

Cuba. Post office established June 23, 1884; discontinued November 30, 1914. Probably named for Cuba, Illinois, or the island of Cuba in the Caribbean.

Duff. Post office established April 14, 1886, with Stephen B. Nelson as postmaster. Discontinued September 9, 1901. Reopened January 20, 1903; discontinued June 30, 1953. Origin of the name not learned.

Elliott. Post office established April 14, 1886; discontinued July 25, 1889. Only postmaster was Gustaf P. Nygren. Origin of the name not ascertained.

Evelyn. Post office established January 16, 1911; discontinued August 15, 1912. Origin of the name not learned. Only postmaster was Mike Popp.

Grace. Post office established February 10, 1886; discontinued September 20, 1886. Origin of the name not learned. Only postmaster was Alexander Schlegel.

Gracie. Post office moved from Loup County 1915; discontinued September 20, 1934. See Gracie, Loup County.

Gurney. Post office established April 10, 1912; discontinued April 30, 1913. Possibly named for Cassius Gurney, first postmaster.

Hammond. Census not available. Post office established August 19, 1887; discontinued 1937. Name given by U.S. Post Office Department to this former town. One source says named in honor of J. R. Ammon, who didn't wish the office to be named for him. Friends gave it a name similar to his.

Horsefoot. Post office established December 26, 1905; discontinued March 1930. William A. Best, first postmaster, named office for his cattle brand, a horse's foot.

Ingallston. Post office established February 10, 1886; discontinued July 1, 1895. Probably named in honor of James W. Ingalls, first postmaster.

Kirkwood. Post office established June 2, 1882; discontinued 1922. Origin of the name not learned. When office was established, Samuel Jordan Kirkwood was United States secretary of the interior under President Chester Arthur.

Malvern. Post office established June 2, 1882. Named for Malvern, Iowa, or for the middle name of Clarence Malvern Anderson, first postmaster, who held the office until January 13, 1912.

Mariaville. Census not available. Post office established May 9, 1882; discontinued 1957. Former town named in honor of Harriett Maria Peacock, daughter of Mr. and Mrs. Thomas Peacock. Peacock was first postmaster.

Menlo. Post office established September 23, 1879; discontinued October 4, 1883. Simeon Huffman was first postmaster. Probably named for Menlo, Iowa.

Metzinger. Post office established February 13, 1925; discontinued 1934. Probably named in honor of Marian M. Metzinger, first postmaster.

Newport. Peak population (1940), 275. Post office established January 22, 1884. Town named after Newport Bridge built across the Niobrara River about twelve miles north of the townsite.

Perch. Post office established January 11, 1886; discontinued April 15, 1915. Origin of the name not learned.

Pony Lake. Post office established June 8, 1910; discontinued August 15, 1929. Named after a lake one-half mile from the office. Legend states that in the early days an Indian boy was thrown and killed on its banks by a wild pony.

Rock. This place was never a post office but a locality sometimes known as Rock Center. Named for the county and at one time proposed for a county seat site.

Rose. Census not available. Post office established September 25, 1905. Town named by C. A. Davison, first postmaster, for the wild roses in the vicinity.

Selden. Post office established May 27, 1889; discontinued January 31, 1930. Named in honor of William A. Selden, first postmaster.

Shebesta. Established September 9, 1908; discontinued January 6, 1920. Named in honor of Charles Shebesta, early homesteader.

Spragg. Post office established September 15, 1888; discontinued November 15, 1912. Named in honor of Christopher Spragg, first postmaster.

Stoner. Post office established February 29, 1912; discontinued April 1914. Probably named in honor of Eva B. Stoner, first postmistress.

Sybrant. Post office established April 25, 1895; discontinued February 29, 1932. Named in honor of David O. Sybrant, first postmaster.

Thurman. Post office established January 20, 1886; discontinued March 31, 1919. One source says named for Senator Allen G. Thurman, a Democrat of Ohio, by the postmaster.

Tracy. Former locality named for a local settler.

SALINE COUNTY

Named for supposed salt deposits in the area. County created by an act of the first Nebraska Territorial Legislature, which convened January 16, 1855. Permanent organization was effected in 1867, the year Nebraska became a state.

Adamson's Sawmill. Swan Creek location used as a temporary election place before official organization of county government.

Albany. Post office established June 15, 1871; discontinued October 20, 1871. Probably named for one of fifteen places in the United States and Albany.

Atlanta. Post office established June 15, 1871; name changed to Tobias March 17. Probably named for one of the twelve places in the United States having this name.

Blue Island. Post office established August 26, 1868; discontinued August 11, 1873. Probably named for a small island in the Blue River.

Blue River City. Former name of Crete before Crete became a post office. Plat for the town recorded August 3, 1870, by J. C. Bickle.

Blue River Lodge. Present Saline County locality.

Castor. Tobias was first called Castor, but postal authorities said name would conflict with Custer, another Nebraska post office.

Center. This name was placed on the ballot for county seat in election of September 4, 1877, in an unsuccessful attempt to locate courthouse in the center of the county.

Crete. Peak population (2000), 6,028. Post office established August 26, 1868. City named by J. C. Bickle because he and his wife had come from Crete, Illinois. He platted a townsite called Blue River City. The South Platte Land Company then purchased a section of land northeast of Blue River City, filed a town plat, and gave the Bickles the privelage of naming its town. The two sites were consolidated under the name of Crete. Crete vied unsuccessfully for county seat in two elections. Doane College founded in 1872 with the financial backing of the Congregational Church.

Crete Junction. Junction for two different branches of the Burlington Railroad.

Danville. Post office established May 2, 1872; discontinued July 17, 1873. Probably named for one of seventeen Danvilles in the United States.

Dennison. Former name of DeWitt but did not last long enough to be established as a post office.

DeWitt. Peak population (1890), 751. Post office name changed from Swan City March 12, 1872. First called Dennison and then changed to Swan City. Town probably named for a railroad official.

Dorchester. Peak population (2000), 615. Post office established July 6, 1871. Named by Burlington Railroad officials (1) for Dorchester, a suburb of Boston, Massachusetts; or (2) for the home town of a railroad engineer who came from Dorchester, England. Dorchester fit the railroad's A-B-C-D system of naming towns. Town platted in 1870.

Ellison. Community near Friend which was centered around a Methodist Church in 1878 or 1879.

Equality. Post office established October 6, 1868; name changed to Western on December 19, 1870. Named for the theme of a speech by President Lincoln during the Civil War.

Fairview. Post office established September 11, 1871; discontinued February 5, 1878. Descriptive term. Twenty states have post offices with this name.

Friend. Peak population (1890), 1,347. Post office name changed from Friendville April 6, 1874. Named in honor of Charles Friend, first postmaster and storekeeper.

Friendville. Post office established August 1, 1871; name changed to Friend April 6, 1874. See note on Friend.

Girard. Post office established April 28, 1875; discontinued October 7, 1887. Possibly named for Girard, Ohio, or for Girard, Illinois.

Goldrensey. Post office established December 31, 1873; discontinued March 19, 1884. Origin of the name not learned.

Hornsdale. Post office established September 10, 1874; discontinued August 19, 1875. Origin of name not learned.

Jacksonville. Proposed town in the original county of Jackson, named before the organization of Saline County.

Le Grand. Post office name changed from Swanville February 7, 1877; discontinued January 23, 1882. Possibly named for Le Grand, Iowa.

Loudon City. Locality west of Swanton in early county history.

Lucieville. Post office established December 30, 1871; discontinued October 16, 1896. Origin of name not learned. First postmaster was John Waugh.

Mandano. Post office established November 4, 1879; discontinued September 1, 1881. Origin of name not learned.

Morgan Island. Locality named in early Saline County history.

Morris. Name of Swanton before a post office was established. The name was not accepted by postal authorities because of prospective conflict with an office called Norris within the state.

North Fork. Post office moved from Seward County July 13, 1877; name changed to Repose January 17, 1881. See note on North Fork in Seward County.

Plato. Post office established August 11, 1881; discontinued September 25, 1900. Possibly named for Plato, Illinois, or for the Greek philosopher.

Pleasant Hill. Peak population (1900), 246. Post office established February 2, 1869; discontinued October 31, 1912. Former town named for the township in which it was located. The name is descriptive. Pleasant Hill was located in the center of the county. It won county seat designation in election with Swanville May 11, 1871, but lost it in an election with Wilber September 18, 1877. Town steadily declined after a railroad was built a few miles away.

Repose. Post office name changed from North Fork January 17, 1881; discontinued October 31, 1888. Origin of the name not learned.

Riceville. Post office established December 28, 1868; discontinued June 19, 1876. Possibly named in honor of John G. Rice, first postmaster. Bertwell Mill, owned and operated by John Bertwell, was located in the vicinity.

Saxon. Post office established January 17, 1872; discontinued April 2, 1887. Origin of name not learned.

Shestak. Post office established December 29, 1893; discontinued October 11, 1894. Former post office and present railroad station named in honor of Vaclav Shestak, pioneer.

Swan City. Post office established January 8, 1866; name changed to DeWitt March 12, 1872. Town named for its location near Swan Creek. Clyner Mill, operated by Thomas Clyner, was located here.

Swanton. Peak population (1910), 285. Post office established May 29, 1884. Named for its location on Swan Creek.

Swanville. Post office established June 10, 1872; name changed to Le Grand February 7, 1877. Former town and county seat named for its location on Swan Creek. Swanville was made county seat on formation of the county in 1867, but lost it in an election with Pleasant Hill May 11, 1871. The town eventually lost its identity.

Swingle. Present Burlington Railroad Station.

Tabor. Post office established February 13, 1871; discontinued January 24, 1879. Named for city in Bohemia, now in the Czech Republic.

Tobias. Peak population (1900), 672. Post office name changed from Atlanta March 17, 1884. Town named by Lincoln Land Company in honor of Tobias Castor, Burlington Railway official.

Varna. Post office established May 5, 1873; discontinued April 16, 1883. Origin of name not learned.

Western. Peak population (1930), 511. Post office name changed from Equality December 19, 1870. Named in honor of a Mr. West, a homesteader on whose premises the town was built.

Wilber. Peak population (2000), 1,761. Post office established August 11, 1873. County seat named in honor of Professor C. D. Wilber of Illinois. Wilber and H. Mann erected a flour mill on the Blue River in 1874. Named county seat in election with Crete and Pleasant Hill September 18, 1877. Wilber won another election from Crete in 1927.

SARPY COUNTY

Named in honor of Col. Peter A. Sarpy (1804-65), a notable figure in early Nebraska history. Sarpy County was once a part of Douglas County but was organized into a new county by an act approved February 7, 1857.

Avery. Post office established April 29, 1891; discontinued October 4, 1908. Present railroad station and former post office probably named for a settler.

Bellevue. Peak population (2000), 44,382. Post office establishment date unknown. Fur trading records first mention Bellevue by name in 1824, but it was founded in 1822 by Joshua Pilcher of the Missouri Fur Company. The settlement was a fur trading post as well as the Council Bluffs Indian Agency after 1832. The famous fur trader Manuel Lisa had business dealings in the area prior to the founding of the town. The name Bellevue (beautiful view) results from early French influences. Bellevue was made a city in March of 1855 by the Nebraska Territorial Legislature and is therefore the oldest town in the state. Bellevue wanted the territorial capital located there but lost to the new city of Omaha. It became the first county seat of Sarpy County, then lost to Papillion in 1875.

Belnap. Former station on the Burlington Railroad, located east of Portal.

Camp Gifford. Place mentioned in Sarpy County history.

Chalco. Peak population (2000), 10,736. Post office established January 19, 1888; discontinued 1953. Present railroad station and former town probably named for a lake or town in Mexico.

Childs. Former station on the Omaha and Southwestern Railroad.

Fairview. Census not available. Post office established May 8, 1858; discontinued December 13, 1859. Short-lived town, probably named for its location, which was designated as a county seat at one time. Fairview was platted by the Rev. C. C. Goss.

Forest City. Post office established August 30, 1858; moved to Gretna September 18, 1886. Origin of name not learned.

Fort Crook. Peak population (1900), 600. Post office established July 23, 1888; made a station of Omaha, 1965. The village of Fort Crook was named after adjoining Fort Crook military post which honored Gen. George Crook (1828-90), commander in the Civil War and the Indian campaigns of the West. The fort, established as a military reservation by an act of Congress on July 23, 1888, had 545 acres of land. During World War I it served as a training center. Most of the post later became Offutt Air Force Base.

Gates. Former railroad station probably named for Amos Gates, a settler.

Gilmore. Peak population (1880), 60. Post office established June 15, 1869; discontinued May 31, 1909. Former town and present railroad station on the Union Pacific Railroad, named for an official of the line.

Greens. Former station on the Missouri Pacific Railroad located near Louisville.

Green's Switch. This may have been Greens.

Gretna. Peak population (2000), 2,355. Post office established September 18, 1886. Name is of Scottish origin and probably derived from Gretna Green, Dumfriesshire, Scotland. Town was platted by Lincoln Land Company in October 1887.

Hazleton. Post office established March 3, 1863; discontinued March 4, 1863. Possible named for a settler.

Hendrix. Post office established December 2, 1896; discontinued date not known. Origin of name not learned.

La Platte. Post office established September 22, 1855. Moved to Larimore City March 2, 1858. Former town established about December 21, 1855. Because of its proximity to the Platte River, the town was subject to overflows. To avoid flooding, a new place was platted west of the original site and called Larimore City on March 2, 1858.

La Platte. Peak population (1950), 150. Post office established 1870; discontinued 1954. Town was located on part of the former townsite of Larimore Mills by the Omaha and Southwestern Railroad in 1870. It was named for its proximity to the Platte River Valley.

Larimore City. Census not available. Post office established March 2, 1858; discontinued March 31, 1860. Former town named in honor of a settler.

Larimore Mills. Post office established July 18, 1865; moved to La Platte 1870; named in honor of a settler.

La Vista. Peak population (1990), 9,840. New subdivision of Omaha established in 1960s.

Lisbon. Post office name changed from Platte Valley December 9, 1867; name changed to Sarpy Center June 25, 1875. Probably named for one of eight places in the United States called Lisbon.

Lyman. Former station on the Missouri Pacific Railroad situated near Louisville.

Meadow. Census not available. Post office established March 27, 1894; made a station of Louisville, 1910. This is also a railroad station on the Chicago, Rock Island and Pacific line. The townsite was platted on a meadow and therefore called Meadow.

Melia. Post office established March 23, 1905; discontinued January 31, 1910. Named in honor of Peter Melia, settler.

Merrill Mission. Baptist mission established by the Rev. Moses Merrill in 1833 for teaching the Oto Indians. Location was seven miles southwest of the present town of Bellevue.

Nasby. Post office established August 29, 1872; discontinued September 19, 1887. Origin of the name not learned.

Offutt Air Force Base. Post office established, 1948; made an independent station of Omaha, 1949. This area was an army air field when established adjacent to Fort Crook in 1924. Named in honor of Lt. Jarvis B. Offutt, first air casualty from Omaha in World War I. The U.S. headquarters of the Strategic Air Command was moved here from Boling Air Force Base, Washington, D.C., in November 1948 and named Offutt Air Force Base with Gen. Curtis E. LeMay as commander.

Papillion. Peak population (2000), 16,363. Post office established March 6, 1862. County seat named after nearby Papillion Creek. The name is French, meaning butterfly. According to local tradition, early French explorers named the creek for the many butterflies found along its banks. Papillion won county seat from Bellevue and Sarpy Center in 1875 election. Post office made a branch of Omaha, 1974.

Papillion City. First site of this proposed city was laid out two and one-half miles northeast of present location of Papillion. It did not last long enough for a post office.

Pappio. Station on the Burlington Railroad.

Park Mills. Early settlement in Sarpy County.

Paynters. Early settlement in Sarpy County. Probably the name of Larimore before a post office was established.

Peach Grove. Post office established March 23, 1878; discontinued November 17, 1886. Named for a peach orchard in the area.

Platford. Peak population (1860), 135. Post office established May 8, 1858; discontinued October 1879. Named by the Platford Town Company that established the town.

Platona. Town platted by Daniel Gant that did not last long enough for a post office.

Platte River. Station at the junction of the Chicago and North Western Railroad.

Platte Valley. Post office established August 7, 1865; name changed to Lisbon December 9, 1867. Named for the Platte River Valley.

Plattford. Post office established May 8, 1858; discontinued October 1879.

Portal. Peak population (1890), 25. Post office established April 23, 1887; discontinued August 24, 1898. Town platted by the Portal Land and Town Lot Company and supposedly named for the portal of the western gateway.

Richfield. Peak population (1900), 65. Post office established April 15, 1890. So named because it is situated in the heart of one of the richest farming areas in the West.

Rumsey. Station on the Chicago, Rock Island and Pacific Railroad, named in honor of Rumsey Saling, a settler.

Saling's Grove. Picnic and camp meeting place probably named for Jefferson Saling, a settler.

Salinte. Early proposed town in Sarpy County.

Santee. Site of the Santee Hotel, stone structure used as a wayside rest by early travelers.

Sarpy. Post office established June 24, 1864; discontinued March 22, 1866. Named for the county.

Sarpy Center. Peak population (1880), 43. Post office name changed from Lisbon June 25, 1875; discontinued May 9, 1883. Named for the county. Town lost its identity when nearby Springfield was built on a railroad line. Sarpy Center vied for county seat wlth Papillion and Bellevue.

Sarpy's Trading Post. Early trading post established by Peter Sarpy on the east edge of present Bellevue.

Springfield. Peak population (2000), 1,450. Post office established December 7, 1881. The Missouri Pacific Railroad surveyed and platted the town in November of 1881 on land owned by J. D. Spearman, who named the new town Springfield because of the abundance of springs in the region.

St. Columbans. Post office established July 21, 1922. Seminary founded by the Society of St. Columbans for the educating of Catholic priests for the mission fields of China. There are two hundred acres of park-like grounds overlooking the Missouri River and valley. Location is near Bellevue.

Traders Point. Trading place and ferry crossing on the Platte River for immigrants. It was managed by a Mr. Wheeler.

Triqua. Proposed town on the Missouri River that never got beyond the platting stage.

Willview. Former station on the Missouri Pacific Railroad located near the Cass County line.

Woodworth. Former station on the Missouri Pacific Railroad near Louisville.

Xenia. Post office established June 15, 1869; discontinued October 1, 1887. Named by James Bates for Xenia, Illinois, his former home town.

SAUNDERS COUNTY

Named in honor of Alvin Saunders (1817-99), governor of Nebraska Territory from 1861 to 1867. The county was originally called Calhoun, but the name was changed by an act of the Legislature approved January 8, 1862. The original county was established and the boundaries defined by an act approved January 26, 1856, and redefined November 3, 1858.

Alvin. Name proposed for the town of Mead, but there was already a post office in the state so named.

Anoka. Early locality in Saunders County.

Ash Bluffs. Post office established May 16, 1872; discontinued April 17, 1873. Named for native ash trees overlooking the bluffs in the area.

Ashland. Peak population (1980), 2,274. Post office established November 13, 1866. Named for Ashland, Kentucky, by a Mr. Argyle in honor of the home of his favorite statesman, Henry Clay. Town was at one time in Cass County, but on formation of Saunders

County, it was separated from Cass and became county seat for the new county. Ashland lost an election with Wahoo for county seat October 14, 1873.

Attica. Post office established July 5, 1870; discontinued August 28, 1872. Possibly named for one of six places in the United States called Attica.

Benton. Post office established June 8, 1868; discontinued April 2, 1877. Possibly named for Senator Thomas Hart Benton (1782-1858) of Missouri, who was prominent in the affairs of the West.

Bradford. Post office established October 20, 1873; discontinued July 15, 1879. Possibly named for one of thirteen places in the United States called Bradford.

Cedar Bluffs. Peak population (1980), 632. Post office established July 10, 1868. Possibly named for an abrupt bluff in the vicinity on the Platte River where some cedar trees were growing.

Cedar Hill. Post office name changed from Slavonia May 13, 1874; discontinued March 10, 1888. Named for cedar trees growing on a hillside.

Ceresco. Peak population (2000), 920. Post office established August 10, 1869. Named by two settlers—Richard Nelson, the first postmaster, and Hod Andrus—for their former home of Ceresco, Michigan.

Charlotteville. Former locality in western Saunders County.

Chaslaw. Post office established December 30, 1880; discontinued August 3, 1882. Origin of name not learned.

Clayton. Former station on the Union Pacific Railroad.

Clear Creek. Post office established June 15, 1871; name changed to Yutan June 6, 1884. Named for a nearby creek.

Colon. Peak population (1910), 193. Post office established January 3, 1872. Named by Postmaster Leander Taylor for his former home of Colon, Michigan. The post office was orignally two miles from present site.

Crowder. Post office name changed from Wautisca February 18, 1874; discontinued April 1, 1879. Post office named for the Rev. Thomas Jefferson Crowder, who came from Springfield, Illinois, and promoted the later town of Crowder.

Edensburgh. Post office established October 1, 1883; discontinued November 3, 1886. Swedish Lutheran settlement possibly named for a place in Sweden.

Eldred. Post office established April 8, 1869; discontinued September 25, 1874. Named in honor of J. Eldred, first postmaster.

Estenia. Post office established October 28, 1869; discontinued January 22, 1883. Origin of the name not learned. First postmaster was William A. Esty.

Excelsior. Former locality listed in early Saunders County history.

Firestone. Station on both the Burlington Railroad and the Union Pacific Railroad. Location is near Memphis.

Headland. Post office established August 26, 1868; discontinued October 31, 1877. Origin of the name not learned.

Hill. Former station on the Union Pacific Railroad located near Wahoo.

Isla. Post office established January 8, 1875; discontinued November 11, 1886. Named for a small town near Malmo, Sweden.

Ithaca. Peak population (1910), 171. Post office established February 14, 1870. Named for Ithaca, New York, at the suggestion of the county surveyor when the town was established.

Kenton. Early locality in Saunders County.

Krumel. Station on the Union Pacific Railroad.

Leshara. Peak population (2000), 111. Post office established February 26, 1906. Village named for a former Pawnee leader, Petalesharo. He and his tribe once lived in this locality. Postal authorities spelled the name Leshara.

Lone Valley. Post office established February 8, 1870; discontinued March 2, 1874. Name is descriptive in meaning.

Lothair. Post office established April 7, 1871; discontinued March 6, 1872. Origin of name not learned.

Loupville. Locality mentioned in early Saunders County history.

Malmo. Peak population (1900), 259. Post office established December 22, 1887. Town named by Swedish settlers for Malmo, Sweden.

Marrietta. Locality in early county history.

Mead. Peak population (2000), 564. Post office name changed from Saunders August 4, 1880. Named for an official of the Union Pacific Railroad.

Melrose. Post office established January 13, 1873; moved in name to Harlan County in January 1874. Possibly named for one of thirteen places in the United States called Melrose.

Memphis. Peak population (1920), 186. Post office established May 15, 1888. Named for Memphis, Tennessee, which was named for the ancient Egyptian city.

Milton. Post office established February 2, 1870; discontinued March 29, 1886. Origin of name not learned. First postmaster was David W. Folsom.

Morse Bluff. Peak population (1920), 216. Post office established January 20, 1888. Named in honor of Charles W. Morse of North Bend, Nebraska, who owned the land on which townsite was located. "Bluff" is not descriptive of the place, but was added to prevent confusion with another Morse on the same railroad line.

Neapolis. Place selected as the capital of Nebraska Territory in January 1858 when the Territorial Legislature decreed that the seat of government was to be removed from Omaha to a site not less than fifty miles west of the Missouri River and not more than six miles from the Platte. Through political maneuvering, however, the proposition was soon voided. Neapolis was to be near the site of Cedar Bluffs. A hill near the proposed city is still called Capitol Hill.

Newton. Post office established February 7, 1872; discontinued April 6, 1894. Probably named for one of fourteen places in the United States bearing this name.

Phase. Locality listed in Saunders County history.

Pilzen. Post office established February 15, 1877; name changed to Poitsam April 28, 1884. Named for Plzen, a city now in Czech Republic, by a local settler who formerly lived there. The English spelling is Pilzen.

Plasi. Peak population (1890), 40. Post office established June 13, 1884; discontinued April 14, 1904. Named for Plasy in Bohemia, now in Czech Republic. Postal authorities spelled the name Plasi.

Platte River. Station at the junction on the Chicago and North Western Railroad.

Platteville. Census not available. Post office established June 20, 1870; discontinued March 19, 1874. Former hamlet named for its location on the Platte River.

Pohocco. Post office established September 20, 1869; discontinued February 9, 1871. Named for the precinct whose name was derived from the Pawnee word pahuk, meaning headland or promontory. It was the Pawnee name for a prominent local hill on the Platte.

Poitsam. Post office name changed from Pilzen August 28, 1884; discontinued June 13, 1884. Origin of the name has not been learned.

Prague. Peak population (1930), 421. Post office established December 10, 1887. Named for Praha, the capital of the Czech Republic. The Czech residents of the town requested the name Prague when the railroad was being built to the site.

Raccoon Forks. Name of Valparaiso before a post office was established.

Rescue. Peak population (1930, 1940), 25. Post office established June 23, 1874; discontinued 1934. Former hamlet possibly named for a rescue in the neighborhood at the time the post office was named.

Ricker Spur. Former station on the Burlington Railroad located near Ashland.

Rose Hill. Post office established June 11, 1873; discontinued September 24, 1879. Possibly named for wild roses growing on a hillside.

Saline Ford. Probably a stage stop for early freighters where the town of Ashland now stands. Ford over lower Salt Creek.

Sand Creek. Post office established December 8, 1870; discontinued July 16, 1903. Locally descriptlve name of the creek in the area.

Saunders. Post office established February 15, 1877; name changed to Mead August 4, 1880. Named for the county.

Slavonia. Post office established December 12, 1872; name changed to Cedar Hill May 13, 1874. Probably named for the Slavonian region of Europe by settlers.

Strauss. Post office established April 3, 1873; discontinued July 21, 1873. Origin of name not learned.

Success. Post office established July 3, 1900; discontinued April 30, 1904. Possibly named for patrons' success in securing a post office.

Swedeburg. Peak population (1940), 102. Post office established August 19, 1873. Town platted by Pioneer Town Site Company and named for the large settlement of Swedes in the area. Post office discontinued in 1973; mail served from Wahoo.

Touhy. Peak population (1940), 102. Post office established June 9, 1890; discontinued 1956. Mail served from Valparaiso. Named after Patrick Touhy, for many years a local employee of the Union Pacific Railroad, who advanced from section hand to section foreman, and afterward to higher positions.

Troy. Post office established April 14, 1873; name changed to Weston July 23, 1877. Possibly named for Troy, Davis County, Iowa, from which Jacob March and other Saunders County settlers had come.

Valparaiso. Peak population (1900), 614. Post office established September 27, 1871. Andrew Johnson considered this locality the "vale of paradise" and so named the town Valparaiso. There is also a Valparaiso, Indiana.

Veda. Post office established July 23, 1884; discontinued December 28, 1887. Origin of the name not learned.

Wahoo. Peak population (2000), 3,942. Post office established July 15, 1869. There is some dispute over the origin of the name Wahoo. One explanation is that it is derived from the euonymus or wahoo shrub, commonly known as the "burning bush," which grows on the banks of Wahoo Creek. The plant was used medicinally by the Indians, according to tradition. Another theory is that Wahoo stems from pahoo (not very blufflike). This is not probable considering the rugged appearance of the country. Henry Gannett's work on place names states that Wahoo is an Indian word meaning a species of elm. Wahoo was made county seat in election with Ashland October 14, 1873.

Wahpco. Present Union Pacific Railroad station.

Wann. Peak population (1940), 52. Post office established May 26, 1908; discontinued 1951. Mail served from Ashland. Town named in honor of a settler.

Wantiska. Post office established February 8, 1870; name changed to Crowder February 18, 1871. State and county records show the spelling Wautisca. Postal authorities received the spelling as Wantiska. Other spellings were Watiska and Wautiska. This was probably an Oto Indian word.

Weston. Peak population (1900), 426. Post office name changed from Troy July 23, 1877. Named by Union Pacific Railroad officials. The town was to be the western terminus of this branch.

Willow Creek. Post office established March 6, 1872; discontinued March 10, 1888. Name describes a creek in the area.

Woodcliff. Former station on the Burlington Railroad.

Yutan. Peak population (2000), 1,216. Post office name changed from Clear Creek June 6, 1884. Town named for the Oto Indian Chief Ietan, whose people had a village of some seventy lodges located near the present village site. English pronunciation of Ietan's name is Yutan. The first Sunday school for the Oto Indians was established in this vicinity.

SCOTTS BLUFF COUNTY

Named for Scott's Bluff, noted landmark named for Hiram Scott, an early trapper who perished at the foot of the bluff. Scotts Bluff County formed from a part of Cheyenne County by vote November 6, 1888.

Bailey View. Former station on the Union Pacific Railroad named for a settler.

Baxter. Post office established August 6, 1887; discontinued 1888. Former post office and present station on the Burlington Railroad named for a settler.

Bellingar. Station on the Union Pacific Railroad named for a settler.

Bradley. A station on the Burlington Railroad.

Brockoff. Station on the Union Pacific Railroad named for a settler.

Caldwell. Post office established March 11, 1890; discontinued June 15, 1915. Named in honor of a settler.

Camp Mitchell. This military post name changed from Camp Shuman in October 1864. See Fort Mitchell.

Camp Shuman. Military post located three miles west of present city of Scottsbluff and named in honor of Capt. J. S. Shuman sometime prior to 1864. Name changed in October 1864 to Camp Mitchell.

Carlson. Station on Burlington Railroad.

Clouse. Station on Burlington Railroad.

Collins. Post office established January 22, 1889; discontinued May 29, 1899. Probably named by homesteaders from Fort Collins, Colorado.

Costin. Station on the Union Pacific Railroad near Haig.

Covert. Station on the Burlington Railroad.

Dorrington. Post office established, 1890; discontinued 1899. Probably named for Capt. F. M. Dorrington, surveyor for the U.S. Land Office.

Doyle. Station on the Burlington Railroad near Mitchell.

Dutch Flats. Colony of German settlers who were the first to homestead on tableland in Scotts Bluff County.

Ficklin Springs. Pony Express Station No. 35, located one mile west of present town of Melbeta. Named for Benjamin Ficklin, superintendent of Pony Express line.

Fort Fontenelle. Temporary fort located at foot of Scott's Bluff, the historical landmark. Named for Lucien Fontenelle of the American Fur Company. Probably established in the early 1860s.

Fort John. This post was established in or near Robidoux Pass, Scotts Bluffs, in the summer of 1849 by employees of Pierre Chouteau and Company. The following spring the post was moved several miles to the southeast but late in 1851 it was moved again to near the original location. The business at the post included trade with overland trail emigrants as well as with Indians.

Fort John. Post office established January 24, 1854; discontinued December 27, 1857. Named for the original Fort John.

Fort Mitchell. Army post formerly called Camp Mitchell and renamed Fort Mitchell in late 1864, in honor of Brig. Gen. Robert B. Mitchell. A subpost of Fort Laramie, it was probably abandoned in 1868.

Gering. Peak population (1990), 7,946. Post office established April 1887. County seat town named in honor of Martin Gering, a Civil War veteran, banker, and member of the original townsite company formed in 1887. Gering became the county seat in election with Mitchell in February 1889.

Granger. Post office established February 26, 1887; discontinued prior to 1895. Named for the first Grangers (members of a farmers' fraternal organization), who advocated fencing the open cattle ranges.

Haig. Peak population (1960), 80. Post office name changed from Haigville November 16, 1925. Town named in honor of Harry Haig, friend of John Clay who was a cowboy in the early days with the Two Bar Ranch. Haig belonged to the family whose most distinguished member was Sir Douglas Haig (1861-1928), British field marshal during World War I and founder of Poppy Day, annual fundraising drive to aid war veterans. Post office made a rural branch of Scottsbluff in 1968.

Haigville. Post office established June 17, 1914; name changed to Haig November 16, 1925. See Haig.

Hartford. Post office established November 27, 1888; discontinued 1889. Origin of the name has not been learned.

Hartman. Station on the Union Pacific Railroad located near Lyman.

Headgate. Former railroad station.

Heldt. Former railroad station.

Henry. Peak population (1940), 176. Post office established November 19, 1909. Town named in honor of Henry Nichols, a boy drowned in the Platte River about a year after the town was platted. His father, Yorick Nichols, once owned most of the townsite. Made a community post office of Lyman in 1977.

Heyward. Former station on the Burlington Railroad named for Heyward G. Leavitt, active in establishing the sugar industry in the North Platte Valley.

Hilliker. Station on the Union Pacific Railroad.

Hope. Post office established August 20, 1907; discontinued April 30, 1912. Post office established by Henry Nehne, a Boer who refused to live under English rule in South Africa. Possibly named for the famous diamond found in the South African mines.

Horse Creek. Pony Express Station No. 37 in Nebraska and the last one before entering Wyoming. Location was two miles northeast of the present town of Lyman.

Janise. Station on the Union Pacific Railroad.

Joyce. Station on the Union Pacific Railroad.

Kiowa. Former station on the Union Pacific Railroad situated near Lyman.

Larissa. Post office established May 28, 1891; discontinued May 3, 1896. Named in honor of the daughter of W. B. Cole, first postmaster.

Little Moon. Former station on the Burlington Railroad named for the Little Moon Lakes in the region.

Lyman. Peak population (1970), 626. Post office established February 9, 1921. Named in honor of Charles F. and W. H. Lyman, early residents and bankers.

Marlin. Former station on the Burlington Railroad.

Mathers. Station on the Union Pacific Railroad. Possibly named in honor of Albert Mathers, who owned a number of ranches in Scotts Bluff County.

McGrew. Peak population (1940), 139. Post office established August 30, 1911. Possibly named in honor of Charles McGrew. With a Mr. Atkins, McGrew was in the business of promoting townsite building.

Melbeta. Peak population (1980), 151. Post office established May 28, 1912. This town is a shipping point for sugar beets. Melbeta is of German origin and is locally considered to mean sugar beets.

Millstown. County seat contender with Mitchell located four miles east of present Scottsbluff. Never a post office.

Minatare. Peak population (1940), 1,125. Post office established April 28, 1887. Town named for the Minnetaree Indians, a tribe of Siouan stock.

Mingo. Post office established April 28, 1887; discontinued 1888. Named for Mingo, Iowa, by Frank Beers, a settler from that town.

Mintle. Station on the Burlington Railroad.

Mitchell. Peak population (1940), 2,181. Post office established May 13, 1887. Town takes its name from former Fort Mitchell, named for Brig. Gen. Robert B. Mitchell. Mitchell vied for county seat with Millstown and Gering in 1889 election.

Moon. Station on the Union Pacific Railroad named for Little Moon Lakes in the vicinity.

Morrill. Peak population (1980), 1,380. Post office established December 26, 1901. Town named in honor of Charles H. Morrill, president of the Lincoln Land Company and former regent of the University of Nebraska.

Old Red Cloud Agency. Location of this agency was across the Nebraska-Wyoming line about one mile from the present town of Henry, Nebraska. Named for the famous Oglala Sioux Chief Red Cloud. The agency was in existence from 1867 to 1873 before removal to Dawes County.

Pelton. Station on the Union Pacific Railroad.

Pratt. This locality was once on the present site of the town of Henry before a post office was established. Headquarters for the Pratt and Ferris Cattle Company.

Redus. Station on the Burlington Railroad.

Riford. Station on the Union Pacific Railroad.

Roach. Station on the Burlington Railroad. Possibly named in honor of David J. Roach, an official of the Great Western Sugar Company.

Roberts. Station on the Burlington Railroad named for a local settler.

Robidoux's Trading Post. Famous early trading post consisting mostly of a store and a blacksmith shop to service the emigrant wagons moving on the Oregon-California trails. Named for the French trader Joseph Robidoux.

Roubedeau. Station on the Union Pacific Railroad.

Scottsbluff. Peak population (2000), 14,732. Post office established August 31, 1899. City named for the county.

Scotts Bluffs. Pony Express Station No. 36 in Nebraska. The site later became Fort Mitchell, according to some sources.

Scoville. Station on the Burlington Railroad.

Sears. Station on the Union Pacific Railroad located near Lyman.

Sedan. Post office established August 26, 1891; discontinued January 19, 1897. Origin of name not learned.

Snell. Former station on the Burlington Railroad.

Stegall. Station on the Union Pacific Railroad.

Stewart's Siding. Former railroad station.

Stovil. Former railroad station.

Sunflower. Post office established January 15, 1889; discontinued October 20, 1900. Named for the wild sunflowers growing in the area.

Tabor. Proposed town started by George W. Fairfield, surveyor. It was to be named for his son-in-law, Wian Tabor, but a land dispute caused building operations to cease. The name Tabor remains as the designation of a local precinct.

Terrytown. Suburb and station of Scottsbluff. Named for Terry Carpenter (1900-1978), Nebraska legislator and public figure.

Thomas. Station on the Burlington Railroad.

Thompson. Post office established May 1, 1888; discontinued prior to 1895. Origin of name not learned.

Tony. Station on the Burlington Railroad located near Bayard.

Toohey. Former station on the Burlington Railroad near Morrill.

Trail. Former station on the Union Pacific Railroad located near Haig.

Trout. Station on the Burlington Railroad.

Willford. Post office established August 28, 1890; discontinued August 12, 1905. Named in honor of the son of Mrs. Emma King, first postmistress.

Winters. Former station on the Burlington Railroad.

Woodrow. Post office established July 20, 1913; discontinued December 15, 1917. Named in honor of Woodrow Wilson (1856-1924) who was in office at the time the post office was established.

Wright. Post office established June 29, 1892; discontinued June 29, 1894. Named in honor of William H. Wright, first postmaster.

SEWARD COUNTY

Named in honor of William Henry Seward (1801-72), secretary of state under President Abraham Lincoln. County was originally called Greene, established January 26, 1856. Name was changed to Seward January 3, 1862.

Batesville. Post office established January 9, 1878; discontinued October 15, 1878. Possibly named in honor of L. D. Bates, county commissioner.

Beaver Crossing. Peak population (1940), 550. First postmaster was Roland Reed, appointed January 22, 1868. Town named after a place near the townsite where the Overland Trail from Fort Leavenworth crossed Beaver Creek. Beaver Creek got its name from the numerous beaver in the vicinity. Town platted by Pioneer Town Site Company.

Bee. Peak population (1920), 228. Post office established September 7, 1887. The sixteen precincts in Seward County are lettered A to P. The town of Bee is in B precinct, so a double "e" was added to the initial to coin the name.

Camden. Peak population (1870), 50. Post office established September 8, 1862; discontinued October 29, 1900. Possibly named for Camden, New Jersey.

Carlisle. This place, chartered March 15, 1855, was the proposed county seat of Greene County, which became Seward County in 1862.

Cordova. Peak population (1920), 205. Post office established March 27, 1888. C. W. Hunkins, the postmaster, suggested the town name for Cordova, Spain, because of its dissimilarity to any other post office name within the state. The idea was accepted by both postal authorities and the railroad.

Fouse Ranch. The John E. Fouse Ranch, located on branches of Beaver Creek and Blue River, included an underground stable with trap door to provide protection from Indian attacks and a log house 36-by-16 feet. As many as two hundred wagons stopped at one time at this overland freighting stop.

Garland. Peak population (1920), 279. Post office name changed from Germantown 1918. Named in honor of Ray Garland, soldier who died in France during World War I.

Germantown. Post office established March 19, 1874; name changed to Garland 1918. Named for the German settlers who predominated in the population.

Glendale. Post office established May 10, 1877; discontinued September 23, 1878. Named for the physical surroundings of the neighborhood.

Goehner. Peak population (1990), 192. Post office established March 13, 1888. Named in honor of John F. Goehner of Seward, merchant and member of the Legislature. Platted by Pioneer Town Site Company.

Greenville. Proposed town that never got beyond the platting stage when the region was first formed as Greene County in 1855.

Groveland. Post office established April 5, 1871; discontinued April 7, 1875.

Grover. Post office established November 9, 1885; discontinued October 31, 1908. Probably named for Grover Cleveland, U.S. President when this office was established.

Hartford. Early locality in Seward County.

Hartman. Post office established April 13, 1871; name changed to Marysville December 29, 1873. Named for family in Seward County.

Hunkins. This was Cordova before a post office was established; named in honor of C. W. Hunkins, who became postmaster of the new town of Cordova. The name Hunkins was not accepted because of conflict with Hoskins, Wayne County.

Lafayette. Post office established November 21, 1878; name changed to Tamora October 10, 1879. Possibly named for General Lafayette of France who had aided the American revolutionaries one hundred years before.

Leahey. Former station on the Burlington Railroad. Probably named for Mike Leahey, railroad contractor.

Marysville. Peak population (1892, 1900), 38. Post office name changed from Hartman December 29, 1873; discontinued November 11, 1903. Possibly named in honor of Mary F. Augur, resident.

Milford. Peak population (1980), 2,108. Post office established April 24, 1864. J. L. Davison made the first settlement in the vicinity in the spring of 1864. He built a log house on the site of the present hospital building and opened a ranch on the steam wagon road. Later, Davison improved a ford on the Blue River, then moved a mill from Weeping Water Falls and placed it just above the ford. Thus, the name of Milford originated. Milford held county seat from 1867 to fall 1871 when lost to Seward.

Neldon. Post office established February 13, 1871; discontinued October 13, 1871. Origin of name not learned.

North Fork. Post office established February 4, 1869; moved to Saline County July 13, 1877. Named for its site at the fork of the Big Blue and West Blue rivers.

Norval. Post office name changed from West's Mill March 13, 1882; discontinued December 3, 1884. Named in honor of T. L. Norval, member of the State Supreme Court.

Oakgroves. Post office established December 22, 1874; discontinued July 21, 1884. Probably named for its location near a grove of oak trees.

Orton. Post office established September 8, 1871; discontinued December 11, 1888. Origin of name not learned. There is also an Orton, Minnesota.

Ost. Former station on the Burlington Railroad named in honor of Louis E. 0st, railroad agent.

Pittsburgh. Peak population (1872), 25. Post office established May 2, 1873; discontinued April 23, 1875. Former town surveyed by Chris Lezenby and probably named for Pittsburgh, Pennsylvania.

Pleasant Dale. Peak population (1910), 257. Post office established February 13, 1871. Town named for the beautiful valley in which it is located. Capt. J. H. Culver, U.S. Army, suggested the name for its appropriateness. The town was originally one and one-half miles from its present site and was served by passenger stage coaches and freighters.

Ruby. Peak population (1910, 1920, 1930, 1940), 71. Post office established September 25, 1883; discontinued December 12, 1894. Mail served from Milford. Town probably named in honor of James Ruby, Civil War veteran and county resident.

Seward. Peak population (2000), 6,319. Post office established April 3, 1867. Platted in 1868. Seward was named for the county and became the county seat in 1871. Concordia Teachers College was established here in 1894. In 1973 Seward was designated "Nebraska's Official Fourth of July City" for its annual patriotic observances.

Staplehurst. Peak population (1980), 306. Post office established February 8, 1877. Town named for Staplehurst, England, by Ebenezer Jull who, with his family, came from there in 1873.

Success. Community with a store operated by John C. Tissue, who hoped it would be a success.

Tamora. Peak population (1910, 1920), 205. Post office name changed from Lafayette October 10, 1879; discontinued 1970. Mail served from Seward. Each of three or four donors of land for the townsite wanted the place named for himself. After every discussion about the matter, they would put off the final decision "until tomorrow"; thus, they eventually coined the word Tamora.

Thompson's Ranch. Probably used as a meeting place in early county government proceedings.

Unitt. Post office established 1904; discontinued 1921. Probably named in honor of Philip Unitt, stockman who came from England in 1880.

Utica. Peak population (2000), 844. Post office established June 23, 1874. Town named for Utica, New York, by G. A. Derby. Post office first established in Derby's home; later he platted the town.

Welden. Former locality whose name origin has not been learned.

West's Mill. Post office established January 22, 1868; name changed to Norval March 13, 1882. Named in honor of Thomas West, who with his son Thomas West, Jr., and Orin Johnson established the settlement in June 1859. They erected a saw and grist mill on the West Blue River.

Wickoff. An early community. Origin of the name not learned.

SHERIDAN COUNTY

Named in honor of Philip H. Sheridan (1831-88), Civil War general. Boundaries were defined by act of the Legislature approved February 25, 1885.

Adaton. Post office established January 11, 1886; discontinued December 15, 1930. Named by cowboys of the vicinity for Ada Foster, first postmistress and first white woman to live in Beaver Valley.

Albany. Peak population (1892), 42. Post office established November 19, 1886; discontinued 1939. Former town named after Albany, New York, by William B. McIntyre, first postmaster. His former home was New York state.

Alcove. Probably descriptive of the land which this area represented.

Antioch. Peak population (1920), 764. Post office name changed from Reno August 1, 1891. Town named by the family of W. G. Wilson after a town in Iowa or Ohio from which they had come. Antioch is a familiar biblical name. Five potash factories in the area made Antioch a boom town during World War I.

Appleton. Post office established September 25, 1889; discontinued September 26, 1894. Possibly named for Appleton, Wisconsin.

Billing. Post office established July 1, 1912; discontinued 1934. Possibly named in honor of Henry Billing, foreman on the Creighton Ranch.

Bingham. Peak population (1940), 149. Post office established June 7, 1888. Town named for the precinct. The precinct may have been named for a settler, a railroad official, or for Bingham, Minnesota.

Birdsell. Station on the Burlington Railroad probably named for a railroad official.

Buff. Post office established June 13, 1906; discontinued May 16, 1907. Origin of name not learned.

Burrough. Post office established December 14, 1891; discontinued September 11, 1895. Possibly named in honor of John H. Burroughs, first postmaster, with the last letter of the name omitted.

Camp Sheridan. A military post located one mile below Spotted Tail Agency on the east bank of the west fork of Beaver Creek, tributary of the White River. Named in honor of Gen. Phil Sheridan when founded on September 9, 1874. This post was abandoned about 1880.

Cilicia. Post office established July 12, 1917; discontinued November 15, 1923. Origin of name not learned.

Clinton. Peak population (1930), 157. Post office established August 4, 1885; discontinued 1960. Named for Clinton, Iowa. Platted by Pioneer Town Site Company in 1894.

Colcesser. Post office established May 23, 1899; discontinued January 15, 1924. Named in honor of Henry Colcesser, first postmaster.

Craven. Post office established June 23, 1892; discontinued April 28, 1894. Possibly named in honor of Gus Craven, pioneer settler.

Dewing. Probably the former name of White Clay before a post office was established. Possibly named in honor of C. M. Dewing, rancher.

Dullaghan. Post office established July 24, 1915; discontinued December 31, 1921. Origin of name not learned.

Ellsworth. Peak population (1910), 30. Post office established March 2, 1904. Origin of name not learned. There are towns in Maine and Minnesota having this name. Located on the Chicago, Burlington, and Quincy Railroad, Ellsworth was an early cattle shipping point. For a time it was the headquarters of the Nebraska Land and Feeding Company, operated by pioneer cattlemen Will Comstock and Bartlett Richards.

Gordon. Peak population (1960), 2,223. Post office established March 3, 1884. Town named in honor of John Gordon of Sioux City, Iowa. During the 1870s Black Hills gold rush, Gordon, with a train of wagons under his command, attempted to travel to the Hills when the country was still Indian territory and closed to white settlers. He was overtaken about five miles from the present location of the town by a United States cavalry detachment. Gordon's oxen were turned loose and his wagons burned as an example to other gold seekers attempting to illegally enter the Black Hills.

Grayson. Census not available. Post office established December 9, 1889;, discontinued December 31, 1928. Former village named in honor of Charles Grayson, first postmaster.

Hamilton. Post office established April 8, 1908; discontinued June 30, 1911. Possibly named in honor of Alexander Hamilton, first postmaster.

Hay Springs. Peak population (1950), 1,091. Post office name changed from Moakler September 28, 1885. Town named for its location in the center of meadow country where the soil is moistened by numerous springs.

Hazelton. Post office established November 28, 1913; discontinued November 30, 1914. Probably named in honor of Frederick Hazelton, minister and homesteader.

Hilton. Census not available. Post office established March 14, 1910; discontinued 1932. Former village named by Mrs. Carrie E. Smith, first postmistress, in honor of her nephew, William Hilton Merrill.

Hinchley. Post office established December 1, 1911; discontinued December 15, 1930. Named in honor of E. W. Hinchley, rancher.

Hoffland. Post office established June 13, 1916; discontinued October 15, 1927. Named in honor of the Hoffland family.

Holland. Former station on the Burlington Railroad located west of Antioch.

Holly. Post office established March 5, 1890; discontinued February 11, 1904. Probably named in honor of Thomas Holly, northwest Nebraska pioneer.

Holton. Locality listed in Sheridan County history.

Hunter. Post office established February 5, 1910; discontinued December 31, 1917. Named for the precinct, which was probably named for Hunter and Evans Ranch established by David Hunter, R. D. Hunter, and David Evans at an earlier date.

Ingomar. Post office established September 10, 1885; discontinued August 5, 1887. Origin of the name not learned. First postmaster was Darwin Clark.

Jennings. Post office established January 18, 1913; discontinued April 30, 1920. Possibly named in honor of F. M. Jennings, rancher.

Jess. Post office established March 13, 1890; discontinued August 15, 1913. Possibly named in honor of the wife of the first postmaster, C. C. Joy.

Kenomi. Post office established February 20, 1907; discontinued December 31, 1920. Kenomi was coined from the names of two daughters of Mr. and Mrs. Charles Orr.

Lakeside. Peak population (1940), 152. Post office established July 28, 1888. Town named for a nearby lake when the railroad was built. There are many lakes surrounding the town.

Long Lake. Post office established April 1, 1904; discontinued August 30, 1930. Derives its name from a lake two miles long and one-half mile wide near the post office.

Luella. Post office established March 13, 1890; discontinued March 1, 1907. Named in honor of Luella M. Keller, first postmistress.

Lulu. Post office established July 3, 1913; discontinued November 29, 1914. Origin of name not learned. First postmaster was Birdie B. Zinmaster.

Marple. Post office moved from Box Butte County April 23, 1908; discontinued 1933. See name in Box Butte County.

Mirage. Post office established August 18, 1885; discontinued February 5, 1913. Named for the precinct in which the office was located.

Moakler. Post office established December 16, 1884; name changed to Hay Springs September 28, 1885. Named in honor of a local settler.

Moomaw. Post office established January 28, 1890; discontinued December 15, 1916. Named in honor of Jacob P. Moomaw, first postmaster.

Mosser. Post office established December 22, 1885; discontinued October 22, 1895. Possibly named in honor of Mrs. Emma Mosser, first postmistress.

Peters. Post office established January 17, 1902; discontinued 1934. Named in honor of George S. Peters, first postmaster.

Reno. Post office established July 23, 1888. Name changed to Antioch August 17, 1891. Possibly named for one of two military officers: (1) Maj. Gen. Jesse Lee Reno, Union officer during the Civil War, killed in 1862 at the battle of South Mountain, Virginia; Reno, Nevada, was named for him (2) Maj. Marcus Reno, who participated with Gen. George Custer in the battle of the Little Big Horn. Name of Reno changed to avoid confusing mail directed to Reno, Nevada.

Riggs. Post office established August 6, 1888; discontinued June 14, 1895. Possibly named in honor of John Riggs, first sheriff of Sheridan County.

Roosevelt. Post office established May 10, 1907; discontinued August 17, 1907. Possibly named in honor of Theodore Roosevelt (1858-1919), President of the United States at the time post office was established.

Rosecrans. Post office established June 27, 1888; discontinued September 20, 1890. Probably named in honor of William Rosecrans (1819-98), Civil War general.

Rushville. Peak population (1950), 1,266. Post office established October 17, 1884. County seat was named for nearby Rush Creek. Generally dry, the creek was named for a growth of rushes in its bed.

Russell. Post office established February 3, 1911; discontinued September 30, 1911. Possibly named in honor of Harvey H. Russell, first postmaster.

Sandoz. Post office established August 25, 1885; discontinued December 31, 1895. Named in honor of Jules Sandoz, pioneer and father of Mari Sandoz, Nebraska author.

Schill. Post office established February 28, 1902; discontinued January 31, 1917. Named for the precinct in which it was located. Precinct probably named for the Schill Brothers cattle ranch.

Sharp. Post office established March 4, 1904; discontinued March 28, 1904. Origin of name not learned.

Sioux. Post office established May 20, 1884; discontinued May 7, 1888. Named for the Sioux Indians who lived in this region.

Smoot. Post office established April 12, 1892; discontinued December 14, 1892. Origin of the name not learned.

Spade. Census not available. Post office established June 20, 1908; discontinued September 29, 1923. Town and precinct both named for nearby Spade Ranch, operated by Nebraska cattleman Bartlett Richards.

Spotted Tail Agency. Indian agency located at the junction of Beaver Creek and White River. Served the Brule Sioux from 1873 until its removal to Rosebud Indian Agency in South Dakota in 1878. Named for Spotted Tail. Camp Sheridan was located nearby.

Spring Lake. Post office established April 22, 1907; discontinued July 15, 1907. Named for a spring which fed a lake near the post office.

Strasburger. Post office established December 5, 1908; discontinued July 15, 1916. Named in honor of John B. Strasburger, first postmaster.

Whiteclay. Peak population (1940), 112. Post office established December 22, 1904. Named for nearby Whiteclay Creek. The creek had been named for its clay-like color. The first post office was located one and one-half miles from present site.

SHERMAN COUNTY

Named in honor of William Tecumseh Sherman (1820-91), Civil War general. County was created by legislative enactment March 1, 1871.

Ashton. Peak population (1940), 488. Post office name changed from Zeven March 2, 1880. Named by John P. Taylor for his former home of Ashton, Illinois.

Austin. Peak population (1890), 26. Post office established July 11, 1877; discontinued 1919. Former hamlet named in honor of Austin Butts, settler.

Balsora. Post office established September 9, 1879; discontinued April 6, 1888. Origin of name not learned.

Bentora. Post office established October 2, 1882; name changed to Hazard January 14, 1887. Probably named for the Bent family. Mary Bent was first postmistress.

Bluffton. Post office established April 17, 1879; discontinued May 26, 1888. Origin of name not learned.

Bunnell. Proposed name for the town of Hazard.

Cedarville. Post office established January 14, 1884; name changed to Litchfield June 19, 1886. Probably named for cedar trees growing in the vicinity.

Cleoria. Post office established January 14, 1884; discontinued November 3, 1884. Named in honor of Cleoria Woods, resident.

Denniston. Post office established February 6, 1885; discontinued July 28, 1885. Possibly named for Dewitt C. Denniston, first postmaster.

Divide. Post office established March 19, 1886; discontinued July 11, 1906. Named for the summit of a railroad grade.

Elting. Post office established June 1, 1883; discontinued February 9, 1887. Named in honor of Elting Johnson, first postmaster.

Fern. Post office established August 3, 1882; discontinued February 17, 1887. Name selected by Thomas A. Coverly.

Fitzalon. Post office established January 4, 1880; name changed to Furay April 6, 1882. Origin of name not learned.

Furay. Post office name changed from Fitzalon April 6, 1882; name changed to Paris May 3, 1882. Named in honor of Major Furay, a postal inspector.

Hayestown. Peak population (1880), 100. Post office established January 19, 1877; discontinued July 25, 1899. Former town named in honor of President Rutherford B. Hayes (1822-93), who was in office when Hayestown was established.

Hazard. Peak population (1920), 167. Post office name changed from Bentora January 14, 1887. Town residents had difficulty selecting a name until one resident remarked that they "would hazard some name." Another person took up the comment and proposed the name Hazard.

Jericho. Post office established April 3, 1883; discontinued May 26, 1888. Probably named for the town in the Old Testament.

Litchfield. Peak population (1990), 314. Post office name changed from Cedarville June 19, 1886. Probably named for Litchfield, Connecticut.

Lonelm. Post office established May 26, 1882; discontinued February 29, 1884. Office, located in the eastern part of the county, named for a lone elm tree that survived a prairie fire.

Loup City. Peak population (1940), 1,675. Post office established August 26, 1873. County seat named for the Wolf or Skidi band of Pawnee Indians. Loup is the French translation of the Pawnee word skidi, meaning wolf. Loup City was made county seat in 1873. The town is also the terminus of the Union Pacific Railroad from Grand Island.

McAlpine. Former station on the Burlington Railroad. Possibly named for Thomas Alpine, railroad official.

Noah. Post office established April 19, 1881; name changed to Souleville March 20, 1882. Named in honor of Noah D. Vanscoy, first postmaster.

Paplin. Same location as Polander post office of 1887. Site with store located five miles northwest of Ashton.

Paradise. Post office established September 7, 1883; discontinued February 20, 1884. Named for the descriptive location of the post office.

Paris. Post office name changed from Furay May 3, 1882; discontinued November 25, 1890. One source says post office was named for Paris, Wisconsin, former home of Mrs. A. H. Gray, the postmaster's wife. Another source says named for Miss Lydia French, called Miss Paris.

Rockville. Peak population (1930), 241. Post office established December 1, 1873. Platted by John H. Frease in 1886. The town took the name of the rural post office, which had been named for its site on Rock Creek.

Schaupps. Census not available. Post office established July 27, 1905; discontinued June 15, 1915. Former town named for the Schaupp brothers, who owned the land where the townsite was located.

Souleville. Post office name changed from Noah March 20, 1882; discontinued August 27, 1886. Named in honor of the Soule family.

Verdurette. Post office established January 9, 1880; discontinued December 15, 1897. Named by the Rev. Joshua M. Snyder for the lush vegetation in the area. He was first postmaster, serving from 1880 to 1889. Verdurette was also a stage stop.

Walhelms. Former locality named either for a local settler or for a place in Germany.

Wilhelmshohe. Post office established September 4, 1879; name changed to Zeven November 13, 1882. Possibly named for a town in Germany.

Willamne. Located on CB&Q between Loup City and Ashton in the 1890s, approximately one half mile from Schaupps.

Zeven. Post office name changed from Wilhelmshohe November 13, 1882; name changed to Ashton March 22, 1888. Named for a town in Hanover province, Germany.

SIOUX COUNTY

Named for the Sioux tribe. County boundaries were defined by an act of the Legislature approved February 19, 1877, and redefined February 19, 1885.

Addis. Former station on Burlington Railroad. Post office was Adelia. Post office established May 27, 1891; name changed to Orella November 23, 1910. Origin of name not learned. First postmaster was Andrew P. Rosenburg.

Adelia. Post office established May 27, 1891; name changed to Orella November 23, 1910. Origin of name not learned. First postmaster was Andrew P. Rosenburg.

Agate. Post office name changed from Royville April 26, 1899. Named by James H. Cook after his ranch, the Agate Springs Ranch. Deposits of agate found at this point and there are springs in the area. Post office discontinued in 1970; mail served from Harrison.

Aldine. Post office established December 17, 1899; discontinued August 31, 1929. Named for a female acquaintance of R. H. Brown, first postmaster.

Andrews. Peak population (1910), 45. Post office name changed from Hunter May 8, 1906; discontinued 1953. This former town is said by one source to be named for a Mr. Andrews, who homesteaded the land on which town was platted. Another source says named for Jew Andrews, a locating engineer for the Chicago and North Western Railroad.

Arid. Post office established July 22, 1910; discontinued March 27, 1912. Name descriptive of the locale.

Ashbrook. Peak population (1910), 12. Post office established July 20, 1903; discontinued July 31, 1919. Former town named in honor of Link and Harry Ashbrook, who owned a ranch and had charge of the post office.

Asp. Post office name changed from Curly October 12, 1923; discontinued 1935. Named for the initials of A. S. Powell, first postmaster.

Bell. Post office established July 5, 1894; discontinued August 20, 1901. Named in honor of a local settler.

Bodarc. Census not available. Post office established March 19, 1896; discontinued August 31, 1901. Town of Bodarc was named by John W. Hunter and C. F. Slingerland, partners in a store on Hat Creek. They wanted a post office, and the name of Hunter's little daughter Oressa was suggested. About the same time a Texas community requested that its post office be named Bodarc, a corruption of bois d'arc (a tree native to eastern Texas—the Osage orange tree, commonly known as hedge apple). Postal authorities crossed the names and called the Texas post office Oressa and the Sioux County office Bodarc. Bodarc vied for county seat with Harrison and two other contenders and lost.

Bowen. Name suggested for the town of Harrison, but there already was a post office so named within the state.

Canton. Post office established February 8, 1890; moved to Box Butte County December 28, 1891; reestablished March 10, 1921; discontinued June 15, 1921. Probably named for one of eighteen Cantons in the United States.

Carey. Post office established July 20, 1899; discontinued September 7, 1904. Possibly named for Samuel W. Carey, early settler.

Casmelia. Post office established June 30, 1892; discontinued April 28, 1894. Origin of the name has not been learned.

Coffee. Post office established May 22, 1908; rescinded September 3, 1908. Named for the Charles F. Coffee family, residents.

Coffee Siding. Station on the Chicago and North Western Railroad.

Colville. Post office established April 18, 1907; discontinued October 15, 1908. Said to be named in honor of David Colville, an Australian settler.

Cross. Post office established March 14, 1910; discontinued January 4, 1911. Named in honor of a settler.

Curly. Post office established July 22, 1907; name changed to Asp October 12, 1923. Named in honor of Cyrus H. Henderson, the first postmaster, known as "Curly" for his curly hair.

Dancer's Hill. Stage stop on the old Fort Pierre and Fort Laramie Trail.

Deadman Creek. Locality in Sioux County.

Dome. Post office established April 17, 1911; discontinued December 31, 1915. Named for a land characteristic which resembled a dome.

Dowling. Post office established September 15, 1913; discontinued September 15, 1916. Possibly named in honor of Elizabeth M. Dowling, first postmistress.

Dubert. Post office established May 12, 1911; discontinued March 15, 1912. Probably named in honor of Ada Dubert, first postmistress.

Eckard. Post office established January 18, 1889; discontinued September 25, 1890. Possibly named in honor of John Eckard of Ardmore, South Dakota.

Empire. Post office established October 3, 1906; discontinued March 31, 1911. Probably named for the Empire Cattle Ranch or for the "cattle empire" in the surrounding area.

Gilchrist. Post office established September 11, 1889; discontinued September 20, 1902. Possibly named in honor of L. W. Gilchrist, member of Nebraska's Legislature at the time the office was established.

Glen. Peak population (1940), 50. Post office established August 22, 1887; discontinued 1954. Former town named for its location in a glen.

Gramercy. Post office established February 28, 1887; discontinued June 13, 1893. Probably named for Gramercy, England.

Harold. Name of Adelia before a post office was established.

Harrison. Peak population (1940), 500. Post office established August 6, 1886. County seat named in honor of President Benjamin Harrison (1833-1901). Harrison won county seat in election with Andrews, Bodarc, Montrose and the S. E. Smith Ranch in the first week of January 1887.

Hewitt. Post office established July 1, 1899; discontinued September 4, 1904. Named in honor of a local settler.

Hunter. Post office established March 19, 1903; name changed to Andrews May 8. Named in honor of the Hunter family, well-known in ranching activities. David and R. D. Hunter, with David Evans, established the Hunter and Evans Ranch on the Niobrara River at an earlier date.

Joder. Station on the Burlington Railroad located near Orella.

Kelley. Post office established January 6, 1908; discontinued November 15, 1911. Named in honor of Mattie A. Kelley, first postmistress.

Malinda. Post office moved from Box Butte County August 14, 1910; discontinued December 31, 1916. See note on Box Butte County.

Mansfield. Former station on the Burlington Railroad named for a railroad official.

Montrose. Peak population (1910), 24. Post office established February 28, 1887; discontinued 1949. Former town located on the high, rose-covered banks of Hat Creek. It is a name used in Scotland to describe wild roses. Montrose vied for county seat in 1887.

Mud Springs. Post office established June 9, 1909; discontinued July 15, 1918. Named by a ranchman because of the muddy soil near a local spring whose waters seeped over a large area.

Orella. Post office name changed from Adelia November 23, 1910; discontinued 1956. Named in honor of a young lady resident.

Porter. Former station on the Burlington Railroad.

Royville. Post office established March 29, 1890; name changed to Agate April 26, 1899. Named in honor of Roy Green, son of Mr. and Mrs. John A. Green.

S. E. Smith Ranch. Contender for county seat in early county history.

Spud. Post office established May 27, 1926; discontinued November 30, 1928. Probably named after the slang word for potato. Area was well-suited for growing potatoes.

Story. Census not available. Post office established May 23, 1891; discontinued 1936. Former town named in honor of Solomon R. Story, Civil War veteran and first postmaster.

Townsend. Post office established June 18, 1907; discontinued January 31, 1909. Possibly named in honor of Addie Townsend, first postmistress.

Unit. Post office established April 26, 1906; discontinued August 15, 1927. Origin of name not learned.

Warbonnet. Post office established September 12, 1882; discontinued May 29, 1886. This office established at the Emmons and B. E. Brewster Ranch, probably named for an Indian warbonnet found in the area or for Warbonnet Creek.

White Glen. Former locality in Sioux County.

STANTON COUNTY

Named in honor of Edwin M. Stanton (1814-69), secretary of war under Presidents Abraham Lincoln and Andrew Johnson. Organized by Legislature January 10, 1862, it had previously been called Izard County after Territorial Governor Mark Izard.

Bega. Peak population (1880), 60. Post office established January 30, 1879; discontinued January 31, 1902. Town probably named by Postmaster Andrew Johnson for a locality or subdivision in Sweden.

Berry. Former locality in the early settlement of Stanton County.

Butterfly. Post office established January 14, 1886; discontinued March 15, 1901. Named by area surveyors for the numerous butterflies found around the creeks in dry seasons.

Canton. Post office established July 24, 1868; name changed to Pilger July 10, 1884. Probably named by Irving Layton, first postmaster, who was born in Canton, Ohio.

Clinton. Peak population (2000), 30. Post office established October 19, 1868; discontinued February 24, 1875. Former county seat located three miles east of the present town of Stanton. Town said to be named for Clinton, Indiana, by some of the early settlers from there. Clinton lost its identity when railroad bypassed the town.

Craig City. This former locality did not exist long enough for a post office to be established; probably named for Walter Craig, a settler.

Degen. Post office established January 11, 1886; discontinued September 14, 1886. Origin of name not learned; it is probably British.

Devon. Early community in Stanton County named by Thomas Mortimer, British settler, for the Duke of Devon.

Dimick. Locality was the Marshall Field Ranch and was named in honor of Ed Dimick, the ranch manager.

Donup. Post office established April 3, 1871; moved to Wayne County October 30, 1882. Probably named by early German settlers for a German locality.

Farmington. Post office established September 1, 1875; discontinued September 11, 1876. Probably named for its location in a farming community.

Gassey Hollow. Later site of the Pleasant Run post office.

Haymow. Post office established April 23, 1884; discontinued March 2, 1904. Named for the precinct in which it was located. The word pertains to ricks of wild prairie hay in nearby fields.

Hoosier Hollow. Locality near Pleasant Run named by settlers from the Hoosier state of Indiana.

Horace. Post office established February 13, 1886; discontinued July 31, 1886. Named in honor of Horace B. Wheeler, first postmaster.

Hunton. Designated as county seat for Izard County. Hunton existed in name only.

Kingsburg. Post office established August 4, 1876; discontinued prior to 1885. Office originally called Koenigsberg by early German settlers after a city in Germany.

Orlon. Post office established October 23, 1872; discontinued April 26, 1876. Origin of name not learned.

Pilger. Peak population (1930), 578. Post office name changed from Canton July 10,

1884. Platted by the Valley Land and Town Lot Company of the Sioux City and Pacific Railroad. Named in honor of Peter Pilger, owner of the land on which townsite was platted.

Pleasant Run. Post office established July 11, 1868; name changed to Stanton April 3, 1877. Descriptive name of post office located at the A. J. Bartoff farm.

Schwedt. Post office established August 19, 1873; discontinued August 1, 1895. Probably named by Carl Feyerham for a town in the Prussian province of Germany.

Stanton. Peak population (2000), 1,627. Post office name changed from Pleasant Run April 3, 1877. County seat platted by S. L. Holman in 1871. Holman named the town in honor of his wife, whose maiden name was Stanton. Another source says the town named for the county.

THAYER COUNTY

Named in honor of John Milton Thayer (1820-1906), Civil War general and governor of Nebraska from 1887 to 1892. He was also a U.S. senator from Nebraska from 1867 to 1871. County, originally called Jefferson, was created in 1867. The present Thayer County was established by legislative enactment in 1871.

Alexandria. Peak population (1910), 447. Post office established June 10, 1872. Named in honor of S. J. Alexander, Nebraska secretary of state, 1879-82. Town platted by Nebraska Land and Town Company.

Belvidere. Peak population (1910), 475. Post office name changed from Elm Grove July 17, 1873. Col. Thomas Harbine, an official of the St. Joseph and Grand Island Railroad, named this town in accordance with the railway's A-B-C-D system of naming stations along its route. It may have been named for either Belvidere, Illinois, or Belvidere, New Jersey.

Big Sandy. Post office established March 8, 1872; discontinued April 5, 1875. Named for Big Sandy Creek.

Bruning. Peak population (1990), 332. Post office name changed from Prairie Star February 19, 1884. Town named in honor of Frank Bruning and his three brothers, who settled in the area. A U.S. Army air field was located here during World War II.

Bryant. Post office established August 1, 1871; moved to Fillmore County April 25, 1873. Probably named for Bowater Bryant, a settler from Indiana.

Byron. Peak population (1930), 206. Post office established January 29, 1885. Town named for Frank James Byron, who came from Ohio in the 1870s. Byron was a descendant of English poet George Noel Gordon, Lord Byron (1788-1824).

Carleton. Peak population (1890), 458. Post office name changed from Pioneer February 13, 1873; named in honor of Carleton Emory, son of the owner of the townsite.

Chester. Peak population (1940), 634. Post office established September 2, 1880. Probably named for one of the twenty-six places in the United States called Chester. Town established by Lincoln Land Company.

Coldrain. Name suggested and rejected for the present town of Carleton.

Coleraine. Locality listed in early county history.

Davenport. Peak population (1890), 513. Post office established June 23, 1874. Named by the St. Joseph and Grand Island Railroad for Davenport, Iowa.

Deshler. Peak population (1930), 1,176. Post office established, 1887. Named in honor of John Deshler, who owned the townsite.

Dryden. Post office established June 6, 1870; discontinued September 29, 1879. Possibly named for John Dryden, the English poet. First postmaster was Richard D. Preston.

Elm Grove. Post office established July 5, 1871; name changed to Belvidere July 17, 1873. Named for a grove of elm trees in the vicinity.

Fort Butler. The Indian raids of 1869 caused organization of Company A, 1st Nebraska

Cavalry, numbering sixty-five volunteers. They built a stockade on Spring Creek named Fort Butler in honor of Governor David Butler. In 1870 a company of regulars stationed at Kiowa replaced Company A, most of whom were settlers. The next year, on March 18, the citizens again formed a company subject to the order of the governor. The founding of Fort Butler led to the establishment of the town of Hebron.

Friedensau. Peak population (1910), 30. Post office established May 9, 1878; discontinued April 23, 1903. Former hamlet established by German colonists who named it "the vale of peace."

Gazelle. Post office established June 23, 1874; moved to Fillmore County February 18, 1879. Named for the antelope or gazelle which frequented this region in an earlier period.

Gilead. Peak population (1910), 181. Post office established June 23, 1874. Probably named for Mount Gilead in Palestine or Mount Gilead in Ohio.

Hebron. Peak population (1950), 2,000. Post office established April 25, 1870. County seat located in the valley of the Little Blue River and named for the ancient city of Hebron in Palestine. Named by members of the Disciples of Christ congregation who were among settlers platting the town in 1869.

Hillsdale. Proposed town in early county history.

Hubbell. Peak population (1900), 375. Post office established August 16, 1880. Town named in honor of Hubbell Johnson on whose farm the townsite was platted by the Lincoln Land Company.

Jersey City. Post office established March 8, 1872; discontinued September 30, 1872. Possibly named for Jersey City, New Jersey.

Kiowa. Pony Express Station No. 6 in Nebraska, about ten miles south of Hebron.

Kiowa. Peak population (1875), 25. Post office established July 14, 1870; discontinued April 23, 1903. Former village named for the Kiowa Indians.

Millersville. Nebraska Pony Express Station No. 5, probably located north of Hebron. Sometimes called Thompson's station because it was operated by George B. Thompson.

Pioneer. Post office established July 18, 1871; name changed to Carleton February 13, 1873. Named for the pioneers of the westward movement.

Prairie Star. Post office established December 29, 1873; name changed to Bruning February 19, 1884. Probably named for the Prairie Star school in the vicinity.

Sickler's Mill. Post office established May 8, 1876; discontinued November 4, 1881. Named in honor of a settler who operated a grist mill.

Stoddard. Peak population (1910, 1920, 1930), 56. Post office established May 21, 1886; discontinued 1935. Former town and present railroad station probably named for an official of the Burlington Railroad.

Williams. Peak population (1930), 126. Post office established June 25, 1901; discontinued 1935. Named in honor of William Lamb, son of Mr. and Mrs. Joseph Lamb, who owned the land of the townsite. Postal authorities added the letter "s."

THOMAS COUNTY

Named in honor of George H. Thomas (1816-70), Civil War general. County boundaries were defined by an act of Legislature and approved March 31, 1887.

Comfort. Post office established January 8, 1913; rescinded December 9, 1913. Probably named for the comfort of his home or ranch by Thomas M. Lucas, first postmaster.

Dismal. Post office established September 30, 1916; discontinued August 14, 1920. Named for the Dismal River, on which the office was located near the ranch of Billy and Fred Black.

Halsey. Peak population (1950), 160. Post office established May 11, 1892. Named in honor of Halsey Yates of Lincoln, member of a surveying party for the Burlington Railroad.

Imhof. Post office established April 12, 1919; discontinued 1933. Named in honor of George Imhof, on whose ranch the post office was established.

Natick. Post office established November 30, 1887; discontinued June 15, 1916. Presently a railroad station on the Burlington Railroad. Post office and precinct named by railway officials for Natick, Massachusetts.

Norway. Peak population (1940), 10. Post office established November 30, 1887; discontinued 1936. Former hamlet and present railroad station named for Norwegian settlers.

Purdum. Post office moved from Blaine County, November 19, 1891; moved back May 5, 1894. Named in honor of George F. Purdum, first postmaster.

Robeda. Post office established February 15, 1906; rescinded October 15, 1906. Origin of name not learned.

Seneca. Peak population (1920), 476. Post office established January 23, 1888. One source says town named for the Seneca Indians in New York state. Another source reports the town named by a railroad contractor from Seneca, Kansas. Town established by Lincoln Land Company and vied with Thedford for county seat in 1920 election.

Shidler. Post office established February 11, 1914; moved to Logan County September 15, 1915. Probably named in honor of Richard Shidler, first postmaster.

Summit. Post office established March 9, 1912; moved to McPherson County January 10, 1923. Named by J. W. Shutts for its elevated location.

Sunflower. Post office established March 13, 1909; discontinued April 30, 1913. Named by Fred Maseberg, first postmaster, and John H. Evans, local settler, for a field of sunflowers nearby.

Thedford. Peak population (1980), 313. Post office established November 30, 1887. One source says this county seat named for Thedford, Ontario, Canada. Another source attributes name to Thedford, England, birthplace of the parents of homesteader W. W. Cowles from Massachusetts. Thedford was made county seat when the county was established. It won county seat in an election with Seneca in 1920.

THURSTON COUNTY

Named in honor of U.S. Senator John M. Thurston (1847-1916). The area comprising Thurston was previously known as Blackbird County, a paper county which existed from 1855 to 1856 when the Omaha Reservation was created. Modern Thurston County boundary was established in 1889.

Athens. Post office moved from Cuming County January 29, 1885; name changed to Pender in February 1886. Possibly named for Athens, Illinois; Athens, Ohio; or Athens, Greece.

Blackbird. Post office established April 1, 1856; discontinued December 10, 1858. Named in honor of Blackbird, noted leader of the Omaha.

Flourney. Post office established, 1886; name changed to Thurston July 2, 1895. Probably named for a local settler.

Logan. Former station on the Chicago, St. Paul, Minneapolis and Omaha Railroad located north of Lyons.

Macy. Peak population (2000), 956. Post office name changed from Omaha Agency March 16, 1906. Name was changed from Omaha Agency because much mail was mistakenly sent to Omaha. To form the new name the second syllable of Omaha was combined with the last syllable of agency. The town is an Indian trading post. The Omaha Indian reservation is nearby.

Middle Creek. Former station on the Chicago, Minneapolis, St. Paul and Omaha Railroad. Location was south of Winnebago.

Omaha Agency. Post office established October 9, 1861; name changed to Macy March 16, 1906. Named in honor of the Omaha Indian tribe.

Pender. Peak population (1980), 1,318. Post office name changed from Athens February 1886. County seat named in honor of John Pender, an Englishman noted as a cable builder and director of the Chicago, St. Paul, Minneapolis and Omaha Railroad. Town was moved from old site when railroad built nearby.

Quinton. Post office established June 1892; name changed to Walthill June 15, 1906. Origin of the name not learned.

Rosalie. Peak population (1920), 321. Post office established July 13, 1906. Named in honor of Rosalie LaFlesche, daughter of Joseph LaFlesche, French-Indian leader of the Omaha Indians.

Thurston. Peak population (1930), 236. Post office name changed from Flourney July 2, 1895. Town named for the county.

Walthill. Peak population (1940), 1,204. Post office name changed from Quinton June 15, 1906. Town named in honor of Walter Hill, son of James Hill, builder of the Great Northern Railroad. Walter Hill worked for the building of the Burlington Railroad through the county in 1905. He joined a Mr. Hutchins in organizing the townsite company.

Winnebago. Peak population (1980), 902. Post office established January 16, 1867. Town named for the Winnebago Indians. It lies within the Indian reservation but is not part of it.

VALLEY COUNTY

Named because it was composed mostly of valley land, lying between higher table lands in the North Loup Valley. County was created and its boundaries defined by an act of the Legislature approved March 1, 1871. County was finally established by the Legislature in 1873.

Adair. Post office established March 5, 1878; discontinued March 12, 1879. Possibly name for Adair, Iowa, by an early settler.

Alta. Post office established May 14, 1890; discontinued January 31, 1905. Name is derived from the Latin word "altus," referring to a high or elevated position.

Arcadia. Peak population (1920), 745. Post office established June 23, 1814. Mrs. Samuel A. Hawthorne, postmistress, suggested the name Arcadia, which means feast of the flowers. At that time the valley was filled with wild roses, and the name was appropriate for the season.

Barracks. Post office established October 14, 1874; name changed to Calamus March 25, 1875. Named for the army barracks at nearby Fort Hartsuff.

Boleszyn. Located four miles north of Geranium. Site of St. Stanislaus Kostka Catholic Church and Polish settlement founded in 1884.

Brownville. Proposed name for Arcadia before it was established, but there was already a Brownville post office within the state.

Burris. Former station on the Burlington Railroad. Possibly named in honor of William Burris of Ord.

Calamus. Peak population (1890), 65. Post office name changed from Barracks March 25, 1875; discontinued March 23, 1889. Town platted by Lt. Thomas Capron and located at the southeast corner of Fort Hartsuff. When there were rumors of abandonment of Fort Hartsuff, most of the residents moved to Ord. Calamus is a Dakota Indian word meaning food of the muskrat. Fort Hartsuff is now a state historical park operated by the Nebraska Game and Parks Commission.

Chin City. Former name of Ord before the town was platted. Named in honor of A. T. (Chin) Tracy, first man to live in the area.

Dane Creek. Former settlement made up mostly of Danes.

Eldon. Suggested name for the town of Elyria, but there was already a post office in the state so named.

Elyria. Peak population (1950), 150. Post office established September 26, 1888. Town named by the Lincoln Land Company for Elyria, Ohio.

Fort Hartsuff. Army post located on Knife Creek (also called Lone Tree Creek and later Bean Creek) in 1874. The post was garrisoned by units of the Ninth, Fourteenth, and Twenty-third Infantry and was active until May 1881. Comprised of nine concrete-like grout buildings, the fort was intended for the protection of settlers in the Loup Valley. Named for George L. Hartsuff (1830-74), Union general during the Civil War.

Garfield. Post office established August 2, 1880; discontinued April 5, 1884. Possibly named in honor of James Garfield (1831-81), twentieth President of the United States.

Geranium. Post office established April 28, 1879; discontinued June 5, 1905. Named for the precinct in which it was located. Name is floral in origin.

Goodenow. Former station on the Burlington Railroad named in honor of M. B. Goodenow, early settler.

Ida. Post office established February 1, 1876; discontinued September 19, 1887. Origin of the name not learned. Jonas Sheperd was first postmaster.

Lee Park. Post office established January 15, 1879; moved to Custer County February 13, 1889. Town named in honor of James Lee, first settler.

Manderson. Post office established April 2, 1883; discontinued January 9, 1892. Possibly named for Charles F. Manderson, Nebraska U.S. senator when the post office was established.

Mira Creek. Peak population (1880), 121. Post office established August 17, 1877; discontinued June 15, 1904. Named for nearby Myra Creek—after Myra Babcock. Because there already was a Myra post office in the state, the spelling was changed to Mira.

Netolice. Name of Geranium before a post office was established. Named for a village in Czech Republic.

North Loup. Peak population (1930), 643. Post office established May 7, 1873. Named for its location in the North Loup River Valley. A colony established by Seventh Day Baptists from Wisconsin in the fall of 1871.

Olean. Former station on the Union Pacific Railroad. Possibly named for Olean, New York.

Ord. Peak population (1980), 2,658. Post office established November 17, 1873. County seat named in honor of Gen. Edward O. C. Ord, commander of the military department of the Platte. Town was surveyed in the spring of 1874 by O. S. and O. C. Haskill and A. M. Robbins.

Saunders. Station on the Union Pacific Railroad.

Sedlov. Post office established March 29, 1880; discontinued May 11, 1907. Named for a town in the Czech Republic. John W. Beran, first postmaster.

Spelts. Railroad station and elevator siding named in honor of Louis Spelts, settler.

Springdale. Post office established October 16, 1872; discontinued December 19, 1882. Named by R. W. Bancroft for its site on Spring Creek.

Sumter. Post office established May 24, 1894; discontinued November 12, 1895. Named for Thomas Sumter, a local settler.

Vinton. Peak population (1880), 100. Post office established February 15, 1875; discontinued March 23, 1888. Former village platted by the Vinton Town Site Company from Vinton, Iowa.

Yale. Post office established March 28, 1881; discontinued April 21, 1905. Named by C. H. Young, probably for shortness of the name or for Yale University in Connecticut.

WASHINGTON COUNTY

Named in honor of George Washington (1732-99), U.S. president from 1789 to 1897. Boundaries were defined by an act of the Legislature approved February 22, 1855, on the anniversary of President Washington's birthday and redefined November 2, 1858. The western boundary was redefined by an act approved January 12, 1860.

Admah. Peak population (1880), 40. Post office established January 26, 1874; discontinued January 19, 1901. Former town named for a biblical site near Old Testament city of Sodom. Admah is Hebrew, meaning fortress.

Advance. Post office established August 1, 1871; discontinued October 20, 1871. Probably named by some party in advance of others at its founding.

Amherst. Post office established August 8, 1871; discontinued October 28, 1878. Possibly named for either Amherst College or Amherst, Massachusetts.

Arlington. Peak population (1990), 1,178. Post office name changed from Belle Creek January 16, 1882. Named for a city in Virginia, located on the Potomac River. Town platted by Sioux City and Pacific Railroad.

Belle Creek. Post office established October 2, 1857; name changed to Arlington January 16, 1882. Named for Belle Creek, which was named for the Belle family.

Blair. Peak population (2000), 7,512. Post office established January 7, 1869. Named in honor of John I. Blair (1802-99), of New Jersey, railroad builder and controller of railroad operations. At one time president of the Sioux City and Pacific Railroad, Blair owned the land on which the town is located. Won county seat from Fort Calhoun in 1869. Dana College, first called Trinity Seminary, was founded by the Danish Evangelical Lutheran Church in 1884.

Bono. Post office established August 28, 1867; discontinued July 7, 1875. Origin of name not learned.

Bowen. Census not available. Former town, platted by the Pioneer Town Site Company, was named in honor of John S. Bowen, a settler, in 1886. Mail from nearby Kennard was served to this area.

Calhoun. Name of railroad station for Fort Calhoun.

Cantonment Missouri. Constructed by soldiers of the Yellowstone Expeditionary Force under Col. Henry Atkinson in October 1819 near Council Bluffs. Abandoned in the spring of 1820 for new fortifications nearby, which became Fort Atkinson.

Coffman. Census not available. Post office established January 3, 1891; discontinued June 22, 1901. Former town named in honor of Dr. V. H. Coffman, who owned the land on which it was located.

Cuming City. Post office established February 8, 1856; name changed to Herman January 19, 1872. Town named in honor of Thomas B. Cuming, acting territorial governor of Nebraska when the town was platted.

Dale. Hamlet and station on the Chicago and North Western Railroad eventually moved across the county line into Douglas County.

De Soto. Peak population (1860), 500. Post office established March 2, 1855; discontinued 1934. Former town and present station on the Chicago and North Western Railroad named for the sixteenth century explorer, Hernando De Soto. De Soto was a popular steamer port and boom town on the Missouri River before the advent of the railroad. It dwindled in population after Blair was established. De Soto was made county seat in 1858 but lost it in election with Fort Calhoun in 1866.

Fairview. Post office established June 30, 1892; discontinued May 18, 1895. Locally descriptive name. Twenty states have post offices with this name.

Fletcher. Post office established March 22, 1883; discontinued January 9, 1901. Named in honor of Foxwell Fletcher, first postmaster.

Fontanelle. Peak population (1880), 199. Post office established May 7, 1855; discontinued 1959; mail served from Nickerson. The first settlement in this area, then in Dodge County, was established by a Mr. Leiser of German origin in 1854. During the same year a company was organized at Quincy, Illinois, to settle in Nebraska Territory. The colony paid Logan Fontenelle $10 for the privilege of settling on the land and named the town for him. However, postal authorities misspelled the name, using an "a" instead of an "e." Fontanelle was county seat of Dodge County from March 1855 until county lines were redefined in 1860, putting the village in Washington County. The town once hoped to become the capital of Nebraska Territory. Short-lived Congregational institutions, Nebraska University (1855) and Fontenelle University (1858), were founded here.

Fort Atkinson. Military post located on the Council Bluffs on the Nebraska side of the Missouri River. When established in 1820, it was farther west than any other outpost in the United States. The fort was named in honor of Col. Henry M. Atkinson, appointed by Secretary of War John C. Calhoun as the commander of the military portion of the Yellowstone Expeditionary Force. Fort Atkinson was abandoned in 1827 with troops removed to Fort Leavenworth. It is now a state historical park operated by the Nebraska Game and Parks Commission.

Fort Calhoun. Peak population (2000), 856. Post office established June 15, 1855. Town named in honor of Secretary of War John C. Calhoun (1782-1850). Location was near site of old Fort Atkinson. Fort Calhoun, first county seat of Washington County, lost designation to De Soto in 1858; regained its status in 1866; and lost it three years later to Blair. Railroad name was Calhoun.

Giles. Post office established October 7, 1881; discontinued November 12, 1883. Named in honor of Giles Mead, first postmaster.

Golden Gate. Former locality east of Belle Creek in southern Washington County.

Hayes. Post office established April 16, 1878; moved to Douglas County April 26, 1887. Probably named in honor of President Rutherford B. Hayes (1822-93), whose term of office occurred at the time post office was established.

Herman. Peak population (1940), 427. Post office name changed from Cuming City January 19, 1872. Town platted by Omaha and Northwestern Railroad officials on or near site of Cuming City. Named in honor of Samuel Herman, railroad conductor.

Hiawatha. Townsite located on the Missouri River. Before a post office could be established, the town was washed out by a flood in 1857. Name is of Indian origin.

Hiland. Former station on the Chicago, St. Paul, Minneapolis and Omaha Railroad named in honor of J. H. Hiland, assistant traffic manager of the line.

Hillside. Former station on the Chicago and North Western Railroad near Blair.

Hudson. Town proposed by W. E. Walker, an enterprising citizen of Connecticut. He platted the town and drew imaginary streets, then went back East and sold 8,720 lots at $1 apiece at promotional lectures. However, the scheme failed.

Kennard. Peak population (1980), 372. Post office established, 1871; established first as a rural post office. Town named in honor of Thomas P. Kennard, Nebraska's first secretary of state (1867-70). Town platted by Sioux City and Pacific Railroad in 1895.

Lewisburg. Post office established, 1856; discontinued 1859. Located on Clark Creek. Locality had a grist mill.

Lisa's Post. Founded in 1813 and probably abandoned in 1823. The site has never been precisely identified but was about five miles southeast of Fort Calhoun. Named for Manuel Lisa, trader and sub-agent for the Indian tribes.

Meads. Former station on the Chicago, St. Paul, Minneapolis and Omaha Railroad located north of Blair.

Melrose. Early settlement mentioned in Washington County history.

Miles. Early settlement mentioned in Washington County history.

Mills. Former Omaha and North Western Railroad station located north of Fort Calhoun. Store also located in the area.

Nashville. Post office established October 14, 1922; discontinued June 15, 1929. Probably named for Nashville, Tennessee.

Nero. Post office established June 15, 1871; name changed to Vacoma March 17, 1882. Origin of name not learned.

New York Creek. An early locality or a proposed townsite.

Orum. Post office established June 30, 1890; discontinued March 23, 1904. Named in honor of Robert Orum, first postmaster.

Platteview. Post office established August 19, 1869; discontinued September 25, 1869.

Prairie Oaks. Former locality in Washington County.

Richland. Place listed in 1865 census as having ninety-five people. Probably a river town that did not last long enough to acquire a post office because of a flood.

Rocket. This town on the Missouri River had a short life due to severe floods in the early 1850s.

Rockport. River port on the Missouri. Its existence was brief, probably due to floods.

Sheridan. Proposed town in early county history.

South Blair. Former station on the Chicago, St. Paul, Minneapolis and Omaha Railroad.

Spiker. Post office established June 6, 1890; discontinued May 23, 1902. Possibly named for Samuel R. Spiker, Civil War veteran and early settler.

Telbasta. Post office established March 17, 1890; discontinued September 20, 1900. Origin of the name of this present community not learned.

Tyson. Former station on the Chicago, St. Paul, Minneapolis and Omaha Railroad. Probably named for Watson Tyson, local pioneer.

Vacoma. Origin of the name not learned. There was a store in conjunction with the post office.

Walnut Creek. Post office established August 22, 1853; discontinued September 22, 1855. Location was near Walnut Creek. Named for the black walnut trees growing along the banks.

Washington. Peak population (1910), 150. Post office established August 16, 1871. Named for the county and platted by Pioneer Town Site Company.

WAYNE COUNTY

Named in honor of "Mad Anthony" Wayne (1745-96), Revolutionary War general. County organized in 1870 by proclamation of Governor David Butler and the boundaries defined and legalized March 4, 1871.

Altona. Peak population (1910, 1920, 1930), 45. Post office established May 10, 1898; discontinued 1936. J. G. Bergt and F. G. Panning, both of Hooper, Nebraska, erected a store on land purchased from George F. Theis. Postal authorities granted a petition request for a post office and suggested the name Altona. Theis platted the town in 1898. Some sources say named for a town for the Holstein province of Germany.

Apex. Former station on the Chicago and North Western Railroad, named for its elevated location on or near a divide one mile south and four miles west of Winside. This place was never a post office. A siding was put in Apex so that freight trains could be carried over the point in sections when they were too heavy for one pull.

Bird. Post office established March 30, 1898; discontinued March 23, 1900. Former post office located six miles north of Melvin on the farm of Erwin C. (Bird) Brooks.

Brookdale. Former name of Wayne before the post office was established.

Carroll. Peak population (1920), 448. Post office established August 19, 1887. Town first called Manning for J. R. Manning, an early settler. A difference of opinion arose, according to one source, between the railroad company and landowners over the townsite.

A Mr. Carroll arbitrated the matter, and the railroad company put the name Carroll on the depot. Another source claims that the town was named by E. W. Winter, general manager of the railroad, for Charles Carroll of Maryland, last surviving signer of the Declaration of Independence. Another source says town named for Ed Carroll, former county commissioner and friend of J. R. Manning and the Berry brothers.

Donup. Post office moved from Stanton County November 7, 1879; discontinued and moved to Hoskins October 30, 1882. See Donup, Stanton County.

Gray. Post office established January 11, 1886; discontinued November 9, 1887. Possibly named for Emma E. Gray, first postmistress.

Hoskins. Peak population (1980), 306. Post office established October 30, 1882. Named in honor of a Mr. Hoskins, member of the land company that platted the site. He was from Sioux City, Iowa, and associated with the Peavey Elevator Company. First settled by Germans.

La Porte. Peak population (1875), 300. Post office established February 27, 1871; discontinued June 17, 1876. Town named for La Porte, Indiana, by settlers from that state. Platted by Solon Bevins in May 1874. La Porte was made second county seat of Wayne County in election with Taffe in 1871, but lost in election with Wayne in 1881. La Porte was bypassed when the railroad was built through Wayne, and the place eventually declined in population. Its buildings were dismantled and moved to Wayne.

Leslie. Post office established December 18, 1871; discontinued October 12, 1875. Office said to be named for a judge who served Wayne County.

Logan City. Former locality said to be named for an Indian called Logan, and situated southeast of Wakefield on the Childs place. The Childs family came here in 1880 when Childs and a Mr. Lash built a store, grist mill, and blacksmith shop on Logan Creek. The railroad company constructed a grade through the Childs place, but the line eventually went farther north.

Lorain. Locality situated northwest of Wayne.

Manitou. Proposed town in McNeale County (later Wayne County).

Maze. Post office established May 13, 1890; discontinued July 12, 1893. Origin of name not learned.

Melvin. Post office established March 30, 1898; discontinued 1904. Named in honor of Melvin Benedict, first postmaster.

Northside. Post office established October 3, 1882; moved to Winside December 6, 1887. Named for its location north of Winside. See Winside.

Sholes. Peak population (1910), 100. Post office established April 30, 1902; discontinued 1966. Mail served from Randolph. Named in honor of Lyman Sholes, former official of the Chicago, St. Paul, Minneapolis and Omaha Railroad. Established for use as a shipping point.

Taffe. Peak population (1872), 25. Post office established July 14, 1870; discontinued July 26, 1874. Former town, first county seat of Wayne County, named in honor of John Taffe, who served in the first Territorial Legislature. Taffe lost county seat in election with La Porte and thereafter disappeared.

Wayne. Peak population (2000), 5,583. Post office established August 12, 1881. Named for the county. Wayne won county seat from La Porte in election of 1881. Wayne Normal, founded in 1891, is today Wayne State.

Weber. Census not available. Post office established September 11, 1899; discontinued January 22, 1903. Town named in honor of Frederick Weber, first postmaster.

Winside. Peak population (1930), 479. Post office established December 6, 1887. Winside was founded following rivalry between two locations, the present one and another three miles west called Northside. A side track and temporary depot were secured for Northside, but the competing townsite company induced the railroad to select its location.

The side track and depot were then moved on a Sunday to avoid injunction proceedings. The town was named Winside because that site won the railroad's favor.

WEBSTER COUNTY

Named in honor of Daniel Webster (1782-1852), American statesman. Boundaries were defined by an act approved February 16, 1867.

Amboy. Post office name changed from Webster Centre December 23, 1879; discontinued January 8, 1890. Probably named for Amboy, Illinois.

Batin. Post office established November 8, 1872; discontinued March 3, 1887. Named in honor of the mother of Dr. T. B. Williams; her maiden name was Batin.

Belmont. Probably the name of the community before Blue Hill was established as a post office.

Berne. Post office established February 11, 1884; discontinued October 15, 1884. Probably named for Berne, Switzerland, or Berne, Indiana, where the official publishing house and General Mennonite Conference headquarters were located.

Bladen. Peak population (1900), 1,823. Post office name changed from Wells November 15, 1886. Probably named for a railroad official by the Lincoln Land Company, which platted the town. There is also a Bladen, Ohio.

Blue Hill. Peak population (1980), 883. Post office established December 20, 1878. Named for its location on the hills near the Little Blue River, town was platted by Anselmo B. Smith. It was to be called Belmont, but there was already a town in the state so named.

Blue Hill Junction. Junction for railroads of the Chicago, Burlington and Quincy division.

Bole. Post office name changed from Hicks July 31, 1885; discontinued December 7, 1892. Origin of name not learned. First postmaster was John B. Strausser.

Buffalo. Post office established December 18, 1871; discontinued February 10, 1873. Probably named for the buffalo that roamed the prairie in this region.

Catherton. Post office established May 15, 1876; discontinued August 29, 1877. Named in honor of George P. Cather, an uncle of Willa Cather, noted Nebraska author.

Cloverton. Post office established June 23, 1874; discontinued April 2, 1887. Origin of name not learned.

Cowles. Peak population (1920), 222. Post office name changed from Edna January 27, 1879. Named in honor of W. D. Cowles, general freight agent of the Burlington and Missouri Railroad. Post office made a rural independent branch of Blue Hill in 1959.

Eckley. Post office established October 12, 1874; discontinued April 29, 1879. Origin of name not learned. There is also an Eckley, Colorado.

Edna. Post office established May 10, 1877; name changed to Cowles January 27, 1879. Origin of name not learned. First postmaster was Arando Edson.

Guide Rock. Peak population (1910, 1930), 690. Post office established February 3, 1871. Named for a high rocky bluff about two and one-half miles southeast and across the Republican River from the townsite. The rock served as a landmark to early western travelers.

Hicks. Post office established December 17, 1883; name changed to Bole July 31, 1885. Named in honor of a local settler.

Inavale. Peak population (1930), 252. Post office established April 3, 1873. Named by a vote of the residents: In-a-Vale, the vale being the Republican Valley. W. J. Vance platted the town in 1884.

Lester. Station on the Burlington Railroad named in honor of a local settler.

Negunda. Post office established February 23, 1872; discontinued May 4, 1903. Probably derived from the botanical name of box elder trees.

Otto. Post office established September 12, 1884; discontinued December 22, 1903. Named for Norwegian settler Otto Skjelvar. First postmaster was Francis Payne.

Red Cloud. Peak population (1890), 1,839. Post office established January 14, 1872. County seat named in honor of the Sioux leader Red Cloud. Local tradition states that he held a war council on what is now the townsite. Another source says that Red Cloud was never in the locale. The town was platted by Silas Garber on November 12, 1872. Red Cloud was made county seat upon organization of the county. It probably has the distinction of being one of the last towns to have horse-drawn street cars, which operated from 1889 until October 1917. Red Cloud is the site of the Willa Cather Historical Center, a property of the Nebraska State Historical Society.

Rosemont. Peak population (1930), 202. Post office established June 16, 1890; discontinued 1955. Named in honor of Claus Rose, Sr., who once owned the townsite. Platted by Lincoln Land Company.

Scott. Post office established November 4, 1873; discontinued May 24, 1894. Origin of name not learned.

St. Ann. Post office changed from Wheatland December 14, 1885; discontinued February 9, 1887. Probably named for a local church.

Stillwater. Post office established June 18, 1874; discontinued August 29, 1879. Origin of name not learned. There are places in eight states having this name.

Stockade. Post office established February 16, 1876; discontinued October 17, 1876. Probably named for the stockade built to protect settlers from Indian attacks.

Thomasville. Post office established December 29, 1876; discontinued July 12, 1888. Origin of name not learned. First postmaster was William Longbotham.

Webster Centre. Post office established March 7, 1879; name changed to Amboy December 23, 1879. Named for its location in the center of the county.

Wells. Post office established May 20, 1872; name changed to Bladen November 15, 1886. Named in honor of Silas Wells, early settler.

Wheatland. Post office established March 5, 1875; name changed to St. Ann December 14, 1885. Named for its location in a wheat-growing section.

WHEELER COUNTY

Named in honor of Maj. Daniel H. Wheeler (1834-1912), longtime secretary of the State Board of Agriculture. Boundaries for county were defined by an act of the Legislature approved February 17, 1877.

Arden. Post office moved from Boone County May 15, 1918; discontinued June 1918. See Arden, Boone County.

Baird. Post office established May 17, 1902; name changed to Wheeler February 1, 1909. Town probably named for W. S. Baird. Post office name was changed to avoid confusing mail with Bayard.

Bartlett. Peak population (1940), 176. Post office established July 22, 1886. Town named in honor of Ezra Bartlett, founder and first settler. Bartlett won county seat in election with Cumminsville in 1885. Bartlett vied with Ericson for county seat in election of 1909 and won.

Bliss. Post office established April 29, 1884; moved to Holt County March 4, 1886. Named in honor of Nelson Bliss, first postmaster.

Buffalo. Peak population (1890), 12. Post office established July 31, 1883; discontinued May 1, 1895. Former town named by first postmaster, William J. Riddle, for buffalo bones and horns found in the region. Probably the second county seat of Wheeler County.

Cedar City. Locality did not last long enough to be identified with a post office. Cedar

City became first county seat but lost out in election with Cumminsville in November 1883. The community was named by Ben Johnson on July 19, 1881, for its site on the Cedar River.

Cumminsville. Peak population (1890), 25. Post office established September 23, 1880; discontinued 1937. Named in honor of Frank Cummins, a homesteader. The old location of the town was three miles west of present site. The Union Pacific Railroad wanted to build its line from Albion, but the plan did not materialize. Cumminsville won county seat from Cedar City in November 1883, and then lost in election to Bartlett in 1885.

Deloit. Post office established August 21, 1883; moved to Holt County December 12, 1905. Named for Deloit, Michigan.

Ericson. Peak population (1940), 279. Post office established December 8, 1887. Village named in honor of Chris Erickson and his two relatives Eric and Peter. Postal authorities dropped the "k" from the name. Ericson vied for county seat with Bartlett in 1909.

Farley. Post office established December 22, 1885; rescinded June 1, 1886. Origin of name not learned. First postmaster was Eldridge F. Thisselle.

Francis. Peak population (1900), 180. Post office established August 21, 1883; discontinued April 14, 1917. Former village probably named in honor of a daughter of Mr. and Mrs. Charles Stowell. Stowell was first postmaster.

Gem. Post office established May 15, 1908; moved to Logan County February 1, 1909. Name suggests a place prized by its founder.

Harrington. Peak population (1880), 25. Post office established December 3, 1880; discontinued November 19, 1893. Former town named in honor of John S. Harrington, early settler. U.S. post office directories show Harrington as county seat from 1885 to 1888.

Headquarters. Post office established March 27, 1900; discontinued December 15, 1917. Name is locally descriptive.

Lisle. Post office established April 18, 1907; discontinued September 15, 1922. Named for brother-in-law of Harry Grout, first postmaster.

Middleport. Post office established August 28, 1883; discontinued November 20, 1885. Named by Postmaster Frank Mead because the office was midway between Scotia and Cumminsville.

Moran. Post office established June 20, 1881; discontinued October 7, 1890. Honors Louis Moran, early settler.

Newboro. Census not available. Post office established February 3, 1896; discontinued 1935. Former town named in honor of Joe Newboro, early settler.

Ono. Post office established December 22, 1885; discontinued February 4, 1907. Origin of name not learned.

Pibel. Post office established November 4, 1892; discontinued February 29, 1916. Named in honor of Edwin Pibel, first postmaster, who had the office in his store.

Reilley. Post office established July 21, 1882; discontinued October 15, 1892. Honors William Reilley, first postmaster.

Sandy. Post office established October 9, 1890; discontinued October 15, 1892. Origin of name not learned. First postmaster was Luther Bennett.

Sheridan. Census not available. Post office established February 11, 1885; discontinued 1936. Former village named in honor of Philip H. Sheridan, Civil War general who commanded troops in Indian campaigns in the West.

Thompson. Post office established October 18, 1883; moved to Holt County November 20, 1885. Named in honor of John Thompson, first postmaster.

Walker. Post office established September 5, 1881; moved to Holt County November. Honors Horatio M. Walker, first postmaster.

Wheeler. Census not available. Post office name changed from Baird February 1, 1909; discontinued 1934. Town named for the county.

YORK COUNTY

Organized in April 1870. One source says county named by Alfred D. Jones for York, England. Another source credits the name to early settlers from York County, Pennsylvania.

Aikin's Mill. Post office established September 8, 1870; name changed to Plainfield January 3, 1873. Named in honor of Chauncey Aiken, first postmaster.

Antelope Ranch. Established east of the Porcupine Ranch on the Old Freight Road in November 1865 by James Mathewson.

Arborville. Peak population (1880), 100. Post office name changed from Willard October 19, 1874; discontinued 1943. Former town platted by the Rev. C. S. Harnson, formerly of York. He planted various species of trees to form an arbor along the streets.

Benedict. Peak population (1910), 336. Post office established August 6, 1887. Town named in honor of E. C. Benedict, who was then president of the Kansas City and Omaha Railroad.

Bluevale. Peak population (1890), 42. Post office name changed from Blue Valley January 4, 1895; discontinued April 1, 1901. Name changed to Bluevale after relocation on the north side of the Blue River; another Nebraska office then took the name of Blue Valley.

Blue Valley. Post office established January 24, 1870; name changed to Bluevale January 4, 1895. Name derived from the valley of the Blue River.

Bradshaw. Peak population (1890), 434. Post office name changed from Lenox July 8, 1880. Town platted by Burlington Railroad in 1879. Named after Mrs. Jesse M. Richards, the former Mary Bradshaw.

Charlestown. Peak population (1900), 119. Post office established March 13, 1887; discontinued 1943. Former town named in honor of Charles A. McCloud, railway right-of-way official. Town platted by Pioneer Town Site Company in 1887.

Creswell. Post office established April 21, 1873; discontinued February 4, 1888. Probably named in honor of John A. J. Creswell, postmaster general in President Ulysses S. Grant's Cabinet at the time of the town's founding.

Dana. Post office established December 14, 1874; discontinued January 6, 1888. Named in honor of Charles A. Dana, American newspaperman and author. He was also assistant secretary of war in President Abraham Lincoln's Cabinet from 1863 to 1864.

Danby. Post office established January 28, 1877; discontinued March 2, 1888. Named by John S. Parris, who formerly lived at Danby, Vermont.

Derby. Former elevator siding probably named for an early settler or railroad official. George Derby was a land agent for the Burlington Railroad.

Eureka. Post office established January 26, 1876; discontinued January 26, 1887. Name of this former post office probably derived from the Greek word eureka meaning "I have found it," or from the city of Eureka, Illinois.

Farris. Post office established May 2, 1872; discontinued August 13, 1873. Probably named in honor of John B. Farris, first postmaster.

Gresham. Peak population (1920), 492. Post office name changed from Poston December 9, 1887. Named in honor of Walter Quinton Gresham, secretary of state in President Grover Cleveland's Cabinet. Town platted by Pioneer Town Site Company in 1887.

Henderson. Peak population (1980), 1,072. Post office established February 21, 1888. Named in honor of David Henderson, settler.

Houston. Peak population (1900), 58. Post office established December 22, 1881; discontinued August 15, 1928. Former town platted by Pioneer Town Site Company, honors Joseph D. Houston, settler who immigrated here from England in 1870.

Indian Creek. Post office established August 19, 1873; discontinued June 29, 1888. Named for the creek on which it was located.

Knox. Elevator siding and station on the Kansas City and Omaha Railroad. Probably named for the owner of land on which elevator was established. Located five miles south of York.

Lawrence. Proposed town chartered March 15, 1855, which never got beyond the platting stage.

Lenox. Post office name changed from Plainfield December 11, 1879; name changed to Bradshaw July 8, 1880. Origin of name unknown. There are also places in Massachusetts and New Jersey called Lenox.

Lisbon. Post office established May 7, 1879; discontinued November 13, 1879. Named by T. W. Smith after a town in Kendall County, Illinois.

Long Hope. Post office established December 14, 1874; discontinued March 5, 1883. Said to be named by Gus Gibbs, a homesteader who had cherished a "long hope" for establishment of a post office.

Lushton. Peak population (1910), 205. Post office established August 6, 1887. Town named in honor of William Lush, official of the St. Joseph and Grand Island Railroad and former engineer on the Kansas City and Omaha Railroad. Post office made a rural branch of McCool Junction in 1965; discontinued in 1981.

Mapps. Elevator siding built on the Kansas City and Omaha Railroad five miles north of York. Probably named for William Mapps, settler.

McCool Junction. Peak population (1980), 404. Post office name changed from Niota February 4, 1888. Town named in honor of Daniel McCool, general manager of the Kansas City and Omaha Railroad. Junction point of the Burlington Railroad.

McDonald Ranch. Freight and stage station on Beaver Creek established in the fall of 1864. It was sold to a Mr. Baker in 1865.

McFadden. Post office established January 22, 1868; discontinued April 23, 1884. Named in honor of Fernando B. McFadden, first postmaster.

New York. Town incorporated outside the city limits of York in 1880 and named for the "newness" of its establishment and for New York, New York. The city of York absorbed it as an addition in 1884.

Niota. Post office established June 8, 1887; name changed to McCool Junction February 4, 1888. Probably named for Niota, Illinois.

Palo. Post office established April 8, 1872. Name is of Spanish origin. There are also towns in Iowa and Michigan by this name. This town declined after it was bypassed by the Fremont, Elkhorn and Missouri Valley Railroad. Palo buildings were moved to the new town of Gresham.

Plainfield. Post office name changed from Aikin's Mill January 3, 1873; name changed to Lenox December 11, 1879. Probably called for a place in Illinois, Indiana, or New Jersey by a local settler. Name possibly chosen because it described the site.

Pleasant Home. Post office moved from Polk County November 15, 1877; discontinued February 4, 1888. Name suggests the environment of the locality.

Porcupine Bluffs. Stage stop near Hamilton County line established in 1863 by Benjamin F. Lushbaugh, U.S. Indian agent of the Pawnee tribe and proprietor of the Nebraska Overland Stage Company.

Poston. Site of Gresham was originally called Poston, but the name was not approved by postal authorities.

Red Lion. Post office established March 31, 1884; discontinued January 11, 1888. Named for the Red Lion Flour Mills founded by C. Seeley and E. O. Wright.

Seeley. Post office established August 12, 1874; discontinued July 5, 1881. Probably named in honor of Horace Seeley, first postmaster.

Smith Ranch. This freight and stage station, established by Benjamin F. Lushbaugh on the Jack Smith Ranch in 1864, was managed by a Mr. Chapin.

Stone Ranch. An overland freight station which opened August 1865 on the Jack Stone

Ranch. Named for Jack Stone, whose real name was John McClellan. It was managed for a short while by George Chapman.

Thayer. Peak population (1910), 250. Post office established September 8, 1870, made an independent station of York in 1958. Town commemorates John Milton Thayer, Civil War general and later Nebraska governor and senator.

Waco. Peak population (1910), 310. Post office name changed from Westerfield October 22, 1879. Town named by a Miss Chapin, who owned and donated the land for a townsite. She formerly lived in Waco, Texas, from which the name is taken.

Westerfield. Post office established February 12, 1872; name changed to Waco October 22, 1879. Origin of name not learned.

Wickliffe. Post office established May 2, 1872; discontinued May 7, 1873. Origin of name unknown.

Willard. Post office established February 24, 1873; name changed to Arborville October 19, 1874. Origin of name not learned. First postmaster was John W. Kingston.

York. Peak population (2000), 8,081. Post office established August 22, 1870. City named by a colony of homesteaders from the vicinity of York, Pennsylvania. Townsite taken as a preemption claim by Messrs. Ghost and Sherwood, agents for the South Platte Land Company. The present site of York was platted October 18, 1869. The section of New York was added on the north in 1884. In the spring of 1870, the buildings in the county seat consisted of one sod house and a frame structure called the preemption house. The first courthouse was erected in 1872. York College was founded in 1890 by the United Brethren in Christ Church.

BIBLIOGRAPHY

ATLASES

Asher and Adams. *New Statistical and Topographical Atlas of the United States.* New York: Asher and Adams, 1872.

Black's General Atlas of the World. Edinburgh: Adam and Charles Black, 1885.

Century Dictionary and Encyclopedia. Vol. 10. New York: Century Co., 1914.

Colton, Joseph Hutchins. *Kansas and Nebraska Atlas.* New York: G. W. and C. B. Colton and Co., 1859, 1881.

Cram Atlases. Chicago, New York: George F. Cram Co., 1880-1905.

Everts and Kirk. *The Official State Atlas of Nebraska.* Philadelphia: Everts and Kirk, 1885.

Mitchell. *New Central Atlas.* Philadelphia: Samuel Augustus Mitchell, 1867.

People's Family Atlas of the World. Chicago: People's Publishing Co., 1884.

Rand McNally Atlases. Chicago: Rand McNally and Co., 1882-1970.

BOOKS

Andreas, Alfred Theodore. *History of the State of Nebraska.* Chicago: Western Historical Co., 1882.

Bang, S. D. *Centennial History of Sarpy County, Nebraska.* Papillion, Nebraska: Papillion Times, 1876.

Bassett, Samuel Clay. *Buffalo County, Nebraska and Its People.* 2 Vols. Chicago: S. J. Clarke Publishing Co., 1916.

Biographical Historical Memoirs of Adams, Clay, Hall and Hamilton Counties, Nebraska. Chicago: Goodspeed Publishing Co., 1890.

Burton, William R. and Lewis, David J. *Past and Present of Adams County, Nebraska.* 2 Vols. Chicago: S. J. Clarke Publishing Co., 1916.

Buss, Rev. William H. and Osterman, Thomas T. *History of Dodge and Washington Counties, Nebraska and Their People.* 2 Vols. Chicago: American Historical Society, Chicago, 1921.

Chase County Historical Society. *History of Chase County Centennial.* Imperial, Nebraska, 1965.

Cox, W. W. *History of Seward County, Nebraska.* Lincoln: Lincoln State Journal Co., Printers, 1888.

Curry, Margaret. *A History of Platte County, Nebraska.* Culver City, California: Murray and Gee, 1950.

Dobbs, Hugh J. *History of Gage County, Nebraska.* Lincoln: Western Publishing and Engraving Co., 1918.

Edwards, Lewis C. *History of Richardson County: Its People, Industries, and Institutions.* Indianapolis: B. F. Bowen, 1917.

Faris, John (ed.). *Who's Who in Nebraska.* Lincoln: Nebraska Press Association, 1940.

Fitzpatrick, Lilian L. *Nebraska Place-Names.* Lincoln: University of Nebraska Press, 1960.

Foght, Harold Waldstein. *Trail of the Loup.* Washington D.C.: Library of Congress, 1906.

Frederick, James Vincent. *Ben Holladay, Stage Coach King.* Glendale, California: Arthur H. Clark Co., 1940.

Gaffney, Wilbur G. (ed.). *Fillmore County Story.* Geneva, Nebraska: Community Grange No. 403, 1968.

Graff, Jane, project coordinator, *Nebraska, Our Towns.* 7 Vols. Seward, Nebraska: Second Century Publications, 1988-92.

Huse, William. *History of Dixon County.* Ponca, Nebraska, 1896.

Jones, Lillian. *Early History of Brown County.* Ainsworth, Nebraska: Brown County Democrat, 1916.

Kaura, J. W. *Saline County Nebraska History 1858.* Lincoln: Nebraska Farmer Co., 1962.

Mattes, Merrill J. *The Great Platte River Road.* Lincoln: Nebraska State Historical Society, 1969.

McCoy, Mike. *History of Cedar County.* Hartington, Nebraska, 1937.

McDermott, Edith Swain. *Pioneer History of Greeley County, Nebraska.* Greeley, Nebraska: Greeley Citizen Printing Co., 1939.

Morton, J. Sterling and Watkins, Albert. *An Illustrated History of Nebraska.* 3 Vols. Lincoln: Western Publishing and Engraving Co., 1907-13.

Nebraska, A Guide to the Cornhusker State. American Guide Series. New York: Viking Press, 1939.

Nebraska Blue Book. Lincoln: Nebraska Legislative Reference Bureau, 1915.

Nyberg, Dorothy Huse. *History of Wayne County.* Wayne, Nebraska: Wayne Herald, 1938.

Perkins Historical Society. *History of Perkins County.* Grant, Nebraska, 1969.

Phillips, George Walter. *Past and Present of Platte County, Nebraska.* 2 Vols. Chicago: S. J. Clarke Publishing Co., 1915.

Rapp, William F. *Postal History of Nebraska.* Crete, Nebraska: J-B Publishing Co., 1985.

Rapp, William F. and Janet. *The Post Offices of Nebraska: Territorial Post Offices.* Crete, Nebraska: J-B Publishing Co., 1992.

Reece, Charles S. *A History of Cherry County, Nebraska.* Simeon, Nebraska, 1945.

Rock County Nebraska Centennial, 1888-1988. Bassett, Nebraska: Walsworth Publishing Co., Inc., and Rock County Leader, Inc., 1987.

Rosicky, Rose. *A History of Czechs in Nebraska.* Omaha: Czech Historical Society, 1929.

Scoville, C. H. *History of the Elkhorn Valley, An Album of History and Biography.* Chicago, 1892.

Sheldon, Addison E. *Nebraska, The Land and the People.* New York: Lewis Publishing Co., 1931.

Shumway, Grant L. *History of Western Nebraska and Its People.* Vols. 2 and 3. Lincoln: Western Publishing and Engraving Co., 1921.

Snider, Luree. *Boyd County History.* Lynch, Nebraska: Lynch Herald, 1938.

Steele, D. A., Howson, Elmer T., and Tebo, J. B. *Who's Who in Railroading in North America.* New York, 1922.

Stough, Dale P. *History of Hamilton and Clay Counties, Nebraska.* 2 Vols. Chicago: S. J. Clarke Publishing Co., 1921.

Sutherland, Douglas L. *History of Burt County, Nebraska.* Wahoo, Nebraska: Ludi Printing Co., 1929.

Sutton, E. S. *Tepees to Soddies, History of Dundy County.* Benkelman, Nebraska, 1968.

Talbot, E. H. and Hobart, H. R. *Who's Who in Railroading in North America in 1885.* Chicago: Railway Age Publishing Co., Chicago, 1885.

Van Ackeren, Ruth (ed.). *Sioux County, Memoirs of Its Pioneers.* Harrison, Nebraska: Ladies Community Club, 1967.

Wakeley, Arthur C. *Omaha, the Gate City, and Douglas County.* Vol. 1. Chicago: S. J. Clarke Publishing Co., 1917.

Warner, M. M. *History of Dakota County, Nebraska: From the Days of the Pioneers and First Settlers to the Present Time.* Dakota City, Nebraska, 1893.

Williams, Henry T. *The Pacific Tourist.* New York: Union Pacific Railroad Co., New York, 1879.

Wood, Asa Butler. *Pioneer Tales of the North Platte Valley and Nebraska Panhandle.* Gering, Nebraska: Courier Press, 1938.

Yost, Nellie Snyder. *Before Today, A History of Holt County, Nebraska.* O'Neill, Nebraska: Miles Publishing Co., 1976.

CHAMBERS OF COMMERCE

Literature from Alliance, Bridgeport, Columbus, Falls City, Grand Island, Hastings, Kearney, Lexington, Nebraska City, Ogallala and Plattsmouth.

DIRECTORIES

United States Post Office Department. *Directory of Post Offices.* Washington, D.C.: U.S. Government Printing Office, 1885-1971.

Nebraska: Census of Population and Housing, Final Population and Housing Unit Counts. Washington, D.C.: U.S. Department of Commerce, Bureau of the Census, 1980.

Nebraska Blue Book 1992-93. Clerk of the Legislature, State Capitol, Lincoln, Nebraska, 1993.

LETTERS

Sizer, Mr. and Mrs. Robert L. A letter on history of Arthur County, Arthur, Nebraska, 1963.

MAGAZINES

Nebraska History. Nebraska State Historical Society, Lincoln.

MANUSCRIPTS

Link, J. T. *The Origin of the Place-Names of Nebraska.* Lincoln: Nebraska State Historical Society, 1933.

MAPS

Nebraska Highway and Road Maps, 1940-70.

MICROFILM

National Archives and Records Service, *Postmasters of Nebraska Territory and State of Nebraska.* Washington, D.C.: General Services Administration, 1854-1929.

NEWSPAPERS

Beatrice Times. Jubilee Issue, Beatrice, Nebraska, July 31, 1949.
Crete News. Jubilee Issue, Crete, Nebraska, August 17, 1967.
Custer County Chief. Jubilee Issue, Broken Bow, Nebraska, November 26, 1942.
The Frontier. Jubilee Issue, O'Neill, Nebraska, June 1949.
Keith County News. Ogallala, Nebraska, March 24, 1941.
Norfolk Daily News. Norfolk, Nebraska, April 27, 1895.
Omaha World-Herald. Omaha, Nebraska, September 11, 1932.
Plainview News. Plainview, Nebraska, November 11, 1978.
Republican Register. Jubilee Issue, Aurora, Nebraska, April 3, 1942.

PAMPHLETS

Black Hill Trails Through Custer County.
National Society of the Daughters of the American Revolution in Nebraska. *Historical Markers in Nebraska.* Beatrice, Nebraska: Franklin Press, 1951.
Sizer, Mrs. Robert L. *A Pioneer Nebraska Community.* Arthur, Nebraska, 1962.

THESIS

Jelen, Josephine. *Towns and Townsites in Territorial Nebraska, 1854-1867.* Thesis for University of Nebraska, Lincoln, 1934.

INDEX

Name of county follows name of town.

Ash Bluffs, Saunders
Ashbrook, Sioux
Ashby, Grant
Ashford, Banner
Ashgrove, Franklin
Ashland, Saunders
Ashton, Sherman
Askotope, Otoe
Asp, Sioux
Aspinwall, Nemaha
Assumption, Adams
Asylum, Lancaster
Aten, Cedar
Athena, Cheyenne
Athens, Cuming
Athens, Howard
Athens, Lancaster
Athens, Richardson
Athens, Thurston
Atkins, Morrill
Atkinson, Holt
Atlanta, Phelps
Atlanta, Saline
Atlee, Franklin
Attica, Saunders
Auburn, Nemaha
Aucoria, Otoe
Audacious, Cherry
Augur, Douglas
Augustus, Logan
Aurich, Gage
Aurora, Hamilton
Austin, Gage
Austin, Sherman
Avery, Sarpy
Avoca (1), Cass
Avoca (2), Cass
Avon, Hamilton
Avondale, Otoe
Axelson, Phelps
Axtell, Kearney
Ayers, Cherry
Ayr, Adams
Ayr Junction, Adams
Bachelor, Cherry
Baden, Gage
Badger, Gage
Badger, Holt
Badger Lake, Cherry
Bailey, Cherry
Bailey View, Scotts Bluff
Bainbridge, Harlan

Baird, Nuckolls
Baird, Wheeler
Baker, Boyd
Baker, Buffalo
Balfe, Cherry
Ballagh, Garfield
Balsora, Sherman
Bancroft, Cuming
Bangs, Dodge
Banksville, Red Willow
Banner, Banner
Banner, Cherry
Barada, Richardson
Barbor, Antelope
Barkey, Gage
Barneston, Gage
Barney, Otoe
Barnum Ranch, Platte
Barracks, Valley
Bartlett, Wheeler
Bartley, Red Willow
Barton, Deuel
Bartonville, Frontier
Basford, Burt
Basin, Boyd
Bassett, Rock
Batesville, Seward
Batin, Webster
Battle Bend, Custer
Battle Creek, Madison
Baxter, Scotts Bluff
Bayard, Morrill
Bayonne, Cherry
Bay State, Dodge
Bazile Mills, Knox
Beachamville, Nuckolls
Beacon, Kimball
Bear Creek, Gage
Beardwell, Brown
Beatrice, Gage
Beaver, Boone
Beaver City, Furnas
Beaver Creek, Buffalo
Beaver Crossing, Seward
Beck, Lincoln
Becker, Morrill
Bedford, Lancaster
Bedford, Nemaha
Bedford, Platte
Bee, Seward
Beechville, Custer
Beemer, Antelope

Beemer, Cuming
Beer Man Spur, Dakota
Beet, Morrill
Bega, Stanton
Behlen, Platte
Belden, Cedar
Belfast, Greeley
Belgrade, Nance
Belknap, Holt
Bell, Butler
Bell, Sioux
Belle Creek, Washington
Belle Prairie, Fillmore
Belleville, Polk
Bellevue, Sarpy
Bellingar, Scotts Bluff
Bellwood, Butler
Belmar, Keith
Belmont, Cass
Belmont, Dawes
Belmont, Lancaster
Belmont, Otoe
Belmont, Webster
Belnap, Sarpy
Belt Line Crossing, Hall
Belvidere, Thayer
Benedict, York
Benewa, Grant
Benkelman, Dundy
Bennet, Lancaster
Bennett, Kimball
Bennett's Ferry, Otoe
Bennett's Station,
    Lancaster
Bennington, Douglas
Benson, Douglas
Benson Acres, Douglas
Benson Gardens, Douglas
Benton, Colfax
Benton, Saunders
Bentora, Sherman
Berea, Box Butte
Berg, Buffalo
Berks, Lancaster
Berlin, Otoe
Berne, Webster
Berry, Stanton
Bertha, Burt
Bertha, Keith
Bertrand, Burt
Bertrand, Phelps
Berwick, Hall

Berwyn, Custer
Best, Chase
Best, Rock
Bethany, Lancaster
Bethany Heights, Lancaster
Bethel, Kimball
Bethel, Merrick
Beulah, Nuckolls
Beulah, Polk
Beverly, Hitchcock
Bevier, Keith
Big Creek, Cherry
Bighorn, Banner
Bignell, Lincoln
Big Sandy, Jefferson
Big Sandy, Thayer
Big Springs, Deuel
Billing, Sheridan
Billingsville, Red Willow
Bingham, Sheridan
Birch, Pierce
Bird, Wayne
Birdsell, Box Butte
Birdsell, Sheridan
Birdwood, Lincoln
Biscuit, Holt
Bishop, Pierce
Bismarck, Cuming
Bissell, Colfax
Bixby, Fillmore
Blackbird, Burt
Blackbird, Holt
Blackbird, Thurston
Blackroot, Box Butte
Blacksmith's Point, Dodge
Blackwood, Hitchcock
Bladen, Webster
Blaine, Adams
Blaine, Blaine
Blaine, Gage
Blaine Center, Blaine
Blaineville, Kearney
Blair, Washington
Blake, Garfield
Blakely, Madison
Blakesly, Douglas
Blanche, Chase
Bliss, Holt
Bliss, Wheeler
Bloomfield, Knox
Bloomington, Franklin
Blue Hill, Webster

Blue Hill Junction, Webster
Blue Island, Saline
Blue River City, Saline
Blue River Lodge, Saline
Blue Springs, Gage
Bluevale, York
Blue Valley, York
Bluff Center, Hall
Bluff City, Gage
Bluff City, Garfield
Bluffdale, Cass
Bluffton, Richardson
Bluffton, Sherman
Blyburg, Dakota
Blyville, Knox
Bodarc, Sioux
Boelus, Howard
Boheet, Platte
Bohemia, Colfax
Bohemian, Knox
Boiling Spring, Cherry
Bole, Webster
Boleszyn, Valley
Bondville, Red Willow
Bone Creek, Brown
Bonhomme City, Knox
Bonn, Gage,
Bonner, Morrill
Bono, Washington
Bookwalter, Pawnee
Boone, Boone
Bordeaux, Dawes
Bosler, Keith
Bostwick, Nuckolls
Boulware, Cherry
Bow Creek, Dixon
Bowen, Sioux
Bowen, Washington
Bower, Jefferson
Bowerville, Jefferson
Bow Valley, Cedar
Box Butte, Box Butte
Boxelder, Red Willow
Boyd's Ranch, Buffalo
Boyer, Cheyenne
Boys Town, Douglas
Bracken, Nemaha
Braden, Arthur
Bradford, Saunders
Bradford City, Cass
Bradish, Boone
Bradley, Scotts Bluff

Bradshaw, York
Brady, Dakota
Brady, Lincoln
Brady Island, Lincoln
Brady's Crossing, Dakota
Brainard, Butler
Branch, Cedar
Brandon, Perkins
Brass, Merrick
Brass Spur, Howard
Bratton, Nemaha
Brayton, Greeley
Breckenridge, Knox
Breckenridge, Richardson
Brennans, Adams
Breslau, Pierce
Brewer, Holt
Brewer, Keya Paha
Brewer's Ranch, Merrick
Brewster, Blaine
Brickton, Adams
Bridgeport, Morrill
Bridgeton, Adams
Briggs, Douglas
Briggs Ranch, Hamilton
Brighton, McPherson
Bristow, Boyd
Britt, Cherry
Broadwater, Morrill
Brock, Cherry
Brock, Nemaha
Brockman, Keya Paha
Brockoff, Scotts Bluff
Brocksburg, Keya Paha
Brodie, Holt
Broganville, Keith
Broken Bow, Custer
Bromfield, Hamilton
Brookdale, Wayne
Brookfield, Platte
Brooklyn, Cass
Brooklyn, Franklin
Brooklyn, Otoe
Brooks, Howard
Brownlee, Cherry
Brownson, Cheyenne
Brownville, Nemaha
Brownville, Valley
Brule, Keith
Bruning, Thayer
Bruno, Butler
Brunswick, Antelope

Bryant, Fillmore
Bryant, Thayer
Bryant's Grove, Merrick
Bryson, Johnson
Buchanan, Box Butte
Buchanan, Colfax
Buchanan, Lincoln
Buckau, Cuming
Buckeye, Hamilton
Buckley, Jefferson
Bucktail, Arthur
Buda, Buffalo
Buda, Lancaster
Buell, Rock
Buff, Sheridan
Buffalo, Dawson
Buffalo, Furnas
Buffalo, Webster
Buffalo, Wheeler
Buller's Ranch, Buffalo
Bunker Hill, Hamilton
Bunker Hill, Platte
Bunnell, Sherman
Burbank, Box Butte
Burchard, Pawnee
Burgan, Brown
Burge, Cherry
Burkett, Hall
Burlingame, Merrick
Burnett, Antelope
Burnett, Madison
Burnham, Lancaster
Burnham, Lincoln
Burns, Box Butte
Burntwood City, Dundy
Burr, Otoe
Burress, Fillmore
Burris, Valley
Burroak, Custer
Burr Oak, Otoe
Burrough, Sheridan
Burrows, Platte
Burton, Keya Paha
Burton Creek, Holt
Burton's Bend, Furnas
Burwell, Garfield
Bushberry, Cass
Bushnell, Kimball
Butka, Loup
Butka, Rock
Butler, Buffalo
Butler, Johnson

Butler, Pawnee
Butler Center, Butler
Butte, Boyd
Butterfly, Stanton
Buxton, Fillmore
Buzzard's Roost, Dawson
Byron, Thayer
Cabanne's Trading Post,
    Douglas
Cache Creek, Holt
Cactus, Hayes
Cadams, Nuckolls
Cairo, Butler
Cairo, Hall
Caladonia, Cass
Calamus, Loup
Calamus, Valley
Caldwell, Gage
Caldwell, Scotts Bluff
Calf Creek, Cherry
Calhoun, Washington
California City, Otoe
Calla, Pawnee
Callaway, Custer
Callison, Dundy
Calora, Arthur
Calvert, Dundy
Calvert, Nemaha
Cambridge, Furnas
Cambridge, Otoe
Camden, Seward
Cameron, Hall
Camoak Park, Douglas
Campbell, Franklin
Campbell, Red Willow
Camp Cameron, Franklin
Camp Canby, Dawes
Camp Clarke, Morrill
Camp Creek, Lancaster
Camp Creek, Otoe
Camp Custer, Dawes
Camp Gifford, Sarpy
Camp Harriet Harding,
    Cass
Camp Mitchell, Scotts Bluff
Camp Ogallala, Keith
Camp Red Cloud Agency,
    Dawes
Camp Redwillow, Red
    Willow
Camp Robinson, Dawes
Camp Sergeant, Lincoln

Camp Sheridan, Sheridan
Camp Shuman, Scotts Bluff
Campville, Custer
Canada Hill, Howard
Canby, Red Willow
Cannonville, Harlan
Canotia, Cass
Cantella, Dawson
Canton, Box Butte
Canton, Sioux
Canton, Stanton
Cantonment Missouri,
    Washington
Capawell, Cherry
Capay, Rock
Capitol City, Cass
Carey, Hall
Carey, Sioux
Carisbrooke, Furnas
Carleton, Thayer
Carlin, Rock
Carlisle, Cass
Carlisle, Fillmore
Carlisle, Seward
Carlos, Lancaster
Carlson, Scotts Bluff
Carlyle, Box Butte
Carman, Arthur
Carmel, Butler
Carney's Station, Dawes
Carns, Keya Paha
Caroline, Jefferson
Carpenter, Box Butte
Carpenterville, Kearney
Carrico, Hayes
Carrie, Keya Paha
Carroll, Wayne
Carson, Garfield
Carson, Holt
Carson, Nemaha
Carter, Harlan
Cartney, Buffalo
Cascade, Cherry
Cascade, Howard
Case, Cedar
Case, Hamilton
Cashswan, Cherry
Casmelia, Sioux
Cassville, Cass
Castor, Saline
Catalpa, Holt
Catherine, Chase

Catherine, Cuming
Catherine, Hayes
Catherton, Webster
Cattaragus, Merrick
Cayuga, Platte
Cedar, Holt
Cedar Bend, Gage
Cedar Bluff, Cass
Cedar Bluffs, Saunders
Cedar City, Wheeler
Cedar Creek, Cass
Cedar Hill, Saunders
Cedar Island, Cass
Cedar Rapids, Boone
Cedar Rapids, Nance
Cedar River, Nance
Cedar Valley, Hamilton
Cedarville, Keya Paha
Cedarville, Sherman
Celia, Holt
Centennial, Buffalo
Center, Knox
Center, Saline
Center Bow, Cedar
Centerpoint, Frontier
Centerville, Cass
Centoria, Kearney
Central Bluff, Burt
Central City, Burt
Central City, Kearney
Central City, Merrick
Centre Valley, Cass
Centreville, Lancaster
Centropolis, Banner
Ceresco, Saunders
Ceryl, Gosper
Chadron, Dawes
Chalco, Sarpy
Chambers, Holt
Champion, Chase
Chandler, McPherson
Chapman, Merrick
Chappell, Deuel
Charleston, Gage
Charleston, Johnson
Charlestown, York
Charlotteville, Saunders
Chase, Chase
Chase, Greeley
Chaslaw, Saunders
Chasta, Richardson
Chautauqua, Dodge

Cheese Creek, Cheyenne
Chelsea, Holt
Cheney, Lancaster
Cherry, Cherry
Cherry Creek, Buffalo
Cherry Grove, Platte
Cherry Hill, Platte
Chester, Lancaster
Chester, Thayer
Chesterfield, Cherry
Chicago, Antelope
Chicago, Douglas
Chicago, Gage
Childs, Douglas
Childs, Sarpy
Chimney Rock, Morrill
Chin City, Valley
Chloe, Madison
Chojnice, Howard
Chris Creek, Perkins
Christena, Kearney
Christmanville, Knox
Cilicia, Sheridan
Cincinnati, Pawnee
Cio, Otoe
Circle Ranch, Dundy
Clara, Cheyenne
Claramont, Cedar
Claremont, Cedar
Clarendon, Howard
Clarence, Phelps
Clarion, Madison
Clark, Burt
Clarks, Merrick
Clarkson, Colfax
Clarks Point, Loup
Clark's Station, Morrill
Clarksville, Merrick
Clatonia, Gage
Clay Center, Clay
Clay City, Cass
Clayton, Jefferson
Clayton, Lancaster
Clayton, Saunders
Clear Creek, Saunders
Clear Spring, Antelope
Clearwater, Antelope
Cleman, Morrill
Clement, Cherry
Clenard, Arthur
Cleoria, Sherman
Cleveland, Cass

Cleveland, Holt
Cleveland, Platte
Cliff, Custer
Clifton, Holt
Clifton, Nemaha
Clifton Grove, Holt
Climax, Custer
Cline, Knox
Clinton, Sheridan
Clinton, Stanton
Closter, Boone
Cloudy, Cuming
Clouse, Scotts Bluff
Cloverton, Webster
Clyde, Antelope
Clyde, Banner
Clyde, Dodge
Clyde, Franklin
Clyde, Phelps
Cobb, Lancaster
Coburgh, Custer
Coburn, Dakota
Cody, Cherry
Coffee, Sioux
Coffee Siding, Sioux
Coffman, Washington
Coker, Knox
Coker, Lincoln
Colberg, Chase
Colbergen, Pierce
Colcesser, Sheridan
Coldrain, Thayer
Cold Springs, Lincoln
Cold Water, Cheyenne
Cold Water, Lincoln
Coldwater, Furnas
Colebank, Frontier
Coleraine, Thayer
Coleridge, Cedar
Colfer, Dundy
College View, Lancaster
Collins, Arthur
Collins, Scotts Bluff
Collinsville, Dundy
Colon, Saunders
Colona, Otoe
Colton, Cheyenne
Columbus, Platte
Colville, Sioux
Colyer, Morrill
Comfort, Thomas
Compton, Cherry

Comstock, Custer
Concord, Cass
Concord, Dixon
Condit, Otoe
Cone, Platte
Congdon, Dawson
Conkling, Burt
Conkling, Polk
Conley, Holt
Connell, Butler
Conner's 25 Ranch, Dundy
Conquest, Cherry
Conrad, Merrick
Constance, Cedar
Conterra, Cherry
Cook, Johnson
Cooleyton, Loup
Coon Creek, Red Willow
Coon Prairie, Boone
Cooper, Blaine
Cooper, Cherry
Copenhagen, Antelope
Coplant, Hall
Cora, Gosper
Corbin, Box Butte
Cordova, Seward
Cormick, Garden
Cornell, Hitchcock
Cornlea, Platte
Corral, Cherry
Cortland, Gage
Costin, Scotts Bluff
Cotesfield, Howard
Cottage Grove, Richardson
Cottage Hill, Gage
Cottage Home, Cuming
Cottonwood, Butler
Cottonwood, Lincoln
Cottonwood Falls, Lincoln
Cottonwood Springs,
    Lincoln
Courthouse Rock, Morrill
Cove, Hitchcock
Covert, Scotts Bluff
Covington, Dakota
Cowles, Webster
Coxville, Dawes
Coy, Nuckolls
Coyote, Dawson County
Cozad, Dawson
Crab Island, Dundy
Crab Orchard, Johnson

Craft, Morrill
Craig, Burt
Craig City, Stanton
Crane, Loup
Craven, Sheridan
Crawford, Dawes
Creighton, Knox
Crescent, Hooker
Creston, Platte
Creswell, York
Crete, Saline
Crete Junction, Otoe
Crete Junction, Saline
Crockett, Knox
Crockwell, Dakota
Crocy, Burt
Crofton, Knox
Crookston, Cherry
Cropsey, Gage
Cross, Sioux
Crossbar, Kimball
Crossing, Gage
Crounse, Lancaster
Crow Butte, Dawes
Crowder, Saunders
Crowell, Dodge
Crowellton, Buffalo
Croy's Grove, Knox
Crystal Lake, Pierce
Cuba, Rock
Cub Creek, Jefferson
Cudahy, Harlan
Culbertson, Hitchcock
Cullinan, Arthur
Cullom, Cass
Cuming, Cuming
Cuming City, Washington
Cummings, Perkins
Cummings Park, Custer
Cumminsville, Wheeler
Cumro, Custer
Cupid, Frontier
Curlew, Cedar
Curlew, Cherry
Curly, Sioux
Curry, Colfax
Curry, Hamilton
Curtis, Frontier
Cushing, Howard
Cushman, Lancaster
Custer, Custer
Custer Center, Custer

Cutler's Park, Douglas
Cyclone, Polk
Cyrus, Antelope
Cyrus, Morrill
Dahlburg, Boone
Daily, Dixon
Daily Branch, Dixon
Dakota City, Dakota
Dakota Junction, Dawes
Dale, Custer
Dale, Douglas
Dale, Washington
Dalton, Cheyenne
Dana, York
Danbury, Red Willow
Danbury Station, Red
    Willow
Danby, York
Dancer's Hill, Sioux
Dandale, Cherry
Dane Creek, Valley
Daniel's Ranch, Jefferson
Dannebrog, Howard
Dannevirke, Howard
Dansey's, Lincoln
Danville, Gage
Danville, Saline
Darnall, Keya Paha
Darr, Dawson
Davenport, Thayer
Davey, Lancaster
David City, Butler
Daviesville, Gosper
Davis, Clay
Davis Creek, Greeley
Davis Creek, Howard
Davis Quarry, Gage
Davison, Richardson
Dawes City, Dawes
Dawson, Dawson
Dawson, Richardson
Dawson's Mill, Richardson
Day, Deuel
Daykin, Jefferson
Dayton, Boone
Dayton, Nemaha
Deadman Creek, Sioux
Dead Timber, Cuming
Dean, Cherry
Deans, Adams
Debolt, Douglas
Debolt Place, Douglas

Decatur, Burt
Deep Well Ranch,
    Hamilton
Deer Creek, Dakota
Deer Creek, Lincoln
Deer Creek, Madison
Deerfield, Douglas
Degen, Stanton
De Graw, Morrill
Delaware, Otoe
Delaware City, Otoe
Delay, Lincoln
Delight, Custer
Deloit, Holt
Deloit, Wheeler
Delphi, Nuckolls
Delta, Otoe
Denison, Boone
Denman, Buffalo
Denman, Phelps
Denmark, Lincoln
Dennison, Gage
Dennison, Otoe
Dennison, Saline
Denniston, Sherman
Dent, Cherry
Denton, Lancaster
Derby, York
Deshler, Thayer
De Soto, Washington
Deverre, Garfield
Devon, Stanton
Devries, Howard
Deweese, Clay
Dewey, Dawson
Dewey, Garden
Dewey, Holt
Dewey Lake, Cherry
Dewing, Sheridan
Dewitt, Cuming
DeWitt, Saline
Dewitty, Cherry
Dexter, Lincoln
Diamond Springs, Keith
Dickens, Lincoln
Dike, Hitchcock
Diller, Jefferson
Dilworth, Clay
Dimick, Stanton
Dismal, Thomas
Disney, Holt
Divide, Sherman

Dix, Kimball
Dixon, Dixon
Doane, Dundy
Dobson's Landing, Knox
Dobytown, Kearney
Dodge, Dodge
Dodge, Douglas
Dogtown, Kearney
Dolphin, Knox
Dome, Sioux
Donald, Hooker
Doniphan, Hall
Donovan, Colfax
Donup, Stanton
Donup, Wayne
Dooley, Dawes
Dorchester, Saline
Doris, Custer
Dorp, Logan
Dorrance, Platte
Dorrington, Dawson
Dorrington, Richardson
Dorrington, Scotts Bluff
Dorsey, Box Butte
Dorsey, Holt
Doss, Dawson
Doty, Boyd
Dough Boy, Cherry
Douglas, Cherry
Douglas, Douglas
Douglas, Lancaster
Douglas, Otoe
Douglas Grove, Custer
Dover, Gage
Dover, Otoe
Dowling, Sioux
Doyle, Scotts Bluff
Dresden, Otoe
Dressen, Knox
Driftwood, Hitchcock
Druid Hill, Douglas
Dry Creek, Gage
Dry Creek, Madison
Dryden, Douglas
Dryden, Thayer
Dubert, Sioux
Dublin, Boone
Dublin, Howard
Dubois, Pawnee
Dudgeon, Furnas
Dudley, Fillmore
Duff, Rock

Dukeville, Knox
Dullaghan, Sheridan
Duluth, Grant
Dumas, Garfield
Dunbar, Otoe
Duncan, Platte
Dundee, Douglas
Dundee Place, Douglas
Dundy Centre, Dundy
Dunlap, Dawes
Dunlap, Madison
Dunn, Lancaster
Dunning, Blaine
Dunwell, Hooker
Durant, Polk
Dustin, Holt
Dutch Flats, Scotts Bluff
Dwight, Butler
Dye, Cheyenne
Dye, Kimball
Eagle, Cass
Eagle, Holt
Eagle Island, Platte
Earl, Butler
Earl, Frontier
Earth Lodge, Dawes
East Barton, Deuel
East Ellsworth, Butler
East End, Dodge
East Meridian, Jefferson
Easton, Garfield
Easton, Hall
East Strang Junction,
    Fillmore
Eastwood, Morrill
Eaton, Kearney
Echo, Lincoln
Eckard, Sioux
Eckley, Webster
Eclipse, Hooker
Economy, Polk
Edbell, Blaine
Eddy, Hayes
Eddy's Switch, Nemaha
Eddyville, Dawson
Eden, Clay
Eden, Fillmore
Eden, Nemaha
Edensburgh, Saunders
Eden Springs, Cherry
Edgar, Clay
Edgar, Otoe

Edholm, Butler
Edison, Furnas
Edith, Blaine
Edna, Polk
Edna, Webster
Edward, Arthur
Edward, Garden
Edwards, Cuming
Eight Mile Grove, Cass
Ela, Otoe
Elba, Howard
Elberon, Otoe
Elders, Keya Paha
Eldon, Clay
Eldon, Valley
Eldora, Clay
El Dorado, Cass
Eldorado, Clay
Eldorado, Colfax
El Dorado, Greeley
El Dorado, Johnson
Eldorado, Platte
Eldred, Saunders
Eldridge, Chase
Elgin, Antelope
Elgin City, Cass
Eli, Cherry
Elizabeth, Cherry
Elizabeth, Dodge
Elizabeth, Lincoln
Elk City, Douglas
Elk Creek, Johnson
Elkdale, Merrick
Elkhorn, Douglas
Elkhorn City, Douglas
Elkhorn Junction, Douglas
Elkton, Nuckolls
Elkton, Richardson
Elk Valley, Dakota
Elliott, Rock
Ellis, Dixon
Ellis, Gage
Ellison, Saline
Elliston, Perkins
Ellsworth, Butler
Ellsworth, Greeley
Ellsworth, Sheridan
Elltown, Cass
Elm, Custer
Elm Bridge, Custer
Elm Creek, Buffalo
Elmer, Dundy

Elmer, Hayes
Elm Grove, Cedar
Elm Grove, Keya Paha
Elm Grove, Thayer
Elmont, Cuming
Elmore, Richardson
Elmwood, Cass
Elmwood City, Otoe
Elora, Nuckolls
Elsie, Perkins
Elsmere, Cherry
Elting, Sherman
Elton, Custer
Elva, Grant
Elvira, Merrick
Elwood, Gosper
Elyria, Valley
Emerald, Lancaster
Emerick, Madison
Emerson, Dakota
Emerson, Dixon
Emerson, Dodge
Emerson, Otoe
Emmett, Dakota
Emmet, Holt
Empire, Fillmore
Empire, Sioux
Emporia, Holt
Enders, Chase
Enders Lake, Brown
Endicott, Jefferson
Enfield, Greeley
Enlow, Cherry
Enola, Madison
Enterprise, Keya Paha
Enterprise, Lancaster
Epworth, Banner
Equality, Frontier
Equality, Saline
Eri, Custer
Eric, Cheyenne
Ericson, Wheeler
Erie, Otoe
Erik, Cherry
Erina, Garfield
Ernst, Custer
Ernst, Johnson
Essen, Burt
Essex, Frontier
Essex, Gosper
Estelle, Hayes
Estenia, Saunders

Esther, Dawes
Esther, Dawson
Ethel, Cherry
Etna, Custer
Eudell, Custer
Eureka, Burt
Eureka, Lincoln
Eureka, York
Eustis, Frontier
Eva, Fillmore
Eva, Harlan
Evelyn, Rock
Everett, Dodge
Evergreen, Brown
Everson, Harlan
Ewing, Holt
Excelsior, Saunders
Exeter, Fillmore
Factorville, Cass
Factoryville, Cass
Fairbury, Jefferson
Faires, Otoe
Fairfield, Clay
Fairmont, Fillmore
Fairview, Cass
Fairview, Lincoln
Fairview, Madison
Fairview, Pawnee
Fairview, Red Willow
Fairview, Saline
Fairview, Sarpy
Fairview, Washington
Falls City, Richardson
Fandon, Frontier
Fardale, Howard
Fargo, Richardson
Farley, Wheeler
Farmers, Adams
Farmers Valley, Hamilton
Farmersville, Merrick
Farmersville, Otoe
Farmington, Dakota
Farmington, Stanton
Farmvale, Hamilton
Farnam, Dawson
Farrall, Platte
Farris, York
Farwell, Howard
Favors, Gage
Fay, Cherry
Febing, Nemaha
Fee, Cherry

Ferguson, Loup
Fern, Cherry
Fern, Sherman
Ferndale, Holt
Ferrens, Adams
Ferry, Dakota
Fetterman, Grant
Ficklin Springs, Scotts Bluff
Field, Kimball
Filley, Gage
Fillmore, Fillmore
Finchville, Custer
Finley, Morrill
Finnerty, Dakota
Firestone, Saunders
Firth, Lancaster
Fitzalon, Sherman
Flats, McPherson
Fleming, Box Butte
Fletcher, Washington
Flickville, Adams
Flickville, Clay
Flint, Perkins
Flora City, Cass
Floral, Gage
Florence, Douglas
Floss, Greeley
Flourney, Thurston
Flowerdale, Richardson
Flowerfield, Banner
Floyd, Dakota
Floyd, Knox
Folden's Mill, Cass
Foley, Butler
Folsomdale, Kearney
Fontanelle, Washington
Fora, Arthur
Ford, Holt
Ford, Logan
Fordyce, Cedar
Forest City, Sarpy
Forks, Lincoln
Forks, McPherson
Forney, Richardson
Fort Atkinson, Washington
Fort Butler, Thayer
Fort Calhoun, Washington
Fort Charles, Dakota
Fort Childs, Kearney
Fort Cottonwood, Lincoln
Fort Crook, Sarpy
Fort Fontenelle, Scotts Bluff

Fort Grattan, Garden
Fort Hartsuff, Valley
Fort Helvey, Jefferson
Fort Independence, Hall
Fort John, Scotts Bluff
Fort Kearny, Kearney
Fort Kearny, Otoe
Fort McKean, Lincoln
Fort McPherson, Lincoln
Fort Mitchell, Knox
Fort Mitchell, Scotts Bluff
Fort Niobrara, Cherry
Fort Omaha, Douglas
Fort Robinson, Dawes
Fort Rodney, Loup
Fort Sidney, Cheyenne
Foster, Pierce
Fouse Ranch, Seward
Fowler, Douglas
Fowling, Box Butte
Fox, Loup
Fox Creek, Lincoln
Foxley, Douglas
Francis, Wheeler
Frank, Blaine
Frank, Phelps
Frankfort, Clay
Frankfort, Knox
Frankfort, Otoe
Franklin, Cass
Franklin, Colfax
Franklin, Dakota
Franklin, Dodge
Franklin, Franklin
Franklin, Richardson
Franklin City, Dakota
Franklin City, Franklin
Fraser, Phelps
Frease, Chase
Frederick, Nemaha
Fredericksburg, Kearney
Fredonia, Dodge
Freedom, Frontier
Freeling, Richardson
Freeman, Gage
Freeport, Banner
Freeport, Jefferson
Freewater, Harlan
Fremont, Dodge
Fremont Springs, Lincoln
Frenchtown, Antelope
Frickel, Holt

Friedensau, Thayer
Friend, Saline
Friendville, Saline
Froid, Deuel
Frontier, Hitchcock
Fullerton, Nance
Fulton, Colfax
Funk, Phelps
Funston, Howard
Furay, Sherman
Gables, Garfield
Gage, Buffalo
Gage Valley, Howard
Galena, Dixon
Galena, Dodge
Galena, Hayes
Galley's Ranch, Platte
Gallop, Cherry
Galnes, Adams
Galva, Platte
Gandy, Logan
Gandy Station, Logan
Gannett, Lincoln
Garber, Harlan
Gard, Cherry
Garden, Garden
Garden, Phelps
Gardiner, Platte
Gardiner Station, Merrick
Gardiner Station, Platte
Gardner's Ranch, Butler
Garfield, Lincoln
Garfield, Valley
Garland, Seward
Garman, Cheyenne
Garner, Boone
Garrat, Lancaster
Garrison, Butler
Gartner, Pawnee
Gary, Banner
Gasco, Gage
Gaslin, Lincoln
Gasmann Springs, Custer
Gassey Hollow, Stanton
Gates, Custer
Gates, Madison
Gates, Sarpy
Gavin, Custer
Gazelle, Fillmore
Gazelle, Thayer
Geer, Richardson
Gelston, Douglas

Gem, Logan
Gem, Wheeler
Genet, Custer
Geneva, Fillmore
Geneva, Richardson
Genoa, Nance
Genou, Richardson
Georgetown, Clay
Georgetown, Custer
Georgetown, Jefferson
Georgetown, Keith
Georgia, Cherry
Geranium, Valley
Gering, Scotts Bluff
German Settlement,
    Cherry
Germantown, Seward
Germanville, Cuming
Gibbon, Buffalo
Gibraltar, Richardson
Gibson, Douglas
Gifford, Kimball
Gilaspie, Cherry
Gilchrist, Sioux
Gilead, Thayer
Giles, Blaine
Giles, Brown
Giles, Cherry
Giles, Washington
Gillespie, Antelope
Gillespie, Holt
Gill's, Keith
Gilltown, Furnas
Gilmans, Lincoln
Gilmore, Sarpy
Gilson, Adams
Giltner, Hamilton
Ginn, Box Butte
Girard, Box Butte
Girard, Saline
Glade, Polk
Gladstone, Jefferson
Glasgow, Howard
Gleason, Platte
Glen, Sioux
Glenalpine, Antelope
Glenaro, Antelope
Glenaro, Madison
Glenburne, Lincoln
Glencoe, Dodge
Glendale, Antelope
Glendale, Burt

Glendale, Cass
Glendale, Seward
Glengarry, Fillmore
Glenrock, Nemaha
Glenrose, Arthur
Glenrose, Keith
Glenvil, Clay
Glenwood, Buffalo
Glenwood, Nance
Glenwood Park, Buffalo
Glover, Hamilton
Goehner, Seward
Golden, Burt
Golden Gate, Washington
Golden Spring, Burt
Golden Spring, Nemaha
Golden State, Dodge
Goldrensey, Saline
Goldville, Blaine
Goodenow, Valley
Goodland, Garden
Goodstreak, Morrill
Goodwin, Dakota
Goodyear's Ranch, Custer
Goose Creek, Cherry
Gordon, Sheridan
Gosper, Gosper
Gothenburg, Dawson
Gottenburg, Dawson
Gould, Dawson
Gouldale, Keya Paha
Gould City, Platte
Grace, Rock
Gracie, Loup
Gracie, Rock
Graf, Johnson
Graft, Harlan
Grafton, Fillmore
Grainton, Perkins
Gramercy, Sioux
Granada, Cass
Grand Island, Hall
Grand Island City, Hall
Grand Island Station, Hall
Grand Lake, Box Butte
Grand Prairie, Platte
Grand Rapids, Cass
Grand Rapids, Holt
Grandview, Furnas
Grandview, Gage
Grandview, Harlan
Granger, Scotts Bluff

Grant, Custer
Grant, Franklin
Grant, Nemaha
Grant, Perkins
Grantville, Howard
Granville, Platte
Gravel Pit, Holt
Graveldale, Kearney
Gray, Wayne
Grayson, Sheridan
Grayson's, Jefferson
Greeley, Greeley
Greeley, Holt
Greeley Center, Greeley
Green, Custer
Greenberry, Clay
Greendale, Buffalo
Green Island, Cedar
Green Meadows, Douglas
Greens, Sarpy
Green's Switch, Sarpy
Green Valley, Holt
Greenville, Seward
Greenwood, Cass
Greenwood, Dakota
Greenwood Station,
    Cheyenne
Greenwood Station, Morrill
Greer, Gage
Gregg, Box Butte
Greggsport, Otoe
Gregory, Cherry
Gregory's Basin, Lancaster
Gresham, York
Gretna, Sarpy
Griffin, Cuming
Griffith, Antelope
Grimton, Knox
Gross, Boyd
Groveland, Otoe
Groveland, Seward
Grover, Seward
Gruetli, Platte
Grunewald, Platte
Guide Rock, Webster
Guilford, Custer
Gulfoil, Merrick
Gunderson's Crossing,
    Douglas
Gurley, Cheyenne
Gurney, Rock
Gurnsey, Dawson

Guthrie, Morrill
Hadar, Pierce
Haig, Scotts Bluff
Haigler, Dundy
Haigville, Scotts Bluff
Hainesville, Holt
Hale, Madison
Halestown, Knox
Halifax, Greeley
Hallam, Lancaster
Halloran, Adams
Halsey, Thomas
Halstead, Brown
Hamburgh, Red Willow
Hamilton, Chase
Hamilton, Dawes
Hamilton, Gage
Hamilton, Hamilton
Hamilton, Otoe
Hamilton, Sheridan
Hamlet, Hayes
Hammond, Boone
Hammond, Rock
Hampton, Cheyenne
Hampton, Hamilton
Hancock, Dundy
Hancock, Franklin
Hanlon, Lancaster
Hanover, Gage
Hansen, Adams
Harbine, Jefferson
Hardy, Boone
Hardy, Nuckolls
Harlan, Cherry
Harlan, Custer
Harlan, Harlan
Harmony, Cherry
Harmony, Kearney
Harney City, Dakota
Harold, Holt
Harold, Sioux
Harriet, Holt
Harrington, Wheeler
Harrisburg, Banner
Harrison, Sioux
Harrop, Loup
Hart, Holt
Hartford, Scotts Bluff
Hartford, Seward
Hartington, Cedar
Hartman, Garden
Hartman, Scotts Bluff

Hartman, Seward
Harvard, Clay
Hashman, Box Butte
Haspur, Hall
Hastings, Adams
Hatton, Lincoln
Havana, Frontier
Havelock, Lancaster
Havens, Cedar
Havens, Merrick
Hawkeye, Dixon
Hawley, Blaine
Hawthorne, Lancaster
Haydon, Phelps
Hayes, Douglas
Hayes, Washington
Hayes Center, Hayes
Hayestown, Sherman
Hayland, Adams
Haymow, Stanton
Hayne's Station, Morrill
Haypoint, Holt
Hay Springs, Sheridan
Hazard, Sherman
Hazel Dell, Adams
Hazelton, Sheridan
Hazle, Dixon
Hazleton, Sarpy
Headgate, Scotts Bluff
Headland, Saunders
Headquarters, Wheeler
Heartwell, Kearney
Heath, Banner
Heber, Merrick
Hebron, Thayer
Hecla, Hooker
Hedrix, Jefferson
Heldt, Scotts Bluff
Helena, Johnson
Helper, Dawes
Helvey, Jefferson
Hemingford, Box Butte
Henderson, York
Hendley, Furnas
Hendricks, Otoe
Hendrix, Sarpy
Hennigan, Butler
Henrietta, Nuckolls
Henry, Cheyenne
Henry, Fillmore
Henry, Scotts Bluff
Hering's Mill, Antelope

Herman, Washington
Herndon, Cheyenne
Herrick, Knox
Hershey, Lincoln
Hesperia, Fillmore
Heun, Colfax
Hewarts, Gage
Hewett, Garden
Hewitt, Sioux
Heyward, Scotts Bluff
Hiawatha, Butler
Hiawatha, Dundy
Hiawatha, Washington
Hickman, Lancaster
Hickory, Morrill
Hicks, Webster
Higgins, Cheyenne
High, Custer
Highland, Custer
Highland, Gosper
Highland, Hayes
Highland, Lancaster
Highland, Phelps
Highland, Richardson
Highland Park, Lancaster
Hiland, Washington
Hildreth, Franklin
Hill, Saunders
Hillier, Gosper
Hilliker, Scotts Bluff
Hillsdale, Garden
Hillsdale, Nemaha
Hillsdale, Thayer
Hillside, Arthur
Hillside, Washington
Hill Siding, Platte
Hilton, Dawson
Hilton, Sheridan
Hinchley, Sheridan
Hinckley, Custer
Hindrey, Lincoln
Hiram, Madison
Hire, Cherry
Hoag, Gage
Hoagland, Logan
Hobson, Lancaster
Hodges, Kimball
Hoffland, Sheridan
Holbrook, Furnas
Holcomb, Phelps
Holdrege, Phelps
Holland, Lancaster

Holland, Sheridan
Hollinger, Furnas
Hollinsburg, Burt
Hollman, Holt
Holly, Sheridan
Holmesville, Gage
Holstein, Adams
Holt Creek, Holt
Holton, Sheridan
Home, Hall
Homer, Dakota
Homerville, Gosper
Homestead, Burt
Homestead, Douglas
Homestead, Greeley
Homond, Richardson
Hood, Cherry
Hooker, Gage
Hooper, Dodge
Hoosier, Custer
Hoosier Hollow, Stanton
Hoover, Dundy
Hope, Hayes
Hope, Madison
Hope, Scotts Bluff
Hopeville, Phelps
Hopewell, Frontier
Horace, Greeley
Horace, Stanton
Hord, Merrick
Hord Siding, Antelope
Hordville, Hamilton
Horn, Dawes
Hornsdale, Saline
Horse Creek, Scotts Bluff
Horsefoot, Rock
Hoskins, Wayne
Hough, Dawes
Houston, York
Howard, Gage
Howard, Greeley
Howard, Nemaha
Howard City, Howard
Howe, Nemaha
Howells, Colfax
Hubbard, Dakota
Hubbell, Thayer
Hudson, Hayes
Hudson, Phelps
Hudson, Washington
Huff, Dawes
Huffman, Brown

Hughes, Dawes
Hughes, Jefferson
Hull, Banner
Humboldt, Richardson
Humpback, Dawson
Humphrey, Platte
Hunkins, Seward
Hunt, Frontier
Hunter, Sheridan
Hunter, Sioux
Huntington, Hamilton
Huntley, Harlan
Hunton, Pierce
Hunton, Stanton
Huntsman, Cheyenne
Huskerville, Lancaster
Hutchison, Garden
Huxley, Custer
Hyannis, Grant
Hyersville, Lancaster
Ickes, Cheyenne
Ida, Dawes
Ida, Valley
Idella, Cherry
Ihno, Dodge
Imhof, Thomas
Imperial, Chase
Inavale, Webster
Inco, Douglas
Independence City, Cass
Indian Creek, York
Indianola, Red Willow
Industry, Phelps
Inez, Holt
Ingallston, Rock
Ingells, Holt
Ingham, Lincoln
Ingleside, Adams
Inglewood, Dodge
Ingomar, Sheridan
Inhelder Station, Cass
Inland, Adams
Inland, Clay
Inman, Holt
Inman's Grove, Holt
Integrity, Phelps
Iola, Otoe
Ionia, Dixon
Iowa City, Cass
Iowa Ford Mills,
    Richardson
Ira, Boone

Ira, Keya Paha
Ireland's Mill, Douglas
Irish, Douglas
Iron Bluffs, Douglas
Irvine, Keith
Irving, Morrill
Irving, Nuckolls
Irvington, Douglas
Irwin, Cherry
Isla, Saunders
Ithaca, Saunders
Ivanhoe, Lancaster
Ives, Dundy
Jacinto, Kimball
Jackson, Dakota
Jackson, Platte
Jacksonville, Greeley
Jacksonville, Pawnee
Jacksonville, Saline
Jacobs, Dundy
Jalapa, Dodge
Jamaica, Lancaster
Jamestown, Dodge
Jamison, Keya Paha
Janesville, Custer
Janise, Scotts Bluff
Jansen, Jefferson
Jeffers, Adams
Jefferson, Custer
Jefferson, Jefferson
Jelen, Knox
Jenkins' Mill, Jefferson
Jennings, Sheridan
Jericho, Sherman
Jersey City, Thayer
Jess, Sheridan
Jessup, Antelope
Jewell, Dawson
Joder, Sioux
Johnson, Nemaha
Johnson's Ranch, Gosper
Johnstown, Brown
Jones Trading Post,
    Garfield
Joong, Clay
Jordan, Garfield
Joseph, Pierce
Josephine, Lincoln
Josie, Holt
Josselyn, Dawson
Jovian, Dawson
Joy, Holt

Joyce, Scotts Bluff
Judson, Furnas
Judson, Gosper
Julian, Nemaha
Junction Ranch, Merrick
Junctionville, Hall
Junctionville, Kearney
Juniata, Adams
Junod, Cherry
Justice, Dixon
Kaiser, Blaine
Kalamazoo, Madison
Kam, Gage
Kanosha, Cass
Kaufman, Kimball
Kaw, Dundy
Kearney, Buffalo
Kearney City, Kearney
Kearney City, Otoe
Kearney Junction, Buffalo
Kearney Station, Kearney
Keatskatoos, Platte
Keefer, Kearney
Keeler, Lincoln
Keene, Kearney
Keith, Lincoln
Keithleys, Nuckolls
Kelley, Box Butte
Kelley, Morrill
Kelley, Sioux
Kelso, Hooker
Kelso, Howard
Kemma, Knox
Kemp, Morrill
Kendall, Dawes
Kenesaw, Adams
Kennard, Washington
Kennedy, Cherry
Kenomi, Sheridan
Kent, Loup
Kent, Nance
Kenton, Saunders
Kent Siding, Madison
Kenyon Spur, Howard
Keota, Custer
Kesterson, Jefferson
Ketchum, Dodge
Kewanee, Cherry
Key, Garfield
Keya Paha, Boyd
Keya Paha, Holt
Keystone, Dawson

Keystone, Keith
Kilgore, Cherry
Kilgravel, Merrick
Kilmer, Lincoln
Kim, Garfield
Kimball, Kimball
King, Cherry
King Lake, Douglas
Kingsburg, Stanton
Kingsley, Keith
Kingston, Adams
Kingston, Butler
Kingston, Custer
Kingston, Frontier
Kingston, Johnson
Kingville, Cass
Kinkaid, Boyd
Kinney, Gage
Kinneyville, Cherry
Kiowa, Scotts Bluff
Kiowa (1), Thayer
Kiowa (2), Thayer
Kirk, Banner
Kirkwood, Rock
Kirsch, Logan
Klump, Custer
Knievels Corner, Holt
Knowles, Frontier
Knox, York
Knoxville, Knox
Knoxville, Otoe
Kola, Holt
Koller, Kearney
Korty, Keith
Koshopah, Brown
Kowanda, Garden
Kramer, Lancaster
Krider, Gage
Kronborg, Hamilton
Krugman, Holt
Krumel, Saunders
Kuester's Lake, Hall
Kuhn, Morrill
Lackey, Cherry
Laclede, Polk
Ladora, Blaine
Lafayette, Nemaha
Lafayette, Seward
La Forest, Hayes
Laird, Frontier
Lake, Cherry
Lake, Phelps

Lake City, Holt
Lakeland, Brown
Lake Quinnebaugh, Burt
Lakeside, Sheridan
Laketon, Dakota
Lakeview, Cuming
Lakeview, Garden
La Loup, Platte
Lamar, Chase
Lamartine, Greeley
Lambert, Colfax
Lambert, Holt
Lamb's, Hall
Lamo, McPherson
Lamont, Dundy
Lamore, Custer
Lancaster (1), Lancaster
Lancaster (2), Lancaster
Lander, Douglas
Lane, Douglas
Lanham, Gage
Laona, Gage
Lapeer, Cheyenne
La Platte, Sarpy
La Porte, Wayne
Largo, McPherson
Larimore City, Sarpy
Larimore Mills, Sarpy
Larissa, Scotts Bluff
La Ruhe, Keith
Laska, Holt
Latrobe, Dodge
Latrobe, Johnson
Latrobe, Kearney
Lattin, Keya Paha
Laura, Cheyenne
Laura, Holt
Laurel, Cedar
Lavacca, Cherry
Lavinia, Holt
La Vista, Sarpy
Lawn, Box Butte
Lawn, Dawes
Lawn, Douglas
Lawnridge, Cedar
Lawrence, Nuckolls
Lawrence, York
Leafdale, Cheyenne
Leahey, Seward
Leat, Cherry
Leavitt, Dodge
Lebanon, Red Willow

LeBlanc, Knox
Lee Park, Custer
Lee Park, Valley
Lee Valley, Douglas
Le Grand, Saline
Leigh, Colfax
Leland, Gage
Lemley, McPherson
Lemon, Gage
Lemonville, Jefferson
Lemoyne, Keith
Lena, Arthur
Lena, Blaine
Lena, Custer
Lennox, Chase
Lenox, York
Leonard, Custer
Leonard, Dawes
Leonard, Hamilton
Leonie, Holt
Leota, Franklin
Leoti, Dawson
Leo Valley, Greeley
Leroy, Adams
Lerton, Hamilton
Leshara, Saunders
Leslie, Lincoln
Leslie, Wayne
Lester, Merrick
Lester, Webster
Letan, Box Butte
Level, Adams
Level, Dawson
Lewanna, Cherry
Lewellen, Garden
Lewellen, Keith
Lewis, Cheyenne
Lewisburg, Washington
Lewisburgh, Dodge
Lewisburgh, Harlan
Lewistown, Cass
Lewiston, Pawnee
Lexington, Dawson
Lexington, Franklin
Lexington, Johnson
Libby, Box Butte
Liberty, Cass
Liberty, Gage
Liberty Farm, Clay
Liberty Farms, Clay
Lightner, Morrill
Lilac, McPherson

Lillian, Custer
Lily, Dodge
Lime Creek, Dixon
Lime Grove, Dixon
Lincoln, Dodge
Lincoln, Lancaster
Lincoln Army Air Field,
    Lancaster
Lincoln Air Force Base,
    Lancaster
Lincoln Valley, Hamilton
Linden, Hamilton
Lindsay, Platte
Lindy, Knox
Linn, Lincoln
Linpark, Lancaster
Linscott, Blaine
Linton, Pawnee
Linwood, Butler
Lisa's Post, Washington
Lisbon, Fillmore
Lisbon, Perkins
Lisbon, Sarpy
Lisbon, York
Lisco, Garden
Lisco, Morrill
Lisle, Wheeler
Litchfield, Sherman
Little, Holt
Little Blue, Adams
Little Blue, Jefferson
Little Cottonwood, Dawes
Littlejohn, Gage
Little Moon, Scotts Bluff
Little Papillion, Douglas
Little Salt, Lancaster
Little Sandy, Jefferson
Little White Clay Creek,
    Dawes
Little York, Nemaha
Livingston, Banner
Lockwood, Merrick
Locust, Franklin
Locust Grove, Nemaha
Lodgepole, Cheyenne
Lodi, Custer
Lodi, Dakota
Logan, Dakota
Logan, Dodge
Logan, Logan
Logan, Thurston
Logan City, Wayne

Logan Grove, Dixon
Logan Valley, Cedar
Loganville, Johnson
Loma, Butler
Lomax, Custer
Lombard, Cherry
Lomo, Keya Paha
London, Nemaha
Lonelm, Sherman
Lone Star, Butler
Lone Tree, Merrick
Lone Tree, Nance
Lone Valley, Saunders
Long, Frontier
Longa Valley, Cuming
Long Branch, Platte
Long Branch, Richardson
Long Den, Franklin
Long Hope, York
Longhorn, Dawes
Long Lake, Sheridan
Long Pine, Brown
Longwood, Custer
Looking Glass, Platte
Loomis, Phelps
Lorain, Wayne
Loraine, Banner
Loran, Boone
Lorenzo, Cheyenne
Loretto, Boone
Lorton, Otoe
Lost Creek, Platte
Lothair, Saunders
Loudon City, Saline
Louisville, Cass
Loup City, Sherman
Loup Fork, Howard
Loupville, Saunders
Lowell, Kearney
Loyal, Custer
Loyal Hill, Lancaster
Loyd, Knox
Loyola, Hall
Lucas Siding, Pierce
Luce, Buffalo
Lucerne, Holt
Lucerne, Knox
Lucieville, Saline
Lucille, Hayes
Lucky Valley, Grant
Lucy, Blaine
Ludlow, Adams

Ludlow, Clay
Luella, Cass
Luella, Sheridan
Lulu, Sheridan
Lund, Cherry
Luray, Red Willow
Lushton, York
Lute, Phelps
Lutes, Keya Paha
Lutherville, Garden
Lux, Dundy
Lydia, Custer
Lyman, Fillmore
Lyman, Sarpy
Lyman, Scotts Bluff
Lynch, Boyd
Lynden, Furnas
Lynden, Keith
Lynn, Morrill
Lyon, Garden
Lyons, Burt
Lytle, Garden
Mabelo, Brown
Machette's, Lincoln
Macon, Franklin
Macy, Thurston
Madison, Madison
Madrid, Perkins
Magnet, Cedar
Magoon, Custer
Mahala City, Butler
Mahilla, Buffalo
Mahlon, Polk
Majors, Buffalo
Malcolm, Lancaster
Malinda, Box Butte
Malinda, Sioux
Malmo, Saunders
Malvern, Rock
Manchester, Custer
Manchester, Dawes
Mandano, Saline
Manderson, Chase
Manderson, Valley
Manhattan, Cuming
Manhattan, Dodge
Manitou, Wayne
Mankato, Boyd
Manley, Cass
Manleyville, Fillmore
Manning, Knox
Mannland, Cass

Mansfield, Knox
Mansfield, Sioux
Maple Creek, Dodge
Maple Grove, Holt
Mapleville, Dodge
Mapps, York
Marengo, Hall
Marengo, Hayes
Margaretta, Lancaster
Margate, Cheyenne
Mariaville, Rock
Marietta, Otoe
Marion, Franklin
Marion, Colfax
Marion, Red Willow
Markel, Dawson
Marks' Mill, Jefferson
Marlbank, Keya Paha
Marlin, Scotts Bluff
Marlowe, Cheyenne
Marmora, Cherry
Marple, Box Butte
Marple, Sheridan
Marquette, Hamilton
Marrietta, Madison
Marrietta, Saunders
Marrowville, Pierce
Mars, Antelope
Mars, Knox
Marseilles, Cass
Marshall, Clay
Marsland, Dawes
Martell, Lancaster
Martha, Holt
Martin, Chase
Martin, Keith
Martindale, Cherry
Martins, Cass
Martinsburg, Dixon
Martinville, Adams
Martinville, Hall
Martland, Fillmore
Marvin, Custer
Mary, Brown
Marysburgh, Jefferson
Marysville, Seward
Mascot, Douglas
Mascot, Harlan
Maskell, Dixon
Mason City, Custer
Mathers, Scotts Bluff
Matson, Platte

Matteson, Cherry
Matthews, Holt
Mauston, Boone
Max, Dundy
Maxwell, Lincoln
May, Kearney
Mayberry, Pawnee
Mayflower, Adams
Mayflower, McPherson
Mayville, Lancaster
Maywood, Frontier
Maywood, Harlan
Maze, Wayne
McAlpine, Sherman
McCaffery, Holt
McCandless, Douglas
McCandless, Nemaha
McCann, Cherry
McClean, Keya Paha
McCook, Red Willow
McCool Junction, York
McDonald Ranch, York
McDonald's Track, Hall
McFadden, York
McFarland, Lancaster
McGrew, Scotts Bluff
McGuire, Keya Paha
McKinley, Custer
McLean, Pierce
McNaughton, Hayes
McPherson, Lincoln
McPherson, McPherson
McWilliams, Otoe
Mead, Saunders
Meads, Washington
Meadow, Sarpy
Meadow Grove, Madison
Meadville, Keya Paha
Medicine, Lincoln
Medicine Creek, Furnas
Meek, Holt
Meeker, Hitchcock
McGeath, Keith
Melbeta, Scotts Bluff
Meldon, Cherry
Melia, Sarpy
Mellroy, Gage
Melpha, Cherry
Melrose, Arthur
Melrose, Douglas
Melrose, Harlan
Melrose, Saunders

Melrose, Washington
Melvin, Wayne
Memphis, Saunders
Mendotte, Hall
Menlo, Rock
Menominee, Cedar
Mentorville, Antelope
Mentzer, Merrick
Mercer, Douglas
Merchiston, Nance
Meriden, Dawson
Meridian, Jefferson
Merles Ranch, Richardson
Merna, Custer
Merom, Dawson
Merrick, Merrick
Merrill Mission, Sarpy
Merriman, Cherry
Meserveville, Gage
Mesopotamia, Platte
Metz, Platte
Metzinger, Rock
Mick, Gosper
Middlebranch, Holt
Middlebranch, Knox
Middleburgh, Richardson
Middle Creek, Lancaster
Middle Creek, Thurston
Middleport, Wheeler
Middle Prong, Cherry
Midland, Colfax
Midland, Knox
Midvale, Brown
Midway, Dawson
Midway, Furnas
Midway, Harlan
Midway, Holt
Midway, Howard
Midway, Lincoln
Midway, Morrill
Milburn, Custer
Miles, Washington
Miles Ranch, Richardson
Milford, Seward
Millard, Douglas
Milldale, Custer
Miller, Buffalo
Millerboro, Knox
Millers, Douglas
Millerton, Butler
Millersville, Thayer
Milligan, Fillmore

Millington, Adams
Millis, Dakota
Millis Beach, Dakota
Mills, Keya Paha
Mills, Washington
Millspaw Ranch, Hamilton
Mill Spur, Nuckolls
Millstown, Scotts Bluff
Millville, Lancaster
Millville, Platte
Milton, Custer
Milton, Gosper
Milton, Saunders
Minatare, Scotts Bluff
Minden, Kearney
Mineola, Holt
Mineral, Holt
Minersville, Otoe
Minerva, Nemaha
Mingo, Scotts Bluff
Mintle, Scotts Bluff
Mira Creek, Valley
Mirage, Kearney
Mirage, Sheridan
Miramichi, Hamilton
Mission, Pawnee
Mitchell, Scotts Bluff
Moakler, Sheridan
Moffitt, Cass
Moffitt, Garden
Mohler, Morrill
Moline, Franklin
Momence, Fillmore
Monond, Richardson
Monowi, Boyd
Monroe, Platte
Monterey, Cuming
Monterey, Richardson
Montevalle, Cass
Montrose, Sioux
Moody, Frontier
Moomaw, Sheridan
Moon, Scotts Bluff
Moore, Holt
Moore, Hooker
Moorefield, Frontier
Moorehouse, Pierce
Moorman, Platte
Morrallton, Nemaha
Moran, Wheeler
Morgan, Knox
Morgan Island, Saline

Moritz, Adams
Morrallton, Nemaha
Morrill, Scotts Bluff
Morrilville, Knox
Morris, Hayes
Morris, Saline
Morse Bluff, Saunders
Morseville, Adams
Morton, Boyd
Morton, Gage
Moscow, Franklin
Mosser, Sheridan
Mosside, Boone
Motala, Kearney
Moulton, Loup
Mound, Howard
Mount Clare, Nuckolls
Mount Hope, Cass
Mount Michael, Douglas
Mount Pleasant, Cass
Mount Vernon, Nemaha
Moval, Douglas
Mud Springs, Morrill
Mud Springs, Sioux
Mullahla's Station, Dawson
Mullen, Hooker
Mumper, Garden
Munson, Loup
Munson, Madison
Munson, Richardson
Munt, Keya Paha
Murdock, Cass
Muriel, Adams
Murphy, Hamilton
Murray, Cass
Myers, Dawson
Mygatt, Cherry
Mynard, Cass
Myra, Banner
Myra, Boone
Myra, Nance
Myrtle, Custer
Myrtle, Lincoln
Nacora, Dakota
Nantasket, Buffalo
Naper, Boyd
Napoleon, Harlan
Napoleon, Lincoln
Naponee, Franklin
Narcissus, Red Willow
Nasby, Sarpy
Nasco, Douglas

Nashville, Washington
Natick, Thomas
Nea, Custer
Neapolis, Saunders
Nebo, Platte
Neboville, Platte
Nebraska Center, Buffalo
Nebraska City, Otoe
Nebraska Station No. 31,
　Cheyenne
Neel, Dundy
Neenah, Colfax
Negunda, Webster
Nehawka, Cass
Neldon, Seward
Neligh, Antelope
Nelson, Nuckolls
Nemaha, Nemaha
Nemaha, Richardson
Nemaha Falls, Richardson
Nemo, Custer
Nenzel, Cherry
Neoma, Boone
Nero, Washington
Nesbit, Keya Paha
Nesbit, Logan
Nesbit, McPherson
Nesuma, Otoe
Netolice, Valley
Nevens, Keith
Newark, Kearney
Newboro, Wheeler
New Callaway, Custer
Newcastle, Dixon
New Era, Furnas
New Helena, Custer
Newhome, Pawnee
Newington, Dawson
Newman Grove, Madison
Newmarch, Adams
New Philadelphia, Cuming
Newport, Dakota
Newport, Dawson
Newport, Rock
Newton, Burt
Newton, Cherry
Newton, Lancaster
Newton, Saunders
New York, York
New York Creek,
　Washington
Ney, McPherson

Nichols, Lincoln
Nickerson, Dodge
Nimberg, Butler
Nims, Richardson
Nine Mile Station, Deuel
Niobrara, Knox
Niota, York
Noah, Sherman
Noark, McPherson
Nobesville, Lancaster
Nodine, Cherry
Noel, Custer
Nohart, Richardson
Nonpareil, Box Butte
Nora, Nuckolls
Noraville, Richardson
Norden, Keya Paha
Norfolk, Madison
Normal, Lancaster
Norman, Dixon
Norman, Kearney
Norris, Cedar
Norris, Frontier
Norris, Hayes
North Auburn, Nemaha
North Bend, Dixon
North Bend, Dodge
North Blue, Adams
North Branch, Otoe
North Cedar, Cuming
North Creek, Dixon
Northfield, Hall
North Fork, Saline
North Fork, Seward
North Franklin, Franklin
North Independence, Cass
North Loup, Valley
North Nebraska City, Otoe
North Omaha, Douglas
North Platte, Lincoln
Northport, Morrill
North Rock Bluff, Cass
Northshore, Dakota
Northside, Wayne
North Star, Nance
Northville, Otoe
Northwood, Furnas
Norton, Dundy
Norval, Seward
Norway, Dixon
Norway, Thomas
Norwich, Platte

Norwood, Holt
Nowy Poznan, Howard
Nunda, Loup
Nursery Hill, Otoe
Nye, Box Butte
Nysted, Howard
Oadland, Boone
Oak, Nuckolls
Oakchatam, Douglas
Oakdale, Antelope
Oak Grove, Jefferson
Oak Grove Station,
　Nuckolls
Oakgroves, Seward
Oakland, Burt
Oak Springs, Dodge
Oasis, Cherry
Obert, Cedar
Oberton, Cedar
Obi, Custer
Oconee, Platte
O'Connor, Greeley
Oconto, Custer
Octavia, Butler
Odell, Gage
Odessa, Buffalo
O'Fallons, Lincoln
O'Fallon's Bluff, Lincoln
Offutt Air Force Base,
　Sarpy
Ogallala, Keith
Ogan, Dodge
Ogden, Antelope
Ogden, Madison
O'Gorman, Dakota
Ohiowa, Fillmore
O'Kane, Phelps
Okay, Platte
Olathe, Lancaster
Olax, Custer
Oldenbusch, Platte
Old Mill, Douglas
Old Red Cloud Agency,
　Scotts Bluff
Old Wyoming, Otoe
Olean, Colfax
Olean, Valley
Oleyen, Colfax
O'Linn, Dawes
Olive, Nance
Olive Branch, Lancaster
Oliver, Kimball

Ollie, Butler
Olnes, Boone
Olson, Otoe
Omadi, Dakota
Omaha, Douglas
Omaha Agency, Thurston
Omaha Barracks, Douglas
Omaha City, Douglas
Omaha Heights, Douglas
Omarel, Holt
Omega, McPherson
Omro, Nance
Oneida, Dakota
O'Neill, Holt
O'Neill City, Holt
Ong, Clay
Ono, Wheeler
Opequon, Lancaster
Opportunity, Holt
Optic, Buffalo
Ora, Butler
Orafino, Frontier
Oram, Furnas
Orange, Franklin
Orchard, Antelope
Orchard, Hall
Ord, Valley
Ordville, Cheyenne
Oreapolis, Cass
Orella, Sioux
Oren, Keith
Orient, Knox
Orient, Lancaster
Oriental City, Douglas
Orkney, Kimball
Orlando, Garden
Orlando, Lancaster
Orleans, Harlan
Orlon, Stanton
Ormsby, Custer
Orshek, Dakota
Ortello, Custer
Orton, Seward
Orum, Washington
Orville City, Hamilton
Osage, Cass
Osage, Franklin
Osage, Otoe
Osborn, Frontier
Oscar, Phelps
Osceola, Polk
Osco, Kearney

Oshkosh, Garden
Osmond, Pierce
0st, Seward
Otis, Hamilton
Otoe, Otoe
Otoe Agency, Gage
Otoe City, Otoe
Otoe Mission, Johnson
Otopolis, Cass
Ottman, Deuel
Otto, Webster
Ough, Dundy
Ouren, Burt
Over, Custer
Overland, Hamilton
Overton, Dawson
Ovina, Hall
Ovitt, Loup
Owasco, Kimball
Ox Bow, Nuckolls
Oxford, Boone
Oxford, Furnas
Oxford Junction, Harlan
Pacific City, Dakota
Paddock, Holt
Paddock, Merrick
Padonia, Richardson
Page, Holt
Paisley, Otoe
Palestine, Platte
Palestine Valley, Platte
Palisade, Hitchcock
Pallas, Lincoln
Palmer, Merrick
Palmyra, Otoe
Palo, York
Panama, Lancaster
Panhandle, Cheyenne
Papillion, Sarpy
Papillion City, Sarpy
Paplin, Sherman
Pappio, Douglas
Pappio, Sarpy
Parabell City, Cass
Paradise, Sherman
Paragon, Cedar
Paris, Gage
Paris, Lancaster
Paris, Sherman
Park, Kearney
Park, Lancaster
Parker, Holt

Parker, Kimball
Parkersburgh, Platte
Parkhill, Dixon
Park Mills, Sarpy
Parks, Dundy
Parkvale, Douglas
Parkview, Hall
Parma, Cass
Parnell, Greeley
Parmer, Cherry
Parry, Madison
Pass, Cherry
Patrick, Dodge
Patron, Butler
Paul, Otoe
Pauline, Adams
Pawlet, Garden
Pawnee, Douglas
Pawnee, Hall
Pawnee, Lincoln
Pawnee, Loup
Pawnee, Platte
Pawnee City, Pawnee
Pawneeville, Richardson
Paxton, Keith
Paynters, Sarpy
Peach Grove, Sarpy
Peak, Burt
Peake, Buffalo
Pearl, Chase
Pearl, Perkins
Pearson, Cherry
Pebble, Dodge
Pebble Creek, Dodge
Pebble Creek, Nemaha
Peck, Platte
Peckham, Lincoln
Peck's Grove, Lancaster
Pekin, Keya Paha
Pella, Lancaster
Pelton, Scotts Bluff
Penbrook, Cherry
Penbrook, Keya Paha
Pender, Thurston
Penitentiary, Lancaster
Penn, Garden
Penn, Hamilton
Peora, Richardson
Peoria, Knox
Pepper Creek, Dawes
Pepperville, Butler
Perch, Rock

Perdu, Deuel
Perkins, Perkins
Perrin, Morrill
Perry, Boyd
Perry, Red Willow
Perryville, Holt
Perth, Franklin
Pershing, Brown
Peru, Nemaha
Peters, Sheridan
Petersburg, Boone
Peterson, Cuming
Pencie, Dawson
Pezu, Chase
Phase, Saunders
Phebe, Perkins
Phelps, Phelps
Phelps Center, Phelps
Phillips, Hamilton
Phillipsburg, Custer
Phillips Station, Hamilton
Phoenix, Holt
Pibel, Wheeler
Pickard, Keith
Pickens, Cass
Pickletown, Furnas
Pickrell, Gage
Pierce, Pierce
Pike, Brown
Pilger, Stanton
Pilot, Custer
Pilzen, Saunders
Pinecamp, Keya Paha
Pine Glen, Brown
Pine Ridge, Dawes
Pink Prairie, Dundy
Pioneer, Thayer
Piper, Morrill
Pishelville, Knox
Pittsburgh, Seward
Plainfield, Cedar
Plainfield, York
Plainview, Pierce
Plano, Keith
Plasi, Saunders
Platford, Sarpy
Plato, Saline
Platona, Sarpy
Platteau, Douglas
Platteau City, Cass
Platte Center, Platte
Platte River, Sarpy

Platte River, Saunders
Platte Valley, Douglas
Platte Valley, Sarpy
Platteview, Washington
Platteville, Saunders
Plattford, Sarpy
Platt's, Buffalo
Plattsmouth, Cass
Pleasant Dale, Seward
Pleasant Hill, Cherry
Pleasant Hill, Custer
Pleasant Hill, Saline
Pleasant Home, Polk
Pleasant Home, York
Pleasanton, Buffalo
Pleasant Ridge, Harlan
Pleasant Run, Stanton
Pleasant Valley, Dodge
Pleasant Valley, Pawnee
Plum Creek, Dawson
Plum Creek, Phelps
Plum Creek Station,
    Dawson
Plum Grove, Madison
Plum Valley, Cuming
Plum Valley, Knox
Plymouth, Jefferson
Podunk, Nemaha
Poe, Hitchcock
Pohocco, Saunders
Poitsam, Saunders
Polander, Howard
Pole Creek No. 2,
    Cheyenne
Pole Creek No. 3,
    Cheyenne
Polk, Polk
Ponca, Dixon
Ponca Agency, Dakota
Ponca City, Dakota
Pony Lake, Rock
Poole, Buffalo
Poole Siding, Buffalo
Poor's Ranch, Cherry
Popens, Nemaha
Porcupine Bluffs, York
Portal, Sarpy
Porter, Richardson
Porter, Sioux
Porterville, Douglas
Portland, Cuming
Posen, Howard

Poston, York
Postville, Boyd
Postville, Platte
Poteet, Richardson
Potter, Cheyenne
Potter, Dawson
Powder Creek, Dixon
Powell, Jefferson
Power, Hall
Prague, Saunders
Praha, Colfax
Prairie, Polk
Prairie Camp, Hamilton
Prairie Center, Buffalo
Prairie Center, Butler
Prairie Center, Custer
Prairie City, Hall
Prairie City, Otoe
Prairie Creek, Merrick
Prairie Dog, Harlan
Prairie Hill, Platte
Prairie Home, Lancaster
Prairie Oaks, Washington
Prairie Star, Thayer
Prairo, Fillmore
Pratoulowski, Douglas
Pratt, Scotts Bluff
Precept, Furnas
Prentice, Cherry
President, Platte
Preston, Richardson
Prime, Loup
Primrose, Boone
Primrose, Douglas
Primrose, Hamilton
Princeton, Lancaster
Prinz, Morrill
Pritchard, Blaine
Prosser, Adams
Pullman, Cherry
Pumpkin Center, Holt
Pumpkin Creek Station,
    Morrill
Purdum, Blaine
Purdum, Thomas
Purple Cane, Dodge
Putman, Cherry
Putman, Gage
Quick, Frontier
Quinton, Thurston
Quiz, Box Butte
Raccoon Forks, Saunders

Rackett, Garden
Raeville, Boone
Ragan, Harlan
Rain, Hayes
Ralston, Douglas
Ralton, Deuel
Ramsey, Garden
Ranch, Boyd
Randall, Banner
Randolph, Cedar
Randolph, Dakota
Ranger, Logan
Rankin, Blaine
Raven, Brown
Ravenna, Buffalo
Ravenna, Cass
Rawhide, Dodge
Ray, Holt
Raymond, Lancaster
Read, Arthur
Read, Boyd
Reading, Butler
Rebecca, Lancaster
Redbird, Holt
Red Cloud, Webster
Red Cloud Agency, Dawes
Red Deer, Cherry
Redfern, Custer
Redington, Morrill
Red Lion, York
Redus, Scotts Bluff
Redville, Polk
Redwillow, Red Willow
Redwillow Station, Morrill
Redwing, Nance
Reed, Box Butte
Reeves, Cherry
Regency, Douglas
Reidsville, Knox
Reilley, Wheeler
Remington, Dawes
Reno, Colfax
Reno, Sheridan
Repose, Saline
Republican City, Harlan
Republican Forks, Dundy
Rescue, Saunders
Reservation, Kearney
Reserve, Gage
Rest, Custer
Rex, Cherry
Rexford, Furnas

Reynolds, Jefferson
Rhoid, Banner
Rice, Arthur
Riceville, Saline
Richfield, Sarpy
Richland, Colfax
Richland, Washington
Richling, Knox
Richmond, Furnas
Richmond, Holt
Ricker Spur, Saunders
Ridgeland, Butler
Ridgeley, Dodge
Riege, Cherry
Riford, Scotts Bluff
Riggs, Sheridan
Riley, Morrill
Rill, Hitchcock
Rimmer, Frontier
Rimrock, Keya Paha
Ringgold, Dawson
Ringgold, McPherson
Rising City, Butler
Rita Park, Cherry
River, Hall
Riverdale, Buffalo
Riverside, Burt
Riverside, Dodge
Riverside, Holt
Riverton, Franklin
Riverview, Buffalo
Riverview, Keya Paha
Roach, Scotts Bluff
Roanoke, Douglas
Robbinsville, Dodge
Robeda, Thomas
Robert, Hayes
Roberts, Scotts Bluff
Robidoux's Trading Post,
    Scotts Bluff
Robville, Custer
Roca, Lancaster
Rochester, Boyd
Rochon, Polk
Rock, Hamilton
Rock, Rock
Rock Bluff, Cass
Rockbrook, Douglas
Rock Creek, Cuming
Rock Creek, Jefferson
Rock Creek, Lancaster
Rocket, Washington

Rock Falls, Holt
Rock Falls, Phelps
Rockford, Gage
Rockford, Holt
Rock House, Jefferson
Rockland, Cass
Rockport, Washington
Rockton, Furnas
Rockville, Sherman
Rogers, Colfax
Rohrs, Nemaha
Rokeby, Lancaster
Rolf, Cherry
Rollwitz, Dundy
Rome, Holt
Romeyn, Phelps
Roosevelt, Sheridan
Roperville, Gage
Rosa, Nuckolls
Rosalie, Thurston
Roscoe, Keith
Rose, Rock
Rosecrans, Sheridan
Rose Creek, Jefferson
Rosedale, Adams
Rosedale, Boyd
Rosedale, Garfield
Rosedale, Hall
Rosefield, Nemaha
Rose Hill, Saunders
Roseland, Adams
Roselma, Boone
Rosemont, Webster
Rosenburg, Platte
Roseview, Pierce
Roseville, Pierce
Rosewater, Dundy
Ross, Holt
Roten, Custer
Roubedeau, Scotts Bluff
Roudeu, Knox
Round Grove, Custer
Round Valley, Custer
Rouse, Harlan
Roxby, Cherry
Royal, Antelope
Royville, Sioux
Ruby, Seward
Rudy, Jefferson
Rugby, Dawson
Rulo, Richardson
Rumsey, Sarpy

Rundlett, Hall
Runelsburg, Hall
Running Water, Knox
Running Water Station,
 Dawes
Rupert, Hitchcock
Rush, Franklin
Rushville, Sheridan
Ruskin, Nuckolls
Russia Town, Franklin
Russell, Frontier
Russell, Sheridan
Ruth, Knox
Ruthton, Garden
Ruthton, Keith
Rutland, Dawes
Ryedale, Antelope
Ryno, Custer ·
Sac, Richardson
Sacramento, Phelps
Sad Corners, Franklin
Salem, Richardson
Saline City, Lancaster
Saline Ford, Saunders
Saling's Grove, Sarpy
Salinte, Sarpy
Salona, Butler
Salt Basin, Lancaster
Salt Creek, Cass
Salt Creek, Lancaster
Saltillo, Lancaster
Saltville, Otoe
Sanberg, Dodge
Sanborn, Dundy
Sandalia, Boone
Sandburg, Hamilton
Sand Creek, Saunders
Sandcut, Grant
Sandell, Dodge
Sander, Douglas
Sand Hill, Adams
Sand Hill, Franklin
Sandoz, Sheridan
Sandpit, Dodge
Sandwich, Dundy
Sandy, Wheeler
Sanford, Keya Paha
San Francisco, Nemaha
Sangco, Colfax
Santee, Knox
Santee, Sarpy
Sappa, Harlan

Saratoga, Douglas
Saratoga, Holt
Sarben, Keith
Sargent, Custer
Sarles, Dawes
Saronville, Clay
Sarpy, Douglas
Sarpy, Sarpy
Sarpy Center, Sarpy
Sarpy's Trading Post, Sarpy
Sartoria, Buffalo
Saunders, Saunders
Saunders, Valley
Savage, Antelope
Savannah, Butler
Sawyer, Fillmore
Saxon, Saline
Scandia, Custer
Scandinavia, Harlan
Schaupps, Sherman
Schauppsville, Hall
Scheding, Blaine
Schell, Nuckolls
Schermerhorn, Morrill
Schill, Sheridan
Schimmer, Hall
School Creek, Clay
Schuyler, Colfax
Schwedt, Stanton
Scotia, Greeley
Scotia Junction, Greeley
Scott, Webster
Scottsbluff, Scotts Bluff
Scotts Bluffs, Scotts Bluff
Scottville, Holt
Scoville, Scotts Bluff
Scratchpot City, Furnas
Scribner, Dodge
Scudder, Hitchcock
Seabrooke, Grant
Sears, Scotts Bluff
Seaton, Hamilton
Seberger, Polk
Secret Grove, Knox
Sedan, Nuckolls
Sedan, Scotts Bluff
Sedlov, Valley
Seeley, Lincoln
Seeley, York
Selden, Rock
Seneca, Custer
Seneca, Thomas

S. E. Smith Ranch, Sioux
Sett, Furnas
Set Up, Custer
Seward, Seward
Sextorp, Cheyenne
Seymour, Douglas
Seymour Park, Douglas
Shafer, Buffalo
Shaffer, Pawnee
Shamrock, Holt
Shank, Polk
Shannon, Pierce
Sharon, Buffalo
Sharp, Sheridan
Shasta, Richardson
Shaw, Gage
Shea, Jefferson
Shebesta, Rock
Shelby, Buffalo
Shelby, Polk
Sheldonville, Platte
Shell Creek, Colfax
Shelton, Buffalo
Sheridan, Garfield
Sheridan, Nemaha
Sheridan, Washington
Sheridan, Wheeler
Sherman, Brown
Sherman, Furnas
Sherman, Nemaha
Sherman Barracks, Douglas
Sherwood, Franklin
Sherwood, Phelps
Shestak, Saline
Shickley, Fillmore
Shidler, Logan
Shidler, Thomas
Shiloh, Hamilton
Shinn's Ferry, Butler
Shippee, Red Willow
Shirley's Station, Lancaster
Shoemaker Point, Merrick
Sholes, Wayne
Shrule, Fillmore
Shubert, Richardson
Shylock, Knox
Sicily, Gage
Sickler's Mill, Thayer
Siding, Cherry
Sidney, Cheyenne
Silas, Lincoln
Silver, Gage

Silver, Lancaster
Silver Creek, Burt
Silver Creek, Merrick
Silver Creek, Red Willow
Silver Glen, Merrick
Silver Lake, Adams
Silver Ridge, Dixon
Silverthorn, Morrill
Simeon, Cherry
Simla, Morrill
Simonds, Dawson
Simons Siding, Dakota
Simpson, Keya Paha
Sioux, Dakota
Sioux, Sheridan
Sioux Creek, Loup
Sioux Valley, Fillmore
Sizer, Holt
Skinner's, Colfax
Skull Creek, Butler
Slavonia, Howard
Slavonia, Saunders
Slocum, Holt
Slocumb, Jefferson
Sloughton, Red Willow
Smartville, Johnson
Smeed, Kimball
Smithfield, Gosper
Smithland, Cass
Smithland, Cedar
Smith Ranch, York
Smoot, Sheridan
Smyrna, Nuckolls
Snell, Scotts Bluff
Snowflake, Kearney
Snyder, Dodge
Soda Lake, Grant
Sod Hill, Lancaster
Sodtown, Adams
Sodtown, Buffalo
Sodtown, Dawes
Sodville, Box Butte
Solon, Otoe
Somerford, Custer
Somerset, Frontier
Somerset, Lincoln
Sonora, Nemaha
Soudan, Cherry
Souleville, Sherman
South Auburn, Nemaha
South Bend, Cass
South Blair, Washington

South Creek, Dixon
South Cut, Douglas
South Loup, Buffalo
South Loup, Custer
South Nebraska City, Otoe
South Norfolk, Madison
South Omaha, Douglas
South Pass, Lancaster
South Platte, Douglas
South Ravenna, Buffalo
Southside, Holt
South Sioux City, Dakota
South Syracuse, Otoe
Sowser, Garden
Spade, Sheridan
Spading, Greeley
Spafford's Grove, Hamilton
Spalding, Greeley
Spannuth, Lincoln
Sparks, Cherry
Sparta, Knox
Spear, Lincoln
Spearville, Fillmore
Spelts, Valley
Spencer, Boyd
Spencer, Hall
Spencer Park, Adams
Spezer, Richardson
Spiker, Washington
Spitley, Colfax
Sportville, Adams
Spotted Tail Agency,
   Sheridan
Spragg, Rock
Sprague, Lancaster
Spring Bank, Dixon
Spring Creek, Johnson
Springdale, Valley
Springfield, Richardson
Springfield, Sarpy
Spring Green, Furnas
Spring Grove, Harlan
Spring Grove City, Otoe
Spring Hill, Harlan
Spring Lake, Sheridan
Spring Ranch, Clay
Spring Valley, Madison
Spring Valley, Nuckolls
Springview, Keya Paha
Springville, Custer
Springville, Platte
Spud, Sioux

Spuds, Lincoln
Spur, Burt
Spur, Butler
Stafford, Holt
Stamford, Harlan
Stanley, Buffalo
Stanley, Holt
St. Ann, Frontier
St. Ann, Webster
St. Anthony, Platte
Stanton, Dakota
Stanton, Stanton
Staplehurst, Seward
Stapleton, Logan
Star, Holt
Stark, Hamilton
Stateline, Nuckolls
St. Bernard, Platte
St. Charles, Cass
St. Charles, Cuming
St. Charles, Otoe
St. Clair, Antelope
St. Columbans, Sarpy
St. Deroin, Nemaha
Stearns Prairie, Platte
Stebbins, Dixon
St. Edward, Boone
Steelburg, Jefferson
Steele City, Jefferson
Steele Creek, Holt
Stegall, Scotts Bluff
Stein, Nemaha
Steinauer, Pawnee
Stella, Richardson
Stephenson, Keya Paha
Sterbins, Garden
Sterling, Johnson
Steuben, Frontier
Stevens Creek, Gage
Stevens Creek, Lancaster
Stevenson, Buffalo
Stewards, Johnson
Stewart's Siding, Scotts
   Bluff
St. Frederick, Nemaha
St. George, Nemaha
St. Helena, Cedar
Stillwater, Webster
Stircus Creek, Lancaster
St. James, Cedar
St. Joe, Hamilton
St. John, Colfax

St. Johns, Dakota
St. Libory, Howard
St. Mary, Johnson
St. Mary, Platte
St. Michael, Buffalo
Stockade, Webster
Stockham, Hamilton
Stockton, Franklin
Stockville, Frontier
Stockwell, Lancaster
Stoddard, Thayer
Stone, Gage
Stoner, Rock
Stone Ranch, York
Stop, Custer
Story, Sioux
Stovil, Scotts Bluff
Stowe, Frontier
St. Patrick, Dakota
St. Paul, Burt
St. Paul, Howard
St. Peter, Cedar
St. Peter, Dixon
St. Peters, Otoe
Strahmburg, Cedar
Strang, Fillmore
Strasburger, Sheridan
Stratton, Hitchcock
Stratton's Store, Harlan
Strauss, Saunders
Strausville, Richardson
Strickland, Antelope
Strickland, Hayes
Strickland Mills, Lancaster
Stroemer, Adams
Strohl, Loup
Stromsburg, Polk
St. Stephen, Nuckolls
St. Stephens, Richardson
Stuart, Holt
Stumps Station,
    Richardson
St. Vrain, Dodge
Success, Saunders
Success, Seward
Sullivan, Hayes
Summer Hill, Douglas
Summerville, Dodge
Summerville, Otoe
Summit, Butler
Summit, Cass
Summit, Greeley

Summit, Lancaster
Summit, McPherson
Summit, Otoe
Summit, Thomas
Summit City, Cass
Sumner, Dawson
Sumner, Dodge
Sumter, Valley
Sunflower, Scotts Bluff
Sunflower, Thomas
Sunlight, Cass
Sunnyside, Boyd
Sunnyside, Brown
Sunnyside, Otoe
Sunnyslope, Douglas
Sunol, Cheyenne
Sunrise, Merrick
Sunshine, Lincoln
Superior, Nuckolls
Surprise, Butler
Survey, Cherry
Susquehanna, Butler
Sutherland, Lincoln
Sutton, Clay
Swaburgh, Dodge
Swan, Antelope
Swan, Holt
Swan City, Saline
Swanton, Saline
Swanville, Saline
Swedeburg, Saunders
Sweden, Clay
Sweden, Knox
Swedehome, Polk
Sweetwater, Buffalo
Swift, Otoe
Swingle, Saline
Sybrant, Rock
Sylvia, Boyd
Syracuse, Otoe
System, Cherry
Table, Custer
Tableau, Dawes
Table Creek, Otoe
Table Rock, Pawnee
Tabor, Cheyenne
Tabor, Colfax
Tabor, Saline
Tabor, Scotts Bluff
Taffe, Wayne
Taft, Cedar
Talbot, Knox

Talbot, Otoe
Tallin, Custer
Talmage, Otoe
Tamora, Seward
Tangeman, Otoe
Tarnov, Platte
Tate, Pawnee
Taylor, Gage
Taylor, Loup
Taylor's Spur, Hall
Tecumseh, Johnson
Tekamah, Burt
Tekonsha, Nance
Telbasta, Washington
Terrytown, Scotts Bluff
Tewsville, Knox
Thatcher, Cherry
Thayer, York
Thedford, Thomas
The Forks, Garfield
Thelma, Garden
Thirty-one Station,
    Cheyenne
Thirty-two Mile Creek,
    Adams
Thomas, Scotts Bluff
Thomasville, Webster
Thompson, Holt
Thompson, Jefferson
Thompson, Scotts Bluff
Thompson, Wheeler
Thompson's Ranch,
    Seward
Thorn, Holt
Thornburg, Frontier
Thornburg, Hayes
Thornton, Polk
Thorson, Knox
Three Grove, Cass
Thummel, Merrick
Thune, McPherson
Thurman, Rock
Thurston, Douglas
Thurston, Thurston
Tiffany, Keya Paha
Tilden, Madison
Timber Creek, Nance
Timber Hill, Platte
Timberville, Dodge
Tioga, Cherry
Tippetts, Garden
Tip's Branch, Pawnee

Tipton, Lancaster
Tobias, Saline
Tobin, Cass
Todd's, Cass
Tomahawk Hills, Douglas
Tonawanda, Holt
Tonic, Holt
Tony, Scotts Bluff
Toohey, Scotts Bluff
Touhy, Saunders
Tower, Boyd
Towers, Morrill
Townsend, Gage
Townsend, Sioux
Toxword, Burt
Tracy, Greeley
Tracy, Rock
Tracy Valley, Platte
Tracyville, Gosper
Traders Point, Sarpy
Trail, Hitchcock
Trail, Scotts Bluff
Trail City, Hitchcock
Trail City, Perkins
Traill Spur, Hall
Traill, Hamilton
Traill Spur, Hall
Trappers Grove, Dawson
Tredway, Keith
Trenton, Hitchcock
Triangle, Keith
Triqua, Sarpy
Triumph, Custer
Trivey, Cherry
Trocknow, Buffalo
Trouble, Cherry
Trout, Scotts Bluff
Troxel, Dodge
Troy, Cass
Troy, Greeley
Troy, Holt
Troy, Kimball
Troy, Saunders
Trudell, Knox
Trued, Dawson
Trumbull, Clay
Tryon, McPherson
Tuckerville, Custer
Tufford, Custer
Tull, Cherry
Turkey Creek, Fillmore
Turkey Creek, Johnson

Turkey Creek, Pawnee
Turlington, Otoe
Turner, Holt
Turner, Lincoln
Turner Grove, Dakota
Turnip, McPherson
Twing, Holt
Twin Grove, Antelope
Twin Lakes, Holt
Tyghe, Keith
Tynan, Richardson
Tynerville, Howard
Tyrone, Red Willow
Tyson, Washington
Tysonville, Cass
Uehling, Dodge
Ulysses, Butler
Unadilla, Otoe
Underwood, Hall
Underwood Hills, Douglas
Union, Cass
Union, Dundy
Union Center, Gage
Union Mills, Cass
Union Ridge, Gosper
Union Valley, Madison
Unit, Sioux
Unitt, Seward
University Place, Lancaster
Upland, Franklin
Upton, Custer
Urban, Butler
Urbana, Phelps
Usher, Douglas
Utica, Seward
Vacoma, Washington
Vailton, Red Willow
Valentine, Cherry
Valley, Douglas
Valley City, Kearney
Valley Grange, Red Willow
Valley Home, Nuckolls
Valley Ridge, Blaine
Valleyview, Loup
Valparaiso, Saunders
Valyrang, McPherson
Van, Banner
Van, Cedar
Vance, Morrill
Van Wyck, Lincoln
Van Wyck, Red Willow
Varna, Saline

Varner, Lincoln
Vasa, Knox
Vaughn, Gosper
Vaughn's Ranch, Gosper
Vayden, Merrick
Veda, Saunders
Velda, Greeley
Velma, Arthur
Velma, Garden
Velte, Dawson
Venango, Perkins
Venice, Douglas
Venus, Knox
Verdel, Knox
Verdigre, Knox
Verdigris Bridge, Knox
Verdigris Valley, Knox
Verdon, Richardson
Verdurette, Sherman
Vernon, Nuckolls
Verona, Clay
Verona, Dakota
Verona, Hamilton
Vervine, Grant
Vesta, Johnson
Vian, Cherry
Vick, Merrick
Vickory, Antelope
Victoria, Cass
Victoria, Custer
Victoria, Otoe
Vilas, Antelope
Vim, Antelope
Vincent, Furnas
Vinlon, Banner
Vinton, Valley
Violet, Pawnee
Virginia, Gage
Virginia City, Jefferson
Vista, Dakota
Vockery, Morrill
Vroman, Lincoln
Wabash, Cass
Wac, Phelps
Waco, York
Wagner, Logan
Wagner's, Lancaster
Wagners Lake, Platte
Wahoo, Saunders
Wakefield, Dixon
Wahpco, Saunders
Walhelms, Sherman

Walker, Holt
Walker, Platte
Walker, Wheeler
Walker's Ranch, Kearney
Wallace, Dodge
Wallace, Lincoln
Wall's Mill, Knox
Walnut, Knox
Walnut Creek, Fillmore
Walnut Creek, Washington
Walnut Grove, Knox
Walnut Hill, Cuming
Walnut Hill, Douglas
Walters, Fillmore
Waltham, Buffalo
Walther, Boyd
Walthill, Thurston
Walton, Lancaster
Walworth, Custer
Wanatah, Butler
Wanatah, Dawes
Wanda, Adams
Wann, Saunders
Wantiska, Saunders
Warbonnet, Sioux
Ware, Butler
Wareham, Cedar
Warnerville, Madison
Warrack, Platte
Warren, Dawson
Warren, Garden
Warren, Lincoln
Warren, Madison
Warren, Pierce
Warsaw, Howard
Warwick Spur, Nuckolls
Washington, Cedar
Washington, Harlan
Washington, Washington
Washington City, Cass
Waterbury, Dixon
Water Hole Ranch,
  Cheyenne
Waterloo, Douglas
Waterloo, Franklin
Waters, Buffalo
Watertown, Buffalo
Waterville, Boone
Waterville, Cass
Watson, Harlan
Watson, Knox
Watsonawa, Buffalo

Watts, Lincoln
Watt's Mill, Jefferson
Wattsville, Platte
Waucapena, Cedar
Wauneta, Chase
Wausa, Knox
Waverly, Lancaster
Wayland, Polk
Wayne, Custer
Wayne, Wayne
Wayside, Dawes
Weber, Wayne
Webster, Dodge
Webster Centre, Webster
Webster's Town, Garfield
Weco, Douglas
Weeping Water, Cass
Weigand, Knox
Weir, Deuel
Weir, Grant
Weir, Hooker
Weissert, Custer
Welch, Knox
Welch, Lancaster
Welden, Seward
Wellfleet, Lincoln
Wells, Cherry
Wells, Colfax
Wells, Webster
Wells Mill, Richardson
Wellsville, Morrill
Wescott, Custer
West Archer, Richardson
West Barneston, Gage
West Blue, Fillmore
West Branch, Pawnee
West Chicago, Platte
West End, Dodge
Westerfield, York
Western, Saline
Westerville, Custer
Westgard, Nance
West Hill, Platte
West Lawn, Douglas
West Lincoln, Lancaster
Westmark, Phelps
West Oak, Lancaster
Weston, Cass
Weston, Johnson
Weston, Saunders
West Point, Cuming
West Posen, Howard

West Randolph, Pierce
West Salem, Franklin
Westside, Douglas
West's Mill, Seward
West Union, Custer
Westwood, Hall
Weyerts, Cheyenne
Wheatland, Cass
Wheatland, Webster
Wheeler, Wheeler
Whiskey Run, Jefferson
Whitaker, Lincoln
White, Hayes
White Cap, Brown
Whiteclay, Sheridan
White Cloud, Buffalo
White Cloud, Hall
White Elm, Clay
White Glen, Sioux
White Rabbit, Dawson
Whitesville, Gage
Whitewater, Phelps
Whitman, Grant
Whitney, Dawes
Whitney, Furnas
Whitney, Red Willow
Whittier, Lincoln
Wickliffe, York
Wickoff, Seward
Wilber, Saline
Wilcox, Kearney
Wildcat, Gage
Wild Turkey, Furnas
Wilhelmshohe, Sherman
Willamne, Sherman
Willard, Lincoln
Willard, York
Willett, Arthur
Willey, Box Butte
Willford, Scotts Bluff
Williams, Thayer
Williamsburg, Phelps
Williamsport, Cass
Williamsport, Hamilton
Williamsville, Richardson
Willis, Dakota
Willow, Dawson
Willow Bend, Lincoln
Willow Creek, Saunders
Willowdale, Antelope
Willowdale, Nemaha
Willowdale, Pierce

Willow Grove, Red Willow
Willow Island (1), Dawson
Willow Island (2), Dawson
Willow Springs, Garfield
Willview, Sarpy
Wilmot, Furnas
Wilson, Colfax
Wilson, Otoe
Wilsonville, Furnas
Winchester, Chase
Winfield, Brown
Winfield, Holt
Wing, Nemaha
Winnebago, Richardson
Winnebago, Thurston
Winnetoon, Knox
Winside, Wayne
Winslow, Dodge
Winsor, Howard
Winter Quarters, Douglas
Winters, Scotts Bluff
Wirt, Custer
Wisner, Cuming
Wola, Howard
Wolbach, Greeley
Wolf, Platte
Wolf Creek, Pawnee
Wolfington, Dawes
Woodburn, Platte

Woodcliff, Saunders
Wood Lake, Cherry
Woodland, Cass
Woodlawn, Lancaster
Wood Park, Dakota
Wood River, Hall
Wood River Centre,
    Buffalo
Wood River Farm, Hall
Woodrow, Scotts Bluff
Wood Siding, Nemaha
Woods Park, Custer
Woods Stage Ranch, Custer
Woodsville City, Burt
Woodville, Nance
Woodville, Otoe
Woodville, Platte
Woodward, Fillmore
Woodworth, Sarpy
Woody, Douglas
Woolseyville, Johnson
Worcester, Otoe
Worms, Merrick
Wrage, Cherry
Wright, Brown
Wright, Scotts Bluff
Wrightsville, Buffalo
WX Siding, Otoe
Wymore, Gage

Wynot, Cedar
Wyoming, Otoe
Xenia, Otoe
Xenia, Sarpy
Yale, Box Butte
Yale, Valley
Yancton, Richardson
Yanka, Butler
Yankee, Perkins
Yankee, Platte
Yankee Hill, Lancaster
Yeager, Furnas
Yellow Banks, Madison
Yockey, Morrill
York, York
Yossems Paradise Valley,
    Douglas
Yucca, Custer
Yucca Hill, Custer
Yutan, Saunders
Zell, Chase
Zella, Arthur
Zella, Keith
Zeven, Sherman
Zigzag, Platte
Zimmer, Frontier
Zion, Burt
Zurich, Hall
Zyba, Kearney